Remote Delivery

Remote Delivery

A Guide to Software Delivery through Collaboration
between Distributed Teams

Zhengping Qu

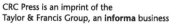
CRC Press
Taylor & Francis Group
Boca Raton London New York

CRC Press is an imprint of the
Taylor & Francis Group, an **informa** business

人民邮电出版社
POSTS & TELECOM PRESS

First Edition published 2021
by CRC Press
6000 Broken Sound Parkway NW, Suite 300, Boca Raton, FL 33487-2742

and by CRC Press
2 Park Square, Milton Park, Abingdon, Oxon, OX14 4RN

© 2021 Taylor & Francis Group, LLC

Published with arrangement with the original publisher, Posts & Telecom Press.
First edition published by Posts and Telecom Press 2020
CRC Press is an imprint of Taylor & Francis Group, LLC

ISBN: 978-0-367-49050-8 (hbk)
ISBN: 978-0-367-74961-3 (pbk)
ISBN: 978-1-003-16049-6 (ebk)

Typeset in Times
by SPi Global, India

Contents

Foreword 1: Taking Up Delivery Wholeheartedly xv
Foreword 2: Pursue Ideal Software Delivery xvii
Preface xix

Chapter 1   Current Situation of Distributed Teams 1

    1.1   Introduction to Distributed Teams 1
        1.1.1   Rapid Development of Distributed Teams 1
        1.1.2   Why Customers Value CMMI Assessment 1
        1.1.3   Types of Distributed Teams 3
        1.1.4   What Kind of Team is a Distributed Team 4
    1.2   Current Situation of Service Outsourcing Industry 4
    1.3   How to Build an Offshore Team 6
        1.3.1   Principles for Building a Distributed Team 6
        1.3.2   Different Composition of a Distributed Team 7
        1.3.3   Investment and Benefit of Building a Distributed Team ... 8
        1.3.4   Matters that Need Attention 9
            1.3.4.1   People are a Key Factor for a Distributed Team ... 9
            1.3.4.2   Mounting Difficulties in Communication Change the
                      Communication Habits of the Team 9
            1.3.4.3   Solutions to Minimize the Negative Impact of Remote
                      Working 9
    1.4   Varying Development Trend of Software Outsourcing Service 10
        1.4.1   The War for Talent has Started 10
        1.4.2   Offshore Delivery Center – Achievement of Strategic Cooperation 10
        1.4.3   New Ways for Customers to Measure Outsourcing Services 11
    Note 11

Chapter 2   Communication between Distributed Teams 13

    2.1   Manage Customer Expectations 13
        2.1.1   Know the Customers 13
            2.1.1.1   Who Are They? 13
            2.1.1.2   What Do They Think About? 15
        2.1.2   Protect the Right to Know of Customers 17
            2.1.2.1   Progress 17
            2.1.2.2   Quality 17
        2.1.3   Maintain Customer Expectations 18
            2.1.3.1   Set Definite Expectations as Early as Possible ... 19
            2.1.3.2   Communicate Frequently and Effectively 19
            2.1.3.3   Take Customers' Business Objective as Our Main
                      Objective 20
            2.1.3.4   Maintain Consistency 21
            2.1.3.5   Reduce the Possibility of Making Mistakes 21
        2.1.4   Exceed Customer Expectations 22
        2.1.5   Case Analysis: Project L 23
        2.1.6   House Splitting Effect 24

2.1.7   Customer Expectations to Decide the Outcome of a Project 24
2.2   Communication is the Biggest Challenge for Distributed Teams 25
2.2.1   E-mail: The Most Basic Means of Communication for
Distributed Teams 25
2.2.1.1   Features of E-mail Communication 27
2.2.1.2   Better Means of Communication are Preferred in
Some Occasions 27
2.2.1.3   View E-mails from the Perspective of Continuous
Improvement 27
2.2.2   Asynchronous Communication and Real-Time
Communication – Both Regular Communications 27
2.2.2.1   Asynchronous Communication 27
2.2.2.2   Real-Time Communication 29
2.2.3   Pros and Cons of Tools 30
2.2.4   Active Communication 30
2.2.5   Conflicts in Communication 31
2.2.5.1   Typical Ways for Distributed Teams to Resolve Conflicts . 32
2.2.5.2   Dare to Say "No" 33
2.2.6   To Be Empathetic 33
2.2.7   Explicit and Candid Communication 35
2.2.8   Other Matters That Affect the Success of Offshore Teams 36
2.2.8.1   Written Communication with Customers 36
2.2.8.2   Paying More Attention to Details Can Improve
Communication 37
2.3   Organization of Meetings 38
2.3.1   Typical Forms of Meeting 39
2.3.1.1   Stand-Up 39
2.3.1.2   IPM 41
2.3.1.3   Inconsistent Criteria for Estimation 42
2.3.1.4   Time of Meeting is Too Long 44
2.3.1.5   Where the Speed of Delivery Drops, the Team Shall
Explain at the IPM that it is Due to the Following
Reasons 44
2.3.1.6   Retrospective Meeting 45
2.3.1.7   Showcase/Iterative Review 49
2.3.1.8   Team Huddle 50
2.3.2   Skills for Offshore Teams in Attending Meetings 51
2.3.3   Summary 52
2.4   Representatives On Site and Short-Term Face-to-Face Visits 52
2.4.1   On-Site Representative 53
2.4.1.1   The On-Site Representative Sent by the Customer to
the Offshore Team 53
2.4.1.2   The On-Site Representative Sent by the Offshore
Team to the Customer 53
2.4.1.3   Matters Need Attention 55
2.4.2   Short-Term Face-to-Face Communication 56
2.4.2.1   Short-Term Visit for Project Start-Up 56
2.4.2.2   Regular Short-Term Visits 59
2.4.3   Review After a Visit to the Customer Site 62
2.4.3.1   Be Clear about Your Purpose of Visiting 63
2.4.3.2   Rear Service Considerations 63

                2.4.3.3   Do Not "Make Commitments" at Will 64
        2.4.4   Summary 64
   2.5   Online Communication Tools 65
        2.5.1   Knowledge Sharing Tools 65
        2.5.2   Instant Communication Tools 66
        2.5.3   Work Collaboration Tools 67
        2.5.4   Process Control Tools 67
        2.5.5   Tools That Integrate Instant Communication and Knowledge
                 Sharing 68
        2.5.6   Summary 70
   2.6   Cases of Failed Communication 71
        2.6.1   McDonnell-Douglas DC-10 Air Crash: A Repeat of the Past 71
        2.6.2   Integration Failure of a Large Energy Company 73
        2.6.3   First User Test Failed in Project L 73
        2.6.4   Summary 73
Notes 74

Chapter 3   Collaboration between Distributed Teams 75

   3.1   A First Look at Teamwork 75
        3.1.1   Relationship between Communication and Collaboration 75
                3.1.1.1   Technical Collaboration 75
                3.1.1.2   Business-Level Collaboration 78
        3.1.2   Unified Opinion is a Prerequisite for Collaboration 80
                3.1.2.1   A Series of Priority Issues 80
                3.1.2.2   Remain Moderate 80
                3.1.2.3   Define "Work Completed" 81
                3.1.2.4   Mutual Code Review 81
                3.1.2.5   View the Process Correctly 81
                3.1.2.6   Agree on Test-Related Issues 81
                3.1.2.7   Consensus on Shared Information 83
                3.1.2.8   Responding to Changes in Requirements 83
        3.1.3   Collaboration Emphasizes Action: Implementation Capacity 83
        3.1.4   Useful Methods for Collaboration 85
                3.1.4.1   Reasonably Arrange the Tasks of Distributed Teams 85
                3.1.4.2   Beneficial Investment 86
                3.1.4.3   Manage the Backlog for Distributed Teams 86
                3.1.4.4   Visualize the Progress of Distributed Teams 87
                3.1.4.5   Make Good Use of Available Resources 88
        3.1.5   Behaviors that Hurt Collaboration 88
        3.1.6   Drive Customers 90
                3.1.6.1   Take the Offshore Team and the Customer as a Whole 90
                3.1.6.2   The Role of Guidance 90
                3.1.6.3   Enhance Persuasion to Customers 92
        3.1.7   Collaboration Skills 94
        3.1.8   Key Collaboration Points 95
                3.1.8.1   Continuous Integration at the Business Level 97
                3.1.8.2   Remote Pairing 97
        3.1.9   Scrum of Scrums Meeting 98
        3.1.10 Collaboration Within the Team 101
                3.1.10.1 Let's Talk About an IPM 101

    3.1.10.2 Prepare for an IPM...102
    3.1.10.3 Intra-Team Interaction 103
    3.1.11   Summary..104
  3.2 Improve the Collaboration between Offshore Teams 104
    3.2.1 Use Assumptions...105
    3.2.2 Two-Way Communication...105
    3.2.3 Use Business Language and Examples 107
    3.2.4 Regularity for Establishing Offshore Teams 108
      3.2.4.1 Regularity in Communication...108
      3.2.4.2 Regularity Brought by Agility 109
    3.2.5 Continuously Improve the Collaboration Level
           of Offshore Teams 110
      3.2.5.1 Strength Collaboration Cross Distributed Teams 111
      3.2.5.2 Idea for Instilling in Customers 112
      3.2.5.3 Focus on User Value in Delivery 115
    3.2.6 Summary 116
  3.3 Standardization Enhances Collaboration between Distributed Teams 117
    3.3.1 Standardization of Business Analysis 117
      3.3.1.1 Standards for Managing User Story 117
      3.3.1.2 Specification by Example (SBE) 120
    3.3.2 Standardization of Technology..121
    3.3.3 Standardization of Testing...123
      3.3.3.1 The Pyramid Principle for Test................................123
      3.3.3.2 Manage Test Cases and Data 124
      3.3.3.3 Manage Bug Reports 124
      3.3.3.4 How to Rate a Bug?..125
      3.3.3.5 Test Strategy 126
    3.3.4 Standardized Automated Test 126
    3.3.5 Summary 127

Chapter 4 Application of Visualization...129

  4.1 Purpose of Visualization 130
    4.1.1 Show Project Status..130
      4.1.1.1 Project Kanban (Physical Kanban and Electronic
               Kanban)...130
      4.1.1.2 Burndown Chart..131
      4.1.1.3 Burnup Chart 131
    4.1.2 Eliminate Deviations in Understanding Requirements 131
    4.1.3 Feedback on the Software Quality 132
      4.1.3.1 Regular Bug Report 132
      4.1.3.2 Software Product Performance Monitoring Curve 133
    4.1.4 Improve Test Coverage of Code...133
    4.1.5 Describe Complex Business Processes 133
    4.1.6 Understand the Project Overall View 134
    4.1.7 Help the Team Think With Mind Maps..135
  4.2 Visualization Method...136
    4.2.1 Showing Project Status: Kanban 136
    4.2.2 Showing Project Status: Burndown Chart and Burnup Chart 140
      4.2.2.1 Burndown Chart..140
      4.2.2.2 Burnup Chart 146

4.2.2.3 Comparison Between Burndown Chart and Burnup Chart 148
4.2.3 Display of Business Process 149
4.2.3.1 Specification of Flowchart 149
4.2.3.2 Extended Application 151
4.2.4 Overall View of Project Requirements 152
4.2.5 Expression of Requirements Stories 153
4.2.6 Use of Mind maps 155
4.2.7 Data Visualization 155
4.3 Use Visualization to Measure Our Work 157
4.3.1 Measurement of Development and Testing Work 157
4.3.2 Suggestions for Measurement of Team Work 157
4.4 Introduction of Visualization Tools for Team Collaboration 158
4.4.1 Brief Introduction to Mingle 158
4.4.2 Brief Introduction to Trello 158
4.5 Summary 159

Chapter 5 Waste in Distributed Teams 161
5.1 Waste Caused by Human Factors 161
5.2 Waste in Inter-Team Collaboration 163
5.2.1 Where Does the Waste Come From 164
5.2.1.1 Waste Caused by Team Collaboration 164
5.2.1.2 Waste Caused by Different Time Zones 165
5.2.1.3 Waste in Different Phases of Project 165
5.2.1.4 Waste in Test Collaboration 165
5.2.2 Ways to Solve Waste 166
5.2.2.1 Just in Time Production 166
5.2.2.2 Timely Collaboration 166
5.2.2.3 Effective Communication 167
5.2.2.4 Do It Right the First Time 167
5.2.2.5 Minimize the Steps of Process 167
5.2.2.6 Manage Time and Reduce Waste 167
5.2.2.7 Record Waste So Everyone Can See It Intuitively 168
5.2.3 Summary 168
5.3 Waste in the Process 168
5.3.1 Shorten the Process 168
5.3.2 Simplify Complex Process 169
5.3.3 An Important Way to Speed Up Progress 169
5.3.4 Over-Design is Also a Common Waste 170
5.4 Waste in Information Processing 170
5.4.1 Waste From Organizational Structure 171
5.4.2 Waste in Knowledge Management 171
5.4.3 Waste Caused by Too Much Information 172
5.4.4 Solve the Waste Caused by Information Processing 173
5.4.4.1 Passive Safety Mode Solution 173
5.4.4.2 Active Safety Mode Solution 173
5.5 Invisible Waste 173
5.5.1 Giving Sea Cucumbers to Mother-in-Law 174
5.5.2 Fail Quickly to Avoid Waste 174
5.5.3 Identifying Invisible Waste Requires Some Insight 175

5.5.4   Invisible Waste: Unaware of Progress 175
5.5.5   Technical Debt and Requirements Debt 175
5.5.6   Lack of Priority 176
5.5.7   Invisible Waste in Distributed Teams 176
5.5.8   Consequences of Invisible Waste 176
5.6   Don't Turn BDD into a Waste in the Team 177
5.7   Summary 178

Chapter 6   Self-Managed Offshore Teams 179

6.1   The Influence of Traditional Culture on the Team 179
6.2   The Driving Force of the Team 182
6.2.1   Where Does the Driving Force Come From 182
6.2.1.1   Objective-Driven 183
6.2.1.2   Team Culture 183
6.2.1.3   A Sense of Security 184
6.2.1.4   Internal Driving Force 184
6.2.2   Establish a Flat Organization 186
6.2.3   People Are the Core of an Organization 187
6.2.3.1   Initiative 187
6.2.3.2   Execution 187
6.2.3.3   "Initiative+Execution" is the Basis of Pull Work Mode ... 188
6.2.4   Does a Flat Team Need Leadership 188
6.2.5   Transform Traditional Organizations to Self-Managed
Organizations 189
6.2.5.1   Recommendations for Traditional Middle Managers 190
6.2.5.2   Three Stages of Self-Management Transformation of
the Delivery Team 190
6.2.5.3   Does the Team Misunderstand MBO 191
6.2.5.4   Three Levels of Self-Management 192
6.2.6   Flattening is Not a Panacea 192
6.2.6.1   Buddy/Sponsor: To Solve Cultural Inheritance in a
Flat Team 192
6.2.6.2   How to Find Someone Who is "Responsible" for a
Thing in a Flat Organization 193
6.3   Shaping the Professionalism of the Team 194
6.3.1   Team Capacity Building 194
6.3.2   Form Good Habits 195
6.3.3   The Positive Impact of Process Standardization within the
Company on the Team 195
6.3.4   Become an Important Contributor in the Project 196
6.3.5   How to Deal with Documents 196
6.3.6   Doing Simple Things Well is Professional 197
6.3.6.1   Details Make a Difference 197
6.3.6.2   Find the Reasons behind the Problem 199
6.3.7   The Team Should be Oriented toward Business Value 199
6.4   Make Information Transparent 200
6.4.1   Blocked Information Flow in Traditional Teams 200
6.4.1.1   What to Do If the Amount of Information is Too Large
Overload? 201
6.4.1.2   What Shall We Do If the Information is Occupied? 201

6.4.1.3   Are Senior Managers More Likely to Make Mistakes?....201
6.4.2   Challenges against Information Transparency 202
6.4.2.1   Upward Communication..202
6.4.2.2   Downward Communication..202
6.4.3   High Transparency is an Irreversible Trend 203
6.4.4   Information Transparency for Offshore Teams 203
6.5   Jump Out of the Comfort Zone 204
6.5.1   Find the Comfort Zone 204
6.5.2   Why Should We Jump Out of the Comfort Zone 205
6.5.3   Team-Motivated to Jump Out of the Comfort Zone 205
6.5.4   Self-Motivated to Jump Out of the Comfort Zone 205
6.5.5   KPI-Motivated to Jump Out of the Comfort Zone 206
6.5.6   Summary 206
6.6   What Does a Project Manager Do? 207
6.6.1   What Does a Traditional Project Manager Look Like?..................208
6.6.2   Project Manager of Self-Organizing Team.................................209
6.6.3   Importance of Project Manager to His Team 210
6.6.4   Importance of Project Manager to Customers.............................212
6.6.5   Successful Project Manager Shall Be the Coach of His Team........213
6.6.6   Successful Project Manager Shall Look at Leadership in the Right Way 214
6.6.7   Successful Project Manager Shall Properly Resolve Conflicts........215
6.6.8   What to Do 215
6.6.8.1   Contribute to Company Management................................215
6.6.8.2   Focus on Products 216
6.6.8.3   Lead the Team to Get on the Right Track 217
6.6.9   How to Do 217
6.6.9.1   Initial Stage 218
6.6.9.2   Later Stage 218
6.6.9.3   Manage Requirements 219
6.6.10   Pay More Attention to Project Risks 220
6.6.11   Summary 220
6.7   Develop a Whole-Team Awareness 221
6.7.1   The Whole Team Shall Correctly Understand Requirements 221
6.7.1.1   Business Analysts 222
6.7.1.2   Development Engineers 222
6.7.1.3   Test Engineers..222
6.7.2   The Whole Team is Responsible for Quality................................223
6.7.3   Development Practice..224
6.7.3.1   The Boundary between Built-In Quality and Built-Out Quality: Code Warehousing 224
6.7.3.2   Philosophy of Code Co-Ownership 224
6.7.3.3   Continuous Integration 224
6.7.4   Awareness of System Security 225
6.7.5   Summary 226
6.8   Feedback is a Propeller for Distributed Teams to Achieve Continuous Improvement 226
6.8.1   Why Should We Value Feedback..226
6.8.2   Key Points in Making Feedback..227
6.8.2.1   Feedback on Personnel Performance................................227
6.8.3   Feedback on Project 228

Chapter 7 Customer-Oriented Offshore Teams 231

    7.1 Establish Mutual Trust with Customers 231
        7.1.1 Objectives 232
            7.1.1.1 Establish Close Cooperation with Customers by Being
                     Frank with Them 232
            7.1.1.2 Customer Trust is a Kind of Asset 233
            7.1.1.3 Avoid Accidents 233
            7.1.1.4 Win Back Customers Who Have Lost Trust in Us
                     without Delay 234
        7.1.2 Build a Trusted Customer Relationship 234
        7.1.3 Tips for Establishing and Maintaining Customer Relationships 235
        7.1.4 Summary 236
    7.2 What Shall We Do When at Odds With Customers? 236
            7.2.1.1 How to "Oppose" Customer Opinions 236
            7.2.1.2 How to Get Prepared to Convince Customers 236
            7.2.1.3 How to Resolve Differences 236
        7.2.2 Settle Differences 237
            7.2.2.1 Business Requirements 237
            7.2.2.2 Technical Realization 237
            7.2.2.3 Results Verification 238
            7.2.2.4 Teamwork 238
        7.2.3 Customer Opinions Determine Delivery Quality 239
    7.3 Delivery Projects Charged by Man-Day 240
    7.4 Fixed-Bid Delivery Projects 240
        7.4.1 Estimation of Workload and Price 241
        7.4.2 Management of Fixed-Bid Projects 243
            7.4.2.1 We Should Know about Team Members 243
            7.4.2.2 What Business Analysis Needs Attention? 244
            7.4.2.3 Make Good Use of Original Story Cards 244
            7.4.2.4 Monitor Progress 244
            7.4.2.5 An Agile Way to Handle Changing Requirements 245
            7.4.2.6 Decisions on Changing Requirements 246
            7.4.2.7 End a Fixed-Bid Project 246
        7.4.3 Business Concerns 246
        7.4.4 Risks of Fixed-Bid Projects 247
        7.4.5 Suggestions, Tips, and Possible Pitfalls 248
    7.5 Connect With Customer's Work 248
        7.5.1 Project Inception 249
            7.5.1.1 Determine the Scope of Requirements with Customers ...249
            7.5.1.2 User Experience Requirements 249
            7.5.1.3 Prioritize All Functions with Customers 249
        7.5.2 Project in Progress 250
            7.5.2.1 Management of Requirements Backlog 250
            7.5.2.2 Customer Knows Project Status in Real Time 251
        7.5.3 Later Stage of Project 252
        7.5.4 Others 253
    7.6 Help Customers Transform into Agile Teams 253
        7.6.1 Capacity Building 253
        7.6.2 Highlight the Advantages of Agile Development and Solidify
            the Beliefs of All Participants 253

		7.6.2.1	Embrace Change	254
		7.6.2.2	Reduce Delivery Risk	254
		7.6.2.3	Legacy System	255
		7.6.2.4	Process Improvement	256
	7.6.3	Establish Cross-Functional Teams		257
	7.6.4	Summary		257

Chapter 8 The Future of Distributed Teams 259

8.1	People in Offshore Teams			259
	8.1.1	Manage Personnel Change		259
		8.1.1.1	Knowledge Transfer	259
		8.1.1.2	Team Migration	260
		8.1.1.3	How to Maintain Team Culture Amid Personnel Change?	260
		8.1.1.4	Create New Culture Amid Changes	261
	8.1.2	Pay Attention to Personal Performance		261
		8.1.2.1	Find the Best Hitting Point	261
		8.1.2.2	Invest in People with Offshore Teams	261
8.2	Remaining Problems in Front of Distributed Teams			262
	8.2.1	Many People Say That Agile Projects Cannot Be Outsourced		262
	8.2.2	Management and Improvement of Domain Knowledge		264
	8.2.3	Effectiveness of Offshore Teams		265
	8.2.4	Learning from History and Facing the Future		265
8.3	The Future of Offshore Teams			265
	8.3.1	Reasons to Hire a Remote Development Team		266
	8.3.2	International Competition		267
	8.3.3	Assist Digital Innovation in Traditional Industries		267
	8.3.4	Agile Model of Offshore Teams		268
	8.3.5	Practice of Innovation with Customers		269
	8.3.6	Summary		270
8.4	Offshore Teams Must Prepare for Technological Change			270
8.5	Low-Cost Offshore Delivery Is a No Return Route			271
8.6	Summary			272
Note				272

Postscript 273

References 275

Index 277

Foreword 1: Taking Up Delivery Wholeheartedly

Three or four years ago, Zhengping Qu said that he planned to write a book on offshore delivery while having a meal with me. At hearing this, I felt so glad that we would finally have a monograph on this subject, and he was just the right person to do so. At that time we had been working at ThoughtWorks for about eight years. It is a company engaged in agile practice and customized software development. After years of dealing with customers coming from different industries and posing different requirements, we have gained rich experiences in software delivery, which is our common interest. Later, both of us left this company, and I transformed from "Party B" into "Party A." A new identity enables me to look at software delivery more comprehensively, but it also makes me confused at the same time.

Half a year ago, Zhengping Qu visited me with the manuscript of this book – a product filled with his wisdom and more than two years' efforts, and told me that it was about to be published. I could hardly wait to finish reading his works.

DISTRIBUTED TEAM

It takes less than three hours to fly from Beijing to Osaka, and about two hours to drive from Wangjing Street to South Third Ring Road (driving across Beijing from northeast to south), but it may take us several months to visit our neighbors or colleagues who live on different floors in the same apartment building. In this day and age, it is no longer accurate to define a "distributed team" simply based on "time" and "distance."

As mentioned in this book, when two teams are more than 30 meters away from each other, they will not communicate frequently and efficiently, a distributed team is then incubated. For example, a team in my company was recently relocated to an office building 200 meters away because of office expansion, since then we seldom connect with it or hear about it. It has to try every means to sustain communication with other teams, but the effect is not desirable.

The theme of this book is "offshore team" – the most "extreme" distributed team, but it tries to solve the problems common to the teams only more than 30 meters away.

SUPPLIERS (DELIVERY TEAMS) BARELY SATISFACTORY

My former employer, ThoughtWorks, is dedicated to excellent software delivery. Working in this company for almost ten years once convinced me that all software development teams were more or less the same. It was not until I left this company and became "Party A" that I came to see the "true colors" of all sorts of software delivery teams. I'm not the person who likes giving lectures, so here I will just share my personal experiences in working with some of these teams.

In each cooperation with a new delivery team, I'd like to ask them for the address of codebase, since it would help me fully learn about the competence of this team. But such a simple request was seldom met. They always made excuses to turn me down. Some teams never used version control tools, but saved codes in shared directories. Some teams were unaware of unit testing; at a code review meeting for a strategic project, I stared at the empty test directory and asked the developer, "Have you done any unit testing?"

"What's that?" he looked at me blankly.

Besides, the work style of their technical supervisors was also worth noting: once a version of software was tested, they would use their personal computer to create a software package for deployment to a production environment.

The above practices, not following industry norms and as primitive as doing manual work, are commonplace in the process of software delivery.

There may be some conscientious suppliers, but most of them are not satisfying: not complying with process specification, making low-quality products, failing to cut high maintenance cost, and ignoring cultivation of employees. These phenomena demonstrate that suppliers pay no attention to the growth of employees while going after interests, and they are too complacent and conservative to make further progress. With such poor performance, they are hard to be counted as specialized software development teams.

"PARTY A" RESTING ON ITS LAURELS

The companies that afford to hire software suppliers are "big" ones, no wonder they have "big company diseases" with varying degrees of symptoms. Lots of business articles have enumerated the typical "diseases," such as heavy department wall, bureaucracy, asymmetry between rights and responsibilities, being content with the status quo, conservative, and less innovative. In addition to the company as a whole, even the subordinate IT division is plagued by these "diseases."

To be frank, the suppliers are somewhat coddled by "Party A" which only wants to stay in the comfort zone, rather than make new breakthroughs. How can it be strict with its suppliers? Of course, not all "Party A" companies stick to established ways. An increasing number of them have started transforming their IT division. It has become an inevitable trend for traditional enterprises to go for digital transformation, but it will not be roses all the way.

The IT division of my current employer (Daimler Greater China) is one of those that seek transformation proactively. But the transformation of such a traditional division with hundreds of employees is no easy job. It calls for the coordination of suppliers, and there are too many things to try and change in the process. The book of Zhengping Qu came at the right time; its pertinent suggestions will help "reformers" avoid detours. All the contents are based on his years of practical experiences, unlike the intangible "golden sentences" preached by those star-like consultants.

PARTY A AND PARTY B NEED A NEW RELATIONSHIP

In fact, I don't like being called "Party A" or "Party B." I think it has created confrontation between the two parties, but there are no better terms to replace them. In outsourcing services, two parties have long been fixing their eyes on contracts, requirement documents, acceptance reports, and PPT files. Party A makes no effort in examining the details of deliverables, and Party B is indifferent to the real thoughts of its customer. Everything is just fine as long as the two parties have no objection to statements and figures.

However, the landscape has shifted in recent years. More and more traditional companies have embarked on digital transformation, making software play an ever more important role in their business and presenting greater challenge to software delivery, which calls Party A and Party B to build a new collaborative relationship. They shall speak frankly and sincerely and make progress together: Party A shall carefully check Party B's deliverables and suggest improvements, while Party B needs to discover Party A's real concern more actively. It is a challenging process for the two parties.

In plain language, this book tells what a professional software development team looks like. With real cases and his personal experiences, Zhengping Qu points out a right direction for his industry peers to improve software delivery.

Han Kai
Chief Software Architect, Daimler Greater China

Foreword 2: Pursue Ideal Software Delivery

After working for years, I have found that many problems in our work are actually caused by people, or more specifically, by communication between people. Though speaking the same language, everyone has his own standpoint, perception, expression and presentation, so the outcome is often not desirable, like the setback in building the Towel of Babel.

In the domain of software development that relies on creativity and multi-party collaboration, especially at the current time when project scale, work pace and distance are several times more than before, the poor communication will widen the gap between requirements and results.

Because of these realistic difficulties, Zhengping Qu is especially admirable for writing a guidebook on offshore delivery. When he made the decision to do so, he was writing the article "Today and Tomorrow of Offshore Delivery" – an entry for the ThoughtWorks Blogger Contest – which seemed like a prelude to the later publication.

"Offshore development" is not something new. When companies look for suitable software implementation, they prefer simple and independent delivery in order to lower cost and ensure quality. But in the past fifteen years, with agile development increasingly popular in China and even becoming the mainstream software development mode, the practices and ideas it promotes have a tangible impact on "offshore development."

This book on offshore development brings together Zhengping Qu's rich work experiences and ThoughtWorks' software delivery practices. It speaks highly of the team that maintains face-to-face communication, implements positive feedback mechanism, employs visualized measurement, eliminates resource waste, and excels at self-organizing. Such a near-perfect team is not only suitable for offshore development.

In my opinion, an energetic and trustworthy team is an ideal condition for software delivery. Domestic teams have made no impressive performances in software delivery over the years; I do hope they could find a clearer direction for doing their work after reading this book.

Many thanks to the writer for bringing us an instructive guidebook!

Zhang Kaifeng
Editor-in-Chief, ThoughtWorks Insights

Preface

The year 2005 was a watershed in my career.

Before that I had been working in a state-owned enterprise for three years, engaged in software development. At that time, the performance of software totally relied on the personal ability of developers; however, the one who was responsible for software debugging in production environment was distracted by welding of circuit board and testing of wireless signal transmission.

Later I found a new job in a software outsourcing company where I met my Waterloo in the first project. I was assigned to develop a warehouse management system before receiving any systematic training. I could understand every function depicted in the technical documents, but the finished product was disappointing. To be honest, I cannot figure out how the customer runs this system until now. While looking back on that period, I came to realize that lack of experience and guidance was the main reason for this failure. First of all, none of us carefully assessed the requirements of the customer. We took for granted that it was enough to do what he asked us to do, instead of making suggestions proactively. All team members had kept busy as the project progressed, but we were unable to deliver rich staged results to the customer. What's worse, we only contacted the customer via e-mail and weekly teleconference, our conversation was all about existing problems and next-week's work plan. We had no more communications on optimization of the project.

Despite of this failure, we soon devoted ourselves to a new project. The same team members were about to deal with another overseas customer, but this time we made a hit, mainly because we learned the lessons from the previous setback and applied the Agile Software Development which we just learned. We even visited the customer's company for deepening mutual understanding. During this tour, we learned lots of practical methods of working that will benefit us in the long run, such as daily morning meetings, test-driven development, iterative development, quick delivery for trial run, feedback collection, and defect management with JIRA. At the beginning, employing these methods, which sounded like empty theories, was no better than wading across the river by feeling for the stones. But in the end, we delivered the project to the customer one month in advance, which caused a stir in our company. We had reserved enough buffer time for pre-delivery testing and defect fixing, which was our years' occupational habit, but it turned out to be unnecessary since not many bugs needed to be fixed near the final delivery. This experience gave us a perceptual knowledge of test-driven development for the first time. When my department head asked me if the software should be tested for two more weeks, I said no, "we've done rounds of tests, the number of bugs have kept declining; it (software) is stable enough." I was so confident at that moment. After a year, one day I received the consumer's e-mail forwarded by the director of our company, he said the software was doing well after a year-long running, and it was one of the best softwares that they had ever used.

You might say I'm self-satisfied. Yes, I am. Whenever I recall this experience, I cannot feel more contented. It proves that as long as we can improve process, enhance communication, and carry on feedback, we will do a better job in software delivery and turn defeat into victory.

Later, we got contracts from more customers and started working together with them during software delivery, rather than all by ourselves. In this process, we not only shared our ways of working with them, but also invented and applied lots of valuable practices, such as Quick Start, Continuous Integration, Continuous Delivery, Behavior-Driven Development (BDD), Lean Management, and Kanban Management. While implementing these core practices, I also found some "micro-practices" suitable for distributed teams based on the features of offshore teams. For example, skillfully communicate by e-mail, listen to the thoughts of customers, play mini-games during remote stand-up meetings, visit customer sites, maintain horizontal communication, Build Quality In, showcase regularly, visualize everything, make full use of distributed teams, think with empathy, and resolve conflicts. These techniques and practices, although they may seem insignificant, are worthy of centralized promotion for their great value in collaboration between distributed teams.

In the past more than ten years, China has seen its software outsourcing industry make great headway; there are lots of large-sized companies and countless employees. At least three years ago, these companies made headlines from time to time; they had recruited top talents and accumulated rich experiences. But recently the development of these companies seems to have entered a period of stagnation, being forced to seek transition or service upgrading. Through observation of China's software outsourcing industry, I have found that the long-lived project teams are mostly the ones cooperating with big customers and capable of independent delivery; these projects are usually not difficult, what the project teams should do is to complete the projects on time at customers' request. But in some start-ups and transitional companies, the project teams are having hard times because they have to take up software in-depth development through working with the customers' technicians or deal with their legacy systems. The quality of their deliverables often fails to satisfy the customers and the process of their cooperation is bumpy and tortuous. If things go on like this, the professional growth of all team members will be mired.

Besides, many companies have substantially adjusted their software outsourcing strategies in recent years. In the past decade, the function of the IT division in a big company was to keep other divisions running smoothly. But nowadays, the development of the Internet is in full swing and agile and flexible software has become a valuable tool, thus motivating big companies to pursue business innovation based on information technology. Therefore, they are paying great attention to the capacity building of their R&D teams rather than outsourcing software development to external contractors as before. In this context, outsourcing companies have to deepen their cooperation with customers and bring forth products with higher technological content. Otherwise, their competitiveness will be compromised. Someone may say the trivial matters, such as strength of the IT division, will not affect the transition of a company as a whole, but I don't think so. Take an engine, for example. When its lubrication system poorly performs or when the air filter does not filter inlet air, how can the engine function normally?

The management books on the market are mostly about the strategies and theories on team management and project management, but hardly any of them focus on offshore teams. Having worked on software delivery for years, I have learned plenty of skills in collaboration between offshore teams. In this book, I will give advice to offshore teams that have cultural and spatiotemporal differences, so as to help them smooth operation and extend service life. This book contains useful contents for all scenarios: customer and project team located in two cities or a multinational company with teams members distributed in all parts of the world.

TARGET READERS

This book will teach readers to effectively communicate with customers and accurately grasp their needs, improve the quality of deliverables, reduce resource waste during collaboration, and cultivate a good working habit. If you take part in outsourced software development as a business analyst, developer, tester, project leader, product manager, or an ordinary team member that desires for promotion, or if you are just a layman having learned relevant theories, you can understand this book thoroughly and may exclaim that "Just so so! I thought it would be more difficult!"

A PRECURSORY STATEMENT

Each theme covered in this book can be further explored and expanded into a separate book, but I've only introduced them out of necessity instead of probing into them. Those who are interested in them can look for their details from other channels.

Some readers may feel familiar with most themes in this book or know much about them. Their effect is really amazing without exaggeration, but few people make good use of them when working on a project.

The practices and cases discussed in this book mainly stem from my own experiences when I was working in or with distributed teams in the past decade. Real stories are unique and able to strike a chord with readers. I think my stories are probably the point that readers are most interested in.

Not everyone can have all of these experiences, that's why I decided to incorporate them into a book so that more people will have an intuitive feeling of them through my description. Almost all the problems and their solutions listed out in this book are pertinent to offshore teams, but they are theoretically instructive to all types of teams.

I hope this book will become a valuable reference book for the readers engaged in software outsourcing. For those not in the software industry, this book will let them learn how software development teams as service providers do their work, which may help to improve the supply–demand relationship. Besides, readers are advised to work with different departments and teams in their company as if they are customers, since in-house cooperation has become ever more important for all companies in the context of globalization.

After spending most of my career in offshore teams, I've accumulated so many valuable experiences. Now the time is ripe for sharing them with everyone, and I can hardly wait to see all the "tactics" in the book be applied to actual combat.

This book explores the key problems in offshore delivery, such as poor communication, inefficient collaboration, changing requirements, incomplete information and data, inferior quality, delayed delivery, and budget overruns. In addition to these problems, outsourcing teams shall figure out how to continue a successful offshore delivery. It is unwise for them to "reinvent the wheel" over and over again. The final point to note is that an ideal delivery is hard to come by, although there are theories depicting the ideal delivery process. "The ideal is full, but the reality is skinny"; we have to find out the solutions for non-ideal delivery.

You may find some verbose expressions in this book if you read it through carefully. I have to clarify that it is intentional. Because an individual theme may contain multiple implications, it ought to be elaborated from different dimensions and perspectives to make readers understand this book comprehensively. It will be the best reward for me if all readers could have real gains from this book, and none of them gets confused or has to go over it to learn something useful.

Let me "blow my own horn" in the end: if you have to work with remote teams or provide services to local customers, this book is highly recommended to be the key to your success.

1 Current Situation of Distributed Teams

1.1 INTRODUCTION TO DISTRIBUTED TEAMS

As the wheels of globalization roll on, we have got so many opportunities to work closely with colleagues and customers in all parts of the world. And the developed Internet has made our collaboration increasingly convenient.

1.1.1 RAPID DEVELOPMENT OF DISTRIBUTED TEAMS

The concept of distributed teams was brought up by the software companies in developed countries more than a decade ago. To reduce labor cost, these companies started outsourcing their noncore operations to the countries with vast human resources at a relatively low cost. At that time, most outsourced software was enterprise application with a relatively fixed demand and a long period of development.

In the early days, when customers intended to hire a contractor in the countries with a developed service outsourcing industry, they had to employ the following methods:

- **Online advertising of contractors.** I used to work in a software contractor, there is a team specialized in online promotion, i.e., sending marketing e-mails to all potential customers in the US based on their contact information on the yellow pages directory, in an attempt to introduce the company's business scope and competence.
- **Word-of-Mouth (WOM) or Business-to-Business (B2B) marketing.** There are many cases in this regard, but it is hard for a company to gain a good reputation in this way. So this method cannot become a conventional marketing strategy for contractors to attract customers.

For a cooperative relationship between customers and contractors built with the above methods, a long time is to be spent on fostering their mutual trust. If the customer is a small- and medium-sized company more vulnerable to potential risks, it may organize an on-site investigation of the contractor. If the customer is a big company, the above cooperative models will be far from satisfying, since it prefers a mature system and sophisticated appraisal methods as the basis of cooperation, which gives rise to the demand for a criterion, and CMMI Assessment came out at a right time.

1.1.2 WHY CUSTOMERS VALUE CMMI ASSESSMENT

Capability Maturity Model Integration (CMMI) was developed on basis of Capability Maturity Model (CMM) born in the late 1980s. It was jointly developed by Carnegie Mellon University and the National Defense Industry Association with the sponsorship of the US Department of Defense

(DOD). It was originally designed as a tool for project implementation and management, but widely used for software process improvement (SPI) since the mid-1990s.

CMMI (and its predecessor CMM) was firstly applied for scientific research and engineering, not exclusively for software. The DOD intended to employ this model to assess the competence of its suppliers so as to lower cost and ensure quality, but the tendering activities of the DOD has increased publicity of CMMI – a model with five levels of maturity, which makes it easier for software companies to lift their management level to the required level. More importantly, they have to do so because more and more tenderees ask bidders to satisfy the requirements of a certain CMMI level, after all, CMMI was the only trustworthy and operable assessment model at that time. To get more orders, companies are increasing input to pass CMMI assessment, which has indirectly promoted its application.

Indian companies are doing particularly well in this regard. To most people's surprise, their promotion of CMMI even surpassed their American counterparts, that's why India is home to a large number of CMMI Level 5 companies, which are qualified contractors of large-scale projects and even core projects of overseas customers, and also the groundwork for the country's developed software outsourcing industry. It can be said that CMMI set the stage for the world's first offshore outsourcing teams, and stimulated their growth and expansion.

To be passed by CMMI assessment, a software company shall create huge amounts of documents to prove its methods and practices for delivering products and services have reached its intentional CMMI level. Appraisers cannot assess the company's project management level simply based on its products. The object of assessment is process; good process management is sure to yield good results. The company usually hires an expert to teach it how to meet the CMMI criteria and how to demonstrate its high-level project management process with documents.

CMMI assessment requires companies and their project teams to spend a lot of energy and time on document writing and maintenance. Such cost can be compensated by the earnings from large-scale and relatively stable projects which need later-stage software maintenance. But for the customers in the Internet industry, such kind of highly documented management may delay their business and technical response.

Readers that are curious about the five maturity levels of CMMI can find more details in Table 1.1.

As shown in Table 1.1, each level below is the cornerstone of the level above. To ascend to a higher level, one shall firstly get over the lower one. Likewise, companies shall pass CMMI assessment level by level. CMMI is in essence a standardized model for process management. By implementing this model, companies can adopt a targeted approach to improve their project management.

From the present point of view, only CMMI Level 5 companies are capable of continuous process improvement through quantification and feedback. As for the Level 5 software companies, how can

TABLE 1.1
Five Maturity Levels of CMMI Based on Staged Representation

Levels of CMMI	Description	Requirements
Level 5	Optimizing	Improve the process proactively upon successful project management, and make sure of continuous optimization.
Level 4	Quantitatively managed	The process is subject to digital management to maintain the stable quality of a project.
Level 3	Defined	A standard process is defined to guarantee the project execution.
Level 2	Managed	The successful outcome of a project is guaranteed by plans, processes, defined distribution of rights and responsibilities, and means of management.
Level 1	Complete	Project goal can be achieved, but it is incidental and non-duplicated.

they make sure of continuous process improvement? There are three principles for them to follow: improve software process to make it more efficient; employ new technologies and new tools to increase productivity; and summarize and resolve existing problems in time to keep from repeating past mistakes.

But there are risks in improving process and introducing new technologies, companies shall think twice before doing so, and try out new process and technology on a small scale before company-wide implementation. While new process and technology are promoted across the company, their implementation shall be monitored and their improvement effect shall be assessed.

For a period of time in the past, distributed teams were mostly offshore contractor teams, and they were managed by someone specially designated by their customers. This person would make plans, assign tasks to the team, check and accept its deliverables. For the offshore team, this person was spokesperson of the customer; but for the customer, this person was responsible for the deliverables of the team.

In recent years, we have seldom heard about CMMI. Is it replaced by a better criterion? The answer is no, it is because Agile Development has become increasingly popular and changes the organization mode and work style of distributed teams. In this context, members of offshore teams shall adapt themselves to different ways of management and cooperation, assume more responsibilities, and create more value to customers.

1.1.3 TYPES OF DISTRIBUTED TEAMS

A distributed team may have different forms of cooperation, including the cooperation with other teams inside the same company, the cooperation with (or competition against) the technical team of the customer, and the cooperation with (or competition against) the consultant team of the customer. Different forms of cooperation correspond to different levels of cooperation, including the cooperation inside the same company.

What if a distributed team is composed of a development team and a testing team which are not in the same place? Such kind of distributed team is not welcome, because its internal communication is further obstructed – the division of development team and testing team is the first barrier for communication – and making it much harder for its sub-teams to work for the same goal. In the past, we thought less communication inside a distributed team might be a good thing, since it would minimize the interdependence between sub-teams and force them to work on their own. But this approach is proved to be unworkable. In fact, we should not build a competent distributed team, but a functional one which performs the functions in an end-to-end manner, i.e., from bringing up an idea, product design, development, testing, and to online running.

Figure 1.1 illustrates the project delivery process of a competent team and a functional team, respectively, based on the Waterfall Model and the Agile Model.

Figure 1.1 shows that the functional team has a great advantage in terms of delivery time, far supervior to the competent team. But if they undertake the projects with fixed requirements but no continuous development, it is the competent team that boasts a cost advantage.

Lots of companies allow some of their employees to work from home. Such personnel arrangement differs greatly from a distributed team; its management of employees is fairly flexible, they can come to the office to work with their colleagues at any time. This "gathering" and "scattering" work style conforms to the realistic need, and reflects the company's humanized management. For example, as long as KPI keeps playing its role, the breastfeeding female employees are able to feed their babies without delaying their work; the employees who are the only child in their family may sometimes work at their parents' home to accompany them; and other employees, especially those who live far away from the company, will not waste time on taking the subway at morning-evening rush hours. "Working from home" boasts so many benefits, no wonder it is to the satisfaction of both company and employees.

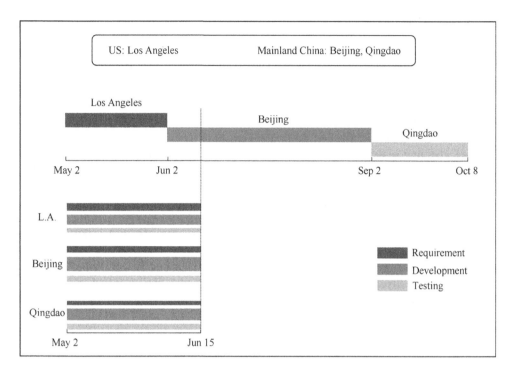

FIGURE 1.1 Project delivery process.

1.1.4 WHAT KIND OF TEAM IS A DISTRIBUTED TEAM

What is a distributed team? Many people will say it is made up of the sub-teams distributed in different places. But they are only partly right. A distributed team may exist in the same building or even on the same floor. An authoritative definition is that as long as the two or more teams are more than 30 meters away from each other, they can form a distributed team. The criteria for "distributed" are as follows: the two teams are out of each other's sight or hard to hear from each other if they have raised their voice, which has blocked their efficient and frequent communication.

Take my own experience as an example, I was once taking charge of a software development project of an automobile manufacturer; my team members were divided into two sub-teams occupied with different microservices, but their office desks were placed at the two opposite corners of the same office area, thus forming a distributed team. As far as I know, although some teams are working on the same floor, they prefer discussing requirement issues via e-mail, rather than exchanging views face to face in front of a whiteboard; they are also a distributed team.

How about the multiple branches of a multinational company? Are they a distributed team? The answer is "no" in most cases. Take Google, for example, the company still insists that all business and technical teams should work together. Although it has set up branches in many parts of the world, they have no substantial collaboration between each other, so they cannot constitute a genuine distributed team. But when they need to collaborate frequently to fulfill the same project, they may take the ways of working for a distributed team as described in this book.

1.2 CURRENT SITUATION OF SERVICE OUTSOURCING INDUSTRY

The benefit of outsourcing is that when customers have a short-term project, they do not have to spend time and money on maintaining a long-term project team.

Even some ambitious companies are in favor of outsourcing noncore businesses (such as business process) to professional service companies, so that they can concentrate on their core business, cut indirect costs, and increase operational efficiency and flexibility.

China is one of the world's leading exporters of outsourcing service. Each year MOFCOM[1] Department of Trade in Services and Commercial Services sums up the data about the national service outsourcing industry in the previous year, and makes them available to the public. The 2017 data are shown as follows:

In 2016, the global investment and trade remained on the downside, but it did not impede the rapid development of China's service outsourcing industry; instead, offshore service outsourcing vigorously drove up China's service exports, played a vital role in optimizing its foreign trade structure and moving national industries up to the high end of the global value chain.

The official from MOFCOM Department of Trade in Services and Commercial Services pointed out that China's service outsourcing presented the following features in 2016:

(1) The industrial scale expanded rapidly, and the newly signed contract value surpassed 1,000 billion yuan for the first time. China's service outsourcing made great headway in 2016, with the contract value and executed contract value hitting 1,021.3 billion yuan and 738.5 billion yuan, respectively, up 20.1% and 17.6% year on year, respectively. Among these, the contract value and executed contract value of offshore service outsourcing reached 660.8 billion yuan and 488.5 billion yuan, with an increase of 16.6% and 16.4%. Moreover, China saw its offshore service outsourcing occupy a global market share of about 33%, retaining its second place in the world; and the executed contract value of offshore service outsourcing account for 1/4 of its total service exports.

(2) The industrial structure continued to be optimized, and the technology-intensive businesses accounted for a higher proportion. With the support of the next-generation information technologies such as cloud computing, big data, the Internet of Things (IoT), and Mobile Internet (MI), the "Internet + Service Outsourcing" development model was rapidly promoted, and the service outsourcing companies were occupied with transformation to undertake high-tech and high value-added businesses. In 2016, the executed contract value of offshore information technology outsourcing (ITO), business process outsourcing (BPO), and knowledge process outsourcing (KPO) reached 229.3 billion yuan, 80.9 billion yuan, and 178.3 billion yuan, respectively, accounting for 46.9%, 16.6%, and 36.5%, respectively, and with an increase of 11.4%, 35.9%, and 15.5%, respectively, year on year.

(3) The companies kept improving their professional services and innovative ability. The service outsourcing companies newly obtained 927 international qualification certifications (including CMMI), increasing 15.3% year on year; and signed contracts with an average unit price of 5.27 million yuan, rising 5.6% year on year. With continuously improved technical capability and professional services, the companies were on the way of gradual transformation from providing single technical services to providing integrated solutions, from project contracting to strategic cooperation, and from being cost-driven to being innovation-driven.

(4) The clustering effect and leading role of the service outsourcing exemplary cities (hereinafter referred to as the "exemplary cities") became more prominent. The executed contract value of the exemplary cities amounted to 456.4 billion yuan, rising 15.9% year on year, and accounting for 93.4% of the national total. Among them, the executed contract value of the four exemplary cities (Beijing, Shanghai, Guangzhou, and Shenzhen) was 138.5 billion yuan, rising 21.3% year on year, and accounting for 28.4% of the national total, marking that these cities were playing an important leading role in innovation of technologies and business model. In 2016, the executed contract value of the ten newly-added exemplary cities reached 38.4 billion yuan, up 32.2% year on year, and faster than the growth pace of all exemplary cities and the country at large, thus becoming a new growth pole in China's service outsourcing industry.

(5) The cooperation with major markets of service outsourcing was strengthened, and the international market was further expanded. In 2016, the executed contract value in offshore service outsourcing from the US, the EU, Japan, and Hong Kong – major markets of service outsourcing – added up to 308.6 billion yuan, up 19.3% year on year; such executed contract value from the countries along "One Belt One Road" reached 84.1 billion yuan, accounting for 17.2% of the

total execution value. Besides, Chinese offshore business had already expanded to 201 countries and regions, with operations all over the world. By undertaking offshore service outsourcing, Chinese companies have built up their R&D strength, promoted their technologies, designs, and criteria to "go global," and deepened international economic and trade cooperation.

(6) The number of employees continued to increase with a great proportion of university graduates. In 2016, newly increased employees in the service outsourcing sector reached 1.12 million, among which 800,000 with college (including junior college) education or above, accounting for 65.9%. As of the end of 2016, the number of employees in the service outsourcing sector totaled 8.56 million, including 5.51 million with college (including junior college) education or above, accounting for 64.4% of the total employees.

According to the official from MOFCOM Department of Trade in Services and Commercial Services, in 2017 MOFCOM would follow the general principle of seeking progress while keeping performance stable, implement new development concepts, accelerate the supply-side structural reform, optimize the layout of service outsourcing industry and regional development in collaboration with competent authorities, establish a dynamic entry-exit mechanism for exemplary cities, promote the first-tier cities to enhance innovative ability and increase industrial added value, transfer the labor-intensive businesses to second- and third-tier cities; conscientiously summarize the development experiences of exemplary cities, and organize studies on duplicating their preferential policies in nonexemplary cities.

Speaking of the software outsourcing in the past, most stakeholders in Party A did not care about how the project was going and how to solve problems; they were only interested in staged deliverables. In recent years, along with the popularization of the Internet, more and more industries are making use of the Internet, especially the MI, to expand their business scope and make innovations. Consequently, the previous software outsourcing models are becoming outdated, now it is common to see that project contractors discuss with customers about sustainable innovation and product upgrading. The two sides are cooperating more closely. Customers value not only the major project results but also the process of cooperation.

More importantly, with sharply rising labor costs, China's outsourcing industry is about to face great challenges in the international market. The report released by MOFCOM Department of Trade in Services and Commercial Services in 2017 confirmed my anticipation of the prospect of software outsourcing and the urgency for industrial upgrading. All practitioners are advised to build up their hard skills and soft skills to stay competitive, there is still a broad stage for them to play on, and the world is to remain flat for them to move about freely. Besides, as China increases input into the supply-side structural reform, more and more talents will throw themselves into software outsourcing industry. If we do not strive for upward mobility proactively, we are bound to be surpassed by new-generation talents.

Service outsourcing industry, mostly software outsourcing, has maintained high-speed growth for more than ten years. It has a powerful magnetizing effect on talents, and in the meantime provides them with sufficient opportunities to improve their professional skills, learn multidisciplinary knowledge and different technology stacks.

Outsourcing industry is a window of opportunity for so many people to start and develop their career. Through this window, numerous young people have come to know how foreign companies operate and how R&D divisions perform their functions.

1.3 HOW TO BUILD AN OFFSHORE TEAM

1.3.1 PRINCIPLES FOR BUILDING A DISTRIBUTED TEAM

The traditional view is that it is appropriate to build domestic and offshore teams according to their work content. For example, the business analysis and design teams are based in the US, the development team is in China, and the test team is also in the US. They will constitute a distributed team that is fit to employ the Waterfall Model.

In recent years, we seldom hear about a separate development team or a separate test team in software outsourcing sector. At present, we usually divide teams according to the functions of products, rather than the competence of teams. A functional team is to develop a functional module from end to end, not just a particular stage. It means that a distributed team shall be split into several sub-teams, and each of them develops a single functional module. Thanks to continuous integration, the interaction between functional modules will not be affected, i.e., as the development proceeds, all modules will gradually integrate together.

For an offshore team, the workplace of the business analyst (usually assuming the responsibility of product manager) is an important issue. He is farther away from both users and product stakeholders if comparing with his counterpart in a local team. The business analyst in an offshore team needs to solve business-related problems on the spot, so that developers will no longer spend a whole day waiting for solutions, and the process of development will proceed smoothly. But it is easier said than done; the business analyst must acquaint himself with the customer's businesses, and exchange views with the customer's business manager on the current project in advance.

The composition of an offshore team is based on the criteria for a full-functional team, which is good for communication. A full-functional team is able to solve most problems inside the team, unlike a single-functional team which fails to do so and has to discuss the matter with other single-functional teams. If two single-functional teams, like a development team and a test team, are located in different time zones, their out-of-sync communication will seriously affect the outcome of the project.

Thomas L. Friedman, author of *The World Is Flat*, says the "flatteners" (including the rise of outsourcing, offshoring, supply chaining, and insourcing) "created a flat world: a global, web-enabled platform for multiple forms of sharing knowledge and work, irrespective of time, distance, geography and increasingly, language."

Some customers have noticed the advantage of distributed teams. When an American team is about to get off work, a new problem or an urgent task suddenly comes up, they can contact the team in another time zone, like the one in China, and hand over the task to their Chinese colleagues. When the Americans come to work the next day, all or part of the work is already completed. The customer, who had to wait for two days to get a result, now finds his concerns addressed in just one day, although it actually costs our teams two workdays.

1.3.2 DIFFERENT COMPOSITION OF A DISTRIBUTED TEAM

When undertaking different projects, a distributed team shall have different staffing and deployment, as shown in the examples below:

There is a team made up of twelve people, ten (DM, PO, QA, BA, Dev) are working in Beijing and two (Dev) in Wuhan. The people in different positions are working independently, but the two Devs in Wuhan are invited to join in team activities every time, and work in Beijing for a while, which helps to deepen their mutual understanding and maintain their relationship. Moreover, the team members in two places are encouraged to work in pair to guarantee knowledge sharing inside the distributed team.

There is a team made up of twenty-eight people, twenty (DM, PO, QA, BA, Dev) are working in Beijing, and eight (BA, QA, Dev) in Xi'an. Unlike the above example, the two sub-teams are engaged in development on their own, and do not often communicate; it is Scrum of Scrums Meeting that coordinates their work and informs them of updates. Their interaction while working is better to be avoided for saving communication cost in collaboration.

The Scrum of Scrums (SoS) Meeting is a complex mechanism that facilitates the sharing of information among various Scrum Teams, so as to help the multiple teams working on a large project better coordinate and integrate their work. Typically, after the daily stand-up meeting held by each Scrum Team is over, a representative from each Scrum Team – usually the Scrum Master – will attend another meeting where he will talk about the work of his team the day before and its impact on the work of other teams, as well as the work plan of his team the next day and its possible impact. This meeting is an occasion for each Scrum Team to deliver its problems without any solution yet, and expect answers from others; it seems like a deeper-level daily stand-up meeting.

1.3.3 INVESTMENT AND BENEFIT OF BUILDING A DISTRIBUTED TEAM

A distributed team is usually built for the following three purposes:

- **Reduce cost**
- **Open up local market**
- **Recruit more talents**

Regarding the issue of building an offshore team instead of recruiting local talents, not only customers have practical concerns, but the software industry has different opinions. Those who prefer an offshore team speak highly of its lower labor cost. Sometimes an offshore team – the extreme form of distributed team as mentioned earlier – is the only choice for us to fulfill product delivery, because no right talents are found locally, which may be the most valid reason for creating a distributed team to carry out product development.

In fact, it is unwise to fixate on labor cost, since it is only a part of total cost. Being a veteran in software industry for years, I can say for certain that the productivity of different people varies more significantly than their salary. Such difference between offshore teams and local teams is more striking, because the former not only has labor cost, but also higher expenses on communication and business travel, meaning that there are greater risks to set up an offshore team than a local team.

Let's look at communication cost first. A distributed team has to deal with a variety of communication challenges, such as impossible face-to-face communication due to long distance, time difference, and weak language expression ability. Because of these challenges, we are prone to misunderstand customers' requirements, and even invent some undesirable functions of software. Although we have adopted many technical means and sent permanent representatives to the distributed team, the offshoring risks still have a negative impact on our entire project team.

If the distributed team adopts a traditional work style rather than an agile approach, the sub-teams will find it more difficult to realize face-to-face direct communication, but send e-mails and files to reach a consensus. Can we say this distributed team has the highest input-output ratio? Of course not. Reducing communication cost by avoiding direct communication cannot build up the delivery capacity of a team. Just like we cannot get rich by saving money, we need to increase inputs into Open Source to create more value.

But the advantages of a distributed team are undeniable. If the offshore teams are distributed in different time zones, they can develop a function incessantly within 24 hours like runners in a relay race. It is a kind of serial working mode unique to offshore teams, and able to speed up the product launch. If the offshore teams are capable of technical support, they will be exceptionally good at solving urgent problems. For example, we were using Salesforce – a third-party platform software – at some time in the past, a technical problem popped up at night. Our Beijing office immediately contacted the technicians in London because they had just started working at that moment. When they were about to get off work, they transferred the remaining work to the Salesforce technical center in California, later the Americans handed the work to the Sydney-based technical division to finish it. Fortunately, when our employees in Beijing came to work the next morning, they received the solution from the offshore team far away in Sydney.

Finally, I'd like to emphasize the value of talents. We can recruit plenty of excellent engineers in many Chinese cities such as Beijing and Shenzhen, even if these people have no plans to settle down in these places. In other countries, it is difficult to find a place where so many talents are concentrated, and they are unwilling to leave their family for working overseas. In view of such reality, building offshore teams is a good idea for attracting the smart minds in all parts of the world. We should never forget that at any time the value of talents must come first, rather than their cost.

1.3.4 Matters that Need Attention

1.3.4.1 People are a Key Factor for a Distributed Team

An entire team should work more efficiently, since all members are working together every day, and they can communicate with each other at any time as they want. How could someone argue that team-working sometimes lowers efficiency? But, unfortunately, this is the fact. An optimal congenital condition is not always leading to a satisfying outcome. For example, a child born with a silver spoon in his mouth may end up as a loser, while those growing up in ordinary families often excel their peers, it is because poor conditions may inspire their fighting spirit and multiply their ambitions.

When something you are longing for is easily obtained, you will not take it as anything special, but when you have it in possession through hard work, you will cherish it as a priceless treasure. Likewise, communication is more valuable for a distributed team than ordinary teams. Those working in a distributed team make full preparations for each communication so as to make it more efficient; it seems as if they are taking every opportunity to make up for the discouragingly objective conditions.

It can be seen that people are one of the key factors for the success of a distributed team. By recruiting talented people, and teaching them to learn self-management skills and implement appropriate practices, we will be able to minimize the negative impact of distance.

1.3.4.2 Mounting Difficulties in Communication Change the Communication Habits of the Team

The previous experiences show that any inconvenient interface may lead to a consequence that when the number of communication decreases, the content of each communication will increase. For example, if it only costs minutes to invite other team members to confirm a request or defect, I can work out an existing problem right away. However, when I have to do so by creating a meeting or sending an e-mail to others, I will prefer putting this problem aside and wait for more problems to emerge, so that I can have all of them discussed and resolved in one time.

1.3.4.3 Solutions to Minimize the Negative Impact of Remote Working

Remote working usually slows down the process of social learning and increases the difficulties in interactive work for cross-functional teams, so we need to invest in some necessary tools (such as Wi-Fi and video telephone) and daily communication processes. And we'd better pair remotely and use SharedView to close the distance between distributed teams. In short, investments in engineering practices, continuous integration and automated testing tools are especially important for distributed teams.

It is important that all consensuses should be reached at the beginning and preserved in the future. For example, the consensus on the principle for distributing work and the one on the roles of each team member will greatly affect the job assignment result among distributed teams.

There are lessons in lacking of consensus: a local team took charge of job assignment or mistakenly believed that it had the power to do so, then it would assign the offshore team to do all tedious tasks, like fixing bugs, but undertake the R&D of new products on its own. Such selfish behavior is detrimental, how can someone keep working passionately when he is treated as a "second-class citizen"!

Regarding the effect of communication, a remote meeting is of course not as good as an on-site meeting, but distributed teams still need to attend remote meetings regularly and even frequently, especially stand-up meeting, iteration plan meeting (IPM), and retrospective meeting.

In the case of distributed teams, the conventional "face-to-face" communication can be realized by means of instant communication tool, video conference, and teleconference, as long as they can communicate with each other directly.

What if our customers themselves exist in distributed teams? If so, we have to properly deal with the two customer teams concurrently, and check and verify their requirements.

1.4 VARYING DEVELOPMENT TREND OF SOFTWARE OUTSOURCING SERVICE

In today's era of digital transformation, the enterprises only providing low-cost commodity services are becoming increasingly marginalized, while more and more enterprises are exploring ways to build a stronger strategic partnership with outsourcing suppliers. Consequently, both the type and quality of outsourcing service contracts have been going through changes gradually.

An increasing number of customers have accepted the ideas of agile development, DevOps, and microservices, and begun to transform into agile enterprises.

1.4.1 THE WAR FOR TALENT HAS STARTED

Outsourcing projects, especially those providing consulting services which have been on the rise, require the participation of more senior experts and consultants. In this context, outsourcing service companies have to pay some attention to attracting and retaining talents.

Purchasing software services in the areas with the lowest cost is no longer a competitive edge, because customers are attempting to raise efficiency and reduce cost through automation and tools. That's why more and more organizations are improving large-scale productivity based on technology rather than labor force.

Nowadays, traditional enterprises, whether they are banks or oil and gas companies, are eager to solve their business problems with innovative, flexible and high-end technologies, and their technical requirements are greatly improved. In the past, outsourcing companies would recommend technologies to customers, but the latter mainly cared about business matters instead of technical realization. At present, customers like talking about cloud computing, big data and AI, and they have more requirements for product design. This is a good news which is sure to add the value of labor force, and break free from the old concept of "cost is king" which had been popular in the past decade or so. An even better news is that customers accept offshore delivery as they did before.

Customers are paying increasing attention to risk aversion, since they find the risks unbearable whenever they put a new product online. That's why customers prefer the "automation-oriented" deliverables which feature automated testing, automated construction, continuous integration, continuous delivery or one-click deployment, in order to eliminate the impact of anthropogenic factors. Automation not only increases efficiency, but also brings proactive problem-solving capabilities before it becomes a business-affecting event, which has created more added value for enterprises than typical cost reduction.

More than that, customers also take more interest in the post-delivery DevOps of software, and the application of virtualization and containerization technologies, which has stimulated the automated and intellectualized development of DevOps.

And customers have become so smart that they have found the "core" of technology-driven innovation, that is, technologies shall be employed to reduce expenditure and increase added value concurrently; such a "two-handed approach" is able to build up enterprise competitiveness.

1.4.2 OFFSHORE DELIVERY CENTER – ACHIEVEMENT OF STRATEGIC COOPERATION

As technology becomes a cross-industry competitive edge, it seems that all companies, including automakers, oil and gas suppliers and retailers, have begun to transform themselves into sci-tech firms. From time to time, we can hear from news that a senior executive introducing his company as a sci-tech firm, although his company is in fact in traditional industry. On the one hand, the Internet-based innovation will motivate more and more IT outsourcing customers to build their own offshore delivery centers. On the other hand, outsourcing service suppliers can grasp this trend to upgrade themselves into delivery centers through deep ploughing of a particular industry and certain technologies.

To be a qualified offshore delivery center, human resources are no doubt important, but it shall also have well-functioning mechanisms for ensuring information security and operation security, and go through an on-site security check by the customer. And all of its environment, regulations, and norms shall meet the requirements of the customer.

1.4.3 New Ways for Customers to Measure Outsourcing Services

During the period of business transformation, one of the biggest changes facing the IT services industry is to quantify services. The contract model is shifting from the traditional one based on investment or transaction to the new one based on business indicators and results. The convincing data acquisition and the design of landmark events are especially important for implementing the new model.

Customer expectations have been developing at a fast pace. When undertaking specific businesses, potential suppliers are asked to offter tailor-made solutions to customers, thus boosting the development of high-end consulting service providers who are skilled in designing better-quality solutions.

The key to transformation of outsourcing services is to replace the arbitrage model by earning a difference with the digitized model, which requires all outsourcing service providers to divert more resources to innovation. Besides, their talent reserve and successful cases are also important indicators to earn the trust of customers.

NOTE

1 Translator's note: MOFCOM is the abbreviation of Ministry of Commerce of the People's Republic of China.

2 Communication between Distributed Teams

2.1 MANAGE CUSTOMER EXPECTATIONS

So many ideas that we take for granted may not be right. For example, it is often said that the people from south China are fond of spicy food, while those from the northern part don't like it. But the fact is just the opposite, most southerners in coastal areas seldom eat spicy food, while the northerners distributed in inland areas enjoy it very much. How could so many people have infinite faith in such misunderstanding? It may be attributed to preconceptions and the mindset of following the herd, but the fundamental reason is "Copinism," that is, we are prone to accepting ready-made viewpoints, rather than check the facts on our own and establish a correct understanding.

Likewise, regarding customer expectations, we should avoid being perplexed by phenomena and see through the appearance to perceive the essence. Lots of people have a personal experience that subjective thinking easily causes misunderstandings, that's why we need to train our ability of objective analysis. This is the first step in managing customer expectations.

The key to good management of customer expectations is to set reasonable expectations for a customer, so that the offshore team and the customer could work in the same direction, and finally achieve a win-win outcome. Reasonable expectations are especially important, it indicates that the judgment made by the offshore team accords with the customer's thinking. If the expectations set by the offshore team are quite at odds with those of the customer, the latter will never feel satisfied no matter how many skills are utilized by the offshore team, because the customer expectations are in essence his requirements for an offshore team.

In order to properly manage customer expectations, we must think and act from the customer perspective. But it is easier said than done. How can we change our own perspective to form a good interaction with customers?

2.1.1 KNOW THE CUSTOMERS

When any project is about to be started, the customer team is obliged to fill in an information sheet, writing down the name of each member, their duty, expertise and work style, etc., as if it was drawing a self-portrait.

2.1.1.1 Who Are They?

Let me take my experience with an offshore team for example. The composition of one of its customers is shown in Table 2.1, and all the personal information is a must-read for the offshore team.

At the beginning, we often confused the responsibilities of Kevin and Ken's. Every time we finished the development of a function, we would contact them for acceptance, but they were seldom available at the same time, so we had to invite either one of them for acceptance. But there

TABLE 2.1

Position and Job Description of Each Member of a Customer Team

Team Member	Position	Job Description
Kevin	Project manager, technical director	Keep an eye on the working progress of the offshore team, and its DevOps solution, technology selection, acceptance functional test, determination of nonfunctional requirements, etc.
Ken	Product manager	Keep an eye on the priority of function launch, user experience, acceptance functional test, etc.
Ben	Tester	Keep an eye on the key points of testing at different stages, the coverage of automated testing, defects found in the product environment, etc.
James	Front-end developer	Discuss with the offshore team on code integration, code review, and technical solution.
Tom	Back-end developer	Discuss with the offshore team on code integration, code review, and technical solution.

were occasions where Ken finished watching the showcase, he would suggest us to confirm it with Kevin. After this acceptance matter was repeated for several times, we found out that if the function was about logic implementation, Ken had no final say but suggested us to turn to Kevin for acceptance; if the function was associated with user experience, Kevin would ask us to consult with Ken. Gradually, we got to be acquainted with their division of responsibilities, and identified which matter was in need of the confirmation and acceptance by both of them.

This story tells that to fully understand a customer, we shall first get to know every member of his team and their respective responsibilities. We can refer to a simple personnel list, or a traditional hierarchical structure diagram that introduces all the members of the customer team, so that the entire offshore team will know whom they are dealing with, what is he responsible for, and which kind of information is he interested in. Only in this way can we carry on our work with a purpose, and identify which member of the customer team needs detailed information and which one only needs an outline.

In case the customer has any stakeholder, we should avoid the situation where this stakeholder puts forward different requirements from the customer. In practice, there are circumstances where the customer agrees to our solution, and then our offshore team starts working upon receipt of his approval; however, when we have reached the halfway stage of the project, this stakeholder says he is against our solution. We can tell him that this solution is approved, or forward him the customer's reply as evidence. But this is only a way of doing things, rather than a strategy. A wise strategy is that when we are about to devise a solution, we shall try our best to get together all members of the customer team, including its stakeholders. Even if there may be someone absent at the meeting, we are ought to inform him of the solution without delay.

- Manage all stakeholders of the customer: draw a diagram that contains the information listed in Table 2.2.
- Background information: time to join in the customer's company, influence inside the company, does he know much about testing or agile practices (or is he certified by Scrum Alliance), and does he have any domain knowledge.
- Major concerns: whether he rejects reconstitution, and whether he values automated testing, test coverage, and rate of development.
- In what ways can he help the offshore team: what is his expertise, which business problems can he address, and does he know about the architecture of the legacy system.

TABLE 2.2
List of Customer's Stakeholders

Name of Stakeholder	Position	Background	Major Concerns	In What Ways Can He Help the Offshore Team?	Immediate Superior

So, when dealing with different members of the customer team, we need to adjust the content of communication. For example, when discussing with a technician, we need to explain the specific technical implementation. A more challenging task is to convince the business staff inside the customer team, since he is usually the decision maker. In my opinion, the most effective approach is "storytelling." In this process, we can explain the purpose of our solution, and try to remind him of any pain points in their businesses, so as to enable him to resonate with us.

For example, if a user intends to save data in the system, and export them in a fixed format, we will advise him to use the existing Excel format, instead of developing a new Form Control which is a lengthy and costly process. After he has edited the data in Excel spreadsheets – the easiest tool for most users, he can have them exported in CSV format, which will significantly shorten the development cycle. To export data in CSV format is for the sake of availability, since one user can export up to 500,000 pieces of data each time, but such a huge amount of data, if coupled with user concurrency, are inoperable in Excel due to the limitations on its performance.

We carried on the development according to the above scheme; however, we later found that the exported CSV data were unusable. For example, the CSV format does not support multiple languages, thus making the non-English text shown as garbled characters. Given this, we were forced to solve the performance problems of Excel, and fortunately, we worked it out with a disruptive solution.

When making explanations to the customer team, we compared the development workload and the advantages and disadvantages of user experience between this disruptive solution and other solutions, rather than tell them how to integrate Excel workbooks and how to develop Excel spreadsheets from a technical perspective. In this way, it would be easier for each member of the customer team to convey our intention to his colleagues, thus paving way for our team to implement this solution.

In the late stage of development, if the solution failed to meet the customer requirements, we could make technical explanations and adjustment to maintain the customer satisfaction, even though our final solution might change greatly from the original one.

2.1.1.2 What Do They Think About?

Making customers satisfied is the biggest wish of all offshore teams. After all, customers are the ones on whom our livelihood depends. Their consent will assure us of doing our work according to established criteria, including the introduction of new practices. This is a virtuous circle. And the key to form or sustain such a virtuous circle is to know what the customers think about.

How to satisfy customers? The first step is to know what they are thinking about from their perspective. Some people may say it's as easy as a piece of cake. But in fact, we cannot truly and fully read their minds unless we have the collective strength of a team and set all of our wits to work.

We should start to understand customers from the following aspects:

(i) **Priority.** All of us have endless work to do, but no one is inexhaustible to accomplish everything. Therefore, when we are about to start working, we shall have each task prioritized. Especially for our offshore team, we shall establish correct work priorities and make them consistent with those of the customer. If we have been doing something that the customer doesn't think important, while putting aside what he wants the most, how can we make the customer satisfied!

(ii) **Progress.** We need to be aware of the desired delivery speed of the customer team. Due to the application of test-driven development (TDD), the work of our offshore team is relatively slow for the delivery by story kick-off. We have taken several measures to raise our efficiency, e.g., developing some functions easier for showcasing or some ready-to-use functions, but our development may still lag behind the absolute development speed required by the customer team. Some customers may take this as an excuse to challenge our working method, or even question the cooperation with us. Under such circumstance, some senior members in our team will defend us by saying that our product has less bugs, lower maintenance cost, or a higher delivery value (rather than a larger number of delivered functions), so as to convince the customer team. Of course, our defense needs to be supported by available statistical data.

(iii) **Quality.** As far as the quality expectations are concerned, our offshore team must identify which kind of defects are negligible, which are ought to be repaired immediately, and which are completely unacceptable. We'd better work with the customer team on developing a set of criteria for evaluating defects. The issues about defects (including severity of defects) and prioritization are to be elaborated in Chapter 3.

(iv) **User experience.** Customers may change their expectations in the process of cooperation with service providers. In recent years, customers have paid increasingly higher attention for user experience, forcing the project teams to specially assign someone to take charge of this matter, which was a kind of blank in the past. As result of the development of mobile Internet, user experience design (UED) was no longer an extra bonus point, but an essential requirement, no customer will say he chooses a software product regardless of user experience.

Therefore, when we are about to work on a project, we have to create some high-fidelity prototype drawings of typical pages to win consent of the customer team, especially a formal approval of its team leader. Then the front-end developers of our offshore team can adopt this design style throughout the development process.

During the process of project implementation, after the product functions are partially completed, the customer may shift attention to the product performance. If the customer expectation is perceptual, e.g., "the faster, the better," then we need to guide him to quantify the perceptual performance metrics into measurable ones.

In order to achieve the above purposes, we need to draw up a formal communication plan with our customers.

Making a communication plan is an important strategy (as important as the testing strategy and the quality assurance strategy), and its supreme goal is to convey the right information to the right person at the right time. Different stakeholders have different information requirements, e.g., they have different requirements for data type, mode of presentation, frequency of data collection and reporting, and richness of details. When dealing with different stakeholders, we must define a specific form of communication (reporting) to ensure that they can be informed of the project progress in an understandable manner. In short, the communication plan is not only for daily communication but also for management of stakeholder expectations.

After the project is started, a formal communication plan shall be produced to be submitted to all participants of different levels and roles. This plan shall define the timing of all meetings and activities throughout the delivery process. These meetings and activities include, but are not limited to, daily stand-up meeting, IPM, functional acceptance activity, showcase, and reciprocal visits between the customer and offshore teams.

Thanks to the communication plan, the offshore team is given the opportunity to hear the customer's thinking, while the customer is given the opportunity to see the performance of the offshore team. These opportunities are divided into the following two categories:

- **Opportunity for customer comment:** start-up, stand-up, defect classification, and IPM
- **Opportunity for customer feedback:** showcase, retro, and code review

We must make full use of these routine communication opportunities. Don't take for granted that offshore teams can complete their jobs perfectly every time, almost all of them have let their customers down. Seemingly, it is because of improper solutions brought forth by the offshore teams, poor quality of deliverables (poor built-in quality is due to inferior code quality, and poor built-out quality is due to inferior application quality), or slow delivery. But these evaluation indicators are relative, which means that we must gain sufficient knowledge of customers, and learn about their criteria for these indicators, only in this way can we make up for the shortcomings and satisfy their requirements.

2.1.2 Protect the Right to Know of Customers

It is extremely important for us to remain honest with customers, since no one wants to be kept in the dark. Whenever there are any bad news, we should inform our customers of the truth and face the trouble with them. In case of hard times, we should not hide or conceal anything, there is no better way than we unite with our customers and find a way out with them.

Part of the customer expectations are formed in the process of working with the offshore teams. To help customers form reasonable expectations, we must make sure that they are accessible to accurate information about the team status.

In reference to the projects I have worked on, customer satisfaction is mainly based on project progress and product quality. Once our performance in these aspects is lower than the customer expectations, we cannot make amends by doing a good job in other aspects. These two aspects, which are easier to be quantified and compared, are taken as rigid indicators by customers. In contrast, nonfunctional requirements, such as better performance and better usability, can greatly increase customer satisfaction, but it is based on the condition that functional requirements are properly satisfied.

2.1.2.1 Progress

The short-term progress mainly indicates the completion of iteration. IPM is an formal occasion to obtain iterative outcome. After updating the iterative data into the burn-down chart and the burn-up chart, we can obtain the progress data at the large scale of product release. Through the prediction of the release date, we will know whether the current progress is ahead or behind.

Since the internal progress of iteration is mainly released at the daily stand-up meeting, it's better for the leader of the customer team to be present at the meeting once in a while. Even if it is impossible for all team members on both sides to attend the stand-up meeting everyday, their representatives shall show up at the status update meeting. The daily stand-up meeting and all kinds of reviews shall be put to good use, so that the factors that cause the overdue project delivery will emerge as soon as possible.

2.1.2.2 Quality

With the support of the defect-tracking system (DTS), can the customer learn about the product quality at a certain stage? I don't think so. The customer is busy with his own work, he can hardly take the initiative to inquire about the work details of the offshore team. So, it is a good option for us to summarize and analyze the product defects to the customer at the IPM or through a weekly report. In addition to existing defects, to inform the customer of the tests that are run in a continuous integration environment can also boost his confidence. The tests can also be carried out in a continuous delivery environment, allowing each code submission to run these tests.

In addition to the above two most important points, there are other factors associated with customer expectations, such as personnel change, requirement change, and work efficiency. In principle, the process of project implementation is a process of constantly looking for balance. What is to be balanced? The answer can be summed up in four aspects: scope, schedule, personnel, and quality. For example, when we fail to adhere to the schedule, we shall manage to fulfill the project by increasing manpower, lowering quality, and narrowing the scope. For most projects, narrowing the scope is a common approach, that is, put aside the less prioritized functions to ensure the on-time delivery of key functions. When dealing with these changing factors, we need more participation of the customer. When one factor changes, although we have more than one countermeasures, or we can just "counter changes with changelessness," the direct customer opinions are especially important at this moment.

Speaking of the projects I have worked on, there had been occasions where the customer increased requirements at will. Given this, we should never loosen the control over the scope of requirements, and manage to help customers build the awareness of scope. Whenever a customer adds a requirement, the iterative development team shall ask him to remove the same number of story cards that are relatively less prioritized from the iteration.

Almost no customer is pleased to see any personnel change inside the offshore team, they think it costs too much for newcomers to become as skilled as their predecessors. Such preconception about the personnel rotation of the offshore team should be altered: it is not simply an issue of "rotation" or "nonrotation," but how often there should be a round of rotation and how to build a benign rotation mechanism, so that the offshore team can adapt to a reasonable rotation cycle. In fact, if all team members repeat their work day after day, they may lose the passion for work or the courage to meet challenges, or even get tired of each other; in the meantime, the people outside the team are deprived of the opportunity to join in this team to learn its technology stack. Any well-planned personnel replacement will bring in new points of view and new skill packages that help to expand the innovation scope of the team. Therefore, customers should comprehend that the management of technicians is of special significance. What we need is not any relaxed and repeated work, but challenges, the latest knowledge, and self-improvement. No company should rest content with stable team composition; otherwise, it will find it hard to retain ambitious employees. And it will be a loss-loss outcome for both the offshore team and customers.

It is a long-term task to enable customers to control the project and personnel information of the offshore team. Of course, we can provide them with incomplete information about the offshore team or conceal such information, but it may undermine their assessment of the offshore team. And when such information is exposed one day in the future, it is sure to set off a bigger storm.

2.1.3 MAINTAIN CUSTOMER EXPECTATIONS

Beyond all question, dealing with the relationship with customers is a more challenging job than solving a technical problem, because human beings are a kind of creature with great uncertainties. Even so, we can still make effort to smooth the customer relationship. Generally, customers will not go mad with us for no reason, unless we have failed their expectations. They can forgive us for not finishing our work, but they cannot tolerate our misjudgment of their expectations. Therefore, the key to proper management of customer relationship is to set reasonable expectations for customers in the first place and reach consensus with them. It is easily understandable, but not that operable.

All offshore teams want to work with the customers that are more agile, rational, and cooperative, but the reality is disappointing most of the time. In view of this, every member in an offshore team has the responsibility and ability to improve this state of cooperation, since we are experts in management of software development projects, while customers may have never joined in the agile software development, and know nothing about the project organization and implementation. Now that we are so skilled in this regard, it is our duty, rather than the customers', to establish shared expectations and a collaborative environment to work for these expectations.

We can maintain customer expectations from the following five aspects:

- Set definite expectations as early as possible
- Communicate frequently and effectively
- Take customers' business objective as our main objective

- Maintain consistency
- Reduce the possibility of making mistakes

2.1.3.1 Set Definite Expectations as Early as Possible

We shall reach an agreement with customers on their bottom lines, necessary practices, and processes in advance, instead of wait customers to point them out. The procedures of the entire project shall be determined at the beginning, including the scope of requirements, risk management, criteria for project acceptance, management structure, and process. Besides, it is better for both sides to agree on the criteria for successful investigations and identification of nonfunctional requirements (performance requirements). On this basis, we can avoid arguments with customers as much as possible while the project is underway. More than that, customers are aware of project implementation, task deployment, and project completion acceptance, it means that if we have muddled through at the early stage, they can find it out at the late stage.

It is not advisable for the offshore team to lower some criteria in order to fulfill the customer requirements on time. The management of customer expectations cannot be taken as the reduction of customer expectations. We should, on the one hand, remain sober-minded when customers are blindly optimistic at seeing their expectations satisfied, and on the other hand, make reasonable explanations to them when our work is unable to reach their expectations.

The ability and productivity of an offshore team is usually overestimated by both customers and even those working in offshore teams. Subconsciously, they tend to take the most ideal situations as prerequisites. However, as the project progresses, our actual performance is often lower than expected. Whenever customers believe that their most important indicator is at risk, our working rhythm will be disrupted. For example, customers are strict with on-time project delivery; when our progress falls behind the schedule, we have to make compromises in some respects, such as product quality, certain solutions, or user interaction function.

For example, lots of teams and people, whether consciously or unconsciously, associate the story point with the number of days. Someone says 1 point is one day's workload, while others believe it is two days' workload. There are people ideally thinking that "one day" is 8 working hours without any meeting or other interferences. How is that possible? Normally, we only work 4–6 hours every workday.

2.1.3.2 Communicate Frequently and Effectively

When the project operation stumbles or encounters difficulties, we are prone to cancel some communication meetings with the excuse of having no time, or avoid the contact with the stakeholder who is not easy to communicate. But it is going to cost us in the long run, because unambiguous, accurate, and frequent communications are a necessary condition for a successful project. Once we have reached consensus on the expectations and project procedures with customers, we shall keep reporting to them on how their expectations are met. Only in this way can we reduce the likelihood of making mistakes in the future.

Therefore, we need to learn about the ways of communication and use these ways effectively, which seems like conveying information to a particular audience. For example, when we are about to send overly detailed information to senior executives, we shall make good use of documents and e-mails. But we are communicating with others in oral form most of the time, with documents and e-mails used for recording the communication results and the decisions that are just made. When writing e-mails, we should be careful with our wording, since the recipients may interpret the emotional words and information therein based on their own thinking.

Maintaining transparency of teamwork is an effective way of communication, which makes the management of expectations easier and motivates the two sides to share responsibilities, it is because if someone has not made his job known to others, he is forced to bear all resulting consequences by default.

But what is transparency? Let me take my own experience as an example:

I am a "Wo Family" package user of China Unicom. When the two-year service expired, I went to the Unicom service hall to renew the contract. They recommended me a new two-year contract with the network speed doubled and a new mobile phone given for free, while the monthly cost only increased by 10 yuan. I signed the new contract without hesitation and went home with great joy. However, in the following month, after I logged in the online business hall to query my bills, I found the fixed-line billing information was missing (in the old "Wo Family" package, the broadband, fixed line, and mobile phone services were bound together). I called the Unicom customer service center, yet the answers of the service staff to my questions were nothing but clever evasions. It took a while for me to understand that my fixed line was untied from broadband and mobile phone, I have to pay additional fees for making calls with a fixed line. Yet I didn't know anything about it. See the differences between the old and new "Wo Family" packages in Table 2.3.

For the business staff of Unicom, they should know very well about their products, including the separate fixed-line charges in my renewed contract. However, they recommended this new package to me without saying a word about the fixed line, and I was simply drawn to the faster broadband speed and the complimentary mobile phone without thinking of the fixed line.

As a Unicom customer, how could I feel satisfied? For whatever the reason, it indeed concealed certain information from me, I must do something to prevent the same thing from happening again. Similarly, when our offshore team proposes a solution to customers, we should inform them of both gains and losses. Otherwise, once they have suffered a loss, they will feel more disappointed or deceived by us. None of the offshore team members should have the fluke mind. The ultimate goal of managing the expectations of customers is to never surprise them.

When the project is progressing smoothly, we need to maintain communication with customers; when any problem arises, such communication becomes more important, though it seems a little more difficult at this moment. Do not try to hide problems, since it will shake customers' trust in our offshore team. Let customers be informed of our investigation of the problem, propose one or two solutions to discuss with them, and decide a final solution with them. If the problem-solving process is honest and professional enough, we can strengthen our relationship with customers. To ensure of professional performance, we must define a timeline for our solution, and customers shall be aware of the corresponding time cost. Under such pressure, it will be unlikely for our offshore team to misjudge the priority of this task.

2.1.3.3 Take Customers' Business Objective as Our Main Objective

How to increase the business value of customers? Can we maximize their business value? Offshore teams shall keep pondering over these two issues. It is easy to stick to our established ways of doing things, but the prerequisite is that they can provide customers with the greatest benefit. We need to distinguish perseverance from stubbornness, and reflect on our work style from the customer perspective, which helps our two sides to work together in the same direction. In addition to doing our own part, we need to ask "how can we maximize the business value of a particular customer under specific conditions." If we believe our ways of working are able to do so, then we need to discuss

TABLE 2.3
Comparison between China Unicom "Wo Family" Old and New Packages

Wo Family	Old Package	New Package
Mobile phone	Including 1 GB of traffic and 200 minutes of talk time per month	The package level remains the same, with increased traffic (4 GB) and longer talk time per month
Broadband	20 MB	50 MB
Fixed line	Including 320 minutes of talk time per month	Canceled

them with the customer with the focus placed on increasing the business value, rather than on the ways themselves or our preferences.

As an offshore team, we are obliged to please our customers, but it does not mean customers are always right. When a customer makes any request that clearly contradicts his business value, or increases the risks of the project and system, we have the responsibility to keep him from doing so. If the customer is too stubborn to be persuaded and we are forced to follow his instruction, we must adhere to his business goal, and try to get his conception aborted as soon as possible by employing the agile development approach, so as to bring him to reason and realize his mistake.

We can never stop on the road of pursuing higher customer satisfaction and achieving higher customer expectations, and we should attempt to provide customers with higher-than-promised value. It implies that we'd better not show all of our cards at the very beginning, but leave ourselves certain leeway. To be specific, when defining the business goal, we shall identify which task is ought be delivered and what one is likely to be delivered; we shall hide our value-added delivery capability at the early stage, and then bring customers surprises from time to time during the project delivery.

Besides, our offshore team must be aware of the level of customer goal, and then appropriately lower their over-high expectations for us, it is a kind of approach to surprise them, just like the effect depicted in Figure 2.1 (the parent on the right is so happy to see his son scored 61 points, since he thought his son could get 55 points at most; while the parent on the left is disappointed although his son scored 98 points, since he expected his son to get a full mark). But it does not mean we will slacken our efforts in working.

2.1.3.4 Maintain Consistency

Different distributed teams shall try to adopt the same criteria. When estimating story cards, judging defect levels, and prioritizing requirements, everyone's understanding shall be unified based on the same criteria, so as to prevent different people from prioritizing the same task differently.

Offshore teams shall remain consistent when communicating with customers. Each team member is likely to discuss problems with customers, and their opinions about the same type of problems shall be coherent. It is unprofessional to convey contradictory opinions to customers or even among ourselves.

2.1.3.5 Reduce the Possibility of Making Mistakes

Whenever we make a mistake, it will impress our customers more than we are doing a good job. Testing personnel are responsible for discovering defects and having other team members fixed them, or else such defects left in the production environment will make our hard work in vain. Such kind of mistake seems unforgivable in the eyes of customers, since they believe that we should have done a perfect job.

In addition to ensuring product quality, avoiding project delay also helps to maintain customer satisfaction. Reduce the length of iteration (one week or no longer than two weeks), so that we can

FIGURE 2.1 Picture composition in one of China's national college entrance exams.

make a more accurate plan and respond to changes more quickly, such as adjustment of priorities (determine the jobs need to be done as soon as possible, and remove those that can be postponed from the iteration).

Distributed teams shall learn to identify what is really urgent and let go of nonimportant things. And they need to broaden the definition of urgency which is subject to influence of so many factors. The impact of urgency should also be taken into account, since it may divert the attention of the team members to some short-term goals, and it is usually too late when they have realized their deviation from larger and more important goals.

However, we cannot satisfy all customers, nor can we satisfy the same customer all the time. In line with this principle, we shall resolutely reject the unreasonable requirements from customers for fear of causing damage to both parties: demoralize the offshore team or indulge the customer team in going too far on the wrong track. Even though there may be considerable benefits in the near future, the long-term goals are likely to undermined. Besides, we must keep our eyes open for something that appears to be correct but done by incorrect ways.

Even we yield to or compromise with their unreasonable requirements regardless of principles, customers may still feel dissatisfied. Given this, offshore teams shall set up a good attitude and insist on a rigorous way of doing things, that is, reject unreasonable requirements and speak out what they don't think right, only in this way can they truly win the respect and recognition of customers.

2.1.4 Exceed Customer Expectations

We should figure out what customers want and will want ahead of them, rather than wait to be told by them, so as to create a good reputation for ourselves. But the core of such reputation is to exceed customer expectations.

We should put ourselves in customers' shoes: Do they often feel "headache" while working with us? If so, where and when does this ache occur? In order to learn about the conditions of customers more accurately, we need to probe into their thinking and cooperate with them more actively. After all, the information customers tell us has been subjectively processed by them.

One of the keys to distributed teamwork is to maintain the trust of both parties. Of course, trust comes from the performance of our offshore teams in usual cooperation, such as problem-solving ability, code quality, and software quality, which are manifestations of hard power. More than that, the soft skills in handling problems and tasks, such as attitude and punctuality, also help to build up mutual trust. Generally, the cooperation between the two sides is established on basis of trust from the very beginning, but such trust may lose or even collapse after we fail to deliver functions or complete tasks again and again.

Offshore teams are encouraged to make more efforts on their own initiative, and what they have done shall be known to customers:

- **Software performance exceeding the indicators required by customers:** faster software response and smoother user experience.
- **Capable of balancing some options and then making a choice.** There is no doubt that customers want offshore teams to possess this ability, so that they can be free from being blocked by any small problem and from waiting for authoritative persons to solve this problem.
- **Better services for innovating businesses of customers.** Offshore teams shall adopt more advanced technologies, such as microservice and cloud computing, to adapt to business changes, shorten the period for product launch, and facilitate the evolution of customer requirements.

If an offshore team intends to control or reduce the amount of low-value work, it shall seize every opportunity to show its abilities. Otherwise, there may be a vicious circle and dampened personnel morale inside the offshore team. When a customer chooses an offshore team, it is usually because he is drawn to its better delivery experience and innovative business solutions.

Of course, our offshore teams should remain cautious when raising customer expectations for us for fear of any potential "trap," because customers may take the additional delivery value as deserved, and dissatisfy at the normal delivery, even if it is within the scope of the contract. Besides, when making decisions, we have to think twice when we are about to subtract something, which is more difficult than adding something. For example, when I register for after-school tutoring classes for my daughter, it only costs me a few minutes to sign up one more class for her, but I have to pause and ponder whether it is appropriate to call off one of her classes.

2.1.5 Case Analysis: Project L

In the past, it had been a consensus in software industry that software development is unpredictable. But now the promotion of agile development method is changing this entrenched perception. In order to provide customers with predictable agile delivery, it is necessary to improve the output predictability of project teams and increase the information transparency among all participants.

While working for Project L, we made the following efforts to manage user expectations, including doing so indirectly through the customer.

- **Keep discussing with the customer until reaching a consensus.** The discussions were about each staged showcase, which functions are about to be completed, and which function blocks are expected to be displayed.
- **Learn about user expectations before testing.** At first, users mistakenly thought there would be a user acceptance test (UAT) in the traditional sense, so they only stressed data integrity. But our real intention was to get their feedback on software functions and use experience through the test.
- **During the first test, users were confused what we expected from their test.** To prevent further confusions, we communicated with the users indirectly before carrying out the second test. For example, we e-mailed the customer to specify which data were available for testing and waited it to be forwarded to the users.
- **Users' insufficient understanding of agile development method was bad for cooperation.** Therefore, we explained to the customer that our development roadmap was business-oriented, we would deliver the basic functions that support business as soon as possible, and then start working on advanced functions; in other words, we developed functions one after another.
- **Putting the test version software online requires software quality and data integrity to meet the relevant criteria. Using the data from the production environment meant that user expectations were the criteria for delivery.**
- **Customer's excessive attention to the development speed was prone to cause problems, yet he was used to measuring production capacity with speed.** I heard the customer repeatedly complaining that "the development speed of the project team has dropped from 30 points in the last iteration to 23 points in the current iteration. Does anything go wrong?" Speed seemed like a performance evaluation tool at that time.

It is important to distinguish customers from users, our expectations from user expectations, and users' reasonable requirements from their unreasonable requirements (rather than customers).

There is likelihood that customers do not know what their users really want. Customers may feel content with simple implementation of some functions, but users actually have higher requirements for experience. In order to avoid such contradiction, we should advise customers to inform their users of our positioning and criteria for user experience at the very beginning, and make it clear that the user experience of our products only meets the basic requirements.

If we have to contact with some colleagues of the customer that are irrelevant to our project, and they propose some requests to us from time to time, such as sending them some documents, then we have to distinguish what they should do on their own and what we can help them as easy as lifting a finger, so that they can have some achievements to show up in front of their leaders, and pave way for our potential cooperation in the future.

2.1.6 House Splitting Effect

The "house splitting effect" comes from a speech delivered by Mr. Lu Xun, a great writer of modern China. In his speech, he depicted the Chinese people as a nation likes to reconcile and compromise. For example, if you tell others in the same room that it is too dark and suggest to open a skylight, all of them will say no; however, when you threaten to demolish the roof, they will rush to make a concession and tell you that the skylight is not a bad idea.

"Opening a skylight" seems like the goal to be achieved, while "demolishing the roof" is a higher or unreasonable requirement. From a psychological perspective, the reason why the "house splitting effect" could be achieved is that when you put forward an unreasonably high requirement, the other party will immediately weigh the gains and losses, and then adjust his psychological expectations to plan for the worst.

If a more reasonable scheme comes out at this moment, the other party will make appropriate compromises to accept it so as to prevent the worst outcome. Moreover, since no one wants to be hated by others, those who have turned you down are unlikely to reject your requirement again, not to mention it is better than the least desired outcome.

We can learn the "house splitting effect" to properly manage customer expectations. When providing service to customers, a wise approach is to set lower expectations for them at the start, they may accept it, although not satisfied. Later, at seeing our deliverable exceed their expectations, they are sure to be overjoyed.

2.1.7 Customer Expectations to Decide the Outcome of a Project

Proper management of customer expectations is the core issue of offshore teams. Therefore, we must balance the value of deliverables, the value received by customers, and the value expected by customers, and try to put them together. For example, a project delivered on time may be regarded as successful, as long as the customer takes punctuality as the foremost indicator for evaluating the project, even if the scope of deliverables is not achieved. There is another scenario, upon delivery of all agreed functions, a project can also be regarded as successful, as long as the customer mainly cares about the integrity of delivered functions, even if the project is not completed on time.

The afore-mentioned Project L was accomplished in the following context: the software we were about to develop was to replace a cloud service system that the customer had bought and would expire on March 10 of the following year. So, the delivery date of this project was fixed. However, the customer reiterated on several occasions that the new system must include all functions of the cloud service system. Could we adjust this project plan? Of course, we could. I discussed with the customer all day during which I consulted with users' employment of the cloud service system and our agreed requirement list, and then identified the requirements that would meet the business needs. Consequently, we found an iteration could be done after the software release, and the workload of this iteration would buffer the software release. In view of this, even though the released software did not contain the functions of the last iteration, the project was still taken as successful.

Even if a project is fully and punctually delivered, it is still likely to be defined as unsuccessful. Do not be surprised, it is probably because our delivery only meets the customer requirements, but fail to satisfy the users at the same time.

If we are not so sure of the customer expectations, the outcome of our project will depend entirely on luck, since we have no idea whether the performance of our team is higher or lower than the customer expectations.

Sometimes we have to identify some traps. For example, after our team completes the promised story card in a certain iteration, and also completes a function point which is not agreed, should we include this newly completed story card into this release plan? If we are too impulsive, we may say "yes" and feel proud that what we have done exceeds the expectations of the customer and will surprise him. In fact, such act is so risky that it will not only increase the workload of testing, but also shorten the test time and inevitably debase product quality.

If we are obsessed with exceeding the customer expectations, we may forget the risks that are associated with them. We need to overcome the temptation to deliver function points as many as possible. Let me set out our plan as follows, and make a correct judgment on the following two delivery results.

- 20 function points: few test points, long test time, and high quality
- 25 function points: many test points, short test time, and low quality

2.2 COMMUNICATION IS THE BIGGEST CHALLENGE FOR DISTRIBUTED TEAMS

As the saying goes "good news never goes beyond the gate while bad news spread far and wide." It tells us that we have to employ some means to let good things known to others, and properly handle bad things, or else the offshore work mode is unable to cover them up. For distributed teams, communication has always been an eternal and focal topic, so I think it's necessary to dig this topic deeper in this section.

- Do a good job no matter how simple it is, and remember there is no trifle for communication.
- Understand the nature of communication from two dimensions (synchronous and asynchronous), which helps offshore team members to explore ways to raise communication efficiency.
- Remain empathetic.

Agile development is characterized by frequent communication, especially face-to-face communication. However, the organizational structure of distributed teams becomes the biggest challenge to communication while adopting the agile development method. Most people believe that as long as the distributed teams in different places could develop functions on their own, it will greatly mitigate the adverse effect of poor communication, which has been a rule in outsourcing industry in the past years. Such distributed cooperation is substantially different from agile development which is based on incremental development and continuous integration. But the good news is that the constant development of communication technologies, especially Internet technologies, enables different teams to collaborate more closely, work in pair remotely, and take part in development of all functions.

2.2.1 E-MAIL: THE MOST BASIC MEANS OF COMMUNICATION FOR DISTRIBUTED TEAMS

I often hear complaint that e-mail is the worst means of communication. But why distributed teams still rely on it? How can we make full use of e-mail by maximizing its strength and minimizing its weakness?

Most people think sending e-mails could not have been much simpler, why should they bother to learn from others to use this tool. But to be honest, I have seen so many occasions where e-mails are improperly sent. See the examples as follows:

- Team members were discussing the pain points of writing work logs through e-mail; but several rounds later, their topic shifted to the security policy of a customer.
- One person sent an e-mail to all of his colleagues in the distributed team, later one of the recipients gave him a reply that contained some personal information, he answered this e-mail and copied it to all the others without the consent of that recipient.
- When discussing a trivial matter, the two sides kept passing the buck in e-mails and failed to make any decision after wasting a long time; what's worse, they forgot to forward the e-mails to the one playing a crucial role.

- Although the requirements were specified in the e-mail, what the other teams had done was poles apart.
- The e-mail subjects were defined randomly, either less relevant to the content or overly broad. For example, there are e-mails carrying the subject as "some recent problems," but they are hard to be searched afterward since there are no keywords at all.

But there are situations where we made good use of e-mail. For example, there were two persons from different teams maintaining single-line contact, but they failed to reach any consensus after rounds of discussion. Later, one of them copied their e-mail to the other one's leader, which apparently upgraded their communication, hoping that some high-level figure would intervene and finalize a scheme as soon as possible.

It is better for each e-mail to focus on one matter or something related. Many people like to discuss several topics in one e-mail. But it will lead to disjointed topics, a long reply list, and ambiguous subjects with inaccurate keywords for finding e-mails.

In addition to text, the e-mail content should also contain screenshots as many as possible, which helps to prevent the recipients from getting confused or suspicious, and reduce the frequency of e-mail exchange.

The offshore teams that I had worked with often complained that they received no reply for a long time after they e-mailed the customer. When they were ready to send another e-mail to the customer to ask for a reply, they would copy it to his leader together with the original e-mail, in order to remind the customer of his procrastination in making any response.

We shall be aware of most functions of e-mails that prevail on the market. First, we must make good use of the mailing list, which will ensure that all e-mails are sent to each member of the distributed teams, especially when they are not familiar with each other. Second, we must learn to use carbon copy (CC) and blind carbon copy (BCC) to make our communication more professional.

HOW TO MAKE FULL USE OF "CC" AND "BCC" TO SEND E-MAILS?

Let me start with CC. I had been working in Singapore-based Creative Technology Ltd where I learned to send and copy e-mails. I was member of a typical distributed team (with testing personnel stationed in Singapore and Beijing) in those years. Shortly after I entered this company, I was present at a meeting and assigned to e-mail the meeting minutes to those concerned. I added almost all of them into the "To" address bar, put my department manager in the "CC" address bar, and then hit the "Send" button. After a short while, a colleague of mine in the same department, who had worked at the Singapore headquarters for more than ten years, came to me and taught me the first lesson of my career. He told me that "when sending the e-mails like meeting minutes, the "To" address bar is left for all participants who are entitled to receive the e-mail, while the "CC" address bar is for those have something to do with the meeting but fail to show up for some reason (including leaders), in order to let them know what the meeting was about."

BCC is a bit complicated. Ordinary recipients and CC recipients cannot see who are in BCC address bar; BCC recipients, although they cannot see each other, are able to see all the other recipients. BCC is mostly used for sending e-mails to outsiders. For example, if you want to send an e-mail to several customers at a time without their detection, you can put them in BCC address bar. Note that when you send an e-mail through BCC, you must not hit the "reply to all" button. So far as I know, two team leaders were arguing over a plan in e-mails, then one of them notified this matter to their supervisor through BCC. Later, this supervisor finalized the plan in their stead and replied to both of them. The result was conceivable, the other team leader was so angry that such a trivial matter was reported to their supervisor. Since then on, they found it hardly possible to work together as before.

2.2.1.1 Features of E-mail Communication

My years' experiences in e-mail communication are summarized as follows:

Considering the information it carries, e-mail is available for nonemergency communication to convey details between each other, and also store the records of communication as evidence for any potential use.

Regarding the dimension of time, e-mail itself is an asynchronous communication process, recipients do not have to answer an e-mail immediately, but have plenty of time to figure out how to reply it.

There are skills in forwarding an e-mail. When we receive an "FYI" e-mail, we will find it contains so many communication records over a period of time, and more than one persons have expressed multiple opinions. It is troublesome to understand all the problems set out in the e-mail without adequate contextual information. Those who forward such e-mail shall make sure of the following two points, which helps to relieve the "headache" of recipients."

- Briefly introduce the problems and how they come into being in the e-mail;
- Summarize all the problems that are raised recently, which were already addressed and how about their solutions.

2.2.1.2 Better Means of Communication are Preferred in Some Occasions

For example, I have mentioned that both parties pass the buck for a small matter in e-mails, and failed to finalize a plan for a long time. In this process, the final scheme is really valuable, yet it is too complicated to be communicated via e-mail. The correct approach is to discuss the plan with a telephone or instant messaging tool, and after we have got a conclusion, it shall be e-mailed to all relevant personnel.

If you still send e-mails in the case of urgent matters, do not expect to get an immediate reply, even if you specially point out that "we will take necessary action if no reply is received before getting off work today."

Many people may have such a misunderstanding: we just need to forward the e-mails to others, and they are sure to read them and learn all the information inside. But for some matters, we'd better call together all parties concerned to have a discussion.

2.2.1.3 View E-mails from the Perspective of Continuous Improvement

If we have to discuss some problems in e-mails, we shall ask a stakeholder of the problems to send each of us a summary e-mail upon the end of discussions. He shall summarize all valuable information in this e-mail for any inquiry and information transmission in the future. In case of no such summary, the newcomers who did not join in the discussions will only get a long list of forwarded e-mails, they have to read them one by one to collect valuable information, which wastes both time and energy.

2.2.2 Asynchronous Communication and Real-Time Communication – Both Regular Communications

Let's first look at the following example:

2.2.2.1 Asynchronous Communication

Many companies now provide their employees with free milk or beverages. But when you want to drink some milk in the morning, you may find several opened cartons in the refrigerator, and you have no idea when they were opened. This situation will be worse on Monday morning. Everyone knows that milk should be consumed within 24 hours after opening to ensure of safely. Given this, when you are not sure when the milk cartons were opened, you have to open a new one, then there will be another opened carton in the refrigerator.

So, is there any easy solution for us to know which carton of milk is safe for drinking? There are ways, of course. On each milk carton, there is a blank area for us to mark the time of opening, which will banish everyone's worries. In this case, some figures (the time) play the role of asynchronous communication.

Theoretically, asynchronous communication means that in the dimension of time, information is generated at one point in time and circulates from one person to another, and another person receives this information at another point in time. Asynchronous communication is off-site communication, that is, two people deal with the same information at different points in time. It is somewhat like the traffic offence penalty, if we break any traffic rules while driving on road, we may receive the on-site penalty by the traffic police, or off-site penalty if our offence is caught on camera.

The offshore teams in different time zones rely on such asynchronous communication most of the time. When adopting this kind of communication, we must, from the very beginning, convey enough information and think from the other party's standpoint, since their context may be different from ours. Although comprehensive and intact information may have something redundant, the foremost thing is to ensure that the other party can get all the required information, and even make a choice.

When working with the offshore teams in different time zones, we need to reduce the adverse impact of asynchronous communication and increase the opportunities for real-time communication. Therefore, the offshore teams are sometimes asked to change their standard commuter time to overlap with the customers' working hours. But such adjustment shall be made carefully, since any change in working hours may affect team members' normal life and even their work morale. We shall not only pay attention to the benefits of changes, but also guard against their potential impact, especially the negative impact.

The method of User Persona, which may be taken as an example for improving communication, is used for analysis of requirements. User Persona itself is the product of information extraction, and it represents a specific group of users. After information extraction, it will be easier for people to draw consistent conclusions on some matters. But we should be careful not to confuse it with User Role. The difference between them is that each User Persona corresponds to a specific person, and such concretization benefits empathic thinking, which is the greatest value of User Persona; while User Role corresponds to software, and it is mainly used to distinguish the permissions of different users technically.

Through the document collaborative approach, we can maintain the documents of the latest version, but do we need to mark the changes in the new version? We should think empathically: when a customer opens a document and finds that it has been updated, but he has to read through the document to identify which part is updated. It would be much convenient if the updated parts are highlighted in different colors.

In addition to information (including requirements), many practices that deal with codes are examples of asynchronous communication. For distributed teams, when they are communicating about the code base, it seems like they are involved in a war without smoke every day. The codes themselves must play a role of communication, while the naming conventions for codes are a basic requirement.

To test an executable document, the name of each test method shall be clear enough to reflect the purpose of the test. For example, if we are going to write codes to test the Magic Guess game in Wenquxing (a kind of electronic dictionary), the codes of the first test method shall be as follows:

should_return_4A0B_when_there_are_four_perfect_numbers_in_the_guessing_ numbers.

As shown the name of the test method, we can know that our method of comparing numbers should return to an appropriate value when certain conditions are met. If we follow the above standards to write codes for testing, then when we manage tests, we can find a set of documents describing software functions.

There are some prerequisites for communication: first, communication should be based on a common understanding of all the conceptual terms involved; second, communication should be based on a common understanding of all the practices involved.

Asynchronous communication means that the two parties do not read the information at the same time. This requires the sender to fully consider the conditions and environment of the recipient, ensure the absolute integrity of the information, and organize the information effectively. The recipient of the information must fully understand some "routines" of the sender, and when the information is incomplete, he can deduce the full picture of the information to the greatest extent possible, because the missing part of the information is often taken for granted by the sender.

Sometimes when we detect a problem, we may immediately reflect it to the customer team, since we are eager to demonstrate our proactivity. But we need to know that the personnel of offshore teams changes from time to time, may be someone has already reported the same problem to the customer and figured out a solution, so we should first try to find ready answers inside our offshore team. In the opinion of customers, they always take our offshore team as the same one despite of any personnel changes. If we discuss with them over the same problem time and time again, they will doubt our communication ability. In a word, active communication is sometimes not a good thing but a blind behavior.

Due to the reliance on asynchronous communication, a principle for remote working is to avoid making decisions at the last minute. It sounds to contradict with the lean theory, but it is actually not. If we have a project that requires for input and decision-making, then we need to collect feedback information before the project implementation. We cannot expect to get an answer right away, since the working hours of collaborating colleagues may differ from those of ours.

We shall spend more time thinking and preparing the topics of asynchronous communication. Although this seems like extra work, it will eventually make asynchronous communication more efficient. For example, the meeting is planned in advance, usually once a week, and its topics are based on the discussion of the entire team, so that all participants may reach an agreement rapidly. This also eliminates those annoying impromptu meetings initiated at any time, which not only deprives offshore team members of the opportunity to participate but also distracts their attention to work, forcing everyone to switch contexts in their minds.

The popularity of shared documents has technically solved the problem of information consistency between different teams. When one team needs a piece of information, it may take the initiative to find the location where the information is saved to get the latest data.

2.2.2.2 Real-Time Communication

Compared with e-mail and shared document, instant messaging software and video phone are more direct and efficient means of communication. And all of them are comprehensive means of communication for resolving the differences in both time zones and geographic locations between distributed teams.

When choosing an offshore team, it is seldom to see the circumstance of no overlap of working hours, because it is one of the key factors in choosing a team at the beginning. Of course, the degree of work time overlaps has a certain impact on the communication mechanism of distributed teams.

- **Few work time overlaps.** Arrange real-time communication as much as possible within the overlapping working hours of both parties, such as stand-up meeting, IPM, seminar, and brief meeting. In addition, they shall learn some skills to improve the efficiency of asynchronous communication.
- **Many work time overlaps.** In this case, we can invest more energy and employ more advanced means in real-time communication. Organize a nonstop video meeting where a large screen is erected to display the work area of all parties, everyone can directly walk to the screen to

make a statement. By performing the automatic answering function of the software, we can simulate the scene where two parties are working together: remain quiet when no one is making a speech, and automatically get through to each other when someone makes a call.

Real-time communication includes direct communication through video, recorded project introduction, or complicated defect recurrence. In many cases, video is the cheapest way to communicate, because it could be no more easier as compared with preparing a separate document for explaining a problem. But most people's understanding is just the reverse, that's why document description is still used most of the time despite of its highest cost and worst effect.

2.2.3 Pros and Cons of Tools

In recent years, remote collaboration tools have become better and better, such as Screenhero, it supports screen sharing, enables two people working remotely to operate concurrently by controlling the mouse and conduct voice chat. Objectively speaking, the functions currently provided by the collaboration tools have basically eliminated the adverse effects brought by remote working, and paved way for us to give our subjective initiative into full play.

It is an annoying process to submit a regular project to all stakeholders, including the status of development and testing, although it is required by our customers. Generally, we have to collect all necessary data and display them in charts or graphs. It takes a long time to use common document tools, and we have to carefully maintain them and sometimes modify the data. But now our job has become quite relaxed thanks to JIRA, Trello, Mingle, and other task management tools that automatically generate reports. It will be perfect if we can persuade customers to log into the system to read the reports on their own.

By employing these tools, we can easily learn about the arrangement of each iteration, since the physical Kanban only allows us to know the content of the current iteration. The virtual Kanban tool can avoid the situation where different teams may see out-of-sync progress indications. In the final analysis, even if we have got a lot of tools, we may not reduce the opportunities for the face-to-face and real-time communications.

2.2.4 Active Communication

While the project is running smoothly, everything seems to go well, but challenges still come out occasionally. After the customer team is more familiar with the offshore team, it starts to ask some interesting questions. For example, have testers done any work after the project started? How about the size of a test case? Why is the priority of defects higher than the priority of story cards? Now that the estimation is so inaccurate, why do we have to estimate the story card? How many codes should be written for an automated test?

Many problems actually arise from customers' misunderstandings, so we must correct their misunderstandings in time to prevent them from spreading and taking root and sprout. Under mature conditions, we can introduce advanced practices to help customers improve the level of practice and enhance their confidence in cooperation.

When customers feel they have lost "control" over the offshore team, they will begin to distrust it. Because of such mentality, whenever customers feel they need some information, they will ask the offshore team to provide to them. Of course, we can send such information to them on time, but we'd better take one more step, that is, discuss with them over all the information that they want, and send it to them regularly, which will avoid randomness and possible omissions. At the same time, the regular information provision is more conducive to horizontal and vertical comparison. In order to prevent customers from not knowing what they are unaware of, we must actively introduce more contexts to them. Project overview or technical architecture is a good start. Such information that "sees both trees and forests" is easier to understand. If customers value product quality very much, but they have no idea of what the offshore team is doing, they are sure to feel anxious. Therefore, we shall regularly discuss the existing defects with customers and let them know about the product quality, the priority of defects may be easily determined if we are lucky enough.

We usually assume that since all information is in the version control system and task management system, customers can take the initiative to look up the information they want. In fact, almost none of them will read it proactively, we still have to send them a status update report to inform them of what they want with a minimum of time and effort.

There are some situations where text communication is used, such as e-mail, content description in story card, and defect description. We can fully understand what we are describing, but those have no context or do not know the cause and effect fail to do so. How to describe something without our familiar contexts is an important skill for customers to accurately understand what we express.

What should we do to deal with different types of collaborative teams?

- The collaborative team is an independent product team, but when it has to develop the tight integration function, how can we cooperate with this team?
- The collaborative is working with us on the same code base. How can we cooperate with each other?
- For distributed teams that do not share the same code base but have a small amount of interaction, can the method of sending periodic reports (such as weekly reports) to each other improve the communication between them?

Many teams are keen on defect analysis, but they should consider how to feed back the analysis results to the development team. Is there any action that the development team can take? Without effective action, the feedback loop cannot be formed, what is the point of doing this kind of work?

Many project teams have met the problem of not reaching the end customers (users), and I believe this is a "common problem" with offshore projects. However, user experience is the only way to test products, so I think we should help customers build a user feedback chain. After undertaking the project, we can create product prototypes before developing the business-related functions, so that customers can show them to users and collect their feedback, which will effectively mitigate risks.

2.2.5 CONFLICTS IN COMMUNICATION

Let's first read two fables:

Fable 1: A fierce fight broke out between the Lion and the Tiger. Both of them were seriously injured in the end. When the Lion was about to die, he said to the Tiger: "if you have not tried to seize my domain, how can I end up like this!" The Tiger replied in surprise, "I've never wanted that. I always thought you were going to invade my territory!"

Viewpoint: Communication with each other is a key element in sustaining different teams. Don't bottle up what you want to say, communicate with others as much as possible, and let your colleagues know more about you, which will help you avoid many unnecessary misunderstandings and contradictions.

Fable 2: There were two birds living together. One day the male bird collected a nest of nuts and asked the female bird to properly store them. Due to the dehydration effect in dry weather, the nuts became smaller and seemed only half of the original amount. The male bird thought the female bird must have eaten them and scolded her. However, several days later, the rainfalls made the air humid and all the nuts swelled into a full nest. At this moment, the male bird was awakened, he felt so ashamed that he apologized to his mate, "I am sorry to have wronged you!"

Viewpoint: Team members must trust each other, since so many teams are ruined by suspicion and mistrust. Therefore, team members must maintain trust and guard against any suspicion,.

The above fables tell that although some problems are caused by a third party, the lack of communication and trust can still lead to conflicts between the two parties, and offshore teams may encounter more complicated situations.

The following situations occur frequently, so we should be prepared in advance in order to take targeted approaches when necessary:

- The customer is not cooperative while working, he only considers his own duties without thinking for our party.
- It is difficult to reach agreement on the timing of meetings, and the party making concessions will blame the other party not considerate enough.
- Language problems make communication with offshore teams more difficult, and offshore teams are often disturbed by information loss.
- Dissatisfaction with a specific problem extends to dissatisfaction with the entire team.
- Disrespect the other party's hard work. It is mainly manifested in neglect of other party's research results, jam through his own solutions, or show no acknowledgment after his expectations are exceeded.
- Throw a wet blanket on others. When someone further asks why a task was completed in certain ways, he gets an answer as "that's our way of making decisions" which lacks the support of data, discussion processes, and quantitative indicators.
- Offshore teams sometimes do things casually and pay less attention to their duties, which affects the daily work of local teams. For example, they do not return the token, thus causing others fail to submit the codes.

If all teams are located in one place, when there is a conflict, they can sit together to solve the problem face to face. But for distributed teams, team members cannot meet each other, it is more difficult for them to resolve conflicts, this is because they cannot observe each other's facial expressions and body language, and have fewer opportunities to understand each other. To resolve conflicts in writing is a bad choice, because we cannot see the other party's expressions or hear their voices. Without the tone of voice, we cannot catch any small emotions. In a company where I had been working, I witnessed the fierce confrontation in e-mails between colleagues, they were mistakenly guessing each other's ideas, and finally had to terminate the e-mail communication. To call in all parties to open a video meeting is a compromise solution, which saves costs and increases the sense of presence.

When it comes to resolving the conflicts in communication, the professional advice is that we should learn to listen. However, in the case that offshore teams are involved, it is not enough to listen, but also to express your thoughts fully and accurately after listening. If you are confident in your own thinking, you may convince others to accept your ideas.

Speaking of the scope of requirements, the depth of each requirement cannot be infinitely expanded. In this regard, we are more prone to argue with our customers, since they often add new requirements, either intentionally or unintentionally. We must know well to which extent each function should be developed. When the user requirements are more complicated than the original plan, we must show them to the customer, and tell him that we are not turning down these requirements, but we need to reprioritize the tasks and shift our attention to truly valuable functions. Such practice is particularly suitable for the fixed-price projects.

2.2.5.1 Typical Ways for Distributed Teams to Resolve Conflicts

The typical ways for distributed teams to resolve conflicts are made up of objective measures and subjective thinking.

Objective measures mainly refer to playing remote ice-breaking games, creating conditions for face-to-face discussion, and seek the intervention of senior officials (they are about to play the role of a coordinator, rather than a judge). The purpose of these measures is nothing more than increasing mutual trust, pushing each other to focus on positive factors, focusing on solutions instead of blaming each other, and discussing the root causes of conflicts only based on facts. The goal of all efforts is to visualize and increase the transparency between different teams. When we have to guess some matters of the other party, we often do not draw conclusions from the optimistic perspective. For an offshore team with some on-site personnel, it may assign these persons to discuss with the customer out of work, because the feeling of tension may be eased after leaving the working environment.

Subjective thinking mainly refers to solving problems by considering something as it stands.

- **Stick to facts and distance oneself from interest relations.** In order to resolve the conflict, if we fail to achieve justice, but influenced by some irrelevant factors, we can never have the two sides sincerely convinced.
- **Seek common ground while reserving differences.** Even if customers blame our working methods or content, we should avoid quarreling with them, which is of no help in solving any problem. We need to seek the common ground between our two parties and find out the parts that we can agree on, and then figure out means to settle differences. The "tit for tat" communication only highlights differences, the right way to do is to seek common ground while reserving and managing differences.
- **Think empathically.** Each party shall try to think about problems from the other party's standpoint, which helps to understand the underlying reasons behind their behaviors.

2.2.5.2 Dare to Say "No"

In order to be recognized by the main stakeholders, we cannot adopt all the ideas and requests without discrimination, because such an approach can only increase unreasonable requirements, distract the goal of the offshore team and disrupt its original plan and rhythm. According to Steve Jobs, innovation is not to adopt all functions, but to retain the most critical ones and delete others. The ability to do subtraction is one of the key factors that Jobs made a hit, which also applies to teamwork. We should keep a sober mind that teamwork is not to meet every requirement of the customer or other teams, but to find out whether the distributed work is reasonable and whether it has a negative impact on us, and help the customer do subtraction when necessary.

If the customer representative who works with us fails to control their requirements, and even indulges frequently changing requirements, we must obtain a written reply from him to confirm the requirements, and refuse to work for any newly-added requirements without such confirmation. In this way, even if the customer keeps changing his requirements in the future, and we have to adjust our workload, we are well-founded to ask him to pay for our increased workload separately.

It is a difficult task to make distributed teams trust each other, and it is even more challenging to repair a soured relationship between them. Therefore, offshore teams are encouraged to immediately expose the contradictions, which leaves room to have them stifled in the cradle. In case of any difficulties, neither party should be a bystander. Both parties shall first examine themselves and reflect on their behaviors since every man has his faults and needs continuous self-improvement.

2.2.6 TO BE EMPATHETIC

The principle of empathy is to put yourself in the place of others, respect and understand their thinking, and form a common feeling between each other. For example, in a romantic relationship, having empathy is an effective way to enhance mutual understanding and mutual tolerance. In case of any setbacks, empathic couples will not complain or blame each other, but encourage, understand, and support each other, so their relationship will become more harmonious. Usually, an empathic person will have a psychological tendency to care and understand everything around him, when he disagrees with others, he can still respect them and tolerate such differences; and when he has any friction with others in behavior, he can understand them with kindness, and is willing to find a win-win solution by integrating factors of both sides from a higher perspective.

To solve communication problems, distributed teams shall think about fostering empathy and emotional resonance. On many occasions, the decisions of other teams will make us feel confused or even dissatisfied, empathy can make us think from their standpoint, then we may discover many facts that we've overlooked. In other words, if we do not switch our perspective, these facts are unlikely to attract our attention. Therefore, empathy indirectly removes barriers to communication in many ways and allows communication to develop in a positive direction. It should be pointed out that both offshore and local teams need to cultivate empathy.

The empathic offshore teams will help us grasp customer expectations more accurately and maximize the value of their work. Offshore teams have a lot of work to be confirmed, if they cannot get a timely reply, what will we think? Is the customer not paying attention to offshore teams, or does he have more prioritized tasks on hand? If we have pointed out some impacts from delayed response, could the customer make a better judgment? As a technical service provider, offshore teams are concentrated on technical architecture and logic implementation. When any change occurs to the requirements, we mainly care about the impact on technologies themselves, while customers only focus on business value and make judgments based on the assessment of business value.

I had been member of an online business hall project entrusted by a foreign telecom company, we used a plug-in to record the user log information, so that we could find the cause of an error as quickly as possible. This function was of great significance for testing and future product environment, so when we arranged the story cards of user functions, we also arranged the related story cards for logging. But the customer opposed such an arrangement, and requested to arrange as many function story cards as possible, and leave the logging story cards in the end. At first, our developers were against this request, because it would increase the debugging difficulties during the test. Later, we learned the customer's standpoint, it turned out that he expected all stakeholders to see the available functions as soon as possible and collect their feedback; without the approval of stakeholders, he would have to change the requirements no matter how perfect the preliminary work was. Later, a consensus was reached between us and the customer, that is, the story cards for functions and logging could be made separately for now, and combined in the future at the request of offshore teams.

If we are a local team without empathy, we may easily shelve or dismiss the recommendations made by offshore teams, and tend to exclude offshore teams from attending the decision-making meetings, since we can cut the odds of trouble. When offshore teams make a mistake, our first reaction is to blame them. In contrast, if the same thing happens to someone at our side, we will look for excuses for him. Given this, if we could learn to be empathic, I think more than half of the communication problems will disappear.

Now that empathy is so important for distributed teams, what can we do to foster empathy step by step? Based on my more than ten years' experiences in working with distributed teams, I'd like to propose some suggestions in the following aspects for different teams to practice:

- **Organize cross-team activities.** We can call in different teams to join in an ice cream social event, or play an ice-breaking game or an across-region treasure hunt game through videophone. Our team and an Australian team once participated in the quiz of the Melbourne Cup horse racing. Both teams bought a lot of snacks and drinks, choosing their favorite horses to guess, everyone enjoyed the process as if they were really being together.
- **Create a photo wall containing people from all teams.** Mark the pronunciation of everyone's name, or write interesting somethings about this person; or post all their photos on a map wall and put each of them at the location of their native place.
- **Cultural exchanges between each other.** These activities can be done in a more interesting way, such as asking offshore teams to introduce the culture of the place where the local team is located, or vice versa. The advantage of doing so is to encourage both parties to learn about each other's culture, customs and habits; in case of any misunderstandings or mistakes, the other party can make correction and explanation, thus creating more opportunities for discussion and interaction.
- **Remote meetings are interspersed with small talks and chats.** Those attending the meetings may once in a while talk about weather, local events, major competitions, or other topics that are not related to work.

- **Send food packages to each other.** This method originated from an event initiated by the Americans during the Second World War. It was designed to send food packages to one's family members fighting on the battlefield in Europe, but now it has become an expression of concern for the people far away from home. At seeing the snacks sent by the other team, the recipient team will be excited for several days, which is good for their bilateral cooperation.
- **Some video conferences can be held in kitchen, activity room, or other venues that are not as formal as workplace, and everyone can discuss some light topics.**
- **Think problems from the other party's standpoint.** Offshore teams differ from our local team in business, environment, and cultural background. What we take for granted may be something new for them; what we feel as easy as pie mean take them a long time to investigate; and our meeting timetable may coincide with their lunch time.
- **Of course, the best way is to create opportunities to visit each other.**

Finally, remember that empathy and respect are complementary, and the supreme guideline read out at the retrospective meeting also reflects this principle. No matter what we have discovered, considering the knowledge category, technologies and capabilities, available resources, and actual situation at that time, we shall understand and firmly believe that everyone has done their best. In other words, in the absence of evidence, we must firmly believe that offshore teams have both eagerness and determination to do a good job, just like our local team. If any outcome does not meet our expectations, we should first make self-examination and ask ourselves "How could a rational and kind-hearted person made those decisions?," "If we've provided them some information or support, can we prevent these things from happening?" "Did we ignore any of their information?"

There are many ways to build trust between teams. Likewise, there are more than one causes that break trust. But the most important thing to watch out for is the formation of the sense of opposition, that is, treat the other party as "counterparty," which is very harmful. We should take offshore teams as part of us, and stress the cultivation of empathy during our collaboration. If this way, the potential obstacles for the collaboration between distributed teams will be significantly reduced.

But we need to understand that empathy is not a shield, a guess or a presumption. We should keep carrying out the user survey, and ask customers to do their own part. We can't imagine the customer scenarios by ourselves, and undertake all of the workload. As compared with offshore teams, our local team is much closer to end users.

2.2.7 Explicit and Candid Communication

When communicating with others face-to-face, it will be easier for us to judge what they are really want to say by observing their body language. For example, when a person says "yes," his body language actually says "not sure"; or when he says "fine," his body language either means "yes" or "no." These observations are unavailable if we talk with each other on the phone. Therefore, when we are present at a teleconference, everyone needs to express his point of view clearly and frankly, and do not leave room for others to imagine and guess.

If there are tasks we are incapable of, we must tell the truth to our customers. Otherwise, as time goes by, our credibility will be damaged. By the same token, when we agree on something, it is important for us to make it clear that "I cannot agree more" or "I like this idea." In this way, the people of other teams will confirm that everyone of us is fully aware of their intention. Similarly, whenever we have finished discussion of a topic, we must summarize it in a timely manner to ensure that no one has any misunderstanding.

When working with distributed teams, we shall not be afraid of exposing problems. Helping others is helping ourselves. If we could remind others of some risks, both of us may keep from a lot of trouble afterward. However, if we remain silent when we notice something wrong, we could only pray that everything will be safe and sound in the future.

Many times, when attending meetings with distributed teams, we will open a text editor or mind map tool to take notes on a shared screen. The advantage of doing so is that if the sound quality is not good, the listeners can still keep up with the rhythm of the discussion based on the meeting minutes. Furthermore, making records can make the participants feel that the problems have drawn everyone's attention, and the follow-up solutions will be introduced soon.

There are omens of failed communication:

- The offshore team members are late for or do not attend the teleconference, or negatively respond to the discussions in the conference.
- A decision or consensus is made through rounds of teleconferences.
- Team members do not pay attention to discussions and often ask the same questions repeatedly.
- Things promised at the meeting are not implemented. It mainly refers to the action plan that is decided in a retrospective meeting, such plan is usually not carried out by the next meeting.

In such a situation, we should waste no time in paying a visit to the other party and conducting a face-to-face communication with them. Some other communication skills are listed as follows:

- **Whether it is a technical or business matter, ensure that there is only one source of truth.** It shall be clearly stated at the beginning, if not, all concerned teams need to calibrate information while working in the future. This also brings additional communication costs and information risks.
- **To maintain a healthy product backlog, and each team shall have a clear division of labor and owner.**
- **Distributed teams must have a clear overall architecture and a set of design criteria, especially a shared code base and information base.**
- **Choose right tools purposefully.** Sometimes many tools are not suitable for distributed development projects, so all teams must be convinced to use the right tools at the beginning.
- **Establish trust across teams through explicit and candid communication.** A healthy environment is a prerequisite for ensuring every person and every team to express their thoughts more openly without fear of consequences. And we shall actively accept feedbacks from others, but carefully provide feedback to others.
- **Make online meetings more efficient.** Since it is difficult to ensure that others have followed the progress of meetings, we should try to use visual aids and high-quality equipment.
- **Keep an open mind about some practices for distributed teams and large-sized teams. Be brave to make experiment, otherwise we can't confirm whether these practices are suitable for our team.**
- **Within each independent team, it is equally important to give the team complete freedom to achieve its small goals,** such as the goal of using a physical Kanban.

2.2.8 Other Matters That Affect the Success of Offshore Teams

In addition to the communication principles and techniques introduced above, many details of communication in the work also need our attention. Small details can often bring unexpected effects. We shall remain sensitive while working and cultivate our ability to discover "beauty" in communication.

2.2.8.1 Written Communication with Customers

Customers generally require regular work reports, that is, updates on team status and work progress. We can report every day, every week, or every iteration, which depends on the nature of our cooperation, the size of project team, and other factors. How to write this report and what should be included is a matter of concern to us. For the technical manager of the customer team, he can verify our work results with the submitted codes, but for any nontechnical manager or other personnel, he has to refer to the documents that record our current work.

A large percentage of customers request a report that is updated daily. If we think about it carefully, it is actually a written form of Scrum of Scrums collaborative practice of multiple agile development teams. What should be emphasized here is what progress we are making, what problems we are encountering, what decisions we make within the scope of our capabilities, and whether we need any external help.

When customers' participation is relatively high, what they need is the daily report as mentioned above. When their participation is relatively low, they need a weekly update report, and the main purpose of which is to report work to their boss. Therefore, in the weekly report, we need to include the information that is finally conveyed to the boss of the customer. For example, which stage we are currently in? Which part of the entire business function have we completed? How does local team support the work? What are we going to do next week?

When our verbal communication with customers is not easy due to language, we must turn to rely on written communication. When dealing with customers, we should carefully manage e-mails and share information, although it has already become a topic of platitude.

2.2.8.2 Paying More Attention to Details Can Improve Communication

We often use assumptions at work, but distributed teams need to be more careful when using assumptions. Distance is easily to cause misunderstandings, and using assumptions too harshly is not conducive to collaboration. And any improper use will also cause the psychology of preparedness of both parties. We should first define a wide range of common points, communicate with as many people as possible, narrow the scope of assumptions, and obtain information directly from team members.

Sometimes it will hurt others if you say "if I were you, I would..." If you are pointing at something that already happened, it is a kind of contempt for others' efforts; but if you are talking about something in the future, it will be readily taken as a kind suggestion.

In cooperation with others, backward induction can be adopted when others do not know how to help you. To accomplish this goal, you need to list out what else shall be done from your perspective, so that others may help you find some suitable work to do.

Promote the first-responsibility system, no matter who receives the customer request, don't ignore it even though you are not the party concerned. Help a customer find the person who can solve his problem, and keeps tracking until someone takes over direct communication with the customer or has his problem addressed in the end.

Helping customers alleviate pressure from end-users is an unshirkable responsibility of offshore teams. For example, users may pressure customers to get a list of end-to-end test scenarios. Although we do not stress documents, in order to help customers alleviate the pressure imposed by users, preparing documents has become a valuable task. As the saying goes, helping customers is helping ourselves.

The members of offshore teams meet with more challenges. Unlike independent teams that are only doing simple jobs, offshore team members have do a good job, and also tell others what they have done and what they know. We all know that oral description of something is often more challenging. You are fully aware of a technology and able to apply it skillfully, but when you describe it to others, you have to prepare for a long time, and cannot guarantee the effect of oral narration.

Stick to all-round communication, different communication strategies should be adopted at different stages of the project. At the same time, all roles of offshore teams are encouraged to conduct more parallel communication to avoid the occurrence of communication bottlenecks, but they should pay attention to the information sharing with their local team after communication. As a knowledge-based team, it is difficult to complete the work without effective communication.

Lead customers to be value-oriented. If customers insist on doing one function, we must help them analyze the business value behind this function. By distinguishing superficial illusions and real value for customers, they will naturally be more convinced.

2.3 ORGANIZATION OF MEETINGS

Offshore teams shall keep taking part in many routine activities, whether it is an internal meeting or a teleconference, whether it is a formal regular meeting or an informal discussion.

I once heard someone teasing that meetings are the best place to waste time. It sounds like a joke, but it actually reflects how people usually feel about participating in meetings. This is because our meetings are often in some embarrassing situations as follows:

- When a remote meeting is started, the equipment and devices are not ready.
- Topics need to be previewed or prepared in advance, and the people who have made no preparation cannot fully participate in the discussion.
- It is difficult to end a topic in a divergent discussion.
- There are often timeouts since the meetings have no time limit.
- The discussions often digress from the key topics.

In fact, we expect to participate in the following forms of meetings:

- Make preparations for the meeting in advance to avoid unnecessary waiting.
- In order to improve the efficiency of the meeting, we encourage sequential discussion or raising hands to speak.
- Principles must be followed at all times, and the issues to be discussed must be purposeful and able to solve the problems of the project.
- The easiest way to meet with customers is to define the meeting agenda in advance. Even if the meeting agenda is finished in a stylized manner, it is considered to have achieved the goal.
- Learn to present issues and then find solutions through divergence and convergence

To achieve the above effects, we need a facilitator. Even in an agile team, the meeting also needs a moderator who is usually called a facilitator. Because of their job responsibilities, project managers, business analysts, and technical directors often serve as a facilitator. In fact, team members can play this role in turn, as long as they fully understand the topics of the meeting.

The reason why the meeting needs a facilitator is mainly for the following purposes:

- Once the discussion digresses from the topics, it could be reminded in time.
- Prevent open issues from being discussed endlessly at the meeting.
- Encourage everyone to participate in the meeting.
- Balance the speeches of participants, in case the opinions of one or two people dominate the opinions of the whole team.
- Handle disputes and conflicts at the meeting.
- Facilitate the offshore team members to fully express their views.
- Keep team members focused and prevent small talks.

The specific requirements for a facilitator are as follows:

- Arrange the time and place of the meeting.
- Collect and prepare topics and distribute them to all participants in advance, which helps everyone preview the meeting agenda and increase participation.
- The facilitator has the right to designate the spokesperson, or only the person who gets the token can speak, so as to ensure that a person's complete statement is not interrupted, and at the same time prevent one or more active persons from dominating the speech.
- The facilitator shall properly control the time of discussion, but he cannot say "our time is up, let's discuss the next topic," since the customer will not agree with it; he'd better put the current topic aside and end the discussion euphemistically.

- The facilitator shall face the audience most of the time, not the blackboard.
- The facilitator shall learn to guide the participants to speak, for example, "Wang, you have proposed a method before, can you explain to everyone why it is able to solve this problem," so as to encourage more people to join the discussion, although it is not sure that everyone has the opportunity to speak at the meeting.

Regarding ordinary participants, they should not only attend the meeting, but integrate themselves into it:

- Try to understand the topics to be discussed at the meeting in advance, and attend the meeting with their own options.
- An ordinary participant shall care about the entire team at the meeting, not just the facilitator.
- Repeat the customer's question, "Can I repeat your question just now," so that he can confirm our understanding of his question.
- Repeat the customer's answer, "Let me summarize your answer just now, please correct me if it is inaccurate," so that he can confirm our correct understanding of his answer.
- Properly take meeting minutes to prevent the loss of information.
- At meeting, especially when answering questions, try to avoid just answering "ok," "yes" or "no," and then saying nothing. Express your own opinion, your viewpoint, even if you just confirm the other person's point of view, so that others can be sure that you really understand the problems being discussed.

The facilitator shall ensure the efficiency of remote meetings, and summarize some divergent discussions in a timely manner. If the participants fail to reach consensus on some problems for a long time, he shall perform his duty of coordination or try other means to suspend such discussion. He shall prevent the participants from spending a long time on one issue, and arrange another meeting which only involves related people, in order to ensure the efficiency of the meeting.

2.3.1 Typical Forms of Meeting

The typical meetings are as follows:

- Stand-up
- Iteration planning meeting (IPM)
- Retrospective meeting
- Showcase
- Team huddle

2.3.1.1 Stand-Up

As the most frequent meeting for distributed teams and a standard means of communication for cross-functional teams, the stand-up meeting is a fairly effective team synchronization mechanism. In case of a remote stand-up, both of its content and time shall be properly prepared to ensure its effect.

Let's learn about the stand-up of an independent team.

We usually choose a suitable time in the morning to do a stand-up upon the consent of all team members. In terms of the content of the stand-up, the updates made by each participant include yesterday's work progress, today's work plan, and expected outcome, as well as the information shared with the rest of the team and necessary assistance.

Compared with the stand-up of an independent agile team, the remote stand-up has to overcome the double difficulties of customer requirements and schedule, so as to achieve its effect. Once distributed teams can solve these problems, the adverse effect of remote stand-up could be eliminated.

Regarding its content, the daily stand-up is definitely not a work report meeting for offshore teams to report their work to the customer team, but a platform for team communication so as to share information, express commitment and point out obstacles (difficulties and corresponding solution), resolve the problem of team coordination rather than a specific problem. In addition, everyone shall brief on his work progress at the stand-up. Do not simply say what you did yesterday and carry on the work today, which is meaningless to other members and teams, since they have no idea when you can finish your job and start the next integration. In short, the goal of stand-up is to make what one team is doing as transparent as possible to other teams.

In a normally functioning team, it is not difficult to guarantee that each stand-up will not exceed 15 minutes. I have attended a stand-up of a team of about 15 people, they easily finished the meeting in 15 minutes, since everyone knew what to say at the meeting and what should be discussed offline. The stand-up is not a place to solve problems, but to list out all problems, and find who can help them, then you will know who you can reach out after stand-up meeting. In order to ensure its efficiency, there must be a token that guarantees that only one person speaks at any time, even with distributed teams. We hand the token to the other party in front of the camera, which seems quite ceremonial.

Regarding the time of stand-up, in general, it is a good attempt to arrange all team members to attend each stand-up, so as to fully understand the situation of other teams. But the jet lag makes it difficult for us to find a suitable stand-up time for all teams. Table 2.4 lists the stand-ups or temporary coordinations I have attended, showing how difficult it is to coordinate all teams to agree on the time of meeting.

Therefore, as long as time permits, we can hold a stand-up joined by all teams every day. If the stand-up of a team has to be arranged beyond working hours, we have to make compromise to organize a weekly stand-up for all teams, and each team can hold its own stand-up at other times.

In case of a cross-team stand-up, some teams may have woken up early, while others may have been busy with a full day of work, we can discuss some light topics to warm up at the beginning of stand-up. For example, when we were working with the customer team in Los Angeles, we would talk about some interesting topics before the start of the weekly stand-up, like the game "two truths and a lie," the most embarrassing moments, the favorite things we had seen, and the meaning of our name.

Sometimes the customer team will not agree to arrange a stand-up during their nonworking hours, so we should get mentally prepared that we have to choose the most suitable time for our team within their working hours. At this time, our team members have to adjust our daily working hours, for example, from 9–18 o'clock to 7–16 o'clock. Such a schedule is hard to be maintained for a long time, so we have to negotiate two sets of stand-up times with our customers. Within its working hours, each team agrees to switch the stand-up time with the customer every two weeks, which is fair to both parties, as shown the project schedule involving the teams, respectively, in Beijing and Los Angeles in Table 2.4. If the customer refuses to make any compromise, we have to abandon the stand-up attended by all team members in exchange for the one only attended by team representatives.

TABLE 2.4
Time for Stand-Ups for Different Distributed Teams

Team 1	Stand-Up Time (Local Time)	Team 2	Stand-Up Time (Local Time)	Team 3	Stand-Up Time (Local Time)
Beijing	17:30	London	9:30		
Beijing	11:00	Sydney	13:00		
Beijing	9:15	Chicago	20:15		
Beijing	19:00/9:00	Los Angeles	7:30 /16:30		
Beijing	10:00	Bangalore	7:30	Sao Paulo	23:00

The organization of remote stand-up has a different manner of execution. Once in a project, the speech of everyone was not directly related to the story card, which making us fail to combine the information with the Kanban, and the Kanban became a background. We began to question whether the rotatory speech was fit for our team. Later, the stand-up was hosted by one person, he would lead us to update the status and problems one by one according to the task cards shown on the Kanban. Naturally, the project manager assumed this important task, but he needed certain skills to let the members of all teams understand the status of each task. When necessary, he had to make some further explanations to ensure that all relevant people fully understand.

Agile development promotes the concept of self-organization and the self-management of teams, while daily stand-up is an important practice in which the team independently conducts status synchronization, risk management, and decision-making. The team learns about the overall status of the project through the stand-up and makes collective decisions on the risks and problems that are exposed. A well-organized stand-up arises from the self-organization needs of the team, not the monitoring needs of the customer.

So, regarding the remote stand-up, I've made the following summary: First, since it is held regularly, choosing a suitable time is the top priority. Second, the agile approach advocates that all team members participate in a brief meeting with regular status updates. Shortness is very important, that's why everyone is standing up at the meeting. As one of the participants of the stand-up, we shall keep in mind the purpose of this meeting: let others know what you are talking about and keep up with your updates. Third, it is more appropriate for some distributed teams to update by card. Making updates by task card makes it easier for the participants to learn about the overall status of the team, in this case the task is the main line. Making updates by personnel makes the participants to know more about a particular person, in this case the person is the main line.

In one of my recent projects, we tried to use Wiki to update the status of each person and each team, which avoided forcing all distributed teams to attend the stand-up at the same time, since their time was unavailable. Fortunately, this worked so well that we got enough information from each other, but only missed the part that needed immediate communication between the teams. We had no choice but to ask any urgent matters to be resolved through other channels. Now, for the projects that do not have overlapping time zones during working hours, we have canceled the cross-team stand-ups. But this does not mean that we have no face-to-face communication, because we still have some discussions attended by a few representatives of each team. The stand-up in the strict sense no longer exists, but a new stand-up attended by team representatives once or twice a week is born.

2.3.1.2 IPM

IPM represents the beginning of a new iteration. Its content is mainly divided into two parts: showing the results of the previous iteration and introducing the tasks of the new iteration. These two parts require the project manager and the business analyst to spend some time making preparations. Prepare your story card[1], give a brief explanation to others, and share your understanding of the story card.

At the IPM, the development team and the product manager will conclude a delivery contract by describing in detail the tasks, respectively, inside and outside the project scope (immediately before the work of the next iteration begins). By the end of the IPM, there should be no hidden assumptions and potential misunderstandings about requirements, solutions or acceptance criteria.

The project manager shall make the following pre-meeting preparations:

- Count the completed story cards and show the status of all story cards in the last iteration.
- Calculate the points of the story card completed in the last iteration, showing the speed of delivery.
- Generate burn down chart and burn up chart.
- Summarize the problems during this period.

The business analyst shall make the following pre-meeting preparations:

- Arrange team huddles for the business analyst of distributed team with the product manager of the customer team, in order to resolve doubts in the requirements.
- Define the scope of story cards delivered by the new iteration.
- Confirm the priority of each story card with the customer.

The agenda of the IPM is usually as follows:

- Show the offshore team and the customer team the results of the previous iteration and the plan for the new iteration.
- Introduce the story cards of new iteration, and let the team estimate the points for each story card.
- The last item of the IPM is the ask-for-leave plan, we can use the visual method to mark the date on the calendar and indicate who is absent that day.

If it is difficult to ask all members of the distributed teams to participate in the IPM, we can separate out the story card introduction and estimation and organize an independent IPM. If project managers, business analysts and technical directors of all teams are about to attend an IPM, then all team members shall take part in the start-up meeting scheduled after the IPM.

The goals of the IPM are shown as follows:

- According to the development speed of the team, choose the appropriate story card to form a new iteration plan.
- Explain the content of the story card to be done in the new iteration.
- Improve the acceptance conditions of each story card.
- Estimate each story card, and the estimated points will affect the iteration plan.
- Define the priority of story cards to be done.

The following problems often arise at the IPM:

2.3.1.3 Inconsistent Criteria for Estimation

It is manifested in the following two aspects:

- Unclear requirements: In case of any domain that no one is familiar with, then the general advice is not to estimate this story card. We need to assign someone to investigate this story card first, divide the tasks after getting the investigation results, and finally make estimation.
- Disagreements on estimation itself: Is the estimation made on basis of workload or relative difficulty?

Many distributed teams have the above doubts, not to mention the customer team. We may fail to explain them clearly when the customer asks. This is often the case when estimating, Wang says, "This story could be completed in two days, let's count two days as one point." In fact, his estimation is based workload (person/day). However, in this book *Agile Estimating and Planning*, Mike Cohn – one of the founders of the Scrum Alliance – says the estimation should be based on relative difficulty.

In fact, it depends on the purpose of our estimation. Usually, our estimation is to arrange an iterative plan and identify delivery risks. For this purpose, we can estimate according to relative difficulty. Our estimated points are all relative values, and the calculated delivery speed is based on previous iterations and experience. If the purpose of our estimation is to count the workload of the team, we can calculate the points in terms of man-days, and such points are an absolute value. This creates a problem, that is, a story card is developed by different people, so the workload is definitely different, and we can only get the average workload of a team.

So far, the estimation in all the projects I have worked on can be divided into the following three categories:

- In the inception phase of the project, quick estimation of all story cards is used to determine the scope of delivery, the date of delivery, and to arrange the story cards into the iteration plan.
- After the project starts to be delivered, the estimation of all developers should be taken at the beginning of each iteration.
- After a story is taken by a developer and before the actual development, the developer can make further refinements based on the results of requirement refinement, and each story card can be refined into a task. Of course, this kind of estimation based on task details is not made by all teams.

The first case should be estimated according to absolute difficulty. At the stage of inception, we need to quickly get the total workload. Usually, the technical supervisor will, based on his own experience, take into account the requirement risks and technical risks, quickly estimate all story cards, and give an absolute value. The purpose of this situation is mainly for commercial needs, that is, used for quotation and bidding.

In the second case, the estimation based on relative workload, which is get supported by the team. This time its accuracy is not important at all, since the principle of estimation here is that the consistency of estimation is more important than the accuracy of estimation. In this case, if our estimation is based on workload, everyone's estimated points of the same story card will be different, since each person's development ability is different. Therefore, we cannot rely on our own development ability to do the estimation, but that everyone uses the sample card of the same criterion and gets the estimated points, so that everyone is comparing the same criterion.

In the third case, the team has a thorough understanding of the details at this time. It no longer makes estimation, but gives the exact time for completing the requirements.

Think it over, you will find that estimation provides a useful mechanism that can initiate and encourage team members to communicate with each other. Estimation meeting can helps us, in different ways, understand the upcoming story, the design direction of architecture and code base. In this case, any story points out of estimation are less important. Similar conversations may take place on many occasions, if these conversations have not happened yet, the team should better to initiate a discussion about estimation. Conversely, if you consider stopping the estimation, you need to ensure that the effective communication during the estimation will be carried on elsewhere.

How to estimate two story cards containing the same basic work? There had been several discussions on this issue in one company where I was working. And it is still being talked about from time to time.

For example, there are two story cards like this: both Story A and Story B contain a basic work C, if story A and story B are estimated separately, they are both 5 points, but if Story A is done first and Story B is done later, then Story B may only take two points, because the basic work C included in Story B has been completed in Story A. Work C cannot be simply split into story cards, because it has no complete business value, the combination of A-C or B-C has independent business value.

There are two views on this issue, one is to split C into a 3-point task card, and A and B into two 2-point story cards; the other is to keep two 5-point story cards for A and B. These two views have their own backgrounds. People who hold the first point of view believe that the value we deliver to customers is 7 points, and we cannot ask customers to pay twice for C, although this method of splitting story cards does not conform to the principle of story splitting. The second view is that from the perspective of user value, A and B are two separate user requirements. When the first one is completed and then the second one is to be done, the cost will be reduced, which means that the complexity is reduced and the development speed is increased, showing the growth of the team's ability. Besides, according to the principle of consistency, we can't give story cards of the same complexity different points only because of their development order.

You may have come to know that the first one is actually a technology-oriented estimation based on workload, while the second is a requirement-oriented estimation based on relative complexity.

THE PRINCIPLE OF STORY SPLITTING: FOLLOW THE INVEST PRINCIPLE OF BILL WAKE

"INVEST" is a combination of independent, negotiable, valuable, estimable, small and testable.

Should the workload of testing be included in the points? The answer to this question depends on the purpose of our story card estimation. If the estimation is to plan for the next iteration, I suggest that it does not include the workload of testers. The reasons are as follows:

- Whether it is a task card or a story card, there are outputs, and the quality is internally contained.
- Regardless of the quality of codes, the test cases are the same.

As can be seen from the above, our views on many practices expressed at this meeting are inconsistent, and unifying these differences is one of the purposes of IPM.

Split subtasks to refine and reduce the points of a single story card. Ideally, each story card can be completed in a day or two. The delivery risk could be mitigated by reducing the number of unfinished story cards at the end of the iteration.

2.3.1.4 Time of Meeting is Too Long

Since the IPM attended by all teams may cause inconvenience to some teams, we need to pay special attention to the efficiency of this meeting. To achieve the goal of IPM in the shortest time, we need to agree to complete many tasks before the meeting.

- The testers complete the test script based on understanding the requirements.
- The developers understand the content of story cards and begin to break down the tasks.
- Record the issues to be clarified.

Therefore, at the meeting, we can pass by the parts with clarified requirements, and focus on the parts where the team has questions.

2.3.1.5 Where the Speed of Delivery Drops, the Team Shall Explain at the IPM that it is Due to the Following Reasons

- There is a serious deviation on estimation.
- The team shall explain to the customer that the estimated points are merely estimates. The purpose of the estimation is for iteration planning.
- The technical debt shall be repaid. The investigation tasks are too much. It may be necessary to make this part of work visible and traceable.

For distributed teams, we may have another kick-off meeting to assign all story cards. Normally, it is the team that take the story card will be responsible for testing too, so that the efficiency will be higher. From my experience, developers and testers are in different places and work on a same story card also happens, but only within distributed teams which have their most working hours overlapped.

One thing I have learned from my experience of tons of projects is that IPM requires all teams to participate, which is of great help to coordinate each other's work afterward.

The annoying time zone issue of distributed teams has become a constraint for team meetings. Although some teams do not have comfortable time, it is definitely worth their sacrifice to attend the IPM, because this meeting is irreplaceable, we have no other means to achieve the same purpose.

Do not let everyone stand up at the IPM, since it may last for a long time. If they have to keep standing throughout the meeting, many people will hope to end this meeting as soon as possible, instead of clarifying all requirement-related issues when everyone is present.

2.3.1.6 Retrospective Meeting

In his *Project Retrospectives: A Handbook for Team* published in 2001, Norman L. Kerth comments that no matter what we've found, considering the knowledge category, technologies and capabilities, available resources and actual situation at that time, we shall understand and firmly believe that everyone has done their best. This has become the supreme guideline for retrospective meeting.

At each meeting, the facilitator will quote this guideline, in an aim to reiterate that the purpose of our meeting is not to settle accounts and investigate someone's responsibility, but to focus on what has happened, let everyone put down their precautions and openly explore the team's gains and losses over the past period of time. Of course, we cannot expect this guideline to solve all problems, but we will find that the people who have been active speakers at the meeting remain so, yet there is an extra sense of disclaimer when they are speaking; the team members who have been cautious still adopt defensive strategies, but they have taken the first step at least. The supreme guideline is reminding our team that everyone's goal is to seek solutions instead of blaming human factors (subjective) and environmental factors (objective). We all know that a guideline cannot change human behavior, but this is a good start. So we continue to advocate the quote of this guideline before each meeting, in order to create an open and more constructive meeting.

For the retrospective meeting to achieve the desired results, there shall be a high degree of trust among the participating team members. It is extremely challenging for distributed teams, without the trust that is already established, it is difficult to ensure that everyone in each team can speak freely. Integrating trust into everyone's blood is not a slogan, this is the goal everyone works for, and it is a tangible goal.

The project manager can get to know each member in a one-to-one interview and promote formal and informal activities to harmonize team relationships.

When building their mutual trust, offshore teams shall pay attention to the following routine activities:

- Transparency of both teams
- Transcend the sense of distance through space through setting up live video
- Regular visits

Safety check is also an important part of the retrospective meeting, and its criteria are shown in Table 2.5.

When the project manager of a team is easy to get along with, the safety check score is relatively high. When the project manager is relatively strong, everyone may not dare to speak out. When some team members feel that the meeting is in an unsafe environment, the effectiveness of such a meeting will be greatly reduced. It is necessary to find a way to make the meeting environment safe, for example, to invite someone "in a high position" out until everyone feels safe. Those who have implemented agile practice will understand these theories, but in a retrospective meeting of a single project, I have never seen anyone was invited out, and the usual outcome is that the participants have to retain certain opinions in the end.

After team members have confirmed the safety of the retrospective meeting, they can start discussing the formal topics. If we want to make everyone active as quickly as possible, playing an

TABLE 2.5

Safety Check Criteria of Retrospective Meeting

Safety Level	Implications
5	Very safe, speak without reserve
4	Relatively safe, but the speaker will consider the future impact, including the impacts on himself and on others (he will speak with reservation in case of any large negative impact)
3	Safe, he only talks about positive things instead of negative things
2	There are no examples for Safety Level 2 and 1 (at least I have never met or heard of it for so many years),
1	since the meeting is meaningless when the Safety Level is below 3.

ice-breaking game is a good option. We usually draw a picture to express our feelings about the project in the past, the time can be 5–10 minutes. If the period for a retrospective meeting is relatively long, we can draw a mood curve with time as the horizontal axis, which helps us recall the typical events and all connections while working on the project.

There are two kinds of retrospective meeting: iterative retrospective and project retrospective, which have different purposes.

- The iterative retrospective focuses on the problems that occurred in the previous iteration and the improvements that need to be made in the next iteration. This is also the retrospective meeting that ordinary teams often attend. The retrospective meeting in this section refers to the iterative retrospective unless otherwise indicated.
- The project retrospective makes a review from a higher level, and it uses the entire life cycle of a project as a starting point to find problems and methods for improving project delivery.

The retrospective meeting can take many forms:

- The most common form is to diverge from the three dimensions: "well," "less well" and "puzzle." It is the most widely used retrospective approach, which simple and easy and free from making explaining to the teams, so it is especially welcomed by relatively large teams, time-bound teams, and distributed teams.
- Use a starfish chart. As shown in Figure 2.2, this dimension is slightly complicated, but it provides participants with several directions of thinking, making it easier to generate action plans.

The role of facilitator in the retrospective meeting

In addition to reading the supreme guideline as mentioned above, conducting safety checks, and leading the team to play ice-breaking games, the facilitator has more important things to do at the retrospective meeting.

(1) Make clear the contents to be covered in the meeting, including everything related to the project, teams, and every team member from the last retrospective to the current one. List important events and milestones for everyone, so as to facilitate team thinking and divergent thinking.

(2) Timing each section of the meeting, for example, 10 minutes for collecting questions.

(3) Group the collected questions. Grouping needs some skills, the same kind of problems should be put together, so that we can think about problems from the dimensions. For example, front-end and back-end technologies, automated testing, performance, communication with customers or other teams, progress, and waste in teamwork.

(4) In the retrospective meeting, some sensitive topics will definitely be mentioned. Make sure all participants to focus on the problems rather than the people.

(5) Lead the teams to analyze the topics which are voted, and guide them to develop an action plan for resolving problems.

(6) Select a responsible person for each action.

(7) After this retrospective meeting and before the next one, an important work is to oversee the implementation of the action plan.

At the beginning of the retrospective meeting, we must first review the implementation of the output of the last meeting. Tick off the completed tasks, and explain those not implemented. Those becoming meaningless can be removed directly; those needs to be continued shall be added into the current execution list.

The retrospective meeting is more in line with the left brain vs. right brain rules. First, the storm of right brain emits as many views as possible, and then the left brain is brought into play, it begins to organize and classify these view into several topics (generally four or five).

It is easy to make everyone speak at this meeting, because most cards require the concerned parties to explain their purposes that they want to express.

Since the fundamental purpose of the retrospective meeting is to make improvement, why should we enumerate and discuss the jobs that have been done well? In fact, in addition to identifying the aspects for improvement, we must affirm the teams' achievements and build their confidence. To adjust the atmosphere of the meeting, we cannot keep talking about the heavy, negative and serious topics.

Speaking from my own experience, in many retrospective meetings, questions such as untimely customer feedback are often raised. In fact, we should not put forward these questions until the

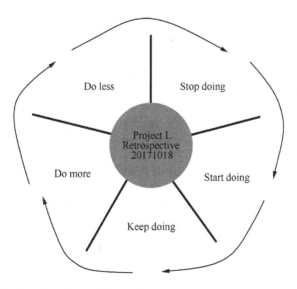

FIGURE 2.2 Starfish chart used in retrospective meeting.

retrospective meeting, but directly show customers the impact of untimely feedback on our plan and schedule, so that they can realize the seriousness of the impact and the resulting waste. Customers are also professionals, they are able to make a better judgment based on enough information. If everyone keeps waiting in silence and hides the information, then no one can know how much the real impact is. In terms of the action plan produced at the meeting, in addition to designating the responsible person for particular tasks, which is a critical link, the time for completing this plan shall be determined. Then we shall convert each action into a task card, add it into the backlog, and prioritize them with other story cards. Make sure that the output of the retrospective meeting is implemented, otherwise the loop of continuous improvement will be broken. This link is easily overlooked, since many people think that this practice is to review the meeting itself. In fact, the output is the goal of the meeting, and efforts shall be made to fulfill this goal. It is because we can rigorously extract value from failure, we can give the team the opportunity to try something new in an iteration cycle.

If the retrospective meeting is attended by a single team (a common practice for most distributed teams), the lessons or experiences summarized by this team shall be shared with other teams, whether sending e-mails to all teams or uploading them to cloud storage. When approved experiences are repeated continuously, we can foster a subconscious and respond to the same problems correctly in the future.

For distributed teams, we usually use Ideaboardz – an online whiteboard tool, which is like a virtual wall with sticky notes. The creation of cards in the system is anonymous and the content of the cards is visible to all participants. Therefore, it can also be used as a safety check tool for distributed teams, both fast and simple. The project manager must build the virtual board for this retrospective meeting in advance so that the team members can post what they want to say in time. In this way, when the retrospective meeting begins, everyone has gone through some thinking, and the discussion is easier to hit the topic.

The simple process of remote retrospective meeting of distributed teams is as follows:

- Time 5 minutes for everyone to create cards on the board, and each card records only one problem.
- The facilitator merges similar cards and ensures that everyone understands every group of problems. When everyone starts voting, the votes on the same topic will not be scattered.
- Within 2 minutes, everyone starts to vote on the topic that they want to discuss in depth. Everyone could have 3 votes, so the voting result is easily define.
- Carry out in-depth discussion of the 3 to 4 topics with the highest number of votes, each of which must have an action plan. If the team is small or has enough time, it can discuss more or even all of the topics.
- At the end of the meeting, designate a person in charge for each action. And this person must ensure the execution and completion of the action before next retrospective meeting.

The retrospective meeting facilitates the exposure of problems in the first place, so that we can keep continuous improvement which is the goal that the agile team always pursues. Never stop in making improvement, which is the core practice directly interpreted by the retrospective meeting, that is, the final output of the meeting is to improve as compared with the past. The retrospective meeting is essentially set up for the self-management team to make up for the lack of professional managers, so everyone should carefully consider what purpose to achieve at this meeting.

Each iteration is equivalent to a small life cycle in the project, and normally an iteration last two weeks, so we could organize a retrospective meeting every two or more iterations.

In short, the retrospective meeting is one of the most valuable and important Scrum meetings. This is a meeting for improvement, through which the team reviews what they have done, and discusses how to ensure all problems that prevent the team from reaching the goal will not happen again in subsequent iterations. At the same time, this is also a practice that can regularly capture changes, regularly adjust the team's general direction and daily work, and make a contribution to "agile development hugs changes." The retrospective meeting reflects the value of PDCA process improvement, which is advocated by the quality management master W. Edwards Deming.

2.3.1.7 Showcase/Iterative Review

As the name implies, this is an opportunity to show the completed work to customers and is a process of collecting customers' feedback. But for some teams, the process where developers show the development results to the business analysts and testers on their own machines is regarded a showcase. But I prefer to call this presentation as desk check. This name sounds more straight-forward and is easier to distinguish from the showcase to customers, free from causing ambiguity and making additional explanation, which is in line with the essence of agile development.

So why does the team need such a showcase?

First, this is a good opportunity to show the team's work results and progress to customers who also welcome such a report-back meeting.

Second, only when we show our achievements to customers, then they will realize which functions are really necessary.

Third, in an agile process, we need customers to eventually accept a story card. Without such a showcase, customers lack the context and motivation to accept the story card. With this routine showcase, customers are happy to accept the completed story cards within a day or two.

Specifically, to do a good showcase, we need to do the following preparation:

- We need at least one drill before showcase, and make sure to restore the data to the status before the drill.
- When a remote showcase is about to start, prepare the environment 15 minutes in advance, including the video conference system and the external independent microphone and sound system.
- It would be much better to have a meeting system with additional backups.
- There should be an agenda of the showcase, so that the entire team will know where the meeting has progressed, and product stakeholders will be aware of the progress of the team's work from the last showcase to the present one.
- We should use a multi-screen display. Currently, most video conference systems support simultaneous display of the team's real scene and the presenter's shared desktop.
- Book a meeting room.

Ideally, each distributed team shall showcase their development results of each iteration, then coordinate with other teams to put the results online based on the outcome of showcase.

The showcase will display the functions that passed the tester's testing. I know that many supervisors of offshore team are eager to show customers what they have made as early as possible, and some customers are also anxious to see what the team has accomplished. However, it is easy to expose problems at the showcase, and turned the showcase to a defect showcase and waste a lot of time. Many teams have suffered losses in this regard, because they arranged this kind of showcase.

If there are remote participants, the showcase script should be sent out in advance. Participants who rely on the teleconference need to know the context in order to get a better effect.

When showing development results to customers, if someone at the customer's site is invited to preside the showcase, the offshore teams shall be fully prepared more carefully, such as helping the presenters prepare the demo script, perfect user scenarios and data. Define the role play of all different users during the entire showcase, just like the cast of movies. If it is a mobile application, use the tools software to map it to the computer so that everyone can see it clearly.

To manage the customer expectations, we must clarify the scope of the showcase in advance. Evaluate the content to be shown, circle the parts that need to be clarified by customers, and let them confirm at the showcase. Make a record of the problems found at the showcase and the customer feedback. Convert the collected feedback into story cards, and prioritize them with stories of the next iteration.

Since we have adopted an agile development approach, the working software is one of the main outputs that customers can see, not documents, it is very important to arrange regular showcase and enable customers to try out the software as soon as possible.

After the functions are shown to customers and stakeholders, it is best that they directly have a try in the test environment of the showcase, so that they may find something surprising while using these functions by themselves.

After the showcase, we need to ask customers to accept the completed requirements as soon as possible. Only when they accept the stories, the staged work is really completed, although many people ignore this matter and shift their focus to new requirements for functions. If this stage is written into contract, the project manager is obliged to have it known by all team members, because any delayed acceptance by customers will directly lead to delayed project billing.

In addition to the above regular and slightly formal showcase, we also encourage customers to further use the functions we have developed in order to receive more in-depth feedback. If conditions permit, such as an established solid customer relationship, we even allow customers to try out the functions not fully completed to get their opinions as early as possible. Many customers understand what they really want after they really use the software. Trust me, such customers are not in the minority.

The essence of showcase is an important node of the feedback loop. Thanks to the iterative development of agile working method, we can invite customers to review period outputs of development team. In an ordinary development team, the general process is like this: business analysts gather requirements, developers implement some functions according to the requirements and then transfer these functions to testers for verification, and finally release the functions to the production environment for customers to use. In an agile team, we can show our customers the functions that are still in development. Customers can find out, as soon as possible, whether the developed functions (or unfinished functions with certain value) are what they want. After our team completes the day's work and submits the work results to the code base, a few hours later the customer's local team will be able to download the latest code. A higher possibility is to directly download the latest packaged applications, install it locally, and then try the latest features. Customers can quickly detect the inconsistencies with their requirements. Although the local team cannot modify the inconsistencies immediately, they can be resolved by distributed teams after they come online the next day.

To make the offshore teams work closely with the customers of local team, we need to give our customers the authority of our development environment and test environment. Besides, it is better to find the easiest way to let customers see our latest achievements. For example, for mobile development projects, we upload all the packages onto Testflight or Dropbox, which is easy for customers to download and install. And what they see is exactly the latest functions that we've finished

2.3.1.8 Team Huddle

In a distributed team, because of the feature team working mode, its stand-up meeting focus on status update of story cards and the obstacles. The members of same role in each team also need to meet regularly to communicate issues of common interest in a horizontal dimension, as shown in Table 2.6. People playing different roles in the host team may actively look for some topics to talk about mostly for half an hour to an hour, or discuss with their counterparts in the customer team, so as to bring the two sides closer.

Distributed team shall take account of time factor for optimizing the communication process. For example, we once hired a Manila-based team to help us do some particular integration work for a project. Before the end of each workday, we would arrange a huddle meeting for all development team members from both sides to discuss the problems encountered during the day; moreover, another purpose of the meeting is to check upon the work of the Manila team.

TABLE 2.6

Usual Forms of Huddle for Distributed Teams

Type of Huddle	Content
Business analysis team	The business analysts of each team unify their needs, discuss whether there are dependencies, interactions, priorities of each function block, and arrange iteration plans.
Development team	The developers of each team discuss the difficulties of some implementations, refactoring plans, review code, learn from each other, etc.
Quality assurance team	The testers of each team share the defects found. Whether the integration of the test task in the near future requires the cooperation of each team, the next stage of the test plan and personnel arrangements

Distributed teams require more preparations for the huddle. In case of the huddle initiated hosted by us, the meeting agenda shall be prepared in advance and send out, stating the expected output of this huddle. For the huddle initiated by other teams, we also need to be fully prepared to understand as much context as possible and get more involved in the meeting.

2.3.2 SKILLS FOR OFFSHORE TEAMS IN ATTENDING MEETINGS

When arranging meetings of different teams, the time selection should minimize the interruption of the working hours of each team. A meeting may cause damage on the working hours of a whole afternoon, because the meeting arranged in the middle divides the afternoon into two time spans, which makes it impossible to finish a large-scale task. Do not call in people to attend any nonurgent meetings, we should ensure all teams of full working hours.

The necessary meetings should be arranged as early as possible. It is recommended that such meetings shall be arranged after the regular meetings like the stand-up, so that it will easier to call in all team members, and it will be less likely to be postponed for someone may be busy with their work at another time.

Sit with the members of the customer team or invite some of them to attend the meeting, do not sit opposite the customer team for fear of causing a sense of opposition. At some informal meetings, try to arrange those nonfamiliar faces to sit together, since there will be small talks when acquaintances are sitting together.

Don't discuss too many topics or invite too many people at a meeting, because control the time of the meeting will be getting harder, which will reduce the efficiency and output of the meeting. It is a good practice to split the meeting into several discussions where only relevant personnel participate.

We expect every meeting to bring about some output or solve some problems. But only keep our eyes on the agenda and deliverables will make the meeting process uninteresting and rigid. We should better take advantage of these opportunities, especially some informal huddles, to bring the teams closer, activate the work atmosphere for them, and maintain their vitality.

Control open discussions at meeting and guide the participants to arrive at a conclusion. For possible open discussions, our solution is to discuss it in a small scale within the team first and then discuss some outputs at the plenary meeting.

For some other training sessions, there is a recommended way to start: First of all, give an introduction to the content and agenda of the session, let all participants raise problems encountered and their expectations around this training subject, then collect the concerns of everyone. At the end of the session, go through all these concerns to identify which are already discussed and which are yet mentioned. If no consensus is reached on a problem, it can be discussed offline.

As mentioned at the beginning of this chapter, not many people are fond of attending meetings, but the meetings of distributed agile teams cannot be ignored, because these meetings are the means for remote teams to maintain daily communication. Regular meetings will strengthen the sense of belonging of all teams, just like our traditional festivals, and they are a moment of team reunion. Don't let the teams make these meetings a burden.

2.3.3 SUMMARY

Past experiences tell us that teleconferencing without video images is difficult to attract the attention of participants, so we should better to use video in all remote daily meetings, code reviews, and pair programming, etc. In addition, if budget allows, we can arrange for people from different teams to communicate face-to-face, for example, to arrange business travels for team members (not project managers). Later, with constant rotation, the members of all teams have experienced such a trip and took some time to get acquainted with each other. For people who work in different places, if they have the opportunity to meet each other face to face, their communication will be improved significantly.

When meetings become a routine activity, team members are getting more quickly form a common point of view, which is a clear signal that the combat effectiveness of the team began to take shape.

Although everyone agrees on the importance of regular communication for project management, once the project is in progress, it is easy for members to forget to meet and communicate with each other or provide other stakeholders with the project updates. Therefore, the establishment of a regular communication meeting mechanism, including who will participate in these meetings and who needs to participate, will help keep the project running smoothly. Only invite necessary participants is very important, because too many people will complicate matters, and a lot of time may be wasted on one issue after another.

The summary after each meeting is both important and effective, whether it is a visual summary photo on the whiteboard on the spot, or a summary by e-mail on the day, because at the end of the meeting, everyone remains deeply impressed by their discussions, and they are easy to reach consensus at this moment. If we commit procrastination, our discussions will fade day by day. When we contact the other party again, they may tell us "I didn't mean that at that time" or "You must have misunderstood, what I mean is…"

2.4 REPRESENTATIVES ON SITE AND SHORT-TERM FACE-TO-FACE VISITS

As long as it is cooperation between teams, there will definitely be a running-in, just like the running-in of a new car. This process is to learn about each other's traits, strengths and weaknesses, and reach a state where both parties cooperate smoothly. The practice introduced in this chapter is to make this running-in more efficient, and to cross this stage as soon as possible to enter the next stage of smooth cooperation.

When a new project starts, we usually go to the office of the customers or invite them to our company to have a better communication at the very beginning. At the start of the project, we shall quickly learn about the customers' business domain, ideas and vision for the future. If possible, our project team also may meet with the end user, which is a rare opportunity for offshore teams far away from customers, and it must be properly used. In addition to requirements, we also need to determine the technical architecture with the customers' technicians. If there is a legacy system, we can deeply understand it's all kinds of information on site.

For a large-scale project, offshore teams have to conduct frequent communications. We may send an on-site representative to work with the customers. He can help us improve the efficiency of communication with customers and achieve better communication results. If there is no such representative, the regular face-to-face communication will become indispensable. We can visit customers for a short period of time, such as two weeks to a month, or invite them to visit the workplace of the offshore teams every six months, or arrange for a face-to-face exchange when the project reaches a milestone.

2.4.1 On-Site Representative

Face-to-face communication makes it easier for the teams to brainstorm or have some complex discussions. When everyone is working in one location, it is easy to call all relevant people to the whiteboard to solve complex problems, because most teams prefer to displaying various states on the sticker strips on the physical whiteboard, rather than using the electronic whiteboard. This is why even if distributed teams have a task management system, they still want to have their own physical whiteboard. It is also easier to build personal relationship with those working at the same place, rather than the ones working remotely.

The approach of sending an on-site representative to the other side is used on many projects, especially the large ones. Through the coordination of the on-site representative, two teams can achieve the seamless integration on a daily basis. This representative bears a heavy burden on his shoulders. He must be familiar with the work of the two teams which means he needs to attend two sides stand-ups, and assess work dependencies of teams at any time. If there is something in need of the cooperation of the other party, this representative has to coordinate the personnel of both parties to complete the collaboration accurately at the right time. Of course, in actual work, the work of the on-site representative is by no means limited to this.

The on-site representative may be the one sent by the customer to the offshore team, or the one sent by the offshore team to the customer.

2.4.1.1 The On-Site Representative Sent by the Customer to the Offshore Team

The outsourcing company that I had worked in has created a large delivery team in Beijing, and divided it into five sub-teams, and each of them is staffed with about ten people. When we were working on a project at the beginning, it was not smooth at all, the communication cost of the entire project was very high, and the effect was not good. Later, we realized the waste of remote communication, so we asked the customer to send an expert to work with us and help to solve the decision-making problems in terms of requirement and technology. The customer adopted our suggestion, and regularly rotated this on-site representative.

The approach that customers send an on-site representative to our delivery team is beneficial to our two sides with less overlap of working hours. This practice has continued to date, lasting seven years.

To which will the customer pay attention when visiting the offshore team?

- The mental outlook of the team
- Professional performance, regular technical communication, team building, learning of customer domain knowledge
- Focus on solving problems that require face-to-face communication

2.4.1.2 The On-Site Representative Sent by the Offshore Team to the Customer

Take the two projects that I have worked on for example:

One project was relatively large, with a total of more than 30 people in offshore teams. Two team members (one was project manager and the other one was business analyst) were sent to the customer. The project manager was responsible for communicating with the customer on the matters about project progress and risk control, task prioritization, and showcase of staged development results, and for collection of customer feedback. The business analyst was responsible for the confirmation and interpretation of the customer requirements and for control of the scope of requirements.

The other project was not large, and the offshore teams were made up of around 10 people. An on-site representative was sent to the customer at the very beginning. Since we were not familiar with the customer's business, we initially sent a senior business analyst to help our offshore teams sort out the customer's complex business logic. It prevented us from misunderstanding the customer requirements from the beginning. Later, this representative was replaced by a senior developer. At this time, our development had entered a critical stage, the requirements had become increasingly clear, but there were more and more technological challenges. Both parties were arguing about the solutions, and the customer started questioning our offshore teams. Given this, appointing a senior developer as the on-site representative to the customer will explicitly convey our views to them, and explain our basis; meanwhile, this representative could timely inform us of the customer concerns.

To which will the offshore team pay attention when visiting the customer?

- Pay attention to the customer's oral views on priority.
- Resolve the questions for offshore teams in time every day and get the exact answers from the customer.
- Provide feedback on the customer's adjustments to offshore teams in a timely manner.
- If there are any bad signs about offshore teams, have them resolved in a timely manner.

What kind of on-site representative can be sent to the customer?

- In terms of roles: All of the senior project manager, business analyst and developer are candidates of a long-term representative to the customer site. They need to continuously communicate with customers, which can effectively reduce the cost of communication and improve the effectiveness of communication at the customer site.
- In terms of technologies: If there is a technical expert at the customer site, he can effectively determine the customers' technology selection, enhance the customer confidence in the technical architecture and solve various technical problems, serve as a bridge to the code review of distributed teams, and effectively mitigate the differences of distributed teams on technical issues and reduce invalid disputes.

Why an on-site representative should be sent?

Agile development highly values face-to-face communication. For distributed teams, we also firmly believe that it will be of great help to send the personnel of offshore teams to the customer and work with them. Of course, when the project starts, we will try our best to bring together all the team members. Even if we fail to do so, we will manage to bring together the core members. But what I want to talk about here is how to plan face-to-face communication between distributed team members during the smooth operation of the project.

At the beginning, we tended to send a person who seems like a representative to stay with the customer to coordinates the general work of both parties. After we did this, we gradually discovered that this person would become the only channel for communication between the two sides; he seemed like a relay station where the communication of distributed teams became a point here. Sometimes, if this person was not reliable enough, he would become a bottleneck. As shown in Figure 2.3, we prefer the channel of communication on the right.

Sending an on-site representative for pure communication will most likely cause the above problem, what should we do? I've witnessed that on-site representative to the customer played a constructive role, but it was based on the following principle: even if there is an on-site representative, the two sides shall maintain direct communication and this representative only plays an auxiliary role. Once we sent a business analyst to the customer to take charge of business analysis, he only coordinated the communication between the two sides, and the substantial work was done directly by both the concerned parties. Since we were a flat team and the members were good at self-management,

FIGURE 2.3 Channel of communication.

we were ready to see that the concerned personnel could directly contact the relevant person with the customer team, which also promoted the customer's work style to become flat. The accuracy of information transfer between teams has increased, so does the efficiency of problem-solving. Since our on-site representative had specific tasks in the project, he could work with someone in the customer team in pairs, which would show our professional capabilities to our customers, and build closer personal relationships.

We tend to rotate the on-site representative every three or six months, or less than three months or more than six months, because if he spends too much time on the other team, he will get more estranged from his own team. For example, he may fail to know half of his team members after rounds of personnel changes. Even if we care no about whether the representative himself wants to stay with the other party, we need to giving more people the opportunity to learn more about the work of another team. There may be another problem here: If someone is selected as the representative, but he does not want to leave his family and work far away from home, we cannot force him to take this task. We must consider this situation when we build offshore teams.

Through the work of an on-site representative, it is easier for us to build trust with the other side, and this trust is also relatively strong. In a world where "the boat of friendship boats are turned over at any time," maintaining this trust is to maintain the cooperation foundation for distributed teams. Therefore, if your project is undertaken by a distributed team, whether it is a team of the same company, a team of customers, or a team of suppliers, you have to take it seriously when there is no personnel exchange for a long time. I suggest to make a visit plan immediately, choose an on-site representative to the other team as soon as possible, and let him work with the other team for some time. All risks must be resolved before the bad signs of communication barriers, misunderstandings or mutual disgust show up between the teams.

2.4.1.3 Matters Need Attention

The communication channel between offshore team and local team must be kept clear, although the local team still has its own work to do.

If we have an on-site representative to the customer team, the information updated by the offshore team to the customer must be informed the representative at the same time or in advance. Avoid the situations where the customer has more information about the offshore team than the representative to the customer.

Improving customer satisfaction is also reflected in the fact that after the customer reports a problem, there is no need to deal with several people from the offshore team to solve the problem. The first-responsible system, through internal tracking and transfer within the offshore team, feedbacks the results to the customer. The clarification, confirmation, resolution, and feedback of problems require timely contact with the on-site representative for assistance.

2.4.2 SHORT-TERM FACE-TO-FACE COMMUNICATION

By sending a business analyst to the offshore team regularly, the local team is able to provide the offshore team with more comprehensive background knowledge about the requirements. In this way, the offshore team, which only knew to work hard on a series of functions before, will be sublimated to understand the reasons why users need these functions. Knowing as much background knowledge as possible is valuable for the offshore team's decision-making in the future.

An on-site representative refers to the long-term retention of a member in the other team during the existence of distributed teams, and all short-term visits by this representative to the other team. If it is difficult to designate a long-term on-site representative to the other team, his short-term visits to the other team will become even more important. The selection of such on-site representative shall be purposeful, ask customer for advice if necessary, which one they are prefer, coding skills, automated testing or agile transformation. We can send the most suitable person to help customers solve their most concerned problems.

There are two main ways of short-term face-to-face communication: One is at the inception phase of the offshore project, which is helpful for all team members to have a consistent understanding of the requirements; and the joint work at the initial stage also creates the conditions for the cooperation between teams after they are separated. The other one is during the smooth operation of the project, which can play a role in maintaining and supporting the cooperation between the two sides.

Developers are more introverted than other team members, so they prefer IM or e-mail communication and flexible working hours. It is highly likely to result in lack of trust and alienation of interpersonal relationships, which are mostly seen in distributed teams. Tools such as Skype are not a panacea, regular face-to-face communication is essential, which can sustain a stronger relationship between members.

2.4.2.1 Short-Term Visit for Project Start-Up

The itinerary and content of the visit need to be planned in advance. We can also consider the cycle of iterations and schedule the visit itinerary for at least one full iteration, such as two weeks. As for the projects I have worked on, one month is a suitable time for such visit. We can arrange various activities with fully engagement, these activities include some discussions and real development activities (the first iteration). During the initial period of the visit, it is very important to arrange the work in need of in-depth cooperation. The team members should learn to collaborate with each other as soon as possible.

Regarding the form of the start-up visits, the business manager and project managers of the local team shall come to the office of the offshore team to work out an initial release plan together. The developers of the local team shall visit the offshore team too, in order to help the offshore team to work on the basis of the existing code base, and pass their previous working experience on this code base to the offshore team.

The business analyst of the offshore team shall come to the customer site as early as possible, devote himself into work, and participate in the customer business analysis from the beginning. Considering the cost of visiting customers' site, first day on customer's office, organize a meeting to let customer know the resource demand list we need to get from them, and what we take to them.

The visit for project inception is so important because this activity is the best chance to bring together as many team members as possible, and the schedule for this visit includes several major and directional decisions, for example, the project release plan, the scope of delivered functions, and the priority of deliverables. Although many customers have done a lot of work in collecting requirements in advance, the quick start mentioned here is an intensive and efficient activity that discusses the core business and requirements of customers.

At this stage, we must identify the key business scenarios of customers. Before completing this visit, according to the results of user persona, we shall find the business scenarios of each key user, and ensure this key output by seizing the moment that customers and users are sitting together.

When the project starts, we shall use all means to sort out the customer requirements, including all users and stakeholders on the customer side. At the customer site, meet with as many stakeholders as possible, and collect as much information as possible. Make good use of second-hand information, since many problems may have been considered and tried by customers.

Guide customers to think about problems and push things forward. Raising questions is the beginning, and leading to conclusions is the end. Don't forget to ask after the heated discussion: "Now what is our conclusion?" When splitting story cards, we should first tell customers what is a story card and the concept of Epic. After all stories are defined, we can post these two kind of cards on the wall of the meeting room to display the entire requirement tree, and help everyone think about the requirements as a whole.

After all the requirements are sorted out, the next step is to ask developers to make a quick and rough estimation. The assumptions for story estimation should be made clear, otherwise it may cause disputes. If they are hard to be clarified, then add a buffer for story, multiply 1.5 or 2 as appropriate. If the customer has a legacy system, when we are prototyping and delivering the design, we must make it clear how to interactive with the customer's system, including the interface design and integration time.

During inception, the most difficult problem is uncertainty, which is even harder to deal with than "difficult" and "limitation." The uncertainty will definitely bring about requirement change in future. Since it is a variable, we need to let customers understand the relationship with scope, time and cost. The delivery plan needs to contain story cards which means nice to have for customer, especially for projects with a fixed launch time. Just like even the simplest software still contains defects, the process of software development is not like moving bricks, and there are always situations that we fail to think about in advance. When the go live time cannot be changed, the scope of requirements or cost must be changeable. As for requirements change, we know that the probability of less consideration of requirements is much greater than the probability of excessive design and excessive consideration.

Customers may sometimes question us when we split the story cards too thinly. We usually respond to them like this: our iteration cycle is very short, and we can't keep a story card for a long time, such as across iterations, since it is easy to cause a lot of semi-finished stories at the end of an iteration; promote frequent code commitment and continuous integration; automate test; avoid parallel working, because it is more efficient for the development to focus on one thing at a time.

At the end of the inception, we will produce an iteration plan report, telling customers the time of UAT, the time window of each stage, and what is included in the monthly planned delivery function and else.

Whatever the purpose of the planned visit, we must remember that the main purpose of our visit is not to do more development work, but to establish a close working relationship and understand each other's work habits and work methods. This is what we need for long-term cooperation. So, before we set off, we should examine our work schedule carefully to see if there are any plans to pursue workload, delete them, and add activities that are conducive to promoting communication between different team members. If it is difficult to establish a good personal relationship at work, we can arrange some informal activities. A sumptuous dinner is a good choice as the host to invite customers to visit local attractions. A good personal relationship can effectively increase trust in the project, which is helpful for asking questions proactively. Without good personal relationships, many problems may be hidden or left aside, and end up with nothing, but give us surprise when we are not paying attention.

2.4.2.1.1 Matters Need Attention

In the first few days with customers, we must grasp the personnel organizational structure and stakeholders of the customer team as soon as possible. Quickly figure out the most critical reason why the customer chooses to work with us, so as to ensure that our direction is not wrong. Take the customer's text confirmation seriously, especially involving third-party dependencies, the scope of requirements and assumptions.

In the Project L, we have seen the requirement points inflate significantly. The story cards of the first iteration was estimated at 25 points totally in the inception, and the number became 49 points at the IPM meeting. Besides we also have to deal with some new requirements, we must replace the same workload from the planned to-do list. When we go to the customer site at the project inception phase, the time is tight, there are many unfamiliar issues or domains, in order to ensure the overall efficiency of our team, we cannot focus on particular issues for too long, we have to establish some assumptions for these issues with the customer, evaluate technology selection and required workload on the basis of assumptions. Even if there are changes in the future, customers will generally understand the decision made at that time. This shows that going to the customer site cannot solve all of our queries. There are times the customer himself cannot make an explanation.

There are usually many people going to visit the customer site during inception. Try to designate a fixed person to contact with the customer, since customer may feel headache to deal with different contact persons, and it is possible that different persons may convey inconsistent information to the customer, then he has to repeat the same thing time and time again.

Team members playing different roles should do well their own part. Do not discuss matters outside of you duties with customers, such as business and price-related issues which should be left to the sales staff to deal with.

Guide customers to do "subtraction." When we seek customer feedback on our design, they usually stand on their own positions to express what they need and ignore those they do not need, which will cause the outcome that we can make sure there will be nothing missing, but we cannot subtract unnecessary things. This is very important for the success of the project. Doing some unnecessary things not only increases our workload (development or testing), increase the possibility of problems, but also affect the product performance. In theory, it may also affect the time for the project to go online.

The education of customers' agile thinking is also a part of communication. The customers shall be educated as early as possible, which is more beneficial to their long-term cooperation with the team. It is a good idea to recommend some books to customers, and arrange some topic seminars.

The time of inception is short, we do not have enough time to discuss all issues clearly, so we must use assumptions and quickly reach consensus based on the assumptions agreed by both parties. All assumptions need to be resolved at the formal development stage, because the assumptions are approved in advance, and the changes caused by the assumptions and conclusions will be easily accepted by the customers at this time.

2.4.2.1.2 Assumptions Made at Inception

The existing SAP system of project L provides a full amount of data of client's business, but no one on the customer side makes sure which data are not needed by the logistics system. So the consequence is no matter it is from technical or usage considerations, it is impossible for us to display more than 1,000 columns of content in a table on one webpage, so if we want to meet the requirements for search performance and data exporting performance, we must determine a number as the basis of our technical solutions. In addition, as for some local business requirements, customers themselves are not 100% sure. However, the start-up time is very tight, and it is impossible to make a complete technical assessment, especially the performance assessment. We finally made the assumptions shown in Table 2.7. In many ambiguous aspects, we made an agreement with the customer in both depth and scope.

TABLE 2.7

A List of Assumptions for a Logistics System

Functions	Assumptions
Waybill search	One search with no more than 50 fields, the response time can reach less than 5 seconds
Users can configure the fields displayed in search results	Field sorting is not supported
Configuration of logistics template	All regions use the same logistics template
Expire a logistics template	The in-progress waybill is not affected, until the user signs the completed waybill
User adds comments to the waybill	Save the added user name and time

2.4.2.1.3 Skills for Making Assumptions

- Unable to know the boundary of requirements, for example, there are certain functions that are required, and other functions are not one hundred percent sure. The requirements only include those determined, and stripping the uncertain part of the demand. Those ones may be added into the requirement list after they are clarified and determined.
- How friendly the interface interaction needs to be? We can use examples to illustrate to customers and decide whether the team need a professional user experience designer.
- There are many options for technical implementation, but we evaluated it based on one solution.
- For the part integrated with a third party, it is assumed that they complete the agreed interface within the specified time, and the customer shall responsible to make sure it is about to occur in time.

After inception, the distributed teams will return to a relatively independent state. However, when making a decision, we must consider it as a whole, and do not make decisions that are only beneficial to our own team. Reasonable decision comes from the goal of maximizing the benefits of the entire team, any team could reject unreasonable decisions made by other teams.

2.4.2.2 Regular Short-Term Visits

2.4.2.2.1 Candidates

Since it is only by sending the right persons to the customer site that the established goal of visiting the customer can be achieved, then if our goal is to establish a good cooperative relationship, we'd better send the members who need to communicate frequently with the customer to the customer site in the future. If our purpose is to help customers to try a new technology or new architecture, we'd better send experienced technicians to the customer site.

For inception, we usually send the most experienced persons to the customer site, so as to leave the deepest impression on the customer and ensure that the general direction of the project is correct from the beginning. While the project continues to run, team members can take turns to work at the customer site, and the customer will have a proper understanding of more members of the offshore team.

Although we do not recommend sending a project manager as an on-site representative to another site, we still suggest regarding the project manager as a candidate for regular and short-term dispatches. The main responsibility of the project manager is to resolve the "conflicts" between the teams, remove the barriers that affect their cooperation and identify problems, and have them addressed before they become obstacles. Familiarity with the team situation on both sides is also very important for solving problems.

If we've already kept an long-term on-site representative on customer's site, do we still need to visit the customer regularly? This representative needs to have a comprehensive understanding of the project team, with a focus on coordination and areas he is good at, such as requirement design. If we are about to work on the next-stage back-end integration architecture, we'd better sent a back-end developer to the customer team.

2.4.2.2.2 Encourage Mutual Visits

For the projects that are underway, we can arrange alternate visits. Encourage customers to visit the offshore team so that both parties have the opportunity to understand each other's working environment and status. For example, customers may visit the offshore team in the first half year, while the offshore team may visit the customers in the second half year. No matter it is customers visit the offshore team or vice versa, if we consider the priority of visit, I suggest that the offshore team shall first visit the customer site, so that it learn all aspects of the customer. Visiting customers is a great opportunity to foster personal relationships, build trust, and exert influence; contact with as many people as possible, and understand the team culture of customers and their capabilities and characteristics, as well as their development process.

The first thing to understand is why we are visiting customers at every time. Of course, a main purpose is to maintain the relationship and morale of both parties. In addition to this, do we have other goals to achieve? Visiting customer needs to be planned in advance, including what we want to show, what we want to get, and what we can bring about. Communicate our plan with the customer's contact person as early as possible to ensure some necessary activities could be carried out during the visit.

If customers are about to visit the offshore team, it helps to establish a good cooperative relationship between the two sides, or provide the offshore team with lots of business knowledge or technical background in the customers' industry. Therefore, it is necessary to arrange the agenda of customer visit in a targeted manner, to a certain extent, customer have ideas with the visiting of their own; on the basis of understanding their plans, relevant activities will be held in an orderly manner.

The focus of short-term visits should include the following points:

- Even if they have met in remote meetings before, the visiting team should be formally introduced to the customer. After all, face-to-face contact is unmatched by videoconferencing, and a formal introduction can pave the way for later cooperation.
- Collect periodic feedback, including customer feedback on teamwork, user feedback on the software we've delivered, and forward feedback from our staff to the customer staff to the customer.
- Introduce new practices which can be continuous integration, continuous delivery, such development methods that use Scrum or Kanban. Face-to-face communication ensures the better effect of knowledge transfer, and helps to persuade customers to try something new.
- Test in the production environment before the phased release, or support the production environment issues after the phased release.
- In case of an offshore team to take over the work of some local teams halfway, we need to acquire as comprehensive knowledge as possible within a limited time. Do not hesitate to send the offshore team to the site and environment of customers.
- If the management of customers changes, we need to establish new contacts.
- People who work on the customer site need to summarize the gains of the day and adjust the plan at any time.

2.4.2.2.3 Knowledge Sharing During Short-Term Visits

- No matter it is we visit customer or the customer visits us, the first day of showcase is very critical, and we need to be clear about what content and skills the team will show to the whole team. We need to show customers that our team can make outstanding software, not only good software.

■ Define the theme of sharing based on what the customers want the most from us, and find ways to show them what we have done and what we are good at. The customers also need to give us some introductions, such as the current status of the customer team, the development process, whether there are pain points, the most desired changes, and the customer's business knowledge and technical architecture. Regarding the time arrangement, in my experience, the lunch seminar is a good opportunity to gather all the people together at this time.

2.4.2.2.4 "Other" Tasks While Visiting the Customer

■ If an on-site representative of our team to the customer happens to be on the spot, we must discuss with him about the plans for this visit and take advantage of the opportunity to have lunch together with him to find useful information about working on the spot.
■ Plan at least one team-building activity outside the office to establish emotional connections. It depends on the preferences of all parties. Exotic food, competitions, and sightseeing activities are all good choices. Hold a retrospective meeting at the customer site. Although you can't get deeply involved, it is still a great opportunity to observe what's happening to the customer team recently.
■ Before leaving, we must make sure that this trip has reached our expectations, and the expected output results are definite.
■ Observe the customer's work style and ways of doing things; speak and act as a member of the local team.

2.4.2.2.5 Value "Relationship"

■ The relationship mentioned here is not the usual human relationships and interests, but to find more common topics by understanding each other's culture and personal interests, especially music and sports. Show yourself boldly and don't let yourself be a boring person in the eyes of others. We will work together for a long time, although the dull cooperation can complete the task, why not make the process more interesting? Several members of our team once went abroad to visit the customer. The dressed as a professional cyclist, since he came to work by bike every day, and he even carried his bike to his work station. One of us said that he was also fond of riding a bicycle, and went to work by bicycle every day. Then the customer invited us to ride a bike to the mountains together on the weekend. All of us had a happy weekend, learned more about local life, and had better relationships with the customer. Private communication is good for any team. Something special will happen among team members during the nonworking hours.
■ If we have the opportunity to go to the customer site, what precautions do we need to know and what preparations do we need to do? This is an issue that everyone who needs to work on the customer site for the first time needs to consider. The following is an e-mail sent to the team who would be working at the customer site.

Hello everyone!
  You are about to work at the customer site, which will be a completely different environment from doing projects in our office. Doing a project on site is both an opportunity and a challenge to the project and the customer relationship. If you communicate more smoothly on the spot and make the work results more visible, you can greatly increase the trust of our customer. But if you do not pay attention to some details in communication and work habits, it may cause a blow to the relationship between the two parties.
  The following are some precautions, please be sure to read carefully, often remind and supervise each other. If there is any omission, please add.

Working hours: Although overtime is sometimes inevitable, the daily working hours must be agreed with the customer on the first day and strictly observed. If you work overtime the day before, it is necessary to agree with the customer on the working time the next day.

On-site communication: Because you are always surrounded by the members of the customer team, you must pay attention to the way and content of internal communication.

For the questions and appeal of the customer, respond them with a professional attitude, do not act impatiently. If you really have no time to deal with such matter, you should set a different time with the customer or transfer it to other colleagues.

Unless there is a special agreement with the customer, do not try out or investigate new technologies on site. At this stage, our technical solutions should be mature and proven, and cannot give the customer the opposite impression.

Although communication on the spot is more direct, important matters and consensus must communicated via e-mail to be served as an archive file and a basis, such as changes in requirements and schedule delays caused by customers.

Speak with one voice at the customer site, and do not argue or challenge your own colleagues in front of the customer. For example, within our company, we may naturally ask the project manager or the requirement staff, "Why do you want to do this, what is the value." But do not act like this in front of the customer. Any different views can be raised after lunch or after work, you must make the same voice in front of the customer.

Don't talk about salary, benefits, and other topics in front of the customer, and don't talk about the personal situation of other colleagues in our company, let alone gossip about the company with the customer.

If you need to take leave, you should first discuss with the project manager, and do not directly talk about this matter with the customer. After internal agreement is reached, the project manager will communicate with the customer in a unified manner.

If you encounter any difficulties in Shanghai, whether it is about work or life, please contact me at the first time, I will help you coordinate and find a solution. I am fortunate to work with you on the first project after our company attempted transformation, let's make joint efforts to make the first productization project of our company fire the first shot!

2.4.3 Review After a Visit to the Customer Site

The content of this subsection is based on a review and summary made by a project team after visiting the customer site, covering various preparatory activities for the visit, work arrangements during the visit and other considerations. Check with this content before each visit, there is sure to be certain reference significance.

The desired goals must be properly set, such as the following goals:

- Scope of project requirements
- Logistics for the business trip
- Project goals, vision, stakeholders and their nuances, their roles and responsibilities
- Clarify the date of some milestones, and other baseline
- Core working hours and stand-up timetable
- Regular reports and reimbursement regulations
- Personnel handover plan

After entering the site, make the following preparations:

- Work ID
- Computer, Wi-Fi

- E-mail account
- Working area
- Confidentiality agreement
- The use of computer, U disk and mailbox must comply with the regulations on the customer site

The customer's other security policies, such as the location of project documents, whether we can use external online collaborative document tools. Whether there are more detailed regulations, such as certain level of content cannot be stored in external space. Therefore, we must confirm the security level of the document we use.

2.4.3.1 Be Clear about Your Purpose of Visiting

Is your purpose in communicating with others about the requirements? Or to pair up with on-site people for development or testing? Be aware of the purpose of the trip, will help us to spend most of the time on.

More than that, arrange meetings with customers to review the important design and requirement issues. In addition to the routine meetings with the contact person in the customer team, arrange meetings with other stakeholders as many as possible so as to collect more feedback from them.

At the customer site, priority should be given to meeting the people who do not frequent contact with us, such as the infrastructure team at the customer side and the staff of our team at the customer site.

Regardless of the main purpose of visiting the customer site, building trust is always a by-product, it can help us gather feedback from customers on the current distributed cooperation, which is more real and frank.

2.4.3.2 Rear Service Considerations

When we select team members, we must ensure that they can travel on time. It should be noted that many people cannot travel due to family reasons. It is not necessary that all people in the team are able to travel, but we need to make sure there are enough people that are capable of doing so, otherwise, it may become a risk.

When we consider the rotation of the entire team, we must take into account the factors and restrictions of their visas in advance. For the whole team, their business visa limits their duration of stay and the types of work in the country of the customer. We may have run out of all the permitted visit time for a project in a year early, then we cannot visit our customer again by the end of the year, so the rules of visas should be considered for personnel rotation.

Make sure that people who are sent to the customer site can start working easily, for example, they know the route to the customer's office, they can easily surf the Internet, and there are enough work stations at the customer's office.

Those who are sent to working overseas will encounter large cultural differences. We shall try our best to make everyone lives an easy and comfortable life:

- How to help the team members on business trip understand the city where they are about to work and appreciate the local culture
- If they have any dietary restrictions, how to make sure of their food safety
- Is there a kitchen in their apartment
- If they have any health problems, how can they get medical care?

Make sure the colleagues on business trips have some personal time. Traveling is a chore. Working in a foreign language environment often make one feel exhausted. In the evening or weekends, try not to assign jobs to them unless everyone agrees.

2.4.3.3 Do Not "Make Commitments" at Will

Customers like to get our "commitments."

A committed goal means that, based on what we know now, we are confident that we can achieve a certain goal. Customers mainly care about the goal, not the prerequisites for the goal, which are the assumptions for our commitment. Software development is an uncertain delivery process, not a standardized production process.

While working on Project L, we had pledged that when the system was officially launched on March 10, the logistics channel template should be ready. But our promise was based on the condition that this template would be share across the world, which was said the customer. However, the users in several large regions of the customer repeated that they refused to use the same template, and each region shall have a specially designed template based on their own situation; there should be separate template for Asia-Pacific, Europe, North America, Central and South America, Middle East, and Africa. It showed that the premise of our commitment had changed, and finally the customer agreed to launch the template for the Asia-Pacific region at the originally planned time. If we had not assumed a universal template for all regions for making the commitment, there will be more or less disputes afterward.

Ideally, we can arrange additional capacity to deal with uncertainty. How much additional capacity is required depends on the following aspects:

- The degree of uncertainty of our workload, as in the example above
- The degree of uncertainty of the environment, whether the priority of tasks will change
- The importance of this commitment to customers and users; the more important it is, the more additional capacity is needed as a buffer.

We will do our best to fulfill the commitments we have made, but we cannot be 100% sure. If at any time we do not believe we can accomplish a certain goal, we should let stakeholders know as soon as possible.

The correct commitment should be the business results we will provide (A), not the functions we will achieve (B). In other words, the commitment should be based on business impact, not system output.

When making commitments to the customer, whether the restrictive conditions are explicitly presented by us, they will remain there. However, a commitment made without any prerequisites usually means that the prerequisites will remain under ideal circumstances and free from any problems. Once the assumptions are biased later, it often hurts product quality and team motivation, and makes planning and forecasting more difficult.

2.4.4 SUMMARY

For distributed teams, I sincerely recommend that we must ensure that local and outsourced teams visit each other regularly, which is a good practice. Through this practice, we can clarify the responsibilities of work visits, and guarantee the effectiveness of the rotation of mutual visits between the two teams. At the same time, the immersive work on the customer site helps us to become familiar with the customer's working language and reduce misunderstandings in communication.

A personnel exchange plan shall is defined at the beginning of the project, and people from different places shall visit each other according to the agreed plan.

Appropriately "catering to someone's pleasure" is essentially a more humane and constructive workplace rule. Customer are also human beings in need of others' recognition.

The purpose of short-term visits will determine the work plan and direction at the next stage. However, it should be noted that in addition to maintaining a good relationship with customers, we may only have time and energy to accomplish one or two other major goals. So, don't plan too many tasks, because more is not always better.

2.5 ONLINE COMMUNICATION TOOLS

I'm not going to sing a different tune.

The Agile Manifesto propagates that individuals and interactions over processes and tools, but it does not deny the importance of processes and tools. In the past few years, team collaboration tools have been constantly upgraded, trying to solve the communication problems in projects and among teams through innovation. Many teams have actually adopted some complicated team collaboration tools in order to reduce the waste in team collaboration and improve the collaboration efficiency. Relative to independent teams, these tools obviously have greater value for distributed teams.

Regarding tools, many industries abide by the same law: there is no best tool, only the most suitable tool. Tools are worthy of the name only after we have formed a habit in using them. We need to determine the tools and usage methods that are most suitable for offshore teams based on their current situation and the available resources of customers.

At present, many large outsourcing projects from Europe and the United States still have strict KPI in cost control. To achieve the goal of cost optimization, one of the common practices is to minimize the travel expenses in projects. In fact, although through various processes and means, such as regular meetings and job reporting, and complemented with the necessary remote communication, it seems that everything is under control, the headquarters still lacks a long-term and dynamic understanding of the status of the outsourcing site, and have no accurate knowledge about problems and risks. Using tools to provide this information, and ensuring the accuracy and legibility of this information, is the goal that all offshore teams have been pursuing.

What tools do a distributed team need? In what ways do they help us? What can these tools help offshore teams achieve? Which inherent defects of the offshore team can these tools resolve? We can find answers in the following categories of tools:

- Knowledge sharing
- Instant communication
- Work collaboration
- Process control
- Tools that integrate instant communication and knowledge sharing

2.5.1 KNOWLEDGE SHARING TOOLS

Online collaboration is the best way to ensure that the documents used by the team are live documents. The local documents of each team member can be synchronized with the cloud storage provided by these tools in real time. In this way, the only source of knowledge for the team can be guaranteed. At the same time, this also requires the continuous maintenance of the team. The information changes obtained by everyone must be placed in the cloud disk on their initiative, rather than saved locally or elsewhere. Only by achieving the above points will the content of the documents not expired and trustworthy.

Many tools not only support document collaboration and sharing between teams, provide simultaneous editing capabilities and editing history, but can also add comments to documents, and some can also support the use of chart functions in documents.

The advantage of using Wiki is that distributed teams can edit the same document online without any learning cost, and the Wiki itself can properly manage the problem of concurrent editing.

Document online collaboration, as a tool for knowledge sharing, is now in a boom, such as shimo.im, Google Drive and Quip. Some task management tools also provide the function of knowledge sharing, such as JIRA's Confluence, users will have the opportunity to manage team tasks and team knowledge in one place.

2.5.2 Instant Communication Tools

Different types of communication tools appear to adapt to different types of communication and solve corresponding problems. If we are in a distributed project, instant messaging tools are essential.

Team instant messaging tools, such as Hangouts, Skype, WhatsApp, WeChat, and Dingding, enable us to ask a question quickly and get an answer quickly. Some instant messaging tools provide a status display function that tells us who is online based on computer, or smart phone. If it is an instant messaging tool for working, we sincerely recommend that we use it at work every day, especially the useful status display function. When our distributed teams have a little overlap of working time, this tool can play the most effective role.

These tools support the establishment of project communication groups to facilitate the discussions within the group and avoid one-to-one discussions. Even if one-to-one discussions are needed, information and conclusions should be updated to others in a timely manner.

If you are using Google's mail system, it will be more convenient to use Hangouts, because you can communicate with anyone in your company instantly without adding contacts. Using Skype to build some groups of projects, you can easily control the scope of a topic to the smallest group of people. For different concerns, you need to create different Skype groups. The characteristic of Skype is that one-to-one communication can be carried out only as a contact, and it has higher security. More than that, Skype can also easily provide instant video communication.

I heard that some companies will block employees from using instant messaging tools, thinking that such tools will distract them from working and affect work efficiency. I really can't understand this kind of regulations, like giving up eating for fear of choking. For distributed teams, it makes us lose the most effective and lowest-cost communication tools. Of course, if they block instant messaging tools to encourage employees to pick up the phone, it is another matter.

Video conferencing is the most commonly used face-to-face communication means for distributed teams, it usually needs to invite the other party to participate in advance. It is often used to explain the project overview, discuss a relatively complex problem, or demonstrate the software functions. If a team cannot attend the live meeting, we can record the meeting and send it to them. Some videos, such as the background introduction of the project and technical architecture, can be preserved as the team knowledge for a long time. When new people join the team, we do not need to explain the background again and again. When people outside the team are eager to share our project experiences, we can send these videos to them for watching. The time it takes to create a video clip is much less than the time required to prepare a document, and the information expressed will be clearer. But we also need to note that the video is not suitable for displaying detailed things, but helpful for displaying an overview or general introduction. Of course, there are exceptions. When we describe a defect to the remote team, we use video recording to show the steps of reproduction, it is easy for people to grasp the key points, and it is difficult for the text to do so.

The most common tool we use for video conferencing is Skype, as well as fee-based software tools such as Zoom, WebEx, and Fuze, which can provide more stable communication effects.

According to my observation, when holding video conferences, not everyone in distributed teams will turn on the camera. But it is important for everyone to see each other's smiling faces (or not). So if the conditions permit, including the speed of the network and the line supported by the video conference, encourage everyone to dial into the video conference individually and turn on the camera. Sometimes when communicating remotely, if you can't see the other person's expression, you may miss some hints. Our rule is that once there is friction at work, we must solve the problem through video communication.

The mind map of ProcessOn supports everyone to collaborate on the same file in real time. The project manager can directly invite his members to participate in the collaboration. The progress of each task every day can be directly marked to the mind map. The collaboration function improves everyone's communication efficiency. At the same time, the progress of the project can be seen in real time, which also saves the time spent on communication. In the past, we shared flowcharts and mind maps in other ways, and now we can promote these two diagrams to the level of collaboration.

2.5.3 Work Collaboration Tools

Collaboration in the team is nothing more than the scenes such as pair programming, code review, bug reproduce, showcase, and retrospective meeting. Using a variety of appropriate tools, distributed teams can easily achieve these practical goals.

Let TeamViewer come on the stage first, it is one of the earliest remote tools I have met. It essentially provides remote control, which is very meaningful for the reproduction of different environmental problems. However, we mainly used it to show the work results of mobile, the other party could easily operate according to the displayed script on their own computers.

Screenhero is a tool that shares screens, chat, and supports input of both parties (including keyboard and mouse). This is very helpful for pairing work, such as code review, problem reproduction, and other scenarios. It can not only collaborate on writing documents, but also collaborate on almost everything.

Teambition is an online collaboration tool that helps teams easily realize daily collaboration, project management, and other needs by sharing and discussing tasks, files, sharing, schedules, and other content in work. To put it simply, if you want to develop a new product, make a copywriting plan, or plan a wedding, then create a project on Teambition and add all relevant team members to the project, Teambition can provide you with management tasks, schedule meetings, file storage, instant discussion, and other collaborative functions required by enterprises and teams, so as to achieve project knowledge sharing, communication, project task arrangement, and progress monitoring, and document storage and sharing of related projects. So this tool will be useful for the teams to reach a small milestone.

Distributed teams also had to resort to online tools when holding retrospective meetings. IdeaBoardz can effectively support remote retrospective meetings and collaborative decisions of different teams. It can also support the secret ballot of the team instead of reviewing the real vote in retrospective meeting.

2.5.4 Process Control Tools

Have you ever encountered the following situations when you need collaboration between teams?

- You don't understand each other's work and plans.
- Due to self-protection consciousness or inertia, some communication barriers have been formed between the teams.
- In case of a task that requires both parties to complete, but you cannot find the person in charge of the other team.
- One team completed a task, and it took a long time for the other team to know this information.

Offshore teams need to be good at using various tools, not only for the purpose of communication, but also for controlling project execution, tracking team affairs (problems), and fast processing of the collaborative tasks. A process control tool shall be good at project execution management, agile development management, system process management, product defect tracking, proposal tracking, requirements management, and customer service.

Collaboration tools will make the work of each team more transparent, especially to enable colleagues on the demand side to see development tasks and scheduling in the system. For example, if the requirements for newly-added functions, which are proposed by customers, are yet executed for a long time, it can be seen from the task arrangement in the system that is not that the remote team is procrastinating, but that the team members are busy with other high-priority tasks, and these new functions need to be scheduled. Such a system can reduce conflicts and misunderstandings and improve communication efficiency. In this way, the business demand side can easily get the information they want, and the originally planned meeting will be much less.

Although most customers are very opinionated, we should not give up the opportunity to recommend a new tool or system to them. For this kind of new things, we can take a lean approach and advance in small steps, but we must consider the customers' usage habits. If they are already using a similar tool, we should be careful when recommending a new tool, even if the new tool has many advantages, because it is often difficult to drive customers to change the status quo, as long as they can meet functional requirements. We'd better be consistent with customers. If we really need to promote new tools, be sure to show the value, risk, and learning cost, so that everyone has enough enthusiasm and set proper expectation at the beginning.

CASE STUDY

There was a traditional customer who was so cautious and so worried about the new working methodology would bring significant changes to his employees' daily work and stimulate their antagonistic emotions. Therefore, the plan at that time was to define two stages in the process of transformation. In the first stage, our goal is to manage product defects, have the product requirements, development, and testing departments work together, especially let some of colleagues in the core department use the new tool first, and get rid of the previous tracking methods such as Word, Excel, and e-mail. The target users of the first stage must be those who were more likely to accept new things and could be taken as seed users. In the second stage, we used this new tool for the task process management of various projects and tasks (including products, design, development and testing) in the entire department, making it a memorandum of the department's work and a record of the work process. Using this online tool, it is easy to implement Dr. Deming's PDCA theory. All the things that are determined to be done must have a final state of completion, so as to avoid those things that the leaders do not urge or ask, then the things are ignored.

After above, we started with combing the relatively fixed project collaboration process of the department, and recommended JIRA to customers at the time for project personalized customization, including the status of key milestones, the division of project roles, the allocation of project resources, the control of each stage, and the deadline for going online. We configurate JIRA workflow to follow the actual business process rules to achieve automated customization, and finally used JIRA's powerful filters to create commonly used analysis statistical reports, and generated permanent links on the JIRA navigation bar as a common entry to provide the access, which surprised everyone at once. In this way, the usual management of defects, requirements, planned timing box, resource allocation, and collaboration between various departments are all connected through JIRA.

Later, the people in the department really felt the benefits of JIRA for actual work, and more and more employees started using JIRA. It was a process where we met resistance in recommending JIRA at the very beginning and then welcome by everyone soon.

With the in-depth use of JIRA, everyone has put forward more and more JIRA application requirements in combination with their actual work. Seeing is believing, other departments of the company were convinced by the benefits in work management brought about by JIRA, so they invited us to help them build, manage, and do the training for them. In this way, the work efficiency and performance of each department and even the entire company were improved.

2.5.5 Tools That Integrate Instant Communication and Knowledge Sharing

Today it is no exaggeration to say that the best tool in this area is Slack. It is a cloud-based communication tool and also a collaboration tool integrated with chat groups and plugins, with an aim to simplify collaboration within teams and organizations, and help to assemble distributed teams into a virtual team. As a daily communication tool, Slack is a collection of chat groups, large-scale tool integration, file integration, and unified search.

Slack is a tool for intra-enterprise communication and collaboration. Its purpose is to integrate all kinds of decentralized information: e-mail, message, files, etc., whether it is internal communication information or files, as long as they are uploaded to Slack, they can be retrieved through its built-in search tool. As of the end of 2016, Slack had integrated multiple tools and services such as e-mail, SMS, Google Drive, Twitter, Trello, GitHub, Zendesk, and Heroku, which can bring together various fragmented enterprise communications and collaborations, and integrate their notification, reminder, defect tracking and other data into the company's internal information flow. The advantage of doing so is that, for example, after binding Google Drive, if a link to Google Doc is sent in Slack, the content of Doc can be directly displayed and automatically updated; after binding Trello, we can synchronize the update of a certain Board to a certain Channel. The mainstream features of Slack also include searching for members of the team, group chats, and document sharing. It is characterized by sharing, allowing team members to share files in the cloud in one place, including Google Drive, GitHub, etc.

Slack provides a message storage and search function. All the notifications used in work can be found at any time by searching, which makes many startups have an extremely convenient experience in collaboration. Slack's flat management model, channel-like classification window, and integration of multi-party interfaces have been doomed from the beginning to do "tiny and pretty" small team collaboration.

More than that, the cloud history and the search of information are of great significance to the service outsourcing team with relatively frequent personnel changes. Ordinary instant chat tools do not support cloud storage and search. If the chat history of the local client is lost, it cannot be traced back. And traceability at any time is very important for the service company, which is also why e-mail mentioned in this chapter remains an important way of communication and contact.

We can imagine Slack as an IRC (Internet relay chat running on the local computer which is very fast) which is open all day, just like a group chat window, you can create a persistent chat room organized by theme ("channel"), as well as private groups and instant messages, in order to discuss with your teammates all day long. You also can know which other groups exist even you are not join, and join those groups proactively.

Slack integrates a large number of third-party application service teams used daily by enterprise teams, so the team can simultaneously receive real-time notifications of the applications other than Slack.

Everything in Slack is easily searchable, including files, conversations, and people. You can drag files and data to share with your colleagues because Slack integrates cloud storage services like Dropbox and Google Cloud Disk.

We all know that the personnel change of the service outsourcing team is remarkable, and Slack is thoughtful about the knowledge acquisition of new members joining the team. The chat history becomes the team's knowledge library, eliminating the hassle of repeating the context when we are halfway through the discussion. Similarly, for team discussions when not online, we can get a complete discussion process after going online.

Why is Slack so popular? Because users can get benefits in two ways:

One is increasing transparency. You can see what others are doing at any time, sometime this makes no need to start a company meeting early in the morning. It also supports cross-departmental cooperation, engineers can see the work of designers, and technical teams can see how customer service is handled. All you have to do is slide your finger gently from message streams of other channels.

The other one is that all communication data in the company is taken as a digital knowledge system. In most systems, knowledge is based on e-mail and is fragmented. But when you provide these to others, they will benefit from now on. So when someone joins in team at any time, his inbox will not be empty. Every decision, discussion, and all resources, companies or organizations mentioned by someone, or even links and exchanged files shared by anyone at any time, all of them are searchable, what you have to do is just looking back. This is very meaningful.

Since Slack will act as a knowledge warehouse, we should take this factor into consideration when we talk, reduce conversations that are irrelevant work, and use accurate keywords for questions and answers.

Many follower vendors also provide many tools with similar functions, such as "Teambition." With more innovators joining in this field, we will see more and more humanized design, which is the gospel of teamwork.

The management and IT team of the company still have a long way to go to make full use of social media to promote collaboration, increase productivity, and stimulate innovation.

2.5.6 Summary

Use the tool as a communication channel, we need to solve the problem of the learning curve at the beginning. The use of learning tools should not cost too much energy, and we can ensure that our energy lies in solving practical problems rather than spending on the tools themselves. Essentially, the ultimate goal of the use of tools is to maintain the connectivity of distributed teams. Connectivity is a prerequisite for collaboration, if properly used, it can play an effective role in promoting collaboration.

Considering the particularity of the service outsourcing industry, time is quite important, and we shall pay attention to achieve substantial results in doing everything, so the learning curve of new tools is required to be low. There shall be a reasonable plan for team learning and growth.

There are more and more team collaboration tools show on market. We should get ready to accept any useful tool which also conforms to the principle of openness that requires to be agile and lean. But sometimes, even under the condition that a tool can help our work become better, we cannot introduce it as we please because customers will prevent its use due to security policy concerns. Sometimes it is just because they are too sensitive to security issues, but more often it is that customers do not understand the real security risks of the tool. We must help customers dispel concerns, rather than stop promoting the tools that our team needs. We should invite a brave supervisor to help make the necessary changes. Since some customers are cautious and doctrine, we have to turn to their managers who have a deeper understanding of risk management and are willing to discuss alternative control to break through some obstacles.

Remote communication is prone to causing misunderstanding, and we must always maintain a positive intention of communication.

Why we still need a physical whiteboard?

When we first adopted the Scrum agile practice, we chose the online agile Kanban on JIRA, it can customize the status, classification, and display mode according to the needs of different teams. The function of an online Kanban is really powerful. But for some time, we found that the interaction between the teams was not satisfactory. At the stand-ups, when one was speaking in front of his computer, others were busy with their own affairs on computer or looking at mobile phones, and then returned to the state of meeting until it was his turn to speak. After a long time, the stand-up looked like a report meeting with the form more important than content, and everyone thought it was a waste of time.

Recognizing this problem, we adjusted our strategy in time. Although we have powerful online tools, we have established a physical Kanban board. It's also amazing to say that since a Kanban was erected next to the team, you will find many things happen naturally. We stand in front of the whiteboard every day, while communicating with the team, while moving the task card and our avatar label on the board. If you have a new issue, write a task card immediately, and then paste your avatar. With the physical Kanban wall, everyone is finally "face to face," and interaction and communication have become "vivid" and "open." So I think that the use of physical whiteboards is really big enough to affect the culture of an organization.

The use of tools is not always successful, and I have witnessed such failures too many times: a manager promoted a tool in the company, and this tool had a specific way of operation, it not only failed to solve the problem, but it also hindered other efforts to solve the problem. The tools should be helpful like this: help us prevent known mistakes from taking place and remember repetitive tasks, rather than replace thinking itself.

Developers may not like to keep running an instant communication tool while working, because it disrupts their deep thinking. How to communicate with remote customers? The status setting of tools can solve this problem so that nonurgent problems will not interrupt the developers. I think we've all heard this story: a craftsman smashed his finger, but blamed the hammer in his hand.

2.6 CASES OF FAILED COMMUNICATION

If there is no communication channel, it is necessary to set up one. When a matter needs coordination of multiple departments, we must strive for end-to-end communication until it is determined. Such a form of communication, like "hoeing one's own potatoes," sounds like everyone has done well his own part, but there are sure to be misunderstandings between teams or between departments, which will eventually lead to overall failure.

2.6.1 McDonnell-Douglas DC-10 Air Crash: A Repeat of the Past

Many of us may not have heard of McDonnell-Douglas Corporation. Many years ago, it was a famous aircraft manufacturer alongside Boeing and Airbus. So why is it gone now?

This has to start with the DC-10, an aircraft launched by McDonnell Douglas, which exposed the flaws in the design of its cargo door soon after it entered the market. The earliest accident of DC-10 occurred on American Airlines No. 96 flight, and a large hole appeared in its cargo door. It was so lucky that this flight made a successful landing without causing casualties. The investigators examined the cargo door of this aircraft and found that its design flaw was the culprit leading to the accident. Under normal circumstances, the door of a jetliner is opened from the outside to the inside, and the area of the door is larger than the area of the door frame. As the altitude rises after the aircraft lifts off, the pressure in the cabin will become greater and greater, and the door will be embedded in the door frame under the effect of the pressure difference. However, in order to increase the cargo volume in the cabin, the McDonnell Douglas DC-10 passenger aircraft had the cargo door open outwards. This requires that after the cargo door of the DC-10 is closed, the lock hook will buckle the latch of the fuselage door frame, and in the end the porter shall also depress the door lever to let the lock pin pass through the lock hook to fix the cargo door.

The accident investigators found that the door latch of the aircraft was not fully tightened, causing the last "safe" lock pin not to be locked in the correct position. As the aircraft climbs, the pressure difference between the inside and outside of the cabin gradually increased, and the cargo door that was not completely locked would be opened by a strong force.

This accident exposed the fatal design flaws of the DC-10 passenger aircraft. The US National Transportation Safety Board (NTSB) responsible for the investigation clearly pointed out the problem of the cargo door and notified all airlines that purchased this type of aircraft. The accident had a huge negative impact on McDonnell Douglas. Unfortunately, after this incident, McDonnell Douglas had not made timely and effective improvements to the cargo door of the DC-10 passenger aircraft. Two years later, Turkish Airlines No. 981 Flight became the victim. While flying from Paris to London, the cargo door exit accident took place, and none of the 346 people on board survived.

The investigators found the aircraft cargo door and six connected seats in the farmland 15 km away from the incident site. These things fell out before the aircraft crashed. At seeing the wreckage of the accident, the NTSB investigators immediately thought of the American Airlines No. 96 Flight accident. What they did not understand was that McDonnell Douglas did not improve the cargo door after the accident, and Turkish Airlines No. 981 Flight seemed to be the recurrence of the same accident.

The accident investigators from both the United States and France immediately conducted a more in-depth investigation into the cargo door of this passenger aircraft. The result showed that Turkish Airlines No. 981 Flight had the same accident as American Airlines No. 96 Flight, because the latch of the cargo door was not locked well. But the luck had gone this time.

When the investigation of Turkish Airlines No. 981 Flight was not over, the NTSB investigators returned to the United States to participate in a special hearing held by the government which ask why the problem discovered on American Airlines No. 96 Flight led to another air crash two years later. In fact, the NTSB made two clear recommendations one month after the American Airlines No. 96 Flight accident: modify the design of the locking device so that the hand lever cannot be depressed when the locking pin is not fixed in the correct position; install vent holes on the floor of DC-10 to prevent the floor from collapsing after explosive decompression in the pressurized cabin.

However, these two recommendations were not adopted before the Turkish Airlines No. 981 Flight accident. The root cause was that the NTSB had no power to force McDonnell Douglas to make improvements, it could only report to the US Federal Aviation Administration (FAA) which would have the improvements carried on in the form of regulations. Owing to the institutional reasons, the solution to the problem became unreachable.

Actually, after the American Airlines No. 96 Flight accident, McDonnell Douglas do modified the design of the cargo door. They opened a glass window at the lock pin position of the cargo door to allow the porters to see if the cargo compartment was locked. Warning signs (in English) were added outside the door. McDonnell Douglas also increased the length of the lock pin and installed a metal plate on the inside of the door. If the cargo door was not locked, the external hand lever could be prevented from pressing down, and the porters would know that the cargo door was not locked. However, these improvements had limitations. Many porters did not know the purpose of the glass hole at the door. The porters in Paris did not understand the specific meaning of the English sign, and this passenger aircraft had no metal plate.

If the accident of American Airlines No. 96 Flight was unexpected, then Turkish Airlines No. 981 Flight was a thorough man-made calamity. Investigators had gone through all the hard work to investigate the accident in order to avoid repeating the same mistakes. Unfortunately, no one had learned from the American Airlines No. 96 Flight accident.

After Turkish Airlines filed a lawsuit against McDonnell Douglas to the court. Later, the R&D documents of the DC-10 aircraft were reviewed by lawyers and related parties. A journalist made a surprising discovery: the leader of the product engineering team of Camfil, the supplier of the passenger cargo door, reminded the cargo door of the potential danger in a memo and warned that the cargo door would cause serious accidents sooner or later. This memo was completed after the American Airlines No. 96 Flight accident. It was recommended to redesign the cargo door of the DC-10 passenger plane. The existence of this memo confirmed the inevitability of the Turkish Airlines No. 981 Flight accident.

The proceedings seemed dramatic after the trial was started. New evidence showed that McDonnell Douglas knew this danger as early as the development of the aircraft. Two years before the American Airlines No. 96 Flight accident, in its pressure test, McDonnell Douglas saw the cargo door burst open, but the company ignored such an obvious design flaw. Although the design of the cargo door was eventually improved, McDonnell Douglas was seriously affected after the air crash, and the sales of DC-10 passenger aircraft plummeted. The entire company was forced to draw a terminator in 1996 and was bought by Boeing at a price of $13.3 billion.

Let's review the entire incident. After the testing department found the problem and completed the test report, their work was completed. As for whether the problem could be resolved and when it was to be resolved, it was a matter of other departments. The design department corrected the problem according to their own ideas, but did not learn about the opinions of users (porters), nor did they train them on how to use the cargo door correctly. It was this style of work collaboration that had created barriers to communication between departments. We need to resolve the design defects as soon as they are discovered. Any delay and ignorance by either party can only cause more serious consequences.

2.6.2 Integration Failure of a Large Energy Company

A large energy company customer, after going through a major defeat, then came to us and become our customer. The background if one of its suppliers took over the function development of a certain part of a large-scale system, but after two teams had finished their respective tasks, they found that the two parts could not be merged at all. The customer made a lot of efforts to rescue this project, but failed to put it online eventually. When we reached the customer site to conduct a preliminary survey, we found that the problems were concentrated on the requirements, because of poor communication between the customer and their vendor, there were many blind spots among the customer requirements.

Requirements are the starting point of all the work in the whole delivery. When there is a communication deviation on the requirements, it will cause a lot of wasted work in the later delivery period, which will dampen the enthusiasm of developers. In severe cases, it will cause the project to fail and restart all over again.

To help distributed teams to correctly and uniformly understand the customer requirements, we set up a special team, which was made up of the members of various roles, to sit with all stakeholders of the customer to dig deeper into the requirements, especially the business purpose behind these requirements. The end result was that everyone really understood all business implications. Thanks to the business value-driven thinking process, each team was very clear about their duties at the time of design implementation, which reduced the disputes and conflicts. After our team and the customer team started their respective work, a continuous integration environment was also established. Through frequent integration of the work of all parties, we could ensure that each team would not deviate from their requirement consensus at any time.

2.6.3 First User Test Failed in Project L

This was a project with an iteration period of two weeks. Every month, an official version would be released to the UAT environment for online user test. Although we showed the completed functions to the users before the field test, the users still reported a large number of unfinished functions and data problems, and some users said that such a system could not satisfy their requirements.

Users did not understand agile delivery methodology and mistakenly thought that all functions had been developed as before. User test was based on their real business goals, but the functions we released for the first time were not end-to-end. The showcase was to tell users what could be done, but they had no idea of what could not be done and which could not meet the test conditions at that moment. For those functions not yet meet the test conditions, we should inform users when they would be ready before ask them to test. From the perspective UAT users, it was necessary to consider how better arrange the development sequence of user story cards[2], as well as the priority of functions.

2.6.4 Summary

Failure to achieve communication will cause many unpredictable results, just like the three cases above. There are a variety of reasons that lead to failed communication. Therefore, improving the communication level of distributed teams is a systematic project and requires a comprehensive plan.

Furthermore, offshore team should not belittle themselves, but to stand up and communicate bravely, customers and us are in one team, and share a same goal. Communicate proactively and covering in collaboration, everyone will see. In the short run, customers may easily increase our budget and give us more core tasks; in the long run, they will pave way for the future cooperation between our two sides.

NOTES

1 Story card is a way for agile development teams to divide functions. Each function that has business implications and can be developed independently can be used as a story card, which is conducive to development scheduling and work delivery.
2 User story cards are the same as story cards.

3 Collaboration between Distributed Teams

3.1 A FIRST LOOK AT TEAMWORK

In today's world, even if you only set a small goal, it usually requires many people or multiple teams to work together to fulfill it. Since it requires effort from all sides, there will be many forms of collaboration. In terms of geographical location, everyone can sit together or collaborate remotely; in terms of time, everyone can work in parallel at the same time or in sequence; in terms of division of labor, people shall play their respective roles in collaboration.

No matter in which form we serve customers, we must face the customer team with an open attitude and a spirit of sharing. This is the premise of collaboration. As compared with cooperation, collaboration stresses the process of interaction between teams.

3.1.1 Relationship between Communication and Collaboration

The significance of communication is mainly to accurately grasp the other party's ideas and desired results, and express our own ideas so that everyone of different backgrounds can accurately understand the information to be conveyed. For example, we want to compile a new version for user test next week. The purpose of communication is to obtain the following goals, including time (sometime next week), location (user environment), and deliverables (software with promised functions), and characters (business users). Collaboration represents the means in the course of action to achieve above goal, such as the development plan of the development team, the environmental preparation of the DevOps team, the quality-assured deliverables of the testing team, and the customer team's selection and training of business users. Many of the delivery stages and job roles may also include the division and cooperation of offshore teams and local teams.

Currently, most of the offshore teams can only be accepted to technical-level collaboration, but as the level of cooperation improves, high-end offshore delivery also begins to involve design and business-level collaboration.

3.1.1.1 Technical Collaboration

Figure 3.1 shows a technology stack for a small project which cost us four months in 2016.

It can be seen that even a small-scale project requires a broad technology stack. This requires that the team composition shall support the entire technology stack, and everyone can work together to complete the entire project. The era of using a single technology to complete a project has long passed.

Each project has its own required technology stack, which is also the weapon arsenal that the entire team needs to possess. Correspondingly, everyone should also have a personal weapons arsenal to complement with the team's internal technical advantages and complete the team's goals in a

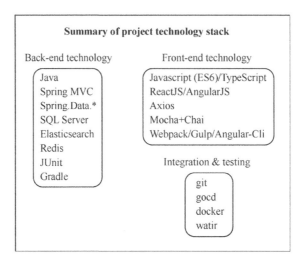

FIGURE 3.1 A technology stack for a logistics query system with a development period of four months.

collaborative manner. In the process of collaboration, individuals can expand their skills by learning from other team members.

When we are invited to the customer site for project inception evaluation, we cannot obtain reliable feedback from common problems in time for us to make the correct action plan. Even the customer has made a careful iteration plan in advance, the integration of the entire system is pushed to the late stage of the project, resulting problems to pile up, so we have to finally stop to solve the accumulated problems. Moreover, because of accumulation of problems, the complexity is also increased accordingly.

For teamwork at the technical level, we need to introduce a package of practices for continuous integration. The goal of continuous integration is to continuously obtain feedback and reduce integration risks. Continuous integration is decisive for the cooperation of distributed teams, and it can reflect the deviation of understanding between teams in a timely manner. The longer the interval between the two code integration, the more painful the final integration will be. Of course, the essence of continuous integration is quick feedback, we can quickly know the impact of the changes we made on the shared code base. Continuous integration has four stages: development stage, submission stage, integration stage, and deployment stage. These four stages seem to be the same as the traditional development integration model, but what we require is to do it continuously and every day, rather than only the final integration throughout the entire development process.

3.1.1.1.1 Development Stage

Test-driven development is essentially protecting the function codes from damage with testing codes. In addition, using the test to provide timely feedback on the quality of the codes, we can easily know whether the required functions are really developed, rather than knowing that some function points are missing until all codes are integrated in the end.

We can use a version control system to manage all things related to software functions, including source code, test scripts, configuration files, database architecture, and installation scripts. We suggest all materials should be included into version control, this will make it very easy to set up a new development environment and build a latest and executable software.

Code review is a code-level collaboration. In this process, the first step is to understand the changes made by others. This context is very helpful for our future development, and understanding the thinking of others in writing codes is also a good learning opportunity. As the code review progresses, the team members' code style and idiomatic usage of some methods will gradually become consistent. When developing a code review principle, a development team can make the following rules:

- Conduct a code review at a fixed time each day or after completing the development of every story card.
- The content of each review is all newly added codes.
- Code style checks should be included in the deployment pipeline.
- Methods and test scenario naming should be simple and easily understood.
- Establish the concept of whole code ownership.

For offshore teams, it is inevitable to implement a remote code review. If it can be done at same time with local team, they shall make good use of the desktop sharing tool; if not, they shall properly use the code management tool to identify everyone and every module's modifications, and compare the modules before and after the changes. Therefore, it can be said that the code review of offshore teams is happened on the next stage, that is, the submission stage.

3.1.1.1.2 Submission Stage

Frequent submissions, at least once a day, and submit large functional modules by several times. The advantage of doing so is that it is easier to track down the problems in fewer modules every time. Therefore, we usually submit the code update related to only one story card or defect at a time.

There shall be certain discipline for continuous integration. To do a good job in code submission for continuous integration, good discipline is indispensable. If the status of continuous integration is red (failed), then the continuous submission of code is not allowed, someone needs to fix it right away; if it cannot be fixed in a short time, we have to roll back to the state before submission. Ensure that the status of continuous integration is green (succeeded) before getting off work.

If the failed modules are not fixed in time, then any work done by developers may be based on an unreliable foundation, and it is impossible to predict how long it will take to fix them next.

Use trunks and branches reasonably. Distributed teams shall make sure that everyone knows which are submitted to the trunk and which are submitted to the branch. When the package is about to be issued, it is difficult to withdraw the wrong submission.

3.1.1.1.3 Integration Stage

Behind continuous integration is continuous verification with an aim to check whether the code on the mainline can achieve the required function, or whether the existing function is damaged by code change. In most of the code building, the verification part is the part that takes the longest time and has the highest cost, but it is also the part with the greatest benefit.

The external quality inspection of the software is an important task in the integration stage. It is necessary to manage the team's integration test scripts and functional test scripts, because these scripts will be run every time the code is built, which is the part with a relatively high usage rate. Therefore, from the perspective of effectiveness, we shall do a good job in auditing automated test scripts to ensure that the test points are truly covered. In terms of efficiency, such scripts take a long time to run, so the number of test scripts should be controlled to cover only the most important business processes.

Increase the speed of building, which could accelerate the speed of building feedback on the basis of ensuring full verification through componentization, parallel building, hierarchical building, and other technical means.

Sometimes we have to face some legacy projects that are really annoying. The test strategy of the legacy project is to protect the core functions from being destroyed and establish a set of functional level tests for the core functions. After protecting the existing core functions, add more tests for newly-added functions and typical defects.

3.1.1.1.4 Deployment Stage

The deployment of large software applications is often a time-consuming, labor-intensive, and error-prone process, because it involves a variety of difficult issues such as data migration and version compatibility. The idea of continuous deployment is to standardize and automate these tasks so that they can run reliably, automatically, and quickly.

Automated scripts can easily deploy the system into a production environment. At the same time, we also need to consider the solution of automatic rollback. Once the deployed version has problems, we can quickly roll back to the previous version. In case of any potential data problems, a well-designed aftercare plan should also be prepared in advance.

3.1.1.2 Business-Level Collaboration

Many projects will have such a result after implementation, that is, the functions developed by our development team are often not used by users. The reason is that users only use the functions that they are familiar with and meet their basic satisfaction. New functions need better guidance and promotion to be accepted by users. Strictly speaking, it is a responsibility borne by the customer side; however, "maximizing the value of deliverables" itself is the value of the project. Therefore, it is necessary for us to distinguish customers from end users and ask customers to listen to the end users' feedback. The thing to do is very simple, when we analyze requirements, clarify these questions, for example, who will use this function? How to uses this function? What is the purpose of users in using this function? These answers will make our implementation more purposeful.

Compared with offshore teams, the personnel in the local team are closer to end users, so they are encouraged to learn more about end users, which is conducive to confirmating the accurate requirements. We need to provide some methodologies to help customers identify their requirements. After all, the real requirements are defined by customers and end users.

Customers often have a common problem. For example, when we want to confirm a set of data, they will tell us what part they know is commonly used, and they feel no shame for not knowing the part that is not commonly used. Not knowing 100% of their work is not block their daily work, but this will block we start to develop the system. For such customers who lack executive force, we have to help them to run the last mile, otherwise we will deliver a feature with 80% function.

The roadmap for requirements confirmation at the inception of the project is to first confirm the role and business of the user and make a user persona. After a user persona is created, you need to think of yourself as a real user and feel it according to the user's perspective. For example, the user persona you created is a salesperson who sells luxury cars for the first time. You think of yourself as this salesperson. Imagine what you will do, maybe you want to try driving the vehicle you sell, and you will also contact some other salespersons. In this process, you will not only find some pain points that may be encountered in the existing process, but also to understand some of the reasons for doing things under the certain conditions.

Let the customer-side business experts introduce all user scenarios, and at the same time sort out information about who, when, and what are the business goals. Figure 3.2 shows the results we sorted out from a customer. Post-it notes in different colors (different shades in the figure) represent different dimensions of information.

In addition to the general business discussions between business analysts and customers, participating in user interview is the best way to extend demand work upstream. Whenever we step forward, we are closer to the truth or there will be less distortion. In essence, user interview is a qualitative method, which discovers requirements through interviews with key sample users.

If you currently have an old system, consider to ask questions like this when doing a user interview: Who you are and what are you doing in this company? What do you usually do with the system and what did you do last time? Are there anything else have you done? What is this for, and how about that? It will be better if the user shares the desktop to demonstrate how he usually uses it, because you can get more real information from the user observation than from the user interview.

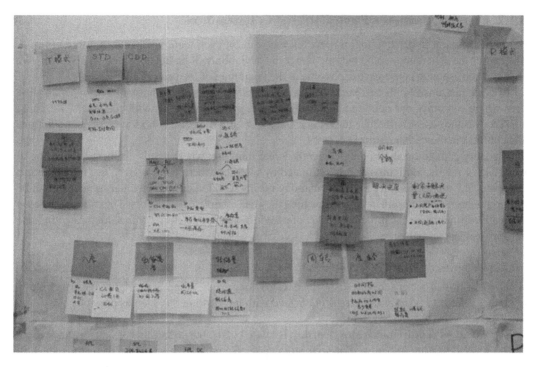

FIGURE 3.2 Results of user interviews.

If there is no existing system, we shall manage to understand how users use other methods to complete their work. In addition to these, are there other pain points? Confirm all the functional modules, start writing user story cards for each functional module, and review with customers after writing and prioritizing.

The above is the method for confirming the requirements at the startup stage. The confirmation of the requirements during the project delivery is mainly to confirm the following details:

- Make a good description of the business background and analyze the requirements from the problem-solving perspective.
- At this time, lots of detail data need to be confirmed, such as the fields displayed on the page and the fields of the search results. We shall design some tables so that the customer can easily know the work needs him to do and track the data list.
- Many times customers are reluctant to "complete" these tasks, we have to find ways to help them make a settlement, at least in stages. For example, they are responsible for confirming the fields displayed on the page. But at the appointed time, only a part of the fields are confirmed. We can say that we only do what has been confirmed. Our estimates are only evaluated according to these confirmed ones. The fields not confirmed yet may be added into the task list after being confirmed. But these information must clearly write down on story cards, and all related customers must be informed.

During the delivery process, we will not reject all the requests of the customer to modify the requirements. Our technicians and business analysts will work together to determine whether the requirements can be modified, how about the impact of the modification and the change in workload. If the workload increases and rework is caused, we must notify the customer.

3.1.2 Unified Opinion is a Prerequisite for Collaboration

Based on different understanding of a matter, the work of each team will yield to different result. The earlier the differences come out, the larger the deviation will be in later stages. This is why we should reach as much consensus as possible at the beginning of the project.

To reach consensus with customers in any aspect, our team needs to have a basic understanding first, which can unify our opinion and save time in reaching consensus with customers. Reaching consensus is the basis of effective teamwork, otherwise, it will become the source of contradictions and conflicts in the collaboration process.

The story estimation shall be based on the same thinking: whether it is estimated according to workload or relative difficulty. If it is estimated by man-day, there is no need to use the Fibonacci sequence, any number is fine. Because man-day means workload, the individual subjective will be too strong, and everyone will estimate how long they can complete every story. The estimation based on relative difficulty is to estimate on basis of one or more sample story cards, which can eliminate personal subjective influence.

3.1.2.1 A Series of Priority Issues

Handling priorities can ensure that distributed teams do the right things at the right time. The following issues related to priority need to be confirmed with the customer as soon as possible.

- **Priority of requirements story card.** It is related to the business value of delivery and preparation for testing. When we prioritize story cards, the product manager needs to know the cost of each story (or backlog item), and the team needs to know the business value of each story.
- **Priority of defect fixing in all tasks.** Usually, the priority of defect fixing task card is higher than the new requirements story card, that is, after completing the story card or task card in hand, developers will take a new card, and he shall get the defect fixing task card in the first place.
- **Deal with the other party's dependence.** When the task of other distributed teams depends on one of our jobs, we shall prioritize this task because earlier integration means less risks.
- **Defect tracking system is a communication tool.** We should agree with our customers on the priority of defects, which is good for later analysis. Defect priority usually adheres to the following rules:
  - ◇ High: The scope of the impact is relatively wide (such as each user will be affected), or affect the achievement of business goals (such as the invoice generated has no tax items), and there is no other way to do the same thing.
  - ◇ Middle: Although the function is important, the scope of its influence is small or there are other ways to accomplish the same task.
  - ◇ Low: The function is not the core function, the influence scope of defects is small, and it does not affect the objective of the customer's' business.

3.1.2.2 Remain Moderate

- **Happy path and sad path.** All the requirements are described in this form. How many sad path are taken as a suitable degree? What is basic common sense? This is determined by the team's own business complexity and the customer expectations, we shall ensure that everyone's thinking depth is consistent.
- **Granularity of acceptance test.** I suggest not leaving a business blank and think about whether too much considerations may restrain the technical solution of developers. That is to say, we should express the comprehensive business requirements, and leave the thinking space for technical realization to developers.
- **In terms of demand, avoid taking too many tasks and making too many promises.** What kind of new requirements can be accepted? What kind of requirements may be put on hold temporarily? These issues should be agreed between offshore teams.

3.1.2.3 Define "Work Completed"

It is very important to clearly define what is "completed," especially when working together between teams. For example, one of our customers Mr. Greg needed a manual to guide the regularly upgrading of the third-party platform every time. I had been thinking from my own point of view to come up with an acceptance list for this test. I uploaded this list to our wiki space for sharing, and I thought I had finished my work. However, one day Greg asked about the status of the manual, and I realized that my work was not 100% completed, because other people could not complete all the upgrade work only by relying on this acceptance test list, and I did not have the list review by him.

A distributed team needs to be very clear about what the other party wants from our side, and show as more details as better about our solution and leave no space for misunderstanding, because even for the same thing, everyone's views are different.

3.1.2.4 Mutual Code Review

Review all codes submitted by all distributed teams refer to the code submission records. Any place that does not conform to the code specifications shall be notified to all team members on the same day, and the parts that affect each other shall also be reminded.

Identifying the key points of the code review in advance will shorten the time for each code review.

3.1.2.5 View the Process Correctly

Most customers have more hierarchical structures, and the purpose of the process is to ensure that everyone's work is controllable in this kind of organizational structure. If you want to transform into a flat agile organization, the purpose of process use will change. The purpose of the process is to ensure the efficiency of the transfer of tasks within and between teams, as well as the effect achieved in each stage. The ultimate goal is to expose the problems at a stage as soon as possible. The more stages a defect crosses, the greater the impact of errors and the cost of correction.

At each time point, if the functions made by different teams need to be integrated, there will always be some unexpected problems. But if continuous integration could be properly persisted, the risks will be dispersed, and the integration will be much smoother every time. That is to say, we should try to submit the code as frequently as possible, and don't submit it all at once after a long time. If a story card can be split into 5 small tasks, we should better to submit it every time we complete a task.

3.1.2.6 Agree on Test-Related Issues

Shall I report it as a formal defect? Fix it directly or report it to the defect tracking system? The agile development team will often encounter such problems. Some concensuses are usually reached in this regard, I'd like to take them as example to illustrate our consistent thinking in dealing with defects.

- If a problem is discovered during the development process, that is, before the story card is "completed," we will continue using this story card to track the problem, instead of creating a defect card. We need to fix this problem, and then re-test the story card, it shall pass the test to prove that it is "completed."
- If the discovered defect originates from the story card of the previous iteration, since the story card has been withdrawn or is already completed, we will write a new defect card to track this defect.

3.1.2.6.1 Not All Defects Need a Defect Card

If a problem is discovered in the story card of current iteration, we usually will not write a new defect card, but have this story card tracked and fixed. We can think of this user story card as not completed. Record the defect reproduction steps and performance, and immediately explain the

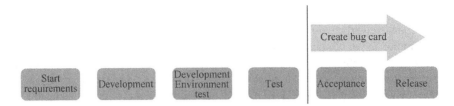

FIGURE 3.3 Demarcation points for creating bug cards in the process.

problem to the developer or demonstrate the problem to him. To be honest, many people are in fact opposed to the reverse movement of the story card on the wall, that is, remove the story card back to the development bar after an error is found in the test. However, if we write a new card to track down the problem, then this story card will stay in place until the new defect card is repaired, so the defect card is put together with the story card. After all, we still need to test both the story card and defect card before we hand over the story card to the customer for acceptance.

We will record a new defect card for the problems found after the story card is "completed," as shown in Figure 3.3, and then put it on the task list for developers to work. The defect found after the story card is "completed" is either proposed by the customer or discovered by us when testing other functions. We need to put these defect cards together with all story cards to evaluate their priority.

For the defects recorded in a defect tracking system (such as JIRA), we can use the system to balance the productivity of distributed teams, uniformly evaluate the priority of all defects, and ensure that the defects with high priority are fixed as soon as possible.

3.1.2.6.2 When to Start Paying Attention to Nonfunctional Issues?

Software response performance and availability are important indicators of software delivery, these factors directly affect the user experience at using the software.

When we are planning tasks, it is hard to consider comprehensive nonfunctional issues. When these issues arise later, we have to make some research passively. The problem that can often be encountered is whether to consider sufficient user experience at the beginning of the project, or to start development with a low experience standard, or focus on availability first, that is, do the basic functions well, and then improve the user experience later .

I once found a performance degradation problem one day before the launch date of a project release: the waiting time for a data processing in current version was 1 minute 15 seconds, and the new version was extended to 3 minutes 30 seconds. If this must be fixed, the code architecture would change a lot, and the launch date would be delayed by nearly a month from the planned date. How to make a choice at this moment? We considered the following aspects: How much value does the new function bring to the customer after this release goes live? Will users frequently encounter the performance problems in actual usage? How many people will be affected? After we get above answers, we will know whether users wait for a longer period to see the function put online after its performance is improved, or they are anxious to see the function put online right away.

Many teams do not pay much attention to the performance indicators during the early development process, and they will not solve the performance problems until customers have reflected. If the performance problems require continuous attention, I recommend adding performance test to the continuous integration pipeline at an appropriate time.

3.1.2.6.3 Define the Production Environment Defects

To deal with the reported production environment defects, if they are introduced recently, they must be fixed as soon as possible. For the defects that have been existing in the production environment for a long time, we need to evaluate whether they need to be fixed or not. Such defects usually have a lower priority, since they have existed in the production environment for a certain period of time, and users have not complained about them, which means that they are rarely used or do not affect the users' normal business.

3.1.2.6.4 Test Rules When Sharing Test Environment

If each team shares one test environment, it is necessary to agree on operating rules in advance to reduce mutual influence and conflict. Otherwise, if the test results are not correct during the test, finally you may find out that it is because other testers have changed the test data you used.

Test the actual environment as soon as possible. The earlier the test is carried out the better, the closer the test environment is to the product environment the better. The principle is not overemphasized at any time, we should avoid such circumstance that serious performance problems are found in the acceptance test when near going online.

In addition to customers, the end users of the product may also participate in the acceptance test, but these end users are far away from the offshore team, and they have not yet directly communicated with the team, so an independent test is required. The offshore team can assist them in preparing test scripts (end-to-end user scenarios) which will help users understand the system early.

3.1.2.7 Consensus on Shared Information

The collaboration on information is mainly to prevent the occurrence of multiple versions and ensure the only source of accurate information.

- Put it in the version control system.
- Use online document management tool.

To achieve the goal of clarifying requirements within distributed teams, sometimes a fixed online storage is needed, and customers can view and edit information at any time. It is the actual implementation of "pull" theory in Kanban, not the "push" concept.

3.1.2.8 Responding to Changes in Requirements

Requirement change is often not to add new requirements, but to the effect of requirements to achieve higher demands. This will definitely increase development difficulties, if this requirement is necessary for customers we must remove the same workload with relatively low priority.

We have always claimed that agile can make us hug changes. How can agile development do it? At the beginning, we will define the general scope of delivered functions. With the accumulation of iterations and the operation of delivered functions, we will adjust the next delivery based on user feedback and data collection during user use in reality. The only principle is to always deliver the functions that currently have the maximal business value.

Unification of opinions is different from retaining opinions, but to express our own thoughts without reservation and reach agreement with the other party on this basis. To maintain team-to-team harmony in daily iterative work and IPM, some teams may choose not to speak out about problems most of the time.

3.1.3 Collaboration Emphasizes Action: Implementation Capacity

The key to execution is a short period before the task is 100% completed. Many people do 80% or 90% of a task and will stop moving forward. The commonly heard saying is "this is what I have done so far, there are..." It seems that he has done a lot of work, but he has not "completed" the work, and other people have to help him finish the work. What we want is what kind of technical solution we should adopt, rather than how about this solution; what we want is the exact fields displayed on a page, instead of knowing how many fields are not needed; what we want is a foundation that allows us to carry on our work, not an uncertain staged conclusion.

The saying as "half of the people who have embarked on a one hundred mile journey may fall by the way side" could be no more applicable. The last part of the work is usually challenging, which calls us to determine the final plan with the business personnel, or make some decisions or assumptions on our own. Many people will stop moving forward at this moment, they only put out all the things they can find, not get the task done.

The following e-mail reply is a communication process when we confirm the requirements with an interface personnel of the customer. Of course, there are also many examples of role exchanges between us and the customer on the issue of execution.

The status update e-mail sent to the customer by the business analyst of our project team is as follows, and of course it is designed to urge the customer:

Hello Xiaoli,
   Regarding the advanced search function: Please refer to the attached document. We need your assistance to complete the contents of columns K, L, and N. Please confirm these fields within this week. Our team will start development based on your confirmation next week.

The reply received one day later is like this:

Hellow Jiaru,
   The attachment is a supplementary table on advanced search.
   Since there are only a few values in the business name column, there is little to add.
   Moreover, this version seems to have changed a lot compared to the version made by Li Jian, so it is best to confirm.
   Best regards,
   Xiaoli

As you can see from the above, we relied on the customer to confirm some fields, but the customer only added some data and kicked the ball back. Perhaps in Xiaoli's opinion, he did a lot of work in accordance with Jiaru's requirements, and even gave Jiaru good suggestions. But it was far from the results we need. We had to take him to find other relevant personnel on the customer side to confirm all the remaining fields, which was also a manifestation of lack of execution.

There are always people in a team who often complain and emphasize problems rather than seek solutions. When faced with a challenge, they think about the reason why the task cannot be completed. Another common mistake made by many people is that they do not know how to converge after they have diverged, that is, they have not completed the last mile to solve the problem.

The action plan produced by the retrospective meeting is a manifestation in this regard. Each issue must have a corresponding action plan, each action plan must have at least one person in charge, and each action plan needs to be completed or yield some staged results by the next retrospective meeting.

Using Kanban in project can track tasks and refine tasks, which is a good place in promoting execution. Kanban is even more important for distributed teams that cannot communicate face to face.

The use of tools can also indirectly increase the productivity and execution of distributed teams. For example, task management tools such as JIRA and Trello can assign tasks to different distributed teams, and track the execution of different teams through the statistical functions of the software (even if the software itself does not have such functions, we can use some plug-ins to complete). Introduce competition to promote the team's execution of tasks, but we cannot emphasize competition too much, it is enough to have data stored there and everyone can see. Too much emphasis on competition may exert the opposite effect.

What other bad effects does offshore work have on execution?

- Time difference lowers the efficiency of execution.
- Increasing difficulties in communication and decreasing frequency of communication will reduce feedback during the execution process.
- The sense of distance will make the offshore team members loosen the demands on themselves.

3.1.4 Useful Methods for Collaboration

After understanding the types of collaboration and the prerequisites for collaboration, we can shift our attention to some ways to promote collaboration. In fact, we can strengthen distributed collaboration from both the internal and external aspects, because we can never stop divergent thinking to look for all methods that can help. In this section, I will share some of my experiences that can actually help distributed teams in teamwork arrangement, software and hardware investment on collaboration, and proper management of major indicators.

3.1.4.1 Reasonably Arrange the Tasks of Distributed Teams

If the collaboration must be distributed, of course, we have no choice in most cases, we must isolate the task of architecture development to minimize the interaction between the different teams. Too much interaction will generate a lot of dependency, good architectural isolation retains only the necessary interfaces. When evaluating a project, the delivery supervisors of many companies will promote the functional team model, they are in fact following the same principle: a large team shall be split, and too many product codes shall be reconstructed and modularized. Ideally, independent evolution and release can be achieved. The popular microservices are also based on the same idea. The above idea is to reduce the degree of coupling between the teams, thereby maintaining the maximum independence of each distributed team, so that the number of interaction is reduced and simplified.

And for better collaboration, will a flat offshore teams be better? This problem can be considered from the following two aspects:

- Parallel communication between the roles in a distributed team. In Section 2.3, we have talked about the importance of huddle between different roles. The direct communication between the relevant personnel embodies the concept of "let front-line staff make decisions for front-line problems" in lean thinking.
- The on-site representative seems to function as a contact window, but the setting of this position is not to meet the management needs for increasing the level or node of communication. Its main purpose is in the following aspects:
    ◇ Eliminate the effect of time difference: not everyone is required to be present at a meeting, and most members of each team do not need to attend a meeting in their break time.
    ◇ Help local and offshore teams have consistent understanding of issues: such as tasks allocation and priority definition.
    ◇ Customers will have a better experience: they have no sense of distance with a representative of the offshore team at their side.
    ◇ Enhance the trust by customers: demonstrate the strength and professionalism of the offshore team to customers by working with them.

As the business develops, offshore projects may extent to many sub-teams. A more reasonable team structure based on project requirement will help on team collaboration for sure.

3.1.4.2 Beneficial Investment

If some technology investment can eliminate the impact of long distance, then this investment must be worthwhile.

(1) **Invest in hardware and software tools to make things easier.** If the time difference allows, our team will set up a camera that is always online, so that we can easily see the other team. We can track a task, discuss problems, and confirm requirements at once, while sending e-mails and messages is sure to cause some delays. If there is a monitor that provides uninterrupted video, you can wave your hand in front of the camera so that you can directly find someone in the other team. If developers want to pair program remotely, they can use shared desktop software to share control of the development environment at anyone's computer.

(2) **Invest in leading software engineering practices.** Continuous integration and automated testing require continuous investment, and these practices are particularly important for distributed teams, and the benefits they bring to distributed teams are also irreplaceable.

If you are preparing to build an offshore team, be sure to learn some experiences in advance. That is, beneficial investment must be poured in, and the choice of remotely connected hardware and software must be reliable. Your investment of thousands of dollars in hardware and software seems expensive, but it is still worthwhile compared to the increased efficiency and reduced waste. We used to spend half an hour to get through a video conference call at a team-to-team meeting. During this process, the team members on both sides were waiting helplessly. Every remote meeting always takes much more time than expected to enter the formal issue.

3.1.4.3 Manage the Backlog for Distributed Teams

The backlog is a collection of tasks planned by the entire distributed team all along. First, it is the goal of the entire team; secondly, it must be assigned to the sub-team to which it belongs; finally, all items in the backlog shall be evaluated and prioritized.

If each sub-team maintains its own independent backlog, each team needs to know where their task is located in the overall goal. At the same time, to ensure the productivity of distributed teams and avoid waiting and repetitive labor across teams, it is very important that each team is clear about what it is responsible for, so that there is no blurred boundary. For an agile team, having a proper backlog is a good start. If it is also a distributed team, the management of the backlog is even more important. When distributed teams assign tasks, the teams on both sides should not depend on their daily work, it is necessary to maintain a clear backlog.

For different teams that need to collaborate, it is best to make the backlog visible to everyone so that they can understand each other's plans. For example, by visualizing the completed list, we can understand the functions that the other party is ready, and then start to consider integration. By visualizing the list of plans, we can make follow-up plans, and when we have interfaces and integration in the future, we can better collaborate. The boundaries of each collaborative team must be definite, and there should be no ambiguities, this is the goal

It's good to let distributed teams work together, but it is equally important to divide their work so that they can work as much as possible without interfering with each other. For the places that need interaction between the teams, we need to identify them in advance and have full discussions and plans before the actual combination.

In addition to story cards, the task list also includes other technical tasks. When the technical cards in the backlog are arranged, they should reflect their original intention to serve subsequent iterations, including subsequent iteration services for other teams, as shown in Figure 3.4.

Clarify the priority of the bug card in the backlog. General bugs have higher priority and are usually higher than ordinary user story cards. But bugs from production environment normally do not have a higher priority, and usually need to undergo a bug triage to determine whether and when they need to be fixed.

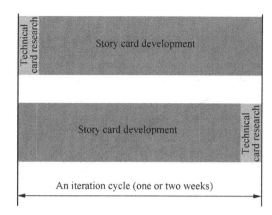

FIGURE 3.4 Arrangement of technology card in an iteration cycle.

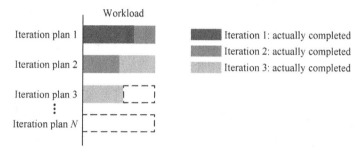

FIGURE 3.5 Planned and actual workload per iteration.

3.1.4.4 Visualize the Progress of Distributed Teams

Dealing with delivery pressure is what every offshore team needs to experience. A manager may need to inquire from time to time and keep checking to keep track of the project progress. A team member is not highly interested in the project progress, since he does not have a grasp of the overall scope of the delivery. We need to use some tools, such as burn-down charts and burn-up charts, to visualize the progress. The team should focus on the progress data and trends of each iteration, by which scatter delivery risks. The online Kanban tool can use various reports to give everyone a comprehensive understanding of the project iteration progress.

The advantage of agile is that the risks to project delivery can be discovered at any time, and delivery pressure is one of the most important indicators, which needs to be handled by team manager in a timely manner. The biggest sign of excessive delivery pressure is that each iteration has more legacy story cards. These legacy story cards often flow into the next iteration. The result may be to make more legacy story cards for the next iteration, as shown in Figure 3.5.

In addition, a visualization tool that finds excessive delivery pressure is the burn-up chart. On the basis of the original delivery scope, draw a straight line from the intersection of the delivery scope and delivery time to the origin, and compare the trend line of "story completed" points. If the slope of the latter is much smaller than the former, it means that the entire delivered deliverable must be far less than the planned delivery, as shown in Figure 3.6.

Take advantage of continuous integration and deployment pipeline. At this stage, this is a best practice for us to work together. To maximize its effectiveness, we need frequent submissions and rapid deployment by various teams to avoid deployment or integration failures and hamper the work of other teams.

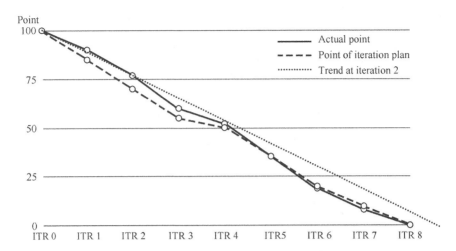

FIGURE 3.6 The impact of actual iteration progress on date of delivery.

Making all tasks visible is the only feasible way to prevent anticlimax. Visible to customers is the driving force for the offshore team to persevere. But using these transparent management methods does not mean that we lack trust in team members.

3.1.4.5 Make Good Use of Available Resources

An offshore team may sometimes have a good luck. The customer pays more attention to our team and gives us access to some of their internal systems and forums. We need to study these systems carefully and make good use of these conditions, whether it is to increase our understanding of this customer or to master more customer background information. These contents will reflect the customer's current concerns, work process and style, and some personal interests. These systems include Salesforce Services, Quality Center, and Jive Forum.

I had been cooperating with an energy exploration company. One business process, including data collection, data processing, and data display, was completed by three teams in three different places. Such problems often occur: different teams may have different understanding of the interface; two teams working on the same thing; each team lacks an understanding of the concept of business overall view and the overall process, as well as its position of in the entire team. Therefore, we shall understand in various ways what is done and how about the project state; such information shall be open to everyone.

If you need help from the other party, such as testing some integrated functions, the best way is to write a task card to the other party and put it in their team's electronic task tracking tool, which will attract its attention and facilitate our tracking.

Make good use of all customer resources. We have done a fixed-budget project. The customer often said that "I have no more money, I cannot increase the budget any more, but the delivery must be on time." For us, because it was a fixed-bid model, if we wanted to increase manpower, it would be difficult to get the support of our company, because increasing manpower meant an increase in costs. But we knew that there might be someone in the customer team that could help us. It is a solution to find some employees of the customer to assist in project delivery, but the premise is that these personnel must be qualified candidates who can provide value; otherwise, the cost of personnel training will drive us crazy.

3.1.5 Behaviors that Hurt Collaboration

The Agile Manifesto is based on the interpretation of distributed teams, which is different from the interpretation of ordinary independent teams. Distributed agile development is a great challenge to every team. If everyone in the team has no consciousness to actively help others, it will be difficult for agile practices to play a role in distributed teams. This requires us to work hard to control behaviors that hurt collaboration, because both communication and trust building is more difficult for distributed teams.

Each distributed team shall be treated fairly. When assigning tasks, we cannot always leave the bug fixing work to the offshore team. Of course, if such a thing really happens, it is also a bad signal for the offshore team, and it may mean that the customer trust in us has decreased.

In case of lack of discipline, its adverse effects may be amplified for distributed teams. In terms of new requirements and new tasks, no matter how small they are, we must use an online task management tool to track their progress. These things seem trivial, but they will be destructive if not done well.

Reduce the impact of subjective factors on the team. We may meet some people who only care about enhancing their personal influence, or those are used to bringing their personal emotions to work. We must oppose individualistic heroism. Although individuals have strong abilities, they also need to learn to cooperate with others. The era of fighting alone and worship of individual heroes is over.

Because of the human-centered principle, it is necessary to create a safe environment so that team members will not shrink back in front of certain things. Only in this way can we get feedback in a more timely manner, and not go further and further on the wrong path.

If something goes wrong, do we have to find someone responsible? It is important for an entire team to share the responsibility. For example, a problem is found after the software is deployed to the production environment, it seems that developers are the most innocent. After we have released a new function, it results in a problem with another function, we will first think that the testers failed to find the bug. But in fact, the fundamental reason is that the design of our system is not good enough and the coupling is too strong, since modifying one function should not affect the code of another function. It is also important to determine the scope of regression testing, a bad design has a great influence on the scope of regression testing.

Well, we can also deduce from the customer standpoint, regarding the management cost incurred by not working together or not working in the same time zone, how much extra effort the customer has made? Many times we are reluctant to discuss these seemingly meaningless issues, but we have to face them. As an offshore team, should we also do something to reduce these management costs? Should we increasing initiative, which may be regarded as creating value for customers? What is initiative? When the other party needs us to do something together, be sure to think about their position and update the status to them in a timely manner. Furthermore their time zone should be taken into account as well.

Reduce friction and internal disputes between different team members, and make constant improvement, so that all team members will cooperate better. I once summed up 10 negative behaviors of developers in a project.

(1) This problem cannot be reproduced on the development machine, it may be the cause of local configuration, I can do nothing with it.
(2) If developers write test code, what will testers do?
(3) Developing functions according to one's own preferences rather than users.
(4) Part of the code can only be modified by himself, others are incapable of the code.
(5) Submit the code by the time to get off work every day, and then tell the tester "the code is available for testing."
(6) Continue to check in code after failed integration.
(7) Request to revise the requirements since the solution is hard to be implemented.
(8) Revoke the relevant test code temporarily to ensure of successful submission.
(9) I didn't do that part.
(10) Easily introduce technology stacks that customers are not familiar with.

3.1.6 DRIVE CUSTOMERS

Make sure that customers participate in our basic agile practices, especially some ceremonial meetings, such as showcase and daily stand-up. If customers found any problem, they can provide us feedback right away.

No matter how many results are achieved by the offshore team, we should say it out loud, otherwise the customer have more negative impressions upon us since people are prone to be impressed by bad things. Just like you buy something online, you may not write many reviews if it is easy to use, but if you have a bad shopping experience, you will definitely write it down in detail. Likewise, let customers pay attention to the merits of the team, which will build up the confidence of the offshore team and benefit the future cooperation between the two sides.

3.1.6.1 Take the Offshore Team and the Customer as a Whole

If we encounter problems that cannot be solved by our team, we should notify the customer as soon as possible. Of course, if the customer attends the stand-up, such a thing is easy to handle. Let customers help us to solve our problems will motivate them to participate in our specific tasks. Customers usually have more understanding of their business and technology stack, so they can give us unexpected tips.

For the sharing of information between teams, do not expect the personnel with the customer team to take the initiative to look for the information about themselves at a designated location or on a designated page. So we have to urge customers frequently, and then deliver information to them through the communication means they are accustomed to. In fact, what we do most is to write a project status update report regularly.

An on-site representative at the customer site has a greater influence on the customer, since he has a geographical advantage that the offshore team cannot match. Such advantage can help the offshore team to explore the root cause of problem. Without an on-site representative, it is difficult for the customer to assist us in in-depth research. Compared with the personnel in the offshore team, the on-site representative has a closer relationship with the customer, and can more accurately grasp the customer complaints, so as to conduct more candid face-to-face communication.

3.1.6.2 The Role of Guidance

We emphasize the role of guidance in many stages of cooperation with the customer team. Guidance usually means that we do not have the hard power to independently solve a problem. The knowledge or ability is on the customer side and is in a dispersed state, but the customer lacks organizational ability. In outsourcing projects, I have experienced the following three typical scenarios where guidance works:

- Start a new project;
- Convene meetings on various agile practices;
- Solve problems in areas we are not familiar with.
  (1) **Guidance at the project inception.** A formal communication plan (see Figures 3.7 and 3.8) is the framework for guiding customers. This is a communication plan discussed and developed with the project manager or responsible person in the customer team, and should be counted as one of the outputs of the inception. The communication plan should confirmed by the senior leadership of the customer, which is the foundation for ensuring the communication and collaboration of distributed teams. The communication plan is a separate plan document, it is usually included into the iteration plan report upon completion of the project inception. With this plan, we can understand the overall communication and the specific communication time in the entire project delivery cycle.
  (2) **Guidance at the retrospective meeting.** In addition to formal guidance, we must also pay attention to the organization and generalization of the problems that are dispersed, as

Type of meeting	Time	Cycle of meeting	Participants
Global synchronization & showcase	Dec 6, Dec 20, Jan 4, Jan 17, Jan 31, Feb 14	Every two weeks	Responsible person and developers at the customer team; our team
Daily standup	Every 10:00 a.m.	Every day	Our team; developers at the customer team
IPM	Nov 17, Dec 1, Dec 15, Dec 29, Jan 12, Jan 26, Feb 9	Every two weeks	Our team; developers and responsible person at the customer team
Local showcase	Dec 6, Dec 20, Jan 4, Jan 17, Jan 31, Feb 14	Every two weeks	Our team (including salesperson); developers and responsible person at the customer team
Retrospective	Dec 2, Dec 9, Dec 30, Jan 13, Jan 27, Jan 10	Every two weeks	Our team; developers and responsible person at the customer team
User test	Dec 19~23, Jan 16~20, Feb 20~24	Every two weeks	Business staff and testers at the customer team

FIGURE 3.7 Communication plan.

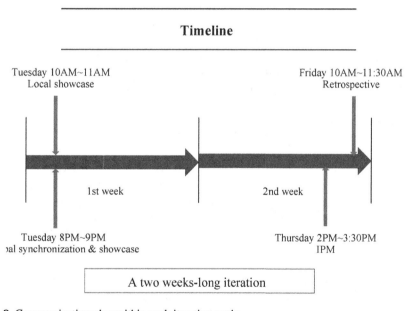

FIGURE 3.8 Communication plan within each iteration cycle.

well as the development of an action plan. Good guidance will have a great impact on the final effect and result.

The same and relevant themes can be combined into a group. In addition to this, a theme may imply multiple dimensions, such as a question about customer cooperation for integration testing, is it teamwork or testing issue? Try to find where the problem is, for this problem it is not in the test, but in team coordination.

(3) **Guidance helps to overcome technical obstacles.** Even if we don't know enough about technology and business, we believe that through good methodology and guidance, we can still analyze problems and finally give a solution or alternative.

I have a colleague who is a project manager, he had been working at the a customer's site for a while to provide consulting service. During this period, he successfully solved a series of technical problems such as system downtime. In this story, this project manager has no relevant technical background, but he flexibly uses the most common methods, such as task decomposition and retrospective meetings to analyze problems, and leads the customer team to tackle the problems, identify the risks at the transaction summit in advance, and have them resolved immediately.

3.1.6.3 Enhance Persuasion to Customers

While working with customers, there are so many aspects that we have to convince customers. For example, why is this technical solution more suitable for us? Why adopt this testing strategy? Why the agile method is able improve software quality and speed up delivery? Does the agile method help performance testing? How does performance testing fit into the agile development process? Also, development and testing is bound together, and why requirements and development is bound together? Although sometimes our claims are far-fetched, and some customers will still accept us, but at this time, they are not yet convinced, but acquiesced with many questions, which is not comfortable for customers.

Customer agility determines the methods we use. If the customer team is a traditional team, we have to explain a lot of terms before doing something, and explain what real benefits this brings and what are the similarities and differences compared with other methods. If the customer adopts the agile method, it will save us a lot of explanation, but the customer's understanding is not necessarily correct, we need to clarify some things in the first place, so that we can reach a consensus on the basic concepts.

Of course, customers have expectations for what they are doing or what they can achieve. We want customers to accept our suggestions; understand and manage customer expectations is the most basic work. Finally we recommend suitable practices based on the customer's agility and acceptance.

We can't be able to convince our customers in all things, but we can't sloppy on some key issues. If we can solve the following key issues, and others problems will be unworthy of mentioning

- **Estimate story card.** If we estimate story card based on relative difficulty, it will facilitate the arrangement of the iteration plan. The points estimated here are the development difficulty estimated by developers and the test difficulty estimated by developers or testers. If we want to better grasp the progress of the workload completed by the team, we can also estimate according to the workload. And the workload for estimation usually includes the workload of development and the workload of testing, while the time spent on business analysis is not included in the estimation.
- **Slow progress at the early stage.** When any project is started, we need to pay attention to the construction of continuous integration environment, the preparation of test framework, and consider the long-term reusability. Only when the foundation is laid firmly can the entire delivery be ensured smoothly. If we are too anxious to develop new functions from the beginning, although many functions can be seen in the short term, when the code integration is involved later, the technical difficulty will mount, the increase in test points and the complexity of interaction will eventually increase the investment in bug fixing. In the final analysis, these are not conducive to delivering a high-quality software on time. Compared with fast delivery, we pay more attention to the quality of software. When a team is pressured to add

more content to the software, it must be able to stick to its values and refute: "we may be able to do more, but our priority is quality, and declining quality will definitely make the team pay a higher price later." At this time, we can make explanations to the customer in the following two aspects to resolve his concerns about our offshore team:

◇ Why there are so many technical research tasks? Explain the purpose of each research task;
◇ Inform the customer of the construction of an integrated environment; the customer cannot quantify these benefits without seeing the direct benefits in doing so.

■ **Arrangement of iteration plan.** Why not make one function perfect at a time, and then work on the next function? But the routine is that we complete the core functions in each module, after all the core functions are completed, then consider how to refine them.

■ **The quantity of bugs found in automated testing.** Regarding the significance of automated testing, this is a question that a normal agile team will ask, not to mention customers. There is a view saying that "automated testing is not primarily used to detect bugs," the main basis for this view is that "automated testing is an automatic regression test strictly in accordance with useful cases." To put it plainly, "it does the same thing every time," so it cannot discover new bugs like manual testing that relies on human subjective initiative. So, the automated test is to guarantee the old function to work normally for every time there is a new submission. This is a kind of passive security. Automated testing is the foundation of continuous integration. How to measure the effectiveness of automated testing? We can use indicators, such as test coverage, the number of test cases and growth trends, the pass rate of each user test, and test run time, to let the team and users notified.

Many people believe they shall break their neck doing a good job, and then a good result will naturally be there, showing that they don't pay much attention to the evaluation of the effect of doing things. It seems like the testability of a piece of code, if it is untestable, what is the significance of this code? A better approach is to test first, consider how to test first, and then implement it.

If we do something by ourselves, it is relatively easy to persist for a long time. However, it is not easy for others or other teams to stick with us. So letting distributed teams collaborate with each other is a big project, and there must be no worries or doubts in their mind, which is a prerequisite.

3.1.6.3.1 Convince Customers to Accept Our Solution

When there are two solutions capable of solving the problems of users, how can we say one is better than the other? "That is not common practice," such explanation is far from enough to convince customers.

For example, when we design a search function, users can save each search condition, and select this search condition directly from a drop-down list when searching next time.

We proposed a new requirement for the customer after doing a user interview: each time user select a search condition, system shall allow the user to modify the search condition before searching. Then the customer directly gave us a solution: each time user select a search condition in the drop-down list, a dialog box pops up to let the user choose whether to perform the search directly or to modify it.

When we heard it, we felt that this plan would definitely not work. No matter how many users need to change the search conditions before each search, it is not only strange to see a dialog window pop up after selecting the conditions from the drop-down list, but also increase the instability of the system. But we could not say like this. We must systematically thinking about users' purpose. The function that customer want is to let user change the search conditions before searching. Look at the nodes from the users' selection of the drop-down menu to the execution of the search results: users click on the drop-down box – the program displays the contents of the drop-down box – users click on a search condition – the system performs this search – the system returns the results to users.

What we want is that after users click on a search condition, before returning the search results, there is still a chance to adjust the search condition. It is indeed possible to add the step of adjusting the search conditions directly after the user clicks. This can achieve the users' purpose. We also need to see that this search is performed automatically by the system. Can we change it to be executed manually by the user? Of course it is possible. In the end, the customer approved our solution.

3.1.6.3.2 Bridge Differences

We should consider the benefits brought to the customer team and the individual customers. The communication with customers must be persuasive, and we have good reasons for doing so.

Think empathically and discover the value of customer opinions. Sometimes, praise customers in a timely manner and recognize the work done by customers, so that they are more willing to cooperate with us.

Only in this way can we view the differences between the two sides from a higher level, extract the common value of both sides, find a goal more suitable for the entire team to achieve, and integrate a result that is better than each individual plan.

3.1.6.3.3 Walking on Two Legs

Some customer teams are very stubborn in their opinions and reject others' suggestions. Even if we recommend the prevailing practices and successful cases in the industry, we still cannot convince them. What should we do?

In opinion, if we can't convince customers to accept our ideas, at least our offshore teams cannot stick to what customers want. We follow our own path, and find ways to let customers see our results, win approval from some open-minded personnel in the customer team, and strive to show the results to the senior decision-makers of the customer team. Those who can really create resistance to us are the leaders in the customer team. They have a certain voice and prestige within the team, and sometimes they regard our offshore teams as a threat. We can only use data and results to impress them.

3.1.6.3.4 Let Customers Give Up Their Doubts

When and under what circumstances will customer raise questions, and how to deal with their questions? This needs to be divided into cases. Some time ago, the media reported that the filter element of Xiaomi air purifier was still "working" with a plastic bag. The truth was that a user bought an Xiaomi air purifier, when he installed the filter element, he forgot to tear off the packaging plastic bag. The media questioned the data of Xiaomi air purifier in this state. As software practitioners, do we need to test the purifier in the same scenario? In other words, even if such a scenario is tested, is it of any value?

3.1.7 COLLABORATION SKILLS

If it is a project that involves the product design process, and there is a time difference, the biggest difficulty is that there is an asynchronous confirmation process for both requirements, prototypes, and design. If we can't solve the problems through face-to-face communication or even quarrel, we need a reasonable collaboration mechanism to facilitate discussion, feedback collection, and tracking.

When customers ask us for our opinions, we should try to avoid saying "I've no opinion" or "whatever," we may really think any solution is ok, but customers may think us indifferent and irresponsible. Instead, we should explain to them the advantages and disadvantages of each solution, and which one is more suitable based on comprehensive consideration.

When doing showcase to customers, the data preparation should not be too arbitrary, but to create a scenario as real as possible. Just like the name given by developers to the test method contains the purpose of the test, the data name of the showcase should also convey our purpose to customers. In the case of a remote showcase, the voice conditions are not good, and there are language and

TABLE 3.1

How to Deal with the "Last Mile" Problems

"Last Mile" Problems	Countermeasure
Deviated understanding or use subjective guessing	Clearly define "completed" and deliver
A brave beginning and weak ending	Visualize the process of task completion, carry something through to the end
A person is doing a lot of things at the same time, but he has completed nothing for a long time	Use Kanban to reduce the generation of multi-threaded work

accent problems, the project team shall manage to use the available information to keep up with the showcase process.

We tend to say that the project inception is a process from 0 to 1, which is a challenge, and we will face many problems that are different from the ongoing project. The tasks we encounter in the course of the project are easy to be executed, but how about the "last mile" problems (from 99 to 100)? In distributed teams, it has more chance to come across some "last mile" problems.

We should pay attention to the "last mile" problems, but our focus is on implementation, rather than theory. Table 3.1 provides some examples for readers' reference.

Only with a sufficient understanding of some key theories, terms, and practical methods of practice can everyone be confident to do it, including customers. Uncertainty cannot stand the scrutiny, nor the challenges of customers. This is also an opportunity for us to study a field specifically of customer's business.

Pay attention to self-protection in offshore teamwork. In other words, it is to find the origin of problems more accurately and avoid the disputes among all parties. We often use technical methods, such as logging and error e-mails, to track the origin of the problems.

One might expect that in any scenario, there is a so-called "tool" or "process" that can solve all problems. Each team should definitely introduce some, but I recommend introducing as few as possible to prevent the occurrence of dependence disorders, because in the end, people still have to rely on their subjective initiative to solve the problem.

If the remote team is not a customer, but a team of our own company, we should still treat them as a "customer" when cooperate with them. For example, we have some functions delivered to them in the end, or sometimes they give us assistance and collaboration. The skills for offshore teamwork are also applicable to these situations.

After knowing so many skills, we still can't immediately improve the collaboration ability of our offshore team. First of all, we should use these skills purposefully in daily work, and find our own handy skills and form our own processes, methodologies and systems. Only when we really benefit from these skills can we become an expert in utilizing these skills. In addition to this, it is necessary to discover new ideas that promote collaboration from the perspective of multi-dimensional collaboration. We shall learn to dealing with problems in collaboration by integrating knowledge of multiple dimensions such as communication skills and risk management.

3.1.8 Key Collaboration Points

Meetings in agile practice are actually the key collaboration points. These meetings have been applied in practice for many years and constitute an architecture for agile teamwork. Table 3.2 lists some typical cross-team meetings I have attended.

At the daily stand-up, everyone is encouraged to take the initiative to think and communicate. The facilitator may ask "are there any accepted functions or newly started functions at the development site?" He is trying to motivate developers to think out this issue and make a plan for the day.

TABLE 3.2

Typical Collaborative Meetings

No.	Meeting and Its Duration	Participants	Agenda
1	Cross-team daily stand-up, 10 minutes per team	Someone with communication needs in each team, generally two to three persons	Status update, whether they need other teams to help them overcome the obstacles, and are there any issues in need of offline discussion
2	Huddle, 0.5~1 hour	Members of different teams playing the same role	Discuss details such as the scope of story card requirements, acceptance conditions, and whether there are dependencies for function release
3	IPM	All team members	The completion of the previous iteration, the description of the content of this iteration plan
4	Iteration reporting, 15–20 minutes per team	All team members	Showcase major functions, long-term plans, and challenges of the team
5	Retrospective, 1.5 hours	All team members	At the meeting, only discuss the topics with the highest number of votes, and develop an action plan

The main content of a stand-up is the results of the previous day and the plan of the current day, meaning that everyone is able to aware of the work progress of others.

It is difficult for everyone to participate in the retrospective meeting of distributed teams, so it is especially important to ask everyone to publish their views to IdeaBoardz in advance, and the participants shall be able to fully express these views. At the retrospective meeting, if some viewpoints are regarded as particularly meaningful, there may be separate meetings for them, and relevant personnel are invited to carry on the research. Only the topics with the highest number of votes are discussed at the meeting, and an action plan is to be formulated.

In addition to the above cross-team regular meetings, each individual team can also develop a communication plan suitable for itself, such as stand-up, huddle, internal retrospective meeting, and showcase.

I have tried some nice methods to facilitate an online meeting, for example:

- Try to use visual method to assist remote discussions. We can use some simple text software or brain map tools to draw some simple charts, or to share the photos with each other in latest physical whiteboard. In this way, we are able to see some real content, which is of great help to raise the efficiency of remote discussions.
- Use online collaboration tools.
- In case of some special discussions, only invite relevant personnel to attend, since agreement is difficult if there are too many people.

The transfer of work across time zones has greater significance for technical support teams. If the duration from the time a problem is raised to the time it is resolved is taken into the KPI assessment, we can improve this indicator through the collaboration between offshore teams in different time zones. For example, the US team took over a technical support job, but did not finish it when they were off work, they could transfer the work to the team in Australia or China. For users, they actually got support from two teams which were working altogether two workdays, but they helped users save half of the waiting time. It should be noted that when any new requirements or new problems are transferred from other teams, we must first confirm clearly what end user's concerns. Otherwise, if an error is found after all tasks are completed, it is sure to hurt the user experience and generate waste.

If the stand-up and other simple practices fail, we can find someone in the team to be an observer, or let everyone take turns to be an observer. Every day they shall record the shortage of team members, monitor the rules of the stand-up, and feedback to the team. If any member are about to attend the stand-up with a remote team the next day, we shall synchronize the physical wall with the online task management tool Trello or Mingle before getting off work the day before, so as to prevent the remote stand-up from deviated understanding and wasting time.

Arranging the tasks in iteration is conducive to raising the efficiency of collaboration. If we have to arrange parallel tasks for multiple teams, more skills are required:

- Prioritize the story cards with dependency.
- Start working on the difficult story cards as early as possible to avoid their incompletion in one iteration.
- The investigation task should be placed at the end of the iteration, and the story cards that depend on it will be arranged in the next iteration.

For the same problem, it may involve communication between multiple people and customers. At this time, we need a team collaboration tool to record the results of each communication with customers. In this way, when others continue to communicate with customers, they can communicate on the basis of existing communication. Currently, many tools are designed to solve this problem, such as Slack. Even so, we still emphasize the subjective initiative of the offshore team members, and calibrate our communication status within the offshore teams without relying on tools.

When all distributed teams complete their own functional modules and start to integrate them together, we need to know that the success of code integration does not mean that the functions are integrated successfully. Testers from different teams still need to carry out a collaborative test to ensure the correctness of integration at the business level. The integration of real business is difficult to achieve through technical means, which requires the testers of each team to complete through cross-team collaboration on basis of an overall understanding of the business. Of course, this work also has many challenges:

- Define the input points of end-to-end test data, start and end points for user operation, and verification points. These points may be on either side of the distributed team. It takes seamless communication to walk the entire path end to end.
- Choose the timing of the distributed test.
- It is necessary to have an environment that can complete this integration test, not an independent environment for each team.
- If a problem occurs, investigate the source of the problem collaboratively. The first step is to find a way to isolate the problem and determine in which team the problem occurred; the second step is to collect information and logs as much possible for developers to solve the problem, because it is uncertain where the useful log information comes from.

3.1.8.1 Continuous Integration at the Business Level

To continue business integration, that is, after completing a requirement story card, we all know what the current overall business is like and verify that all business interfaces are in line with business logic.

To do a good job in technical integration testing and business integration testing is essentially to master the method of isolating problems. Although specific problems shall be analyzed specifically, we still have some basic ideas. We can use the theory of Mock and Stub in automated testing to see if the input and output of each independent part is correct. By means of data transformation, we can find out if there is a problem with the processing of special data.

3.1.8.2 Remote Pairing

Remote pairing is to use technical means to achieve the effect of sitting together as much as possible. Pairing is an important knowledge-sharing behavior, which can even enable the team to reduce the practice of code review, and it can also unify the code specifications of different teams and expose problems in the code. It is these benefits that drive us to create the conditions to develop in pairs even remotely.

Remote pairing is a fashionable topic, but even if time difference is not a big issue for us, we do not recommend using remote pairing as a routine practice. Since during pair programming, two developers are frequently switching control. One person takes the keyboard from the other is a switch, even if he doesn't take the keyboard and just touches a certain position on the screen with his finger, he needs to switch control. In remote operation, switching is more troublesome, frequent switching will seriously affect the enthusiasm of participants in use.

We once used Screenhero, a remote screen sharing tool, which is a great tool that basically achieves the on-site effect. Many of these remote tools focus on sharing and presenting to the other party, while Screenhero is characterized by mutual collaboration. If the network conditions are not good, voice can be provided through other communication tools or by phone.

We've also adopted some other measures:

- Install independent webcams and headsets in workplace to ensure the effect of remote communication.
- Build the meeting rooms that can be used for remote calls, and installed with webcams, microphones, ready-to-use computers, and desktop sharing software.
- Turn on remote video, which is also known as uninterrupted video. At each location there is a large screen that displays real-time scenes of other locations. You can see who is present at the meeting and who are talking. It can enhance the feeling of "we are working together" and facilitate you to discuss with others face to face at any time.

With similar technologies and more means, we can proceed in an orderly way to learn how to hold IPM, showcase, retrospective meeting, and daily stand-up between remotely distributed teams. Like other principles, this is also summed up through continuous practice. In short, the key to multi-team collaboration is to define a series of milestones and collaboration points, and ensure the fulfillment of goals.

3.1.9 SCRUM OF SCRUMS MEETING

When several teams are involved in a project or product development process, Scrum of Scrums (SoS) can be used to extend daily meetings. This is a mechanism for dealing with the complexity of interdependent multi-Scrum teams since its birth. Every day, after each team completes the daily stand-up, a representative of each team will attend an SoS meeting, as shown in Figure 3.9. At this

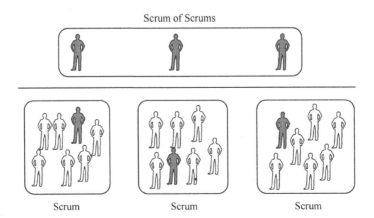

FIGURE 3.9 SoS Team organization.

meeting, each representative reports to the other participants what his team did the previous day and the resulting impact on other teams, and what his team plans to do the next day and the resulting impact. All participants at this meeting main discuss problems, which differs from the daily stand-up. This is to calibrate the interaction content of each team at a higher level, and there is no strict requirement on the meeting time.

The purpose of SoS meeting is to provide transparency to teams that cannot work together and communicate at any time. This meeting allows multiple teams to have an occasion to discuss their work, with particular attention to areas of interdependence and integration. The high-efficiency SoS for large-scale distributed teams and practiced by them will greatly improve the self-organizing skills of each team, and more quickly eliminate obstacles in collaboration and barriers between teams.

Imagine there is a perfectly structured project, it involves four teams, each team has seven members. The four teams independently hold their own daily stand-up, while each team also appoints a representative to attend the SoS meeting. Every team decides who will be the representative of them, usually a technical personnel of the team, such as developer, tester, database administrator or designer, rather than agile coach or product manager. Being sent to attend the SoS meeting is not "life imprisonment," since the participants will be rotated throughout the cycle of the project. The representative selected by the team should be the one who is the best in understanding and explains the most possible problems in the project.

SoS meeting differs from the daily stand-up in the following three aspects:

- No need to be held every day
- No need to be limited to 15 minutes
- Able to solve problems

For most projects, it is enough to hold 2–3 SoS meetings per week, every Tuesday and Thursday or every Monday, Wednesday, and Friday. Although each meeting usually lasts no more than 15 minutes, I suggest it is better extended to 30 or 60 minutes. When a group is talking about a problem and happens to find a right person to solve it, it is allowed to extend the meeting. Think about how many people might be waiting for a solution, there may be almost 100 of them waiting for answers from the SoS meeting. The problems brought to the meeting should be resolved as quickly as possible, which means that the meeting cannot be ended as scheduled to leave the problems to the next meeting.

Of course, sometimes a problem cannot be solved immediately, it may require others to intervene or provide additional information. In this case, this problem may be added into the backlog of the group. This is a list of important issues for the SoS group, it plans to solve it or track it to ensure that another team may solve it. A simple tracking mechanism is usually enough to create a backlog. Some teams record it on a large white paper hanging on the wall of their office, or a spreadsheet, a page of wiki.

SoS meeting and daily stand-up have nothing in common except for their similar names. Daily stand-up is a synchronous meeting where individual team members come together to communicate their work and synchronous progress; while SoS meeting is for problem-solving, it is not as fast-paced as daily stand-up.

The agenda of an SoS meeting is shown in Table 3.3. The agenda is made up of three questions, followed by a discussion of the questions in the backlog. Note that no content of this meeting is dominated by a certain individual.

Just like daily stand-up, the efficient of SoS meeting also needs attention. One technique that can help to do, that is, avoid personal issues. There are two reasons for this: First, when the details of the discussion remains at an appropriate level, everyone expects to learn about the working status of other teams, rather than any personal matters. Second, the length of speech does not equate with its importance. SoS meeting is sure to end quickly if the above two principles are followed.

TABLE 3.3

Agenda of SoS Meeting

Duration	Agenda
Not limit to 15 minutes	Each participant has to answer three questions: • Since the last meeting, what has my team done that will affect the work of other teams? • Before the next meeting, what will my team plan to do that may affect the work of other teams? • For what problems can my team seek help from other teams?

After everyone answers these three questions in Table 3.3, the participants at the meeting can begin to solve problems, difficulties, or challenges that appeared in the previous discussion or on the backlog.

The SoS teams do not organize formal IPM and review meetings. The participants in these meetings are the initial and most important individual contributors of their respective groups. The advanced SoS is a more temporary group, with occasional personnel changes. It is the iteration plans and commitments of a single team that best drive the project towards the right destination.

Even with the guarantee of the SoS mechanism, for the Scrum teams, it is still necessary to consider how to reduce the need for coordination between the teams. In fact, the processing of dependency in Scrum is to eliminate or minimize dependency. Our thinking can be based on (but not limited to) the following key points:

- First, the work of development team cannot be limited to a few number of functional modules, but characterized by spanning all functions. This means that in a product iteration planned to be released, the team has all the capabilities required for this product iteration. The collective ownership of the code is a principle of all team members, so that everyone can touch any line of the code in order to deliver the product increment at the end of the iteration, otherwise we will definitely encounter many unexpected external dependency.

- The requirements and tasks in the backlog should be in the form of end-to-end user story card, dividing the system from the front end to the back end into independent layers to generate functional fragments that can be released separately.

- In the expanded Scrum approach, the team of product owner uses the unique requirements pool to provide input to all development teams for business requirements, and in the meantime ensure that each development team is as independent as possible, so that it can move forward quickly and reduce the need for coordination between each other.

- All plans require the Scrum teams to work together to expose possible dependency as early as possible.

Let the Scrum teams do the above matters, the meeting is not a venue for Scrum experts to report status, but provides an opportunity for people who encounter problems to raise problems and get quick help from other teams. SoS is not an innumerable coordination structure. On the contrary, it is more of an emergency procedure, which plays a role when a team has or will have an influence or dependence on the work of other teams.

Sometimes SoS meeting is like a management review. These review meetings mainly deal with risks and dependency. We can use a separate whiteboard to manage these risks between teams, or open up a separate area on the online task management tool, or create a separate page to manage these risks.

Therefore, the risks that remain on the whiteboard cannot be solved by a single team, because they involve other departments of the company, the customer team, or beyond the control of their own team. The team leader should bear the responsibility to solve these problems. If these external dependency is not properly resolved, the work of the team will be greatly constrained.

We can build a simple Kanban to manage these problems, including four columns: resolved, claimed, accepted, and alleviated. We discuss one risk at a time and make a decision, and then move them to one of the four columns. All risks must be discussed and placed in the corresponding column of the Kanban.

By strictly controlling the dependency between teams, we will find that our daily work will have the following subtle changes:

- Reduced repetitive work. Collaboration between teams is more effective, so less time is wasted on repetitive work.
- Less dependency. Each team has less time wasting on each other's obstacles and on waiting, and teams can cooperate with other departments and stakeholders more smoothly.
- Team leaders can adjust priority and resolve obstacles faster because they know more about the actual situation of multiple teams than ever before.
- Customer trust has improved because they better understand what the teams are doing and why they are doing like this.
- Planning becomes easier, and the rate of achieving commitments is higher, because each team and other stakeholders are aware of our actual capacity and the amount of work that can be promised.

In addition to the need for communication between closely cooperating teams, for offshore teams, such communication is also required between multiple project teams which provide service to the same customer. And it is enough to organize such communication once a week.

3.1.10 COLLABORATION WITHIN THE TEAM

This subsection tells that although we value collaboration with the customer team or other teams, the collaboration of people within the team is also very important, which is the basis of collaboration with customers. If it is not done well, it will cause the following problems: inconsistent voices are heard; internal losses that pull down the progress of the entire team; different methods of doing things from other teams, resulting in deviation in the evaluation data of our team, and so on.

IPM is a milestone time point for an offshore team. Some offshore teams will hold such a meeting on their own. Or if all teams will participate, internal communication of each team is needed in advance, since the successful organization of this meeting calls for too much intra-team collaboration. These collaborations will directly affect whether a team can complete the delivery plan on time, whether it will cause the lack of requirements or even rework, and the acceptance conditions will also indirectly affect the software quality. In this subsection, I will take this as an example to talk about intra-team collaboration.

3.1.10.1 Let's Talk About an IPM

Before holding an IPM, the business analyst of each team shall complete the communication with the requirements stakeholders, or product manager, or domain expert of the team. This is known as backlog sorting in Scrum practice, or requirement refinement in agile business analysis. Collaboration drives us to analyze and refine requirements, and think about other dimensions, standards, and scopes, because two people working together can keep each other better focused and yield higher-quality than one person working alone. This is the benefit of pair-wise programmatic business analysis. We are now well aware that collaboration is the propeller of agile delivery, and the initiative of collaboration is a catalyst.

To enable the team to properly organize an IPM, everyone in the team should receive user story training and understand the relevant knowledge of user stories, in order to meet the following standards:

- Write a user story card in 20 minutes.
- User story card should follow the INVEST principle.
- All developers agree on how to estimate story card.

With these foundations, we have the basic conditions for an efficient and successful IPM. People playing different roles have different ways of thinking. Among the teams that adopt such practices, some teams are willing to pair developers with business analysts to respond to more technically demanding requirements, which is also in line with the concept of a featured team. As long as conditions permit, even some teams will further try to pair with people from different business segments, although they still put their work in the first place. These teams all enjoy such experiences, and new attempts will always fill us with energy. Another windfall of pairing is that more people are involved in the process of requirements refinement. They feel that they have a higher right to speak and a stronger sense of ownership of the story to be prepared.

I've found that when the requirements story is presented to the entire team at the IPM, different requirements proposers can bring new vitality to the meeting and remove the pressure from the business analyst and project manager. Prior to this, the participation of the team was relatively low, and everyone relied on business analyst and project manager to instill requirements.

3.1.10.2 Prepare for an IPM

Although we all know that when the requirements are refined and the acceptance criteria are written, the thinking of two people is definitely better than that of one person. Imagine this scenario: This is an IPM. Almost all the stories we get from the customer are analyzed and verified by the team responsible for designing and delivering solutions. We must digest and absorb these requirements, negotiate and evaluate the work involved, no matter accepting or rejecting, we will put these stories into new iterations. Iteration planning is a guarantee mechanism for agile work. It eliminates hidden assumptions (these assumptions may come from the project early stage, but must be resolved at this time), and promotes communication between the business and development teams. Therefore, this process should ensure that the stakeholders of the customer side have enough time to communicate face-to-face with the developers.

The business analyst of the team has prioritized and scoped the requirements for a new iteration, and story cards or post-it notes have been placed on this iteration's backlog. After the IPM, we still need to communicate further. Therefore, we often encounter the following scenario:

> "We don't need new methods, we are quite skilled in using the requirements design documents," said a team member when he heard the "story" of the user story.
> "So many people estimate story cards, isn't wasting everyone's time? Is it more accurate for more experienced people to do this? ," another person said, looking anxious.
> "Isn't it easier to plan our delivery by estimating story cards based on man-day?" Someone asked this question when estimating.
> "How big a story should be?"
> "How can we split a story?"
> "We've got AC, do we still need to write test cases?"
> "What will happen to these story cards in the future, will they be saved as a knowledge library?"

Although we have encountered all kinds of doubts, this is exactly what we want. The process by which the team splits these requirements is exactly the process by which we test our understanding of its effectiveness and the process by which we try to adapt it to our knowledge and experience.

Discussing the requirements properly is actually examining each user's requirements through the collision of their thoughts and feelings. Once this process is completed, we can understand what users want and why they want them over others. The team will realize which functional points were not part of the core story, but instead of losing them, it is better to split them into new stories for temporary pending. This keeps the stories agile so that they can increase or decrease the priority at a finer granularity. At the same time, we must also remember that research story should be taken first, and then the corresponding story. Although the removed substory has a relatively low priority, it will not affect it as a separate story, but it will stay at the bottom of the backlog with other low-priority stories. It is a good idea to transfer the split requirement to other teams, perhaps its priority would be changed, since other teams may consider the schedule of this requirement, although it may take a long time or never happen.

When an IPM is over, it is clear that everyone knows the story that we will soon work on, we will start discussing this story in a comprehensive manner, and understand the scope of the deliverables and the criteria for measuring the success of the respective deliverable.

If you really want to learn about how a team is doing, you must participate in this meeting, even if you just to observe the iteration plan of other teams. You don't need to be an expert in agile development, but you need to know that this will be driven by incremental requirements use cases (i.e., user stories) or user feedback on the functions of the previous iteration.

Based on the experience and observation of multiple teams, I think it is important for everyone to fully understand the needs for full participation. How well is the team prepared? Are their progress in line with initial expectations? These are the issues that we need to pay attention to.

3.1.10.3 Intra-Team Interaction

From the beginning of the team composition, it means that the people in the team will work hard for the same goal in the future. In this process, we sometimes have to do our own job well, and sometimes we need to help others to do something based on the goals of the team. To make this journey interesting, each one shall get along well with others as soon as possible, know about others' work habits, technical stack level, communication style, or even hobbies. A good team atmosphere can ease everyone's pressure and make communication easy and effective.

The improvement of the collaboration level between distributed teams is inseparable from the collaboration within offshore teams. With initial intra-team collaboration, the efficiency of communication with customers will be higher, and the cooperation experience between customers and offshore teams will be better. This cooperation experience in the delivery process is also a problem that should draw attention of offshore teams, and it is different from the user experience of our delivered software.

Give full play to the internal strength of a team, let everyone fully express their views, and form the collective wisdom of the team. Then, for example, a business analyst can use these views to discuss specific plans with customers.

It should be noted that we'd better pay more attention to the young members of a team, and it is both duty and responsibility of senior employees to give them guidance actively, pass on their wisdom, especially the lessons that prevent them from making the same mistakes. In addition to this, they can discover problems at any time and pair up with each other to figure out solutions. For a newcomer in the team, learning from the senior employees by their side is the best opportunity for their growth. They shall know where they need to improve, do a good job in target management, and develop a phased improvement plan, so that they can have a fruitful teamworking experience every time.

Collaboration is indispensable for agile teams. Cross-role collaboration can be practiced in these teams, but degree control is required. For example, letting developers participate in the preliminary business analysis will certainly have good input, but it cannot affect the productivity of developers.

Do a good job in collecting feedback within the team so that all team members will find and solve problems by themselves. Regarding providing feedback, in fact, the testers' submission of test report is also a kind of feedback, which is to feedback the software quality to developers or even project manager. When providing feedback, specific business scenario should be given, which is helpful to determine the severity of a bug.

3.1.11 SUMMARY

I think we all learned ballroom dancing in college. I want to take a pair of dancers as an example to illustrate the process of collaboration. At the beginning, everyone followed the teacher's demonstration training on their own, and after mastering the essentials of the movement, they could dance with a partner. At first, the boy was not familiar with his partner, he might step on the girl's while training. By adapting to a unified musical rhythm (equivalent to a standardized method) and practicing repeatedly, he and his partner had become good dancers.

We are often forced to make a choice in helping customers to do a remote delivery project: Whether to deliver more functions to users (or result-oriented) or support the team to adopt an agile approach. If a manager have no frontline teamworking experience, they may feel that these two tasks are irrelevant. In fact, in many cases, it may seem simple to change the rules of agile to adapt to the existing management, structure, and operation of customers. However, by changing these rules, it is equivalent to giving up the right to expect the benefits of agile delivery. In the next section, we will study how to improve the agility of offshore team collaboration based on guaranteed delivery.

3.2 IMPROVE THE COLLABORATION BETWEEN OFFSHORE TEAMS

The greatest difficulty is to make up your mind to do something, and the rest is just perseverance.

In essence, there are mainly two types of outsourced projects: one is that we do what customers have told us, and the other is that we tell customers what to do. In case of the first type of project, we cannot bring much value to customers, but simply help them save some labor costs. When working on the second type of project, we will definitely make more effort, but it is more fulfilling. Despite of hard work and sweat in this process, it can better demonstrate our value. At the initial stage, the collaboration and growth of teams is a brutal and extensive way, just like we are pushed into water to learn how to swim. But to a certain stage of development, we need some necessary guidance to improve our swimming skills. This is why many companies claim to adopt agile development method, but in fact only apply some agile tools.

What are the gaps between the teams with general performance team and efficient collaboration? How can we improve our performance? We cannot be self-satisfied for a good performance for a while, since we are pursuing continuous improvement. When doing things, we must not only consider their completion, but also consider the overall and subsequent impact. If it is extended to the technical level, refactoring is an important practice for sustainable development. Phased refactoring not only optimizes the existing code, but also makes the code better prepared to accept new features in the future. If it is further extended to the current software delivery, continuous user feedback and user analysis can also lead the product trend.

Combined with my own experience in offshore outsourcing projects, we will definitely encounter the following problems in our work:

- Uncertainties in demand and technology
- Understanding deviations often occur in communication
- There are too many people at the communication interface, their unprofessional leads to poor customer experience
- Not pay attention to the business value of customers
- Work hard but not work smartly
- Inaccurate grasp of customer requirements
- Some randomness in the work may bring occasional results

The methods and practices presented in this section will address the above problems. Being able to properly solve these problems is a sign of escalated collaboration between offshore teams.

3.2.1 Use Assumptions

Assumption is a future concept, that is, things have not happened yet, and no one knows what will happen. But in project management, we have to make assumptions about our current project, assuming what will happen to its, and then make preparations in advance to reduce unnecessary losses. Let's compare a project to a wedding. The wedding was scheduled to be held on May 1st which might be rainy day, so we must prepare in advance a ceiling or an indoor venue to cope with possible conditions.

Good collaboration should be able to reveal neglected problems. Under normal circumstances, when we have no idea or are uncertain about something, we tend to remain silent, instead of telling others the risk of the uncertainty. We recommend to make the uncertainty visible and put an assumption at this place. Anyone who has familiar with software should know that this assumption can be regarded as "NA" data. No matter whether the data are "NA" or "NONE," they are very different from no data.

Teams may encounter unknown situations, but how to expose these situations? If they cannot be exposed, what measures can be taken to reduce the risk or allow customers to take part of the risk? This requires guiding customers to use formal assumptions. Before that, let's understand the following three-dimensional way of thinking:

- **Horizontal assumption:** limit the scope, such as the scope of requirements and the scope of testing
- **Vertical assumption:** limit depth, such as technical difficulty and level of user experience

Conversely, we also want to avoid the situation that "I have no idea that you don't know this." With assumptions, the work is far from completed. Keep track of these assumptions, and make these assumptions turn to certainty at the right time in the future.

Even if we think we know or firmly believe that we understand the situation, can we avoid these problems in collaboration? Don't be too optimistic, we will also encounter the problem of having grandiose aims but puny abilities.

The original meaning of "having grandiose aims but puny abilities" is to say something is more difficult to do than it seems. But here we need a new explanation. In fact, it reflects the gap between ideal and reality, the gap between estimation and actual result. When you embark on doing something, you will always encounter some unexpected situations. Distributed teamwork will make this gap larger. Using assumptions is a means of reducing risks, but not a fundamental solution to the problems.

Assumptions apply to solving such problems: the requirements are uncertain, there are many options for implementing the plan, and the parties have different understandings of the same problem. Estimating points based on a more difficult implementation plan is also a method of using assumptions.

3.2.2 Two-Way Communication

If we do something just as someone has told us, this is one-way communication. While someone is talking about something, and we ask him questions one after another, which stimulates our both parties to think and even make adjustment, this is two-way communication.

Two-way communication refers to the continuous exchange of positions between the sender and the recipient, and the sender faces the receiver in a context of negotiation and discussion. After the information is sent, the feedback needs to be heard in time, and the two parties can carry out multiple conversations or negotiations if necessary until both parties feel satisfied. The difference between one-way communication and two-way communication is whether there is feedback. Since the recipient has no opportunity to check the accuracy of the information received, he may have a sense of resistance and complain about the sender. Through two-way communication of and feedback, two parties can understand the situation more accurately. Moreover, one-way communication is mostly imperative.

If the local team that owns the information cannot provide useful information, we can proactively describe our understanding of these problems, describe the integration of our offshore team with other teams, and let the right people confirm these perceptions to finally unify the understanding of everyone.

Two-way communication means that our offshore teams will not wait for the customer's local team to provide us with information, but actively inform the customer according to our plan and cognition what we need or how about our current state, they will find out what we have missed from their perspective.

Two-way communication is also used in our daily work. One-way communication is available for some routine jobs and low-level order transmission. In contrast, if the accuracy of work is required and the interpersonal relationship of members is valued, two-way communication should be adopted. Dealing with new and unfamiliar problems, the decision-making meetings of upper-level organizations, the effect of two-way communication is much better.

Where two-way communication is to be adopted, offshore teams must understand the business language of the local team, so as to avoid reaching a false consensus.

> A scholar went out to buy firewood. He shouted at the firewood vendor that "Mr. Firewood Carrier, come here!"
>
> The vendor, though confused at "Firewood Carrier," heard "come here," so he came to the scholar with the firewood.
>
> "How about is pricing?" The scholar asked.
>
> Although failed to fully understand the scholar, the vendor guessed he was asking about the price, so he told him the price.
>
> The scholar continued, "Your firewood is dry on the outside, but wet on the inside. There will be more smoke and less flame when burning. Could you give me a discount?"
>
> The vendor, totally confused, gave up tackling with the scholar and left with his firewood.

Because of the existence of feedback, two-way communication can play a role in ensuring communication, which is conducive to enhancing the understanding of all parties and establishing good interpersonal relationships. In interpersonal communication, we need to accurately understand each other's intention, so that our communication will be more smooth. And communication can make us understand each other, it is a critical factor in interpersonal communication.

Use feedback to strengthen two-way communication, whether it is feedback to individuals, or project retrospective that all team members participate in. In addition, collecting end user's feedback is also the main purpose of user test in agile development.

There was an example in this regard while we were delivering Project L. A user reported a problem, the data of a field that he cared about was not displayed in our system. In terms of such reports, we could not determine whether the problem was caused by data or code. Since there were other users kept reporting similar problems, in order to reduce the number of back-and-forth confirmation and too many single-line communication with a single user, we required all users to submit the following information while reporting the problem:

■ Do these data exist in another parallel system? Due to permissions, our offshore teams cannot view this system with which we use a data source, and we cannot confirm whether there is a problem with the data source or our own system. This first step will quickly rules out a possible cause.

- There are no data in this field for all orders, or is it an individual case? If it is the former, it should be a problem with the code itself; if it is the latter, we need to check the entire data link to see which part of the data processing is wrong.

We use the above methods to communicate with customers who give us their reports according to our requirements, we can quickly handle the data problems reported by different users.

3.2.3 Use Business Language and Examples

Descriptive language is pale, always leaving room for others to develop their imagination, and it is often a divergent imagination. Business language can bring everyone back to the business scene, everyone's thinking will be firmly held by the business value, just like a satellite always revolving around the earth, and will not fly to outer space. But if there is no description of business value, which is left to us will be either the stars out of reach or meteors across the sky.

How to use the business language, Table 3.4 illustrates this issue with a login function that is known to everyone.

As can be seen from Table 3.4, the left column describes a series of behaviors, we cannot literally see the purpose of these behaviors, it is where the business value lies. If the work of technicians is based on the description in the left column as the goal, it is easy to deviate from the goal of business analysts.

Let's look at another case: When I was working on a system related to finance a few years ago, it was sometimes difficult to ask questions due to lack of financial knowledge. What should we do at this time? I tried to use business scenarios to find and expose problems. I had to summarize all the business scenarios I had encountered privately. When I had accumulated enough scenarios, my understanding of the business became more profound.

For example, there are two functions called "postGL" and "Credit Note." Simply put, these functions transmit data to another system, and the other system will then receive the submitted data.

I visited the users engaged in financial work and asked them to explain these business scenarios to me. After fully understanding the business, our description of requirements will be like this:

Essentially these two functions correspond to the same event, the latter is to offset the submission of the former. This is because if the invoice is wrong, we need to correct it. Although we have already had a 3.level audit, we still cannot avoid the inconsistency between the invoice sent to the customer and the customer's own system record. After the offline coordination of the financial staff of both parties, if our data are incorrect, we need to use the "Credit Note" to modify it in the system. This modification is actually to submit a negative number of the general ledger to offset the amount of the last submitted general ledger. After closing the account, the financial staff can regenerate an invoice.

In terms of requirements description, instantiation has a wider use. Let's take the guessing number game on Wenquxing (a brand name of PDA designed for students) as an example to compare the performance of the text description and the example description.

TABLE 3.4

Difference between Language Description from an Implementation Perspective and Business Language

Implementation Language	Business Language
Enter the user name "Tom" and password "psw," click the "Login" button with the mouse, the current user login is successful	A legitimate user login system, the user enters the personal space page

TABLE 3.5
Guessing Number Game on Wenquxing

Number Given by the System	User Guess	Output Result	Explanation
1, 2, 3, 4	5, 6, 7, 8	0A0B	All positions and numbers are wrong
1, 2, 3, 4	1, 6, 7, 8	1A0B	One position and one number are correct
1, 2, 3, 4	6, 1, 7, 8	0A1B	One number is correct, but the position is incorrect
1, 2, 3, 4	1, 2, 4, 3	2A2B	Two numbers and two positions are correct, or two numbers are correct but the positions are not
1, 2, 3, 4	1, 2, 3, 4	4A0B	Four numbers and positions are correct

The rules of the text description are as follows:

(1) After the game starts, the system will randomly give four nonrepeating numbers, and the players will give four nonrepeating numbers.
(2) For each number given by the player, if the number is correct and the position is also correct, the same number of As is returned for the number of correct guesses.
(3) If the number is correct but the position is wrong, the same number of Bs is returned for the number of correct guesses.
(4) If the game returns to 4A0B, it means that players are correct with all of the four numbers, then "You Win" pops up.
(5) In cases of six wrong guesses, the game ends early.

The rules of instantiated questions are shown in Table 3.5.
You can compare which expression is more accurate and closer to the developers' code logic.

3.2.4 REGULARITY FOR ESTABLISHING OFFSHORE TEAMS

"We are what we repeatedly do. Excellence therefore is not an act, but a habit," said Aristotle. Compared with the normativeness to be discussed in the next section, the regularity discussed in this subsection indicates some rules and guidelines that are not easy to implement on paper, but ensures that we can continuously replicate successful repetitive behaviors.

Take an example that is a bit "smelly." We all know that defecation must have regularity, which means that our body is in a good metabolic state. If it is irregular, it may be constipation, which will greatly affect our overall state, we may have a bad mood, lack of energy, and lower work efficiency. Similarly, if our team has no regularity or its health indicators substandard, then the efficiency of the entire team will decline.

We can teach the team what can be done, such as confirmation and reminders between teams, but don't do this all the time, and don't let extra work become a habit and develop into regularity.

3.2.4.1 Regularity in Communication

Some rules are determined with customers from the project beginning, and some are proposed during the cooperation process, like the daily stand-up, regular weekly meeting, IPM at beginning of each iteration, monthly retrospective meeting, and huddle where members playing different roles in all teams will sit together.

Through the above regular communication plans, ensure that different distributed teams could communicate in all directions, and achieve such in the end: the members playing different roles in each team could work together seamlessly, and collaborate naturally at different stages.

Looking at the life cycle of a requirement story card, when a business requirement is proposed by the customer, our business analyst will deeply understand the business value it brings to users, and then write a requirement story card to show the corresponding functions, so as to establish communication with developers.

Looking at the timeline of the daily work of each team and each member, for distributed teams in different time zones, the first thing we do every day is to check e-mails and update the information to the latest state before the stand-up, for fear of any deviated information at the remote stand-up. All of our teams maintain a common continuous integration environment. Any failed submission or test is the first priority. This is a consensus. After a busy day, we need to ensure that all the work of the day is submitted to the code base. The code management system will record all the information. This tool acts as a communication medium.

In terms of a process in which bugs are fixed, the first step is to ensure that the bugs can be reproduced steadily. The conditions and environmental information in which the bugs occur must be accurately provided. In addition, the priority of bugs is higher than that of ordinary requirement story cards. No matter which team they come from, it is everyone's goal to solve these bugs first. In addition to this, the way we deal with bug cards is the same as that of requirement story cards, following the same process until completion.

3.2.4.2 Regularity Brought by Agility

I have been working with the traditional Waterfall Development Method. I'd like to share this experience with you all.

Once we took on a software development project, it was divided into several functional modules to be developed by distributed teams. To ensure of successful integration of all the modules in the end, we elaborately defined their interfaces at the very beginning. It should be noted that such working style means that it is the most time-consuming team that determines the date of module integration. So we were uncertain if we could fulfill this project on time along the project progress. When we finished the development of all functional modules one month before the date of delivery, everyone was overjoyed as if they were going to celebrate a festival. They couldn't help rushing around shouting "let's integrate the modules this afternoon, and test the software from tomorrow!"

But extreme joy begets sorrow, while we were integrating the codes developed by separate teams, we found it was impossible to have them compiled. Until then we saw the codes written by other team members for the first time. When we discussed with each other on how to integrate our codes, each team detected the faults in the codes developed by others. Moreover, it was hard for one team to figure out the codes written by others, since each one had its own coding style and took their codes as benchmark. Some teams made random definitions of global variables, which caused inappropriateness of their codes; and some had their own way in comprehending the setting of environment variables.

After a few days hard working, we compiled the code successfully. Unfortunately, more problems began surfacing as soon as the joint debugging was started. Some modules didn't function at all, since their developers misunderstood the interface or their request failed to reach their partner; some modules had incomplete functions for poor logical thinking; and some modules had dissatisfactory fault tolerance design.

When the joint debugging was over and available for business scenario-based testing, there was only one week left before the delivery date. We had to work overtime to put the software go live by the deadline, although we spent additional energy and cost on the DevOps maintenance.

This instance shows that each distributed team is fully aware of its own responsibility and the overall project goal. In the early stage, everything is going on smoothly, but problems will break out one after another at the time of integration and testing. Such delivering pattern is quite risky, even if they were lucky enough to stand all the tests, they would be exhausted in the end. In most of the time, they have to ask for more budget and postpone the project delivery.

In terms of the agile delivery, it represents a process where delivery is made steadily. Because iterative development is free from notable fluctuations, the workload is evenly distributed throughout the development cycle, codes from distributed teams integrated frequently, and the risks are scattered. Whenever the project progress or quality deviates, the project team will detect it immediately. In contrast, in the process of traditional development, the distributed teams will not integrate the constituent parts until they have completed their separate tasks, and then they will see problems coming out ceaselessly during the integration. They are slack at the beginning and forced to speed up towards the end. The tasks are not evenly divided, there are no uniform criteria for measuring the workload of individuals and how hard it is, no one pays attention to the small problems until they become too big to ignore.

What practices bring regularity?

- **Code review:** We can unify the code styles of different teams, invite some experienced people to detect problems from different perspectives, and ensure high cohesion and low coupling of the code.
- **Agile estimation:** We can use a unified standard to estimate all stories, which is helpful to distribute the work in each iteration, including the sequence and workload.
- **Iterative development:** Iterative development requires that the available functions be delivered at the end of each iteration, so each short iteration we complete is an end-to-end workable function.
- **Continuous integration:** Every day the code submitted by different teams has the opportunity to be integrated together. Even if there are problems, they can be discovered at the initial stage, rather than doing a lot of work in the wrong direction. Everyone gets the code from the code base is the latest integrated code every time.
- **Continuous testing:** Testers are involved in the project from beginning to end. It can help business analysts review requirements early, monitor the development process of the team, and expose problems as early as possible.

Many mature agile practices are helpful for strengthening the regularity of teamwork. Repeated practice and continuous improvement can be regarded as a by-product of regularity.

3.2.5 Continuously Improve the Collaboration Level of Offshore Teams

The purpose of customers looking for outsourcing teams is nothing more than the following reasons: They have no plan or ability to maintain a large-scale software development team for a long time, and the cost of offshore software outsourcing is relatively low. In recent years, with the development of the Internet, many companies have begun to attach importance to improving their innovation capabilities through software technology. Purchasing outsourcing services is their main approach at present. This brings both opportunities and challenges to companies that provide outsourcing services. The goal of the companies that provide software outsourcing services urgently need to move from simple code-stacking work to the goal of industrial innovation with customers.

The big goal is to help customers achieve business growth and meet their expectations, while the small goal is to improve the capabilities of offshore outsourcing teams. More capable offshore teams can bring greater value to customers, the direct manifestation is that the development speed of the development team continues to increase, and there are more deliverables in each iteration. Business analysts understand the basic requirements of customers, and on this basis they are proficient in the industry knowledge about customers and able to provide services that exceed the basic requirements of customers. Relative to documents, more emphasis should be placed on everyone's role in a team. Build a safe, open, and inclusive environment in development to exert subjective initiative and stimulate the interest and creativity of team members.

3.2.5.1 Strength Collaboration Cross Distributed Teams

The purpose of collaboration is to deliver the work that needs to be done on time. We should pay attention to the use of PDCA closed-loop principle to guide our daily work. . Do not guess, but confirm carefully, which is especially important for distributed teams, just like we often hear people say "I thought it should…" when something goes wrong.

Distributed teams share one code base, everyone is responsible for the entire code base, since refactoring is quite challenging. Only by making good use of version control and continuous integration tools to supervise the test coverage of the entire team can safety refactoring be carried out. In addition, some soft skills, such as the trust that is usually established, are also conducive to the work at this time.

I once worked on Project Z with the customer coming from the United States. The team in China would attend the remote stand-up with the customer team every morning. Each team had seven or eight people. After the Monday stand-up, we would play some remote interactive games, such as "two truths and a lie," a 1-minute brief on working experience (it was amazing that everything was especially interesting with a time limit. At the same time, it prompted us to summarize and refine information, after all, too much details would exceed our curiosity), the most embarrassing thing in the past year, and the most intolerable thing in your mind.

If it is an overseas project, there will be language barriers. The offshore project mentioned above had such problem, but we were lucky at that time. The technical director in the customer team, who was responsible for communication with the team in China, attached great importance to the mutual communication and proposed and cooperated with many language problems. Most people agree that the language problem is an objective problem, but they do not think there is any short-term solution that can be implemented. In this project, we tried many ways to improve our communication on language issues. As a native English speaker, this technical director often reminded the spokesperson of his team at the meeting to pay attention to language issues, explain the views of both parties from time to time, and confirm whether the offshore team could understand. He often reminded the speaker to speak louder, slowly, and use simple words and sentences.

The language problem is a fundamental problem that may cause the loss of information in communication, and short-term solutions are not realistic. But this does not mean that we cannot pay attention to language issues. On the contrary, we need to stick to it as a long-term goal:

- Slow down the speed of speech, repeat what was said based on the audience's response, make sure the audience understands, and record the minutes of the meeting.
- Make sure to say "Yes" and "No" correctly, sometimes it causes misunderstandings.

Even if language is offshore team's weakness, we should be brave to call meeting with customers. Evasion does not turn disadvantages into advantages. It is undesirable to be unwilling or afraid to communicate directly with customers.

Communication between each other needs to be done in a certain context. For example, there are wind and dark clouds before we hear thunder. Communication without a context seems like a thunderstorm on a sunny day. Everyone will get frightened? Offshore teams using foreign languages should prepare for the context, which has a significant effect on remote communication.

To improve the level of collaboration with customers, business analysts are a very critical role, In many companies, project manager and technical director assume this role. The project manager focuses on business analysis, and the technical director focuses on technology selection and research. Now, more software outsourcing delivery teams will set up an independent business analyst. This person needs to find ways to influence and guide customers, and transition from requirements reception to real business analysis.

3.2.5.1.1 Acceptance in Development Environment Promotes Quality Built-In

Testers shall do a good job in the acceptance of development environment, so that there will be less and less problems at the later stage of the software. At the beginning of the acceptance of development environment, there must be a lot of repetition, that is, find the problem, modify it, accept it again, find the problem again, and continue to modify it. But we cannot give up or lower the standard until the development environment passes the acceptance. As this practice progresses, developers' quality awareness will get better and better, and these repetitive tasks will be pushed forward to the period when developers have finished developing the functions and are ready for acceptance. When developers are more deeply aware of the acceptance process, they will print this work in their mind more deeply, and make it the last work in function development, and realize the quality built-in. At this time, we will find that the testers of the team seem to be leisurely or have no much work to do, but in fact, this time the testers have enough time to do automated regression testing and valuable exploratory testing.

3.2.5.1.2 Utilize Pyramid Thinking

Each collaboration must have a clear purpose, and subgoals are derived and extended under this big goal, and each subgoal corresponds to a set of arguments or action guidelines. Pyramid thinking has a strong purpose, its advantage is that the audience sees the results and conclusions first, and then see our steps and road maps to achieve such results. With this method of doing things, handling problems will be fairly rigorous, and customers will have more confidence in our work.

Pyramid thinking features "mutually independent and collectively exhaustive," that is, each subgoal or sub-argument is independent, but there is a certain logical relationship between them, and they are combined to exhaust all sub-arguments, and no information is omitted. For example, if you solve a problem for a user, you will first list out the problem, then find all feasible methods, and finally analyze the advantages and disadvantages of each method. In this way, a solid pyramid is created, and when customer see this pyramid, they can fully understand this problem at a glance.

According to this way of thinking backwards, all the work can be inferred completely layer by layer and interlocked, and it is not easy to miss important work by this way.

3.2.5.2 Idea for Instilling in Customers

Our team delivers high-quality software to customers. In addition to the software itself, many ideas in all aspects of daily work should be shared with them. These factors will indirectly have a positive impact on our cooperation.

3.2.5.2.1 Seek Cooperation Instead of Competition

Our teamwork with the customer's local team is for software development, instead of kicking them out. Sometimes the people in the customer team are very sensitive. If we blindly pursue outsourcing and take more work to do offshore, it will make these people oppose us. We must do something in a planned way to let them really understand us and not treat us as competitors. Compromise is sometimes one of the options for improving collaboration with customers.

3.2.5.2.2 Priority

All functions must be prioritized. The customers often believe that all functions are same important to them, and refuses to give them priority from his perspective. If this is the case, it is likely that this is the first phase of a fixed-budget project. All functions are the core functions considered by the customer and not negotiable. Therefore, for the first-phase project, we must add some buffer to the project from the beginning, and we must strictly control the changes in requirements.

Figure 3.10 depicts the consensuses we reached on function priority when helping a customer start a project: The illustration of this pyramid contains the priority of the horizontal and vertical

SCT2.0 project: function priority pyramid

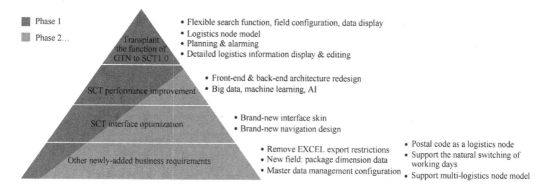

FIGURE 3.10 Priority pyramid of overall project.

dimensions. This figure should be printed out and pasted where all team members can see, especially the customer. It can always remind us not to deviate from these consensuses.

The customer of this project had some long-term plans, and the project were delivered in several phases. So we considered what functions should be arranged in the first phase. The result is shown in the darker area in the upper left and the lighter area in the lower right of Figure 3.10 are the functions arranged in the second and later phases.

Finally we delivered below first phase features to customer:

- Fast search
- Advanced search
- Show details of waybill
- Save search conditions
- Share search conditions with others
- Save search fields
- Share search field with others
- Export search results
- The search result is used as the regular sending function of the report
- User single sign-on (SSO)
- Create a new control panel, put some commonly used information and functions on it
- Use the KPI indicators to predict the date when the goods in the waybill arrive at each node in the route

Among first phase delivery, SSO function is planned at a later iteration, The negative consequence is during the long period of user test, because all users do not need to log in and the generated data shared by everyone, there will be dirty data generated within the system. The reason we plan like this is we want user see more visible functions in the beginning of the project, and we have an easy solution to reload the latest data before go live. In terms of the last function, which is not the core goal of logistics tracking, but a more advanced function with main purpose of evaluation. We convinced the customer to put it in the next phase, so that we could concentrate on the query function in the first phase.

3.2.5.2.3 Roadmap

The entire team needs to know whether we split functions horizontally or vertically, as shown in Figure 3.11. Traditional project development usually completes a function 100% (the top row of post-it notes in Figure 3.11 are function modules), and then turns to another function. The system

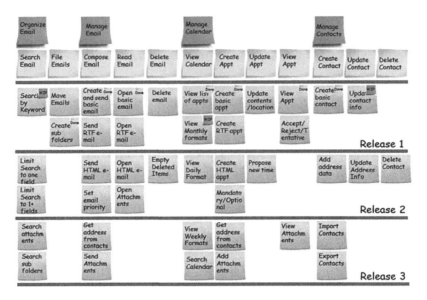

FIGURE 3.11 Function modules and release plans.

needs to be fully developed before it can be used. What agile development pursues is to release a usable version as early as possible, first develop the core part of each function, and then adjust other functions based on user feedback. Therefore, what kind of development roadmap to choose also determines our strategy for preparing user test.

3.2.5.2.4 Respond to User Test

To help customers to support user test is to help ourselves. It is our must-do work to arrange user test in the agile development process, and inform users of the key points of test or have them trained.

Before each user test starts, provide users with a formal user test manual, tell them which functions can be tested and which ones are not yet ready. For users who are familiar with the traditional delivery model, we must explain in detail how user test should be done during the agile development process and how to provide feedback.

For user test, we must pay attention to data integrity. We once had a project, and we thought its functions had been completed, but a lot of misunderstandings were caused by data. If we could think about this problem from the user perspective, it might be avoided.

The user test should be conducted in a production-like environment, or even data from the production environment can be used. A rigorous deployment process should be like this: before deployment, prevent users from logging in with technical means, and then proceed with a step-by-step deployment process; after the deployment is completed, user login is open. This prevents users from reporting some weird problems seen during deployment.

If the customer pays enough attention to user test, we may have the opportunity to create a test script that allows the customer to collect the users' real use scenarios and provide them to us. We shall turn the passive into the positive, rather than waiting for the customer to ask us for the user scenario we plan to test (it will be necessary if he take users serious), it makes more sense for the customer to complete this work.

3.2.5.2.5 Value Horizontal Communication

Individuals in local teams and offshore teams also need some direct communication. Whether it is about business or technology, it has great value.

Hold some remote technology sharing sessions to continuously improve some skills, especially programming. The content of contact in each stage should not be too much, and the selection of topics should be targeted. Repeat until everyone can master it skillfully. With continuous feedback, everyone should know what they have learned this time, where they still need to practice, and what they want to practice next.

Some people may say the effect of this kind of remote sharing is discounted. Wouldn't it be better for a team to share their own results internally? Indeed, some sharing is only suitable for live sharing. However, we do remote sharing for another purpose: demonstrate the capability of offshore team and its learning enthusiasm, it is able to close to the distance between remote teams, and create an up-and-coming atmosphere for the entire team.

In addition to the cultivation of a benign atmosphere, the importance of horizontal communication is also helpful for remote team collaboration. For example, since the offshore team is far away from the customer's team, it is easy to cause misunderstandings when deploying applications. There is a project, each time there are several packages that need to be deployed at the same time, and there are corresponding changes in the database structure. Since not all packages need to be deployed every time, each deployment shall level the latest status of all parties. Direct communication between the parties effectively ensure the accuracy of the information.

What are the benefits of our cooperation if customers accept these ideas?

- When communicating, it is easier to understand each other and avoid the situation of self-talking.
- Distributed teams can work closely together like "one team."
- Have the same understanding of priority and avoid detours.
- Everyone can clearly distinguish what is a functional problem and what is a data problem.

3.2.5.3 Focus on User Value in Delivery

The ultimate goal of delivery is to create value for customers. In the past, we would focus on completing tasks, but now we need to further understand customer business. It is on this basis that we know about the indicators such as priority and importance.

Lean theory talks about small batch production verification, which actually means "small boat is easy to turn around." In the process of offshore development, through the split of business requirements, we can let the core business come online as soon as possible and accept user feedback. Such a process can prevent customers from discovering that they have deviated from the end users' requirements after a large investment. Continuous delivery is a concept that is very conducive to stimulating user value.

To get user value input, we must properly prepare for user test. Please see the case below:

In Project L that I had worked on, the customer paid great attention to user test. Although the customer had collected and investigated the user requirements, they were still not sufficient. Consequently, users still put forward a lot of new requirements in the first phase of the trial. In addition, because of deviations from the users' understanding of agile development, many misunderstandings were caused. Therefore, while we were making preparations for the second user test, we have made the following improvements: On the evening of Tuesday, one day before user testing, overseas users need to do functional demonstration to let users get familiar with the upcoming functions and clarify test purpose. After that, users can log in to the test environment to start official testing.

According to this goal and the pyramid thinking, we have listed the following tasks and their value together with the customer:

- Improve the test data to build up users' true feelings.
- Prepare the test environment and determine the version of each package deployed.
- Delineate the list of functions that users can test. Only 100% of the completed functions can be tested by users, so that users have clear goals when testing.

- Make a list of functions that users do not need to test, tell users which functions will be available in the future, and they will not be confused by some incomplete functions.
- Solve the major problems discovered by users in time, which not only allows users to continue testing, but also does not affect the normal development process of the required functions.
- The test in the internal test environment ensures that the end user will test on a relatively high-quality version, which is conducive to increasing user confidence in product quality. Because if the known bugs reappear after being fixed, it will shake the customer's confidence in our quality control.
- Deploy the user test environment and tell users the status of the currently available data.
- Prepare a list of known problems, so that users do not need to waste time to report them repeatedly.
- Which front-end development work that improves the user experience needs to be completed?
- When everything is ready, send an e-mail to the customer, containing information such as test data availability, list of functions to be tested.

In addition to paying attention to discovering the value of users in the process of continuous delivery, the feedback after the completion of the project is increasingly valued by the industry. We can use some tools, such as Google Analytics, to collect user habits and predicted performance points from the production environment.

What we need to learn from this is to grasp where the system is heavily loaded and where it is lightly loaded. Verify that the software's architectural design is reasonable and whether adjustments are required. According to the users' frequency of use, we can determine which functional bugs have a higher priority.

Customers need to know which functions are used more frequently (i.e., successful), which ones have a relatively low use rate, we can analyze the reason, whether users do not need this function, or its design is not good enough to meet their business requirements.

Here are two suggestions:

- **The team needs to go further and focus on the nonfunctional requirements for business value.** If we can define the necessary nonfunctional requirements at the beginning of the project, this is of course what we want, but many times it depends on the personal experience and performance of the technical directors in the team. This is an area that draws attention too late easily. We strive to discover such requirements without delay to allow time for the resolution of such problems. For this type of new requirements, it is difficult for the team to ask customers to pay for them, because many people think these are included by default. So we should not put these newly discovered problems into the new requirement list, but discover them early and arrange for digestion within the team.
- **Offshore teams have the opportunity to close the distance to end users, but they should pay attention to risks.** When the control of the customer, which connects with our offshore team, is weak, users may communicate directly with us. Although this is helpful for us to understand their requirements more accurately, but some requirements may conflict with the agreement made between us and the customer. So we have to be very careful in handling, and every time we need to invite the responsible person in the customer team to confirm.

3.2.6 SUMMARY

For any team, cooperation is an eternal theme. This cooperation may be the cooperation between the customer and the offshore delivery team, or it may be the cooperation between the branches of a multinational company. Both types of distributed teamwork need to build trust, continuously improve the level of collaboration, and enable offshore teams to embark on a continuous improvement path, although this path is not so easy.

Let's make a definition for "people-oriented" in the offshore delivery team. It means that we shall respect each individual in the team, and encourage them to learn from each other, only in this way can we make sure of being really people-oriented. As an intellectual activity, software development gives everyone space to unleash their abilities and respect everyone's creativity. Another aspect that is easily overlooked is that there should not be some policy and regular factors in the organization to restrict the performance of individuals. It is also important to identify and remove these obstacles.

3.3 STANDARDIZATION ENHANCES COLLABORATION BETWEEN DISTRIBUTED TEAMS

Undoubtedly, standardization can reduce ambiguity, cut the cost of communication, mitigate the impact of personal factors, and reduce the probability of rework. Standardization also keeps our focus on the problem itself, without having to worry about red tape.

The management of uncertainties is a part of risk management, and standardization can significantly reduce its adverse effects. Since the process of software development is ultimately a process of learning and creation, it is inevitable that there are some unpredictable things. However, the adverse effects of unpredictability can be controlled by the following actions:

- Maintain the stability of team staffing
- Keep the iteration cycle consistent
- Use mature business analysis methodology
- Adhere to end-to-end integration frequently
- Eliminate external dependency
- Use techniques such as Test Driven Development (TDD) to avoid unpredictable regression problems

Whether it is the waterfall development process or the agile development process, low-quality code is the source of the pain of unpredictability. In Section 3.3.2, I will talk about how distributed teams manage code.

3.3.1 STANDARDIZATION OF BUSINESS ANALYSIS

A good user requirement shall be perfected in two dimensions of integrality and accuracy. This subsection will ensure the integrality of requirements from their content structure and the accuracy of requirements from their presentation form, in an aim to guide readers to make improvements.

3.3.1.1 Standards for Managing User Story

The writing of each story card must include a background description of this requirement. Based on it, developers and testers can better imagine the scenario of the story when they examine this requirement, which is helpful for understanding the user business value generated by the function to be realized.

The acceptance conditions shall be properly prepared. We advocate using the "Given...When... Then" format, which seems a bit rigid, but this model is not easy to miss information, it will force us to give a more comprehensive content. Whether the acceptance conditions shall reach the level of use cases including happy path, sad path and boundary conditions depends on the impact of this case on specific business requirements. Instantiation is recommended when encountering complex scenarios.

The design of the interface sometimes needs to be standardized to the pixel level, and there must be a standardized design document such as a design style between the teams to guide the work of all designers and front-end developers.

Team members must estimate an entire group of story cards at the same time, which helps to maintain consistency. It is absolutely impossible to estimate it every time when we start to develop a user story card. Although we may have learned more context when starting development, the estimation should be more accurate, but in here, consistency is more important than accuracy.

A 2-point story card is twice as difficult to make as a 1-point story card, and the secondary is that the 2-point story card has twice the workload of a 1-point story card, finally the 1-point story card represents 2 days of workload is the worst idea.

The estimated number of points must follow the Fibonacci sequence of numbers, namely 1, 2, 3, 5, 8, 13, 21, …. The reason is to ensure that when the number is large, the relative size can be easily compared, and it will be more efficient for the team to reach consensus.

The responsibility of business analysis is to split business requirements into specific user stories or tasks. As a business analyst, he needs to follow a standardized thinking process to ensure that all business details can be analyzed and that all points in a story card are not missed. Only if all business analysts follow this principle can we continue to deliver high-quality user stories.

The FANCY method proposed by Li Mo, a former senior business analyst at ThoughtWorks, provides a clearer path for innovative business analysis:

- Functional requirement
- Assumption
- Nonfunctional requirement
- Constraint
- Y-wireframe

3.3.1.1.1 Functional Requirement

In the entire business analysis, the first and most basic aspect is the functional part. Functionality refers to business logic and processes. Business analysts must split user stories into the acceptance conditions of smaller granular that contain details, or smaller story cards. To get comprehensive and thorough details, we need to follow "5W1H" to refine the story cards.

At this stage, the business analysts should already know the target users of this user story and why it is needed:

- Who (target users): user role or user persona
- Why: business value and user goals
- We should also consider the following aspects
- When: prerequisites or preconditions
- Where: entrance to the interface
- What: Input data
- What: business rules and logic in functions
- What: output
- How: happy path
- How: sad paths and boundary conditions
- How: impact on other functions

3.3.1.1.2 Assumption

It is important to grasp the basic assumptions of the development on which the user story is based. These assumptions are usually generated at the beginning of the product concept test and in the early stage of the business analysis. Some technical and architectural assumptions will be made when the team estimates the story card. When our team cannot immediately get an answer to a question, we will make an assumption, and then the team will continue to move forward.

For example, a story card can have this assumption: the database table has been built, or the interface API has been completed or defined before development. Note that once an assumption is established, this assumption needs to be continuously monitored and verified. For example, we can arrange a research to verify the assumption. If it turns out to be not true, the story card needs to be reestimated, and the iteration plan needs to be adjusted accordingly.

Some common assumptions are as follows:

- Basic technical architecture or framework
- Whether third-party APIs or applications are available
- Some uncertain inputs or outputs

3.3.1.1.3 Nonfunctional Requirement

Each project should have a checklist of nonfunctional requirements. These requirements are usually scenarios of cross-functional modules built on a higher level of user stories. Every company should have a recommended nonfunctional requirements checklist. If not, I suggest to issue a standard exception handling specification as soon as possible.

It should be emphasized that some nonfunctional requirements can also be split into independent user story cards and arranged in a later iteration. However, when we write a user story, we should consider the relevant nonfunctional requirements, rather than considering it in later iterations. Failure to consider it in time may cause rework.

3.3.1.1.4 Constraint

Constraint refers to the constraint and boundary of a user story, and it highlights the functions that this user story will not do and cannot do. For example, we will not do some related functions in this user story, since these functions will be in another user story card, or we will not solve a related production environment bug in this user story. This gives other team members, such as testers, a clear scope dimension.

Some typical constraints need to include the following two aspects:

- **Internal constraint:** The functions should be contained in a user story card, but for some other reasons, they cannot be implemented for the time being. For example, there are mistakes in technical selection, or nonsupporting technical architecture. Users need to use these constrained functions until they take advantage of a large-scale refactoring opportunity to solve this problem by changing the technical architecture.
- **External constraint:** The functions should be contained in a user story card, but for some other reasons, they are split into another user card. Users need to have a temporary alternative, or a slightly worse experience, until the other user story is completed.

3.3.1.1.5 Y-Wireframe

Although the name is a Y-wireframe, here I use it to represent all the content related to the front end or user experience contained in a user story.

Broadly speaking, this part needs to include the following content:

- **User interaction process:** how users interact with the system
- **User experience design:** make sure the style, business process, information architecture, and navigation design of the page conform to the standards and logic
- **Device compatibility:** whether any users will use it on mobile devices
- **Browser compatibility:** why it needs to support IE8
- **Auxiliary:** how to make sure of ease of use in design
- **Interface design:** color matching and visual design

A typical Y-wireframe can be a prototype drawing on paper, or an electronic low-fidelity prototype drawn using some tools. It quickly calibrates everyone's understanding of the function by graphically functioning. For developers, a Y-wireframe can better demonstrate user interaction processes and allow end users to confirm availability early, so Y-wireframe is also necessary for a story card.

Whether true visual design can become part of a story card depends on whether the team has prepared design components early in development. To incorporate UI/UX design into each iteration, the team needs a design method to ensure of agile interactive user experience.

The purpose of the FANCY method is to help business analysts and project managers to better understand and systematically analyze requirements. When we need to decompose and refine a user story, we can use this method to split the user story or arrange communication with the local team. Eventually, our output will appear in Trello, JIRA, or other requirements management systems. Of course, the application purpose of these standardized methods is not to produce complex documents, nor to replace dialogue and communication. For an agile team, good communication across roles is an important factor for success.

3.3.1.2 Specification by Example (SBE)

Specification by Example (SBE) is a method of enhancing collaboration to determine requirements and business. By describing requirements with a method of replacing abstract descriptions with real examples, we can achieve the purpose of analyzing, developing, and testing throughout software functions. This method can be applied in the context of behavior-driven development (BDD), and is particularly successful for managing complex domain knowledge and complex business requirements and functional testing of large projects. Using real examples to describe requirements helps to complete high-quality automated tests.

If it is the first time to use SBE, I suggest not to express all acceptance conditions in the form of SBE, unless it is necessary to make further clarification.

SBE is not something new, but using this method to describe requirements is indeed a very thorough practice. This method has always been used for testing, sampling for each equivalence partitioning. When we execute test cases, we always use specific partial data or certain determined paths, because we cannot exhaust all data and scenarios.

With help of examples, people of any roles of team can understand the requirements better. Examples are a good way to communicate, because we can understand these examples without thinking.

The text is sometimes difficult to describe a requirement clearly. We have to adopt a better method decisively. Many times drawing pictures and examples can be used as a better method.

The following is an example of describing requirements in pure language. I wonder if you can understand the requirements without reading this user story for several times.

> The scenario covered by this requirement is how the system generates tax invoices when the sum of all man-hour cards in a project is zero within a charging cycle.
>
> When the financial system crosses months, an engineer's man-hour card will be automatically divided into two sub-cards by the system. If the engineer's work time card does not have charged work hours on the sub-card in the next month, the engineer will have a man-hour card with a total working hours of zero. If the project ends in the previous month, the people in the project do not work on the project in the following month, so the project will generate a tax invoice with zero total working hours in the following month.
>
> When the company issues tax invoices by month, this is a frequently encountered scenario where the project ends in the previous month in the man-hour card. In this case, the invoice in the following month is zero, and it cannot be successfully operated as an account receivable.
>
> If we do not include the zero-hour work card in the bill, there is no need to generate a tax invoice. Eventually, when generating project-level invoices, errors in accounts receivable caused by zero hours are avoided.

In general, the core idea of BDD is to reduce communication deviations and form requirements with examples rather than abstract descriptive language, so communication between teams or individuals will be faster and simpler. The advantage of doing so is that business analysts have enhanced their understanding of the technical challenges of business scenarios, and developers have a clearer understanding of the requirements and what they really want to develop. In addition, as a single source of information in the team, if there are any changes, everyone will know in time.

3.3.2 STANDARDIZATION OF TECHNOLOGY

It is very important for developers to name classes, method functions, and test code. Good naming habits are very helpful to other people on the team in understanding the code. Only other developers can easily understand the intention of the original designer, and subsequent changes to the code will be safer and reduce the guess and speculation of the code. For a distributed team that advocates shared code thinking, these naming conventions are the most basic and fundamental issues, and the first step is to reach consensus.

- **Class naming rules:** The naming of the test class and the tested class should be consistent. Usually, the name of the test class is "the name of the tested class + Test." For example, is the Game class is the tested class, then the test class is named "GameTest."
- **Method function naming rules:** In order to better distinguish the meaning of the method name, we advocate the use of Ruby-style naming methods, that is, use the underscore as a separator to separate each word, rather than the traditional camel-hump style of Java.

The test method should also express the business implications, and reflect the target function of the test, and should be clear and straightforward, so that the test class can become a document. The name of the test method can be long enough to clearly describe the business. It is recommended that the test method name begins with should, in which case the default subject is the class being tested. For example, in the example of guessing numbers, when we write a test NumberComparatorTest, the two methods of all right guessing and all wrong guessing are as follows:

```
@Testpublic void shouldreturn4A0Bwhentherearefournumbersguessedcorrectly()
//... }
@Testpublic void shouldreturn0A0Bwhenthereisnonumberguessedcorrectly()
//... }
```

The method here can be read as:

Game should return 4A0B when there are four numbers guessed correctly.
Game should return 0A0B when there is no number guessed correctly.
Apparently, each one is a natural language describing business rules.

Since we want to drive a method such as NumberComparator, then in the naming of the test method, we should reflect what data this method returns when it meets the conditions. When we use this unified method for naming tests, we can easily get a list of all test methods. This list looks like a document describing all the functions of this method. This document has a good effect on the technicians including developers and testers to understand the integrality of the test.

To achieve this, regular code reviews are essential. The code styles of different developers in a team are different, not to mention the code styles of offshore teams and local teams. Maintaining the same naming convention so that everyone can easily understand other people's code is our basic requirement, which is also a prerequisite for the "code sharing" agile specification. In addition to these basic specifications, when we implement some commonly used functions, the implementation methods commonly used in the industry are also what we need to consider when reviewing the code. Whenever we hear our developers say "This part of the code is written by Zhang," "How can I dare to change this part, it is written by Master Wang" or "I'm not good at this part," I feel a thump on my chest. Code review is a good way to become familiar with software architecture and understand software business logic.

Code review is so important, so how to implement a fast and effective code review meeting? By utilizing the code version management system, developers can enable everyone to see the part of their changes easily, or compare with the code before the change. They can explain their own ideas, the purpose of writing the code, and the business goals to be completed. For the currently popular development method with separate front-end and back-end, code review should also be conducted separately. During the code review process, be sure to record the problems found in the code, using post-it is a convenient way. For some technical task cards generated during the code review, we can directly put them in the backlog. After we have fixed the problems found in the code review, they can be verified again in the code review the next day, of course, we don't have to wait until the next day. Verification must be done, what is reflected here is not a question of trust or not, but a closed-loop theory that guarantees our improved quality after code review.

Generally, code review can take the following two ways:

- **Review the code submitted on the day at a fixed time and better time boxed.** Here we should emphasize the fixed duration, if the end time of the code review is not limited, the team will lack a sense of urgency and the efficiency will naturally decrease.
- **After completing a story card or part of functions, the team will review this part codes.** This method is helpful for others to understand the integrality of the function, but the uncertainty of time is not conducive to others to reasonably arrange their own plans to participate in this meeting. For distributed teams, this approach is unlikely to be implemented as a normal practice. However, for some important integration parts, it is possible to individually appoint a suitable time, and all participants will review the code together.

In addition to naming convention and code review, what else technical specifications do we need to pay attention to? Figure 3.12 is a specification of a team's code packaging and submission. The team should print out this specification and post it next to the display of continuous integration.

Pipeline: red, not submit

Build: failed, not overnight, fix or roll back

Run test before submission

Steps for submission:
1 Git status
2 Git diff
3 Git add
4 Git commit
5 Git pull - rebase
6 Run test
7 Check CI
8 Git push

FIGURE 3.12 Code packaging submission specification.

The problem that refactoring solves is to eliminate messy code. But when is the good time to refactor? Or refactor regularly? We often hear someone asks "Is there any story card for me? I have no card right now, what about I start refactoring right now." It seems that this is a last resort. We always emphasize initiative and the ability to do things proactively. When we feel something wrong in the code, the design and implementation of part of the code have a negative impact on the changes that continue to be on it. When the code is reviewed, everyone has a common view on this part of the code, then we can plan an action as soon as possible and appoint a right person to perform it.

USING TECHNICAL MEANS TO ENSURE EFFICIENCY

Even in small teams, communication and getting along within the team is often difficult, not to mention in distributed teams. However, in the world we live in, the communication of details determines the height that teamwork can achieve. The key to the success of distributed teams is to reduce the complexity of communication and assist them to focus on the truly valuable work instead of solving environmental problems and complicated deployment of problems. This is why Docker deserves our in-depth understanding. Docker has completely released the power of virtualization, and the environment has become part of the release content, which makes testing, deployment, operation, and maintenance efficient and easy.

In the process of learning, I used to think that container virtualization is just an extension of virtualization technology. Later, I learned that it solves not ordinary environmental problems, but more solves the problem of delivery and standardizes the delivery process. We can focus our attention on the needs that really need to be solved, rather than all kinds of environmental problems. Many colleagues who have used Docker found that the part that was originally coupled with the programming framework or environment is now standardized by Docker, so that developers of different languages, different frameworks, and different business scenarios can quickly realize their continuous integration and continuous delivery.

In order to achieve frequent integration, every developer is required to compile, package, and deploy all code every time they submit code to the central code base to ensure that deliverables can be produced. However, frequent integration only proves whether deliverables can be obtained with each submission, but what we really need to know is "how about the quality of this deliverable." If there is a problem with the deliverable, the code that caused the problem is either rolled back or fixed. Of course, such tasks can also be done manually, but the characteristic of manual work is that it is error-prone and time-consuming, so it needs to be automated. In order to do continuous integration practice, it is necessary to write an automated build script to automatically build and run some automated test suites.

3.3.3 STANDARDIZATION OF TESTING

3.3.3.1 The Pyramid Principle for Test

Unit test is the basis for the Test Automation Pyramid. Therefore, it should be the largest and most basic part of a reliable test automation strategy. Automated unit test is great, it can provide programmers with specific error data. For example, if the automated unit test report says "there is a bug on line 86," then the programmer may actually find this bug near line 86. In contrast, the tester can only tell you "there is a problem in the process of retrieving member records from the database," it means you have to find this bug in more than 1000 lines of code. The advantage of automated unit testing is that it can greatly reduce the location of bugs. In addition, because it is usually written in the same language as system development, programmers are more suitable for writing unit tests.

But this does not mean that we do not need to test functional features. What we need is to find a suitable method to avoid performing the interface-based test, this is the origin of the service layer testing in the Test Automation Pyramid. In this test method we use, "service" refers to the application's response to an input or set of inputs, like the two services of multiplication and division in calculator. Service layer test is to test the application services independent of the user interface. Therefore, if we want to test more than a dozen multiplication test cases, we do not use the calculator user interface but through the service layer to execute these test cases. Compared with executing the same test cases at the user level, this is more effective and less cumbersome.

We want to do as little automated test as possible based on the interface. Why? Because automated test of interfaces is more fragile, expensive, and time-consuming. Interface-based test is usually necessary, but it should be used in small amounts. Service layer test fills the gap between unit test and interface test, and meets the team's automated test needs with less effort and cost.

3.3.3.2 Manage Test Cases and Data

The overall management of test cases shall be in line with the management of requirements, and the update of requirements is accompanied with the update of test cases. We should define the priority and types of test cases, so as to ensure that these cases can be used in different test phases, such as the scope of integration tests and regression test after packaging.

The test team should regularly review the use cases of the test. In addition to focusing on what has been tested, we must also understand what it cannot guarantee. According to my experience, there may be surprises when discussing what is not guaranteed.

If the two parties use different data for integration, the data problem will be very painful to solve, so it is necessary to plan the data management of the distributed team to isolate the problems caused by data.

Whenever we need all parties to collaborate to input data, we must define the data format in advance.

3.3.3.3 Manage Bug Reports

Even if Excel (the simplest spreadsheet tool) is used to track and manage our bug list, it generally contains the following information: Which bugs have we fixed until this update? Which bugs are newly discovered? Which bugs are serious and which ones are general? Which bugs need further confirmation? Who is tracking these bugs? When we re-examine these issues the next time, we need to distinguish the new bugs from these remaining ones.

If iterative development is adopted, users on the customer side may start to test early. At this time, it should be noted that the problems they report are of great variety, or simply report a function does not work properly. We not only need to provide them with templates for reporting bugs in advance, but also provide them with more complete information.

A complete software defect description should include the following:

- The environment in which bugs are discovered
- Frequency of bugs
- Steps of reproduction
- Impact
- Use clear signs to indicate the order of the operation steps (number sequence, arrow guidance, etc.)

If there are attachments such as screenshots/logs with errors, they must be pasted/uploaded. This information is more intuitive for those who fixed the bugs.

For better bug description, please refer to the following conditions as appropriate:

- Clear isolation conditions, accurately describing the bugs only occur under specific conditions
- There shall be a summary of the bugs
- Whether there are similar bugs in other scenarios
- Try to describe only one bug in one report
- Do no use any critical language

3.3.3.4 How to Rate a Bug?

After the bug report is completed, rating a bug is also an important task, it determines whether high-priority bugs can be fixed in a timely manner, and whether low-priority bugs have wasted the valuable time of the team. For distributed teams, it is necessary to ensure that everyone works on basis of the same standards. The evaluation of a bug usually depends on two dimensions, one is severity and the other is priority. The severity level reflects the impact of the fault caused by the bug on the software product, as shown in Table 3.6; all the indicators are specified by the tester. Priority refers to the urgency of the bugs that must be fixed, as shown in Table 3.7, and the indicators are specified by the bug allocator (project manager/test manager).

Each bug must be marked with its own functional module, just as every story card has its own functional module. This is helpful for the team that locates the bug quickly, and it is also an important indicator for defining whether a functional module is completed. We need to maintain the configuration of the task management system so that the results used by all users can be more accurate and better guide the work of the entire team.

After the rating, these indicators can guide our follow-up work from the following aspects:

- **Agree with the customer on the conditions for going online or the conditions for applying the patch.** In this way, when we get the bug list, we don't need to discuss the bugs one by one, but just have them filtered according to the conditions.
- **Analyze quality trends.** Before the software is released, serious bugs should show a downward trend until they reach zero.
- **Expose areas of poor quality.** We can know which functional module has the most unstable quality, fix the bugs in a more targeted manner, and easily grasp the key points.

TABLE 3.6
Severity of Bugs

Level of Severity	Explanation
Critical	The error caused a computer crash, a product crash, and the system hangs and becomes inoperable.
Major	There are major functions not implemented, or a function cannot be run, and there is no alternative.
Minor	Whenever a function is unworkable, there is an alternative.
Trivial	The error is superficial or tiny, such as prompt information is not accurate and friendly, typos, page layout, or rare faults has almost no effect on the function, and the product and its attributes can continue to use
Nice to have	Constructive comments or suggestions.

TABLE 3.7
Priority of Bugs

Priority	Explanation
Urgent	Prevent further development activities of relevant developers, immediately have it fixed, and prevent further testing of closely related functions.
Very high	Must be modified before release.
High	Must be modified, but not necessarily immediately, determined to be modified before the end of a specific milestone event.
Medium	It should be modified if time permits.
Low	Allow no modification.

3.3.3.5 Test Strategy

The test strategy/quality assurance plan is the issue that we need to consider carefully at the beginning of the project. This plays a directional role in the quality culture established by the offshore team. Generally, our delivered software does not have a contractual quality indicator. As a delivery party, our quality commitment to customers should be implicit, that is to say, it is included by default. Therefore, in the process of cooperation, customers often ask us questions like this: some directly ask us "do you have any test plans? ." Some care about quality may ask us "how can you ensure the quality of products?" The former question often comes from a traditional customer team that adopts a waterfall development model and runs a test at a relatively independent stage. What he wants is a plan for testing stage. The latter problem is often from the customers with agile development background. We have to explain to them how the test runs through the entire development process, everyone will be responsible for testing, and how to realize built-in and built-out quality.

These contents are recorded in documents, which can make customers feel more comfortable. Customers can review the team's test strategy, and end-to-end test cases also require customer review.

A formal test strategy needs to include the following:

- **Development and test process:** A good process promotes the guarantee of both built-in and built-out quality. During the overall process, there are clarified actions and participants at different stages, preparation and maintenance of the test environment, bug tracking process, the principle of bug prioritization, and the statistics on the number of bugs.
- **Quality-oriented practices:** TDD, code review, development environment acceptance, automated test, and exploratory test.
- **Scope of test:** According to the different nature of each test, such as normal function acceptance test, smoke test, regression test, we are able to define the scope of each test. Doing so is conducive to balancing human resources to achieve the greatest test effect, especially regression test.
- **Security test:** This is an area that is receiving more and more attention. Customers in finance, insurance, and other fields often have more specific requirements for security test.
- **Performance test:** Whoever we are in the team, tester or developer, we must always pay attention to whether there are potential performance problems in the daily function development process. As a developer, we can better understand the code implementation, so we can discover some data processing bottlenecks from an implementation perspective. Testers need to fully understand the business usage scenarios and find some scenarios that require performance monitoring from a business perspective.
- **Prioritize test objects:** The determination of the priority of the test objects is conducive to the final determination of the priority of the bugs. Since the priority of the function is also one of the factors that determine the priority of the bugs.
- **Criteria for system going online:** Define the type and number of bugs that can be tolerated for going online.

3.3.4 STANDARDIZED AUTOMATED TEST

Automated test is a prerequisite for continuous integration and continuous delivery. If this is not possible, we will spend a lot of energy on nonbusiness code. In the process of doing automated test, I have encountered the following problems:

- It is hard to read the test code written by another team or someone else.
- Is this really the code we wrote before?
- We have already implemented the test code method they used.
- New functions developed invalidate the test code.

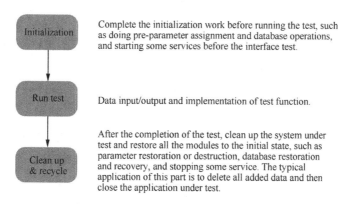

Complete the initialization work before running the test, such as doing pre-parameter assignment and database operations, and starting some services before the interface test.

Data input/output and implementation of test function.

After the completion of the test, clean up the system under test and restore all the modules to the initial state, such as parameter restoration or destruction, database restoration and recovery, and stopping some service. The typical application of this part is to delete all added data and then close the application under test.

FIGURE 3.13 Automated test process.

For the above problems, specific solutions are as follows:

(1) **Standardize the test process:** Standardize the test process to ensure that each test case is independent and does not affect each other. We need to make each test follow the process shown in Figure 3.13.

(2) **Standardize the input and output of test.** It is better to carry out centralized management of data input, so that it is not easy to cause any omission or inconsistent data types.

(3) **Modular expansion.** Considering the reusability of test code, when continuously accumulating test cases, reuse existing methods as much as possible to reduce future maintenance costs.

3.3.5 SUMMARY

Normative approach means generality in this industry, which is also the cornerstone for the collaboration between teams and something that can be directly used for reference. Of course, these norms are not necessarily universal. We still need to combine the characteristics of our team to find the norms that our team should have, so that our team can focus on valuable and creative things. Rather than spend day-to-day communication and quarreling over things beyond value.

Normativity often means automation and routinization. The purpose of these normative work is not to stifle creativity, but to reduce communication costs, improve efficiency, and avoid "reinventing the wheel" without affecting creativity. The best job is definitely manual work, this is the case with cars, since all racers are driving the cars with manual gears; the same is true for driving ships and airplanes. Although there is a convenient automatic system, it is still necessary to switch to manual mode at critical moments. This is true for the landing of ships and the takeoff and landing of aircraft.

4 Application of Visualization

The following game reveals the changes that may occur after the information is transmitted through language. We can also try this game in the team, and feel the degree of change after a message is transmitted, and the difference between language and graphics.

(1) Find a graphic design related to user interaction in the project, and let a team member describe the design in words. Others will independently complete the requirement restoration of this interactive design, and then compare everyone's understanding with the original design for any deviation.

(2) Find a text description with a slightly more complex logic in the project, let a team member show it to all other members in the form of a table or a graph, everyone independently describes their own understanding, and then compare their understanding with the original design for any deviation.

In the above game, the middle team member completes the information transmission. We can compare the difference between using text as a means of transmission and using graphics as a means of transmission.

Of course, if the means of transfer is consistent with the description of the initial information, use text to transfer text and use graphics to transfer graphics, so that information will not be lost. However, there may be deviations in understanding, and deviations in understanding of words are usually greater than deviations in understanding of graphics.

If graphics are used to transfer all types of initial information, supplemented by simple text descriptions, errors in the entire information transfer process can be greatly reduced. This is also the purpose of this chapter. In this chapter, we will focus on the method of visualization used in distributed teams. Of course, we cannot apply visualization to all places, because too much pursuit of visualization will increase our communication costs. We recommend using this method when communicating complex (for text) or important information. We will also learn in this chapter what is beyond the reach of language and text, and why we should apply visualization somewhere, and we hope that in the end, we can naturally apply visualization in the right place at the right time.

I was also confused in early years, especially when I faced with choices. Because in the project, in the distributed team, we may not know whether there are other options, which one to choose, why we should choose this one instead of others. Therefore, I will introduce some basic principles of methods, tools, and means, but I will focus on the comparison between them and the analysis of their advantages and disadvantages, so that we can be more confident when making a choice, and reply customers more convincingly when they ask.

4.1 PURPOSE OF VISUALIZATION

Now when it comes to visualization, many people think about big data –visualization of data. Data visualization converts abstract massive data into easily-perceived data familiar to ordinary users, because users can more easily understand the meaning of graphics. In this way, the data indicators in the system are not only private items that administrators can snoop with specific technical means or tools, making them more intuitive and the data more meaningful. Users can also put forward requirements from their own perspectives, personalize the desired data representation form, and better reflect user value. The goal of letting end users put forward requirements is indispensable for graphics. Without it, end users usually don't know what they can get, because what the data administrator gives is basically conclusive, the user cannot think about them.

In addition to visualizing data, we also need to pay attention to whether we can use a visual method to help distributed teams improve the efficiency and effectiveness of communication in the case of team collaboration, especially the latter. In the teams I have worked with, the main purposes of visualization are as follows:

- Show project status
- Eliminate deviations in understanding requirements
- Feedback on the software quality
- Improve test coverage of code
- Describe complex business processes
- Understand the project overall view
- Help the team think with mind maps

4.1.1 SHOW PROJECT STATUS

To show project status is mainly to discover the risks in the project. Here, the main risk indicates the progress, that is, whether the offshore team can deliver the work within the agreed time. We use Kanban to promote and coordinate work in the team, and track the project progress every day. We use burndown chart and burnup chart to predict the delivery date, including the progress risk is found in the process and measures are taken to continuously evaluate the effect of adjustments.

4.1.1.1 Project Kanban (Physical Kanban and Electronic Kanban)

Kanban allows everyone to understand what the team is doing and planning to do in a delivery cycle, and who is the executor of each task at each stage. Kanban has high transparency of information and status.

The roles of team members are different, and they have different perspectives to look at problems. Especially in distributed teams, it is unrealistic to transmit information to everyone accurately through traditional means. Using a physical or electronic Kanban to transfer information is both accurate and fast, and it can prevent information from being missed. Kanban, as a simple and intuitive existence, unifies everyone's knowledge and instructs the team to work towards a common goal.

In a distributed team, we can only learn about the progress of other teams through the electronic Kanban. This is especially meaningful for distributed teams with high interdependence. We will pay attention to whether other teams arrange the story cards we rely on into their iterations, and the status of these story cards in the remote team iterations. We can use this information to estimate when the story cards will be delivered and how much workload can be delivered in this iteration.

Generally speaking, Kanban mainly has the purpose of continuously improving the work of the team, showing the team's work process, limiting the quantity of Work in Process (WIP), shortening the cycle of story cards from planning to delivery, and so on.

4.1.1.2 Burndown Chart

The burndown chart reveals the trend of the project's entire delivery cycle and can support the prediction of the project's completion date. It graphically shows the relationship between remaining workload (vertical axis) and time (horizontal axis). Ideally, the graph would be a downward curve, and as the remaining workload decreases, "burn" to zero. The burndown chart usually appears in the iteration report, which can be used as a public view to provide project team members and customers with work progress.

The burndown chart is very helpful to the team because it focuses on the remaining workload. As the iteration progresses, the trend it forms provides a basis for predicting the end time of the project and helps us track the project progress.

For customers, the burndown chart is also highly valued. In addition to tracking the project progress, they can learn about the team's development speed from the burndown chart. However, to ensure the accuracy of the data for the development speed, the way of the team to respond to changes in requirements during iterations is to ensure that the backlog could remain constant with the total workload delivered for each iteration plan. For example, if a customer temporarily adds a new requirement, if it cannot be scheduled to the next iteration cycle, it is necessary to remove a task of equal workload from this iteration, together with the same workload with the lowest priority from the backlog.

For distributed teams that adopt agile development practice, each team can draw its own burndown chart independently. Although the standard for estimating the workload of each team is not consistent, but after the workload is divided by the team's delivery speed, the calculated date is relatively accurate. In this way, we can coordinate the common online time from a higher level, and play a strong role in supervising the teams that are behind the development schedule.

4.1.1.3 Burnup Chart

Whether to use the burndown chart or the burnup chart in the project depends on what the customer and the team want from it. The burndown chart focuses on how much work is left in the project, while the burnup chart tells us how much work has been completed and how much is the current total work. Both of these charts are very common in agile development teams or Scrum.

Compared with the delivery time, customers pay more attention to the content of delivery, then the burnup chart is the best choice. The most important purpose of the burnup chart is to flexibly respond to frequent changes in requirements, and even to adjust the requirements to determine the release date at any time. Therefore, the curve of the burnup chart cannot accurately reflect the development speed of the team.

In general, visualization methods such as burndown chart and burnup chart, although they can also be regarded as data visualization in essence, they cannot be separated from the dimension of time. This dimension (horizontal axis) can reveal the time and location of the problem. We can therefore make better use of these charts, for example, to find some improved methods based on the gap between actual results and expected results, or to make some adjustments to future forecasts.

4.1.2 ELIMINATE DEVIATIONS IN UNDERSTANDING REQUIREMENTS

With more and more emphasis on user experience nowadays, we have invested tremendous energy in the design of software interfaces and the design to enhance user experience. More and more front-end development workload has also created the independent position of front-end development engineer. Wireframes can help teams, designers, and front-end development engineers communicate intuitively, especially complex designs.

- **In a distributed team where customers tell us what to do.** We have to use high-fidelity prototypes to communicate requirements, and the content is refined to all aspects, such as the size and position of the control, which will give the specific requirements for pixel value. Since customers have extremely high requirements for user experience, the user experience expert in the customer team usually helps us design the final page effect in their overall style. Such a prototype diagram can accurately express the intention of the customer-side designer. Our team needs to strictly follow the prototype diagram to complete our work.

- **In a distributed team where we tell customers what to do.** Wireframe is a low-fidelity design prototype, which can quickly express the designer's intention, and the details can be left to the development team to deal with. This situation shows that customers trust us, and our team usually has its own user experience expert. In the remote cooperation mode that requires frequent communication, this is a very efficient and low-cost communication method.

The purpose of wireframes is to create a prototype of the page at the minimum cost, and to allow rapid and repeated testing of the design, and finally to quickly collect feedback. The key to wireframes is how the web page or app works and displays, not the visual beauty, so as to avoid the misunderstanding of details in the early stages of project development. Wireframes can be delivered to customers for review early in the project, reducing the designer's workload of repeated modifications during the design phase.

In the field of mobile development, the application of wireframes is particularly widespread. There are many tools on the market to help designers. The advantage is that you can easily see the overall effect of the software by focusing only on the parts you design.

For distributed teams, wireframes are an indispensable tool for daily use. If our team needs to collaborate with another team to solve a problem, we can draw a wireframe to express the idea before writing the code. It is not too late to use wireframes to reach agreement.

Therefore, the main purpose of wireframes is to display the content layout of the page, user journey, functional weights, and the way of communicating information on the interface during the interaction design process. For example, when the password is wrong, how to prompt the users' next action.

4.1.3 Feedback on the Software Quality

4.1.3.1 Regular Bug Report

The report determines the current level of software quality based on the two dimensions of bug severity and incidence trend. These data need to be obtained from the bugs submitted by testers in the bug management system. Many bug management systems can automatically generate the view shown in Figure 4.1.

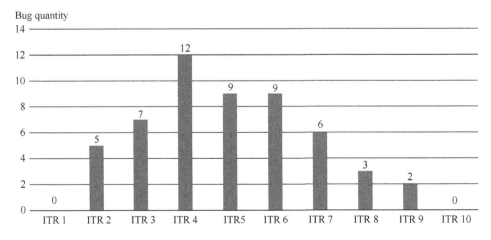

FIGURE 4.1 Trend of bugs.

4.1.3.2 Software Product Performance Monitoring Curve

Track each performance index, observe the trend of performance decline at any time, and adjust the design to make performance to the normal level in time. For customers, keeping abreast of the product performance indicators of the remote team is critical to successfully releasing software on time. If you do not continue to pay attention to performance, you may have to make structural changes before the release to fix performance problems.

4.1.4 IMPROVE TEST COVERAGE OF CODE

Configure a tool for statistical unit test coverage in continuous integration environment, and any user who can log in to the deployment pipeline will see these data. We can also set a technical indicator in continuous integration, for example, any submission that causes a reduction in test coverage will be rejected. This can ensure that the standard of the team's automated testing will not decrease with the project progress. In fact, the projects we have done usually increase the test coverage in stages to pursue higher test integrity. By using different tools, the data given may be different. Choosing a reliable tool based on the team's own technology stack will improve the accuracy of the data.

4.1.5 DESCRIBE COMPLEX BUSINESS PROCESSES

The flow chart is a good indicator for describing complex business details. When developers read code and testers read requirements, they may feel difficult to clearly understand some complex logic. Instead of struggling to explore, we might as well find answers from flowcharts. Looking at the code in conjunction with the flow chart, it will often have a multiplier effect. The flow chart can indeed reduce a lot of unnecessary communication, which is especially meaningful for distributed teams who are always facing communication challenges.

The flow chart can better show the relationship between modules, such as the navigation function of the software. It is a display of the overall business process, and can also show a set of strict business processes, such as the company invoice review process, which shows the roles, timing, and output of all people who need to participate in this process.

The business panoramic process, that is, maintaining an overall business process, can provide guidance for each team member to master the overall process of the project, such as the flow of data. The flow chart can be simple (as shown in Figure 4.2) or complex (as shown in Figure 4.3).

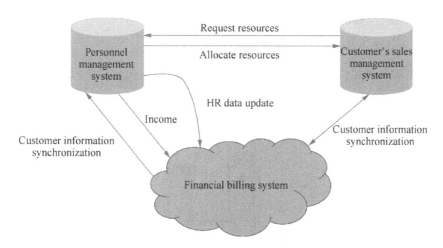

FIGURE 4.2 Simple business process.

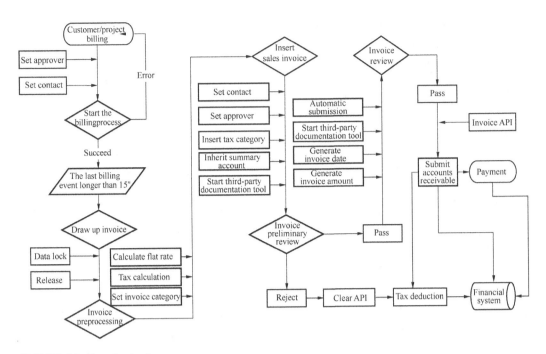

FIGURE 4.3 Complex business process.

4.1.6 UNDERSTAND THE PROJECT OVERALL VIEW

The story card overall view, which I call a tree diagram, shows the various functional modules of the story card level and the hierarchical relationship of the functions. The ordinary flow chart embodies the understanding of business logic. During the operation of the project, we also need to intuitively show the team from the integrality of the project function. We generally divide all business requirements of a project into large functional modules, and each functional module can continue to be split into story cards. Since the agile development model requires value-first and fast online, our online functions always enable the high-priority story cards within every function to go online first.

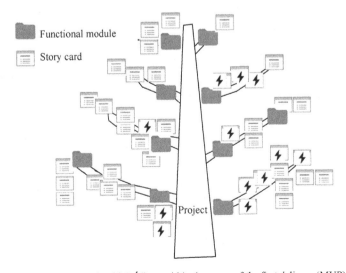

Note: the story cards with "⚡" are within the scope of the first delivery (MVP)

FIGURE 4.4 Relationship between tree function groups and functions.

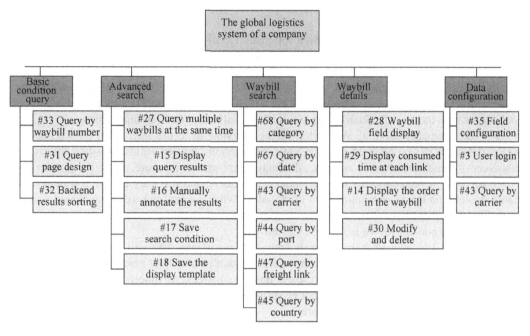

FIGURE 4.5 Requirements split function groups and functions.

Therefore, in many cases, the functions of the functional modules that have been online have not been completely delivered.

Figure 4.4 shows a tree diagram of manual maintenance. In this business requirements tree, each branch represents a large functional module. This large functional module can continue to be split into small functional modules and story cards. The process of completing the entire project is not centered on the functional module, which means the story card on one branch is done after another, but on the business, the priority story cards on different branches are completed first, since they have the greatest business value.

Figure 4.5 shows the structural diagram that can be given by project management software such as Trello or JIRA. It is just another manifestation of the requirements tree.

Referring to Figure 4.5, in each functional group, a part of the functions are put online at the first (such as #33, #31, #15, #68, #67, #43, #28, #14, #35 and #3), there are some story cards with relatively low priority not added into the backlog. Using this diagram or this form of presentation, we can intuitively recognize the completed and uncompleted functions, so as to avoid the omission of functions. At the same time, it has a good auxiliary role in weighing whether to deliver the complete function as soon as possible or the function with relatively high user value. It is only the experienced team that pays attention to reduce the quantity and life cycle of WIP.

4.1.7 HELP THE TEAM THINK WITH MIND MAPS

During meetings, especially when distributed teams are present, using mind maps to make meeting records can achieve multipronged results. The mind map can guide all people to divergent thinking, which is the function of the mind map itself. Since everyone can see the same mind map on the shared screen, it can prevent us from being distracted when we are in a meeting, and everyone's attention is on this growing map. People with language barriers can also follow the discussion according to the hints on the mind map. Mind maps can improve the content and structure of the discussion at meetings, and ordinary meeting minutes may make people forget the association of the issues they talked about after the meeting. As a product of discussion at a meeting, this structured knowledge contains more information, and as time goes by, the rate of information loss is relatively low.

4.2 VISUALIZATION METHOD

Let's look at the simplest example of visual application in a team.

Although the scale of some projects is not large, there are many places for integration. I once experienced a project that often required other teams to collaborate on problem investigation and integration test. When another team was in the US, we were not sure who could help us that day. So sometimes e-mails and messages will not get a reply for a long time, because the person we are looking for took the day off. Such a simple little thing will haunt us from time to time.

How did we finally solve it? We started asking everyone to record their leave on Wiki in text, which did solve the problem of missing leave information between teams, avoiding the sudden discovery of someone's absence one day. Although the information is there, it is in the form of text, which needs to be read carefully to understand it accurately, and it is very easy to misunderstand. Later, we felt that it was very unintuitive to record on Wiki as a list, and we implemented a visual leave form for the team, also known as the team calendar.

Compare the content shown in Figures 4.6 and 4.7.

From Figure 4.6, we cannot immediately know how many man-days will be missing in the next iteration. First, iterations are calculated in weeks. We don't know how much productivity will be reduced each week. Secondly, we don't know how much weekend time is included in the leave period. When valuable information cannot be displayed visually, laziness will make us ignore this information, and Figure 4.7 is much clearer.

Ideally, the mail system we use can manage leave well. For example, when we set a vacation in Google Calendar, others can check the free time and busy time of participants when sending meeting invitation e-mails. This makes it easy to find a time period when all stakeholders are free.

4.2.1 SHOWING PROJECT STATUS: KANBAN

Kanban, as a proper noun, refers to a bulletin board that can be seen by everyone on the production line and demonstrates the status of the production line. People use it to reduce the number of WIPs, shorten their production cycle on the assembly line, find bottlenecks on the production line, and then continuously improve the processes on the production line. If expanding into the field of software development, people can call Kanban an iterative state wall or task board. The purpose of using Kanban is also similar. Kanban is concerned with the delivery process of the team within an iterative range. In the Scrum mode, this process is an sprint. In this process, Kanban helps us track the status of each split story card, tells us that the team has a bottleneck in a certain period of time, gives a signal that the story card is ready to be pulled, and encourages the team to work towards a goal (the goal is in an iteration cycle, all the story cards planned to be delivered are moved to the online state).

In general, a simple Kanban is like the one shown in Figure 4.8. Its purpose is to clearly tell the user the status of each task.

```
Team Leave Plan:
-----------------------------------
Chicago team:
Greg: July 28-Aug 3

Tyler: July 1

Beijing team:
Zhengping: July 16 -July 26
```

FIGURE 4.6 Text leave record.

JULY						
Sunday	Monday	Tuesday	Wednesday	Thursday	Friday	Saturday
					1	2
					Tyler	
3	4	5	6	7	8	9
10	11	12	13	14	15	16
17	18	19	20	21	22	23
	Zhengping	Zhengping	Zhengping	Zhengping	Zhengping	
24	25	26	27	28	29	30
	Zhengping	Zhengping		Greg	Greg	
31	1	2	3	4	5	6
	Greg	Greg	Greg			

FIGURE 4.7 Calendar leave record.

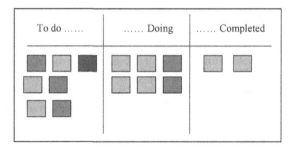

FIGURE 4.8 The simplest Kanban.

In the field of software development, the Kanban we use is usually shown in Figure 4.9: There are more swim lanes on the wall. When a lot of story cards are piled up in the development swim lanes, QA is often in an idle state, and we can know where the current team's bottleneck is. When a story card moves to the "To do..." state, it means that it can be pulled into the following process. So, Kanban is a visual workflow that records the "liquidity" of all tasks.

Let's first create a typical Kanban wall.

According to the typical development activities of the team within an iteration, it is divided into several swimlanes, such as "to be developed," "being developed," "to be tested," "being tested," "test completed," etc. At the beginning of the iteration, we will put the story cards planned to be completed in this iteration into the "to be developed" column. When the developer receives the task, he moves the story card he received from "to be developed" to "being developed," and pastes a small

Backlog	Being analyzed	To be developed	Being developed	To be tested	Being tested	Test completed	Customer acceptance	To be released	Released

FIGURE 4.9 Common swimlane in Kanban.

note with his name. When he has finished the development, he moves the story card to the "to be tested" column. When testers see that there is a story card to be tested in this column, they will take one and move it to "being test" to start the test of this user story. After the test is completed, move the story card to the "test completed" column. If the tester discovers a dug, he can use a red card to write down the bug and put it in the "to be developed" column. On the status wall, in addition to user stories and bugs, there will be some tasks that do not directly generate business value, such as refactoring or setting up a test environment. These three types of tasks are recorded with a card different from the color of the story card and placed on the status wall for unified management.

In this way, our Kanban wall can be used. At the beginning, we can think of the above scenarios, so that we can take the first step as soon as possible. Only by using it as soon as possible, we can find problems in use, and then continuously improve the Kanban wall to make it better serve the team.

When the tester found a bug, we created a red bug card and put it in the "to be developed" column. But how can we deal with the story cards still being tested? We can continue to test the remaining scenarios, if there are other bugs, we will keep creating a red bug card. Finally, we will find that story cards with unrepaired bugs do not belong to any swimlane of the current Kanban wall. We can draw an area in the lower part of the "being tested" column to temporarily store this type of card. After all the bugs are fixed, the tester needs to test the story card again.

The Kanban will be used like this day after day, the team will continue to improve the Kanban wall to make it more adapt to the team's usage habits. As long as we always follow its core philosophy, that is, let all team members know the plan and progress of this iteration in real time, under this premise, the team can freely develop its creativity.

Any team can build an iterative status wall, use it to reflect the progress of a certain iteration plan and tasks, and can design their own Kanban wall based on their own situation. Although I have seen many unique Kanban walls, the basic attributes are the same, and the adjustments are made according to the customers' concerns or the characteristics of the cooperative offshore team. For example, some customers are concerned about the speed of delivery, we must simplify the process as much as possible (that is, the number of swimlanes is as small as possible), the minimum swimlanes are shown in Figure 4.8. If customers have strict quality requirements, we will add more stringent links to promote quality built-in, such as brainstorming before development, desk check after development, automated test acceptance, and performance index review. For teams that are simultaneously transiting to agile development in the delivery process, they shall add a link for agile practice verification, such as user story-level code review.

We can feel the simplicity and ease of use of Kanban Wall, but there are also many doubts that the team has experienced.

Doubt 1: Many Kanbans start with "to be developed," and the state of the requirements before this stage does not seem to receive much attention. Usually, it is the stage of business analysis before development is ready, including "backlog" and "in analysis." What is the value of these two states on the Kanban wall to the team? Is it the project manager who cares about such things as backlog? Do developers and testers need to pay attention? To answer these questions, we first need to declare that the requirements are not the analysts' own business, but the participation of all the team. If there is interaction with a third party, the relevant personnel of the third-party team also need to review our requirements. Therefore, to improve requirements from the perspective of different people has a positive meaning for the correct delivery of requirements. For a self-managed team, we can't wait for the required function to be handed over to us to consider it, but to review its impact on later stages when it is just ready.

Developers can help business analysts from a technical perspective. Choose a reasonable plan to reduce the cost of development or avoid the weakening of software stability. Testers can improve the requirements from the happy path and sad path to reduce the lack of requirements. But what is the value to another distributed team? Understand the plan of the cooperative team, could improve the level of collaboration, reduce waiting and misjudgment in collaboration, and thus reduce waste.

Therefore, the deep problem reflected by the importance of each team on the requirements stage of the Kanban wall is when the team starts to pay attention to the requirements and how much attention is paid. The business analysts of each team will analyze the story card or more of the next iteration plan in advance to ensure that each team has enough work to do. Before the new iteration begins, these cards are prepared according to priority, and demanding developers and testers can go to the online electronic wall system to learn about these story cards in advance.

Doubt 2: Notice the status of block in Kanban. If our work is hindered by the work of another team, then we need to enable them to see the block in real time. Motivate this team to give us their status every day, that is, let them realize clearly that we have a job depending on them. Give them clear information so that this work has an accurate priority in their team. After all, they have priority settings that are considered for their own team.

Doubt 3: How can such a simple tool help us eliminate waste and solve problems in project management? With it, the team has a common goal and a common compliance process. Every time the flow of story cards is a signal of the completion of a job or the start of a new job, it is like an invisible hand guiding the team forward. Statistics such as Cycle Time and the quantity of WIPs are available on Kanban, and these data can also improve our current work, such as reducing the "inventory" function.

Doubt 4: The help of the iterative status wall to the team is that it serves as a tool for visualizing the workflow, telling us all the WIP story cards intuitively. The iterative status wall does not guarantee that the story card to go online as soon as possible, it can only supervise, remind, and highlight problems. So which practices have played a role in reducing WIP and WIP life cycle?

Doubt 5: Do distributed teams still need to maintain their own physical Kanban wall? Regarding intuitiveness, no tool is comparable to the physical wall. We build this physical wall in the simplest way, first of all, find a white wall that the team members can see when they look up or find a whiteboard, the tools needed are also simple, including plasticine, cards or sticky notes, and whiteboard pens.

This subsection shows the use process of the basic physical Kanban wall. If it is a distributed team, this process will be slightly different. In distributed teams, we must first maintain an electronic

Kanban wall, which needs to be synchronized with the physical Kanban wall of each team in real time. The work of synchronization seems small, but if we do not update the electronic Kanban wall in time, the remote team can only read our outdated status information every day, especially when standing at the meeting, they will feel confused and unhappy. Furthermore, the Kanban wall of distributed teams can add some integrated status bars or status bars that are mutually reviewed.

4.2.2 SHOWING PROJECT STATUS: BURNDOWN CHART AND BURNUP CHART

Frankly speaking, the burndown chart has already become a standard configuration for agile projects. The burndown chart can let the team know the remaining workload before the cut-off time in a tracking period. Through this visual method, the risks are displayed as early as possible, so that each team can take timely improvement measures. And after taking improvement measures, the burndown chart can continue to track the effect of the improvement.

For a product stakeholder, it is part of their normal task to analyze information about the team's work progress. If it is an agile team or a Scrum team, the burndown chart or the burnup chart is a good helper for analyzing the progress. It can intuitively tell us some problems, such as changes in requirement scope and whether the development speed has deviated from the plan. When these trends have just emerged, we can detect them on the charts, and then organize discussions immediately to figure out improvement means. At the same time, these charts help customers or managers build confidence in the timely delivery of offshore teams by showing the completion status and progress trends of the project.

4.2.2.1 Burndown Chart

Burndown chart is better known as "iterative residual trend chart." It is the chart showing the total remaining time of all stories (or split tasks) in each iteration, which gradually decreases as the iteration progresses. In the burndown chart, the total number of story points delivered by the team is fixed. Sometimes some teams use the remaining time as the vertical axis, but more teams tend to use the remaining story points as the vertical axis. If the burndown chart takes a sprint as a cycle, these workloads are the amount determined at the beginning of the iteration, which is also a characteristic of adopting the Scrum working method. If an overall delivery cycle is used as a cycle, it is the workload determined at the start of the project, which is also a characteristic of the Kanban working method, that is, the overall delivery volume is fixed, but the delivery volume per iteration is not fixed.

Since the burndown chart is a statistics of the remaining time, we can actually infer the approximate progress and trend of the current work through the chart when the delivery capacity is kept constant. The customer team can use this chart to follow the progress of the offshore team's development in real time, make right decisions, and anticipate risks and adjust plans accordingly. Therefore, the information that the burndown chart can give, coupled with its intuitiveness, is undoubtedly very attractive to customers. It is generally believed that the burndown chart is very simple, and each team is drawing such chart, but have we considered the following issues before we started?

- What data are we going to burn, why choose this type of data?
- Does the vertical axis use hours or story card points?
- Are the data collected accurate? How to guarantee?
- Is there any agreement when distributed teams draw their own burndown chart?
- How to interpret a burndown chart?

We need to understand what we should do with it. Many people think of it as a tool to measure the speed of development. In fact, it can only reflect the speed to a certain extent. Since we estimate the points of story card based on the difficulty level, not according to the workload. If we use the steepness of the curve to evaluate the team's delivery speed, it will mislead the team and may force the

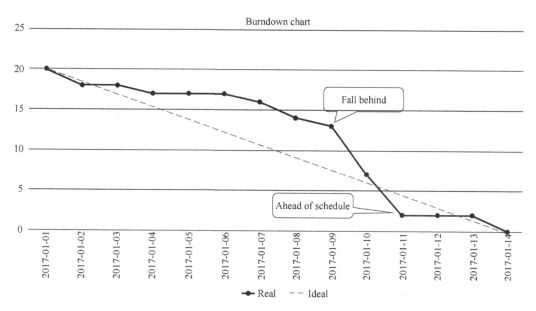

FIGURE 4.10 Theoretical curve and actual curve in burndown chart.

team to disrupt the priority of the requirement story delivery in order to obtain a good-looking curve, which seems to put the cart before the horse.

Based on the burndown curve, imagine a theoretical smooth line from the upper left corner to the lower right corner. In fact, we can draw this virtual line on the burndown chart. This virtual line is actually the theoretical position corresponding to each day or week according to the process of the plan under the theoretical situation. We can compare the actual burndown line with this theoretical line to measure the project progress every day. If the actual line is higher than the theoretical line, it means that the actual progress of the team is behind the planned progress, and vice versa, as shown in Figure 4.10.

At the beginning of the project, we have to think about how to draw a burndown chart. In theory, the horizontal axis of the burndown chart can be days/weeks/months or iteration. Now our vertical axis is generally the points of story card, and working hours are proved to be not a good choice. The purpose of the burndown chart is to quickly present the progress of iteration, which is conducive to identifying risks and take actions. The points on the chart represent the size or amount of work that we still need to complete that day, and the first point is the remaining amount seen on the first day. There is nothing special about it. If we want to draw a burndown chart within an iteration, as shown in Figure 4.10, we need to identify all tasks in this iteration as much as possible at the IPM, and estimate the workload of each task, accumulate the workload of all tasks, get the value of the first point, and take workload as the unit. With the popularity of Kanban, we increasingly use the burndown chart of the delivery cycle. Each iteration is a point, and the first point is the total points of this delivery. In this case, to make good use of the burndown chart, it is necessary to strictly control the total points/workload. In case of any change in requirements, we must ensure that the same workload is moved out of the delivery plan to ensure the accuracy of the burndown chart. If it is not controllable, then the burndown chart calculated by iteration will become meaningless, we'd better replace it with the burnup chart.

What interests us is that the analysis of the burndown chart can reveal many problems, such as how the team performs and how to improve it.

The burndown chart contains two lines showing the theoretical remaining workload and the actual remaining workload. From the trajectory of the burndown chart, although Figure 4.10 has some ups and downs, it is still a relatively perfect burndown chart. In fact, the process for each team to complete the iteration is different. Common situations are enumerated as follows:

- First bulge and then fall: The reason is that the IPM often misses something. Not only does it not burn down after the start of work, but also exposes many new tasks, resulting in increased workload.
- First burn perfectly, then suddenly stop burning: It is a common situation. If the task division is too coarse (or the story points are very large), such as up to 10 days, it is easy to "do it for 1 day, 9 days left"; "do it for another 1 day, with 8 days left... By the time when 2 or 3 days left, oh no, we cannot make it."
- Burn slowly first, and then when it burns out, there are a bunch of unfinished tasks that are to be postponed to the next iteration.

There is a MoSCoW method in the field of agile development. In addition to what is necessary, some stories are secondary and could be given up, so this kind of burndown chart is also very common. But it is often to see that some teams do not use this method, but only passively find that some stories are not completed in the end, which easily causes valuable requirements to fall into the unfinished part, and the project cannot be completed.

We do not have to worry about the imperfection of the burndown chart, because these methods and means are not our purposes, but only a tool for an intermediate process. To accomplish our ultimate goal, these tools and methods can be flexibly changed, instead of pursuing the perfection of tools and measurement data itself, truth is more important.

The goal of the burndown chart is to complete the iteration. What is the goal of the iteration? It is to follow the request of the product manager with the customer team, and deliver the user requirements for the iteration plan. Why can't the burndown chart achieve this goal directly? Because the following potential problems will be encountered during the iteration.

(1) If the burndown chart is completed on time, it may be that the quality of all stories (important and unimportant) is sacrificed in order to complete on time, in exchange for progress.
(2) If the burndown chart is not completed on time, it may not be that one of the stories is not completed, but that all stories have a little work left unfinished, resulting in the failure to deliver all the stories.
(3) If the burndown chart is not completed on time, the unfinished story may include some extremely important business requirements.

Just looking at the shape of the burndown chart, we cannot identify these three problems in advance, so it brings a lot of risks, which will surprise us at the end of the iteration.

To answer the above questions, let's start by analyzing the burndown chart shown in Figure 4.11. My view of Team A in the chart is as follows:

(1) The Team's plan is not good, because the line does not touch the zero point at all, there may be many reasons for this.
(2) The Team's progress has been constantly deviating from the planned progress, and there is absolutely a problem with the estimation at the start of the project, which has caused backward cumulative effects.
(3) Requirements are constantly changing, resulting in a long way from the end of the project. Therefore, for the Team, improvements in delivery planning, requirements control, and self-management are urgently needed.

Team B says that they have achieved their goal, but it is likely that they fail to take the initiative to update the burndown chart figures. The reason may be as follows: they are too lazy to update the

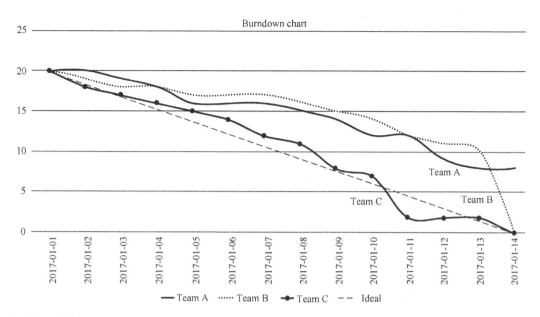

FIGURE 4.11 Burndown chart.

remaining workload; lots of user stories are discarded at the end of the iteration, rather than completed; another possible reason is that the mid-term team has done a lot of research work to speed up the completion of the follow-up requirements, just like the saying goes "more preparation may quicken the speed in doing work."

Team C is a well-planned mature team with burndown workload. This Team features sound self-management and enough stories to be implemented throughout the iteration. This line is close to an ideal state, indicating that the Team is under pressure from the upper level during the project operation, so this burndown chart seems like a work report.

In summary, we can get a lot of information from the burndown chart, but the key lies in its iterative analysis and continuous improvement based on the analysis results. Draw a burndown chart and make it accurately reflect the true state of the team. In addition to faithfully recording the worklog, we also need to deal with the following issues:

(1) Is the vertical axis of the burndown chart story points or working hours? If working hours are used as the object of statistics, it is often the case that working hours are used up and a lot of work is not completed on the project, and counting working hours is very time-consuming. When this method is used, the incentive effect of the remaining work hours on the team members is not obvious, so it is recommended to use the story points as the vertical axis, because the story points are a virtual benchmark unit, which is used for relative statistics. For example, I estimate that there are about 30 story points in an iteration. How many man-days are these 30 story points? Sorry, I don't know, but I can give you a rough estimate before iteration. For example, I estimate that a story point is the workload of about 4 man-days, and the 30 story points are the workload of 120 man-day. In the second iteration, assuming that four people have developed for one week, that is, it takes 20 man-days of workload, it stands to reason that the workload of 5 story points should have been completed, but it is found that only the workload of 3 story points is completed. Well, I immediately amended the estimate of the workload of each story point. We adjust a story point to 6 man-days, then 30 story points would become 180 man-days.

The size of the story point should be calculated properly. It is recommended to take 0.5–1 day (not 1 man-day) as an approximate estimation point. For example, for a four-person development, that one story point contains about 4–8 man-days of work, then we can draw an average of 1–2 story points down every day. Too many story points will make statistics-making troublesome, while too less story points will it hard to observe any change every day.

(2) Should the investment in testing be included in the overall development task? In the famous book *Scrum and XP from the Trenches*, there is a figure describing the iteration relationship (see Figure 4.12).

In fact, each iteration will cost more or less time to fix the bugs of the previous iteration. If the developers' time on fixing bugs is also counted in the burndown chart, although the burndown chart will be smoother and better looking, it will lose its role in reflecting team problems. It is precisely because we first find that the trend line of the burndown chart is flattened and then point out the problem of software quality degradation. Otherwise, customers who are not with the team members every day cannot know the quality decline, and may instead feel happy at seeing this well-done burndown chart.

Observe the above process carefully. The dark part in Figure 4.12 is actually the test and rework part of Iteration 1.

This is actually telling us that the real end time of Iteration 1 is actually the point of 1.01, not 1.00. And if we take 1.00 as the end point, then it must be that when the last end point is reached, our burndown chart is not closed. If you insist on adding the design, development, test and rework into the burndown chart, then this chart will inevitably deviate from the reference line. So is it meaningful to use this as a reference to adjust the workload?

Then look at the last iteration, which is different from Iteration 1 in Figure 4.12. In addition to the bugs of the previous iteration, it has to deal with all the bugs of this iteration, because there are no remaining iterations to continue processing bugs.

Therefore, a more reasonable plan should be like this: Iteration 1 removes the above dark part of workload; Iteration 2 adds the dark part of workload and removes the workload assigned to Iteration 3; the last iteration only adds the workload of the rework part of the last iteration.

Even if the bugs that will cost great efforts of developer to fix should not be included in the burndown chart as task statistics, because this is attributed to the problems left over by the development of the previous story card, it should have been included in the scope of the story card it belongs to. Of course, problems from production are excluded.

For the statistics of the burndown chart, it is very important to define the "Done" state (that is, the state of completion) of the story cards. Take the team as the smallest unit of delivery, that is, the test completion of the delivery state by the team is a sign of the completion of the story card.

Finally, let's look at some extended use cases for burndown chart.

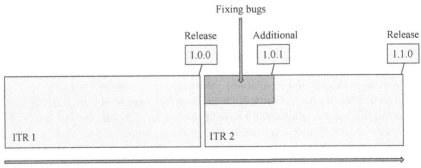

FIGURE 4.12 Iteration diagram.

Through working on an offshore delivery project, I learned that the estimation a new project may be started from a T-shirt number.

We cannot predict the delivery time at the beginning of the project, at this time we can focus on the difficulty of requirements stories, rather than the time to complete the stories. In essence, it is difficult for us to predict the time spent on the stories accurately, but we can compare the difficulty of two different stories, even if we only have a certain understanding of the context of these two stories. When we fully understand the project's requirements, architecture, and technology stack, we can predict with more accurate quantitative points. Perhaps, at the second phase of the project, the estimation can be directly made with points.

When project team members are more concerned about the relative difficulty of stories, the following T-shirt numbers can be used to indicate the relative difficulty of story cards: XS, S, M, L, and XL. If using the Fibonacci sequence 1, 2, 3, 5, 8, these figures are easy to mislead team members to direct their attention to the workload expressed by man-day in the estimation, while the T-shirt number will make the team members more inclined to pay attention the comparative difficulty of the story cards.

As shown in Figure 4.13, use the T-shirt number to estimate the size of the story, and use 3 burnout lines (best, worst, and likely) in the burndown chart to quickly predict the release plan. The advantage of doing so is that it will get a prediction interval, including the reference release date of the best case and the worst case. For the team, this range not only has a certain incentive effect for us, but also draws the bottom line of the team, just like a silent commitment there. A burndown chart with only one burndown line will point to a certain date, but we all know that this is just a prediction, its advance or delay will not greatly affect the team. At this time, the team has neither the incentive to work towards the best outcome nor the pressure to avoid the worst outcome.

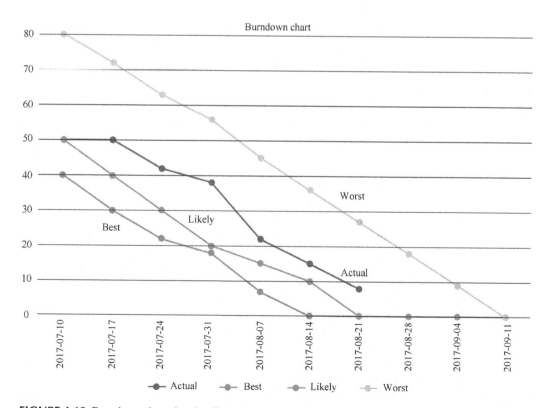

FIGURE 4.13 Burndown chart showing T-shirt number estimation.

TABLE 4.1
Calculation Coefficient of T-Shirt Number Estimation Method

Relative Size	Best	Likely	Worst
XS	0.5	0.75	1
S	0.5	1	2
M	1.5	2	3.5
L	3	3.5	6

So how are the data of these three burndown lines generated? From the project mentioned above, we have summarized the correspondence between the T-shirt numbers and quantified numbers shown in Table 4.1, multiply the planned requirements points by these three sets of coefficients and get three burndown lines: "ideal," "likely" and "worst." Ideally, the "actual" burndown line (the second line from top to bottom in Figure 4.13) should be close to the "likely" burndown line. If the actual burndown line drawn by a team exceeds the interval formed by these three burndown lines, they need to review what went wrong. Perhaps the team failed to select suitable corresponding number; or perhaps some developers failed to understand the requirements correctly, and they might have missed or over-designed certain requirement.

In general, the burndown chart can help guarantee development period and on-time delivery since it is able to acquire and verify progress information, display, disseminate, and promote progress information. The biggest advantage of the burndown chart is its simplicity and directness. Therefore, when presenting and reporting to customers or managers without a technical background, it is often useful to put in a burndown chart. Some managers pay more attention to the incentive effect of the burndown chart on the team. Seeing the line on the burndown chart continue to approach the zero point is like seeing the project continue to make progress. In my opinion, other charts, such as burnup chart, can also play the same incentive role, so from another aspect, the motivation factor is not one of the reasons why we choose the burndown chart.

4.2.2.2 Burnup Chart

Burnup chart is fairly applicable to the projects with changing requirements. Using the burnup chart, we can understand the completed workload and the total workload at that time every day or each iteration. The vertical distance between these two workloads on the chart is the current remaining workload. When the lines representing these two workloads meet, it means that all of the scheduled workload is completed. In general, it means the project can be ended, as shown in Figure 4.14. The burnup chart is simple and powerful, at any time it can tell us how far away from the completion of the project. When dealing with a project with a varying scope of requirements, we cannot know the remaining workload with a burndown chart, but it is easy to do for a burnup chart.

One advantage of the burnup chart compared to the burndown graph is that it contains a requirement range line, which can clearly reflect the situation where tasks are added or removed. By extending the requirement range line and the completed work line, we can get a more visible and more realistic completion date; the point where these two lines meet is the date.

If you are a manager, this requirement range line will allow you to easily locate the point in time when new requirements are added, and then derive the increase in project completion time according to the requirement increment. How is this time increase calculated? Before the new task is added, we record the completion time of the project, and then add the requirement to get an estimated completion time. The difference between these two times is the impact of the newly-added task on the project completion time. When our goal is to put the project online as scheduled, we try to move some tasks out of this delivery range at a certain time point. The change in the requirement range line can match us with a new online date. Overall, the burnup chart is an important tool, it reminds us to sit

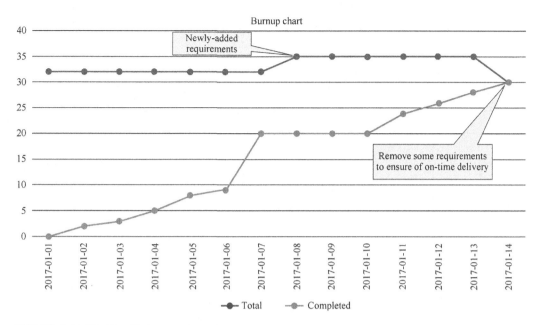

FIGURE 4.14 Workload in burnup chart.

down with customers and teams at the right time to discuss changes in requirements, because it will affect the quality and functionality of the project's delivery. The increase in requirements may bring about a decrease in quality, and the decrease in requirements causes a reduction in the functionality delivered. What we need to do is confirm with the end user that the removed requirement is a low-priority requirement.

Although under normal circumstances, a typical burnup chart contains only two lines, but sometimes we will add other lines. The first thing that comes to mind is an ideal burnup line, which is a straight line drawn from the origin of the coordinates to the intersection of the delivery date and the requirement range line. If the team plans to deliver on time, it can remind the team of the workload that needs to be done every day. This ideal route tells the team whether it is ahead of schedule or behind schedule on the day. The distance from this ideal route represents the workload that deviates from the specific route, as shown in Figure 4.15.

If the project is based on the collaboration among multiple teams, we can superimpose and display the burnup chart of each team on one coordinate. For distributed teams that must release products at the same time point, the teams with the highest progress risk can be identified through horizontal comparisons between the teams.

For a team developing a long-term project, we can track multiple delivery stages of the project on one burnup chart, such as multiple consecutive releases or multiple iterations. The requirement range line of the new delivery stage can accumulate the previous requirement range line. The starting point of the new development stage is the completion point of the previous stage. The advantage of doing so is that we can see the continuity of different development stages. When a task is postponed from the previous release stage to the next release stage, we do not need to adjust the data, so the total range of requirements will not change.

The basic purpose of any chart tool is to better communicate. The burnup chart can clearly show the scope of work and project that is completed. When a stakeholder or customer asks the team to add additional requirements, the burnup chart can effectively tell them the impact of this on the delivery date. In the case of constant requirements, the normal trend of the burnup chart is to ensure the project is delivered on time. In the process of a project, if the customer adds a lot of new requirements, a burndown chart cannot accurately reflect the team's output. The customer may also

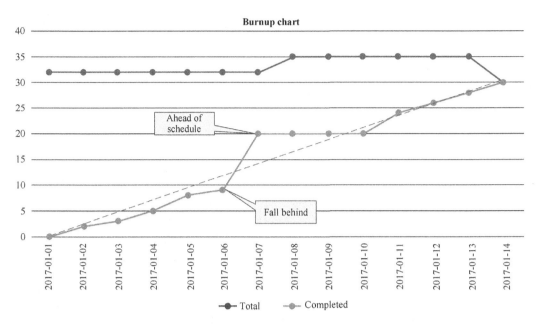

FIGURE 4.15 Progress in burnup chart.

question the team's work, while the burnup chart can avoid these potential traps. The burnup chart is slightly more complicated than the burndown chart. It usually requires a certain explanation to allow all participants in the project to understand the information it displays without deviation.

So, how can we build a proper burnup chart? The team can use a lot of tools to create a burnup chart, a pen and a piece of white paper, or a spreadsheet software like Excel. If our team uses JIRA to manage our story cards and bugs, we can use JIRA's plug-in tool to generate a burnup chart at any time. If the customer needs regular project status reports, the burnup chart generated by these tools can also be easily inserted into the project report.

A normal burnup chart contains 3 lines of total requirement range, expected progress, and actual progress. After there is no problem in the form, we must pay attention to the accuracy of data, which is also the basis for the effectiveness of the burnup chart.

4.2.2.3 Comparison Between Burndown Chart and Burnup Chart

Before deciding which chart to use, our team should ask ourselves more questions to determine what our purpose is. Do we need to show our customers the health of the project? Do we use this chart to motivate team members? Or are we just letting ourselves know the project progress? These purposes determine which chart we choose to use. The focus of the burndown chart is the amount of unfinished work, while the focus of the burnup chart is the amount of completed work. If the contract delivered to the customer specifies the requirements will not change before delivery; however, there is a clear requirement for the delivery time, such as a fixed amount of project, then the burndown chart is a good choice. If the range of customer requirements is not fixed, and there is only a general range, the customer will determine the end date of the project, then the burnup chart is our best option.

The burndown chart and the burnup chart are, respectively, for simplification and comprehensiveness. The burndown chart is so simple that it only has a zero line pointing to the day the project ends. It is so simple that everyone can understand the problems it reflects, but it cannot contain some useful information, such as a change in the requirement range. Responding to changes is an important advantage of agile development. We often encounter situations where, for example, customers suddenly want to add a new function or remove certain functions in order to release on schedule. There is no way to reflect these problems on the burndown chart, but the burnup chart can do it.

The burnup chart can use two lines to track the whole work and the completed work, one records total workload and the other one records the completed workload; while the burndown chart combines the tracking of the work progress into one line. The total workload in the burnup chart is responsible for the communication of an important message. When the agreed or estimated time is reached, if the project has not been completed, the reason may be that the development speed of the team is too slow or there are many new tasks added. Identifying the cause is a critical factor in diagnosing and correcting mistakes in a project.

For our offshore team, if we need to regularly and intuitively show the development progress of the team, the burnup chart is a good choice. It easily explains the progress we have made, even if the customer often adds some new tasks during the project implementation, or the test has exposed some problems that were not considered in the early stage and thereby increasing our workload.

We have to convince customers to control the changes in the requirement range, because an uncontrollable requirement range is a "hot potato" for every project. When the requirement range expands, we will see the team's progress slowing down on a burndown chart. But on the burnup chart, customers can clearly see the changes in the requirement range and notice the team's progress is not slow down. At this moment, the burnup chart is more effective for persuading customers to control the requirement range to ensure of on-time project delivery.

When the requirement range of a project is fixed or the total workload delivered has been kept constant, the amount of information that can be included in the burnup chart is the same as the burnout chart. If the project can guarantee these prerequisites, it is excellent to use a simpler burndown chart.

4.2.3 DISPLAY OF BUSINESS PROCESS

The flowchart includes two parts: process and chart. Process is a series of operations with special logical relationship to meet one or more specific requirements, while chart is to use some of the simplest symbols to standardize these logical relationships. Therefore, the flowchart represents the form of expressing the process through simple and standardized symbols and connections, so as to achieve the purpose of better dissemination, archiving, and reference of information. The flowchart can be used to show not only part of the business process but also complex business overall view. The flowchart, a tool-like method, must be simple and clear in itself, and everyone can have a consistent understanding and no learning cost. Therefore, the standardization of the flowchart is very important.

4.2.3.1 Specification of Flowchart

We use flowcharts to explain the functions of a program, so that people who do not understand a specific programming language can also understand this process, as shown in Figure 4.16.

Although the node symbols used in the flowchart are very simple, they do have usage specification. American National Standards Institute (ANSI) defines a complete set of standard symbols. In fact, we often use only the basic ones as follows:

- Rectangular box: the steps performed by the program, mainly used to represent an operation and behavior
- Diamond box: logic judgment point, which is equivalent to the usage scenario of program assertion, where logic branches
- Circle: The connector of the execution path of the program, making the flowchart easier to understand
- A rectangle with two circular ends: the beginning and end of a flowchart

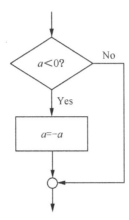

FIGURE 4.16 The simplest flowchart.

The above nodes represent an event or a behavior, and we also need links to represent the connections between each node, such as sequential order, primary and secondary order, and hierarchical relationship. The number of nodes can measure the difficulty of logic. Generally, it is appropriate to include 5–13 nodes in visual communication, and the expression is also clear and easy to read.

After mastering the basic principles, we quickly have the ability to draw a flowchart that looks formal. But to pursue the integral expression of a flowchart, we need to check this flowchart from 6 dimensions to ensure that no information is missing. The six dimensions include process participant (roles), activity, sequence, input, output, and standardization, as shown in Figure 4.17.

(1) Process participant: Which platforms or roles are involved in this process? It can be certain system itself or an external device, but most times it indicates people – people with specific roles.
(2) Activity: Events that have occurred, such as returning the bike, uploading the return information, and unlocking.

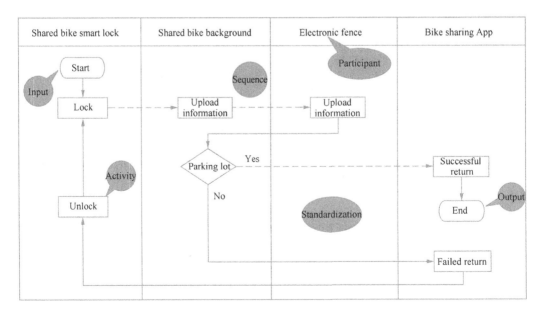

FIGURE 4.17 Six dimensions of information of a flow chart.

(3) Sequence: Some events occur in parallel, but more events occur in sequence, which task is a prerequisite for other tasks? For example, returning the bike outside the electronic fence will not trigger the bike lock.

(4) Input: The start of each activity depends on what kind of input or data, for example, we trigger the bike return activity, sometimes the bike return needs to meet certain conditions, and then start the electronic fence verification.

(5) Output: After each activity, what kind of documents or data will be output to the next party. For example, if the electronic fence is verified, the bike will be successfully locked, and the use of a shared bike will be successfully ended.

(6) Standardization: As mentioned before, in fact, there are internationally accepted symbols. The standard flowchart symbols are used to convey our design, which can be more easily understood by others. Especially in distributed teams, the use of standard symbols will greatly benefit communication.

In fact, we have seen a lot of personalized flowcharts, and they are also well used. They basically do not deviate from their core goals. As long as they can communicate the tasks and sequences, they are good flowcharts. The core of the flowchart is to help us check and fill vacancies, avoid omissions in functions, processes, and logic, and ensure the integrity of business process. However, for distributed team collaboration that relies on communication, we still need to pay attention to the huge impact of standardization on communication efficiency.

4.2.3.2 Extended Application

Essentially, we can treat flowcharts like story cards. We don't need to make a big and complete flowchart every time. We may split the flowchart according to the business split, and let a flowchart show a part of separate business; what we need to do is to correctly define the input and output. In case of any change to the requirements, we only need to update the related flowchart. I often see some teams maintain a super-large flowchart, I'm worried about whether this flowchart can undertake the function of passing on the knowledge to new team members. Higher-order complexity makes the learning curve steeper. And when responding to changes in requirements, whether it will be as slow as an elephant turning around.

At the same time, this also raises another question, how to manage the flowcharts containing different details? We may remove unnecessary details from the overall flowchart, and let its function focus on the relationship between modules and other aspects. All flowcharts need to evolve with iterative development. The characteristic of iterative development is the longitudinal cutting of functions, which is obviously different from the traditional waterfall development that features cross-cutting of functions, the requirements will not change once they are determined. Therefore, when a traditional team uses a flowchart, it will become the final version once it is determined. The difference is that in a constantly changing agile team, the flowchart should continue to increase or change according to the project progress. When necessary, put them into the version control system and treat them as code, test cases, and documents, which is a safe solution.

I once found a bug in a project that I had worked on: When users converted a large amount of raw data into invoices, this process was often unsuccessful. But this problem did not happen every time when an invoice was generated. After analysis, it turned out that our program would conflict when processing the same object when issuing invoices and calculating invoices in the same time. Our fixing method was to avoid the invoicing issuance and the invoicing calculation being executed in parallel, extract the invoicing calculation and execute it separately, and the other unrelated logic kept being executed in parallel to maintain the speed of data processing as much as possible. We used flowcharts to communicate the logical changes brought about by this fixing, and used two flowcharts to mark the changes before and after (as shown in Figure 4.18). Our distributed teams in China and India did not need to spend time on the code, they had a good understanding of our fixing plan, which is especially valuable for teams who cannot communicate face to face.

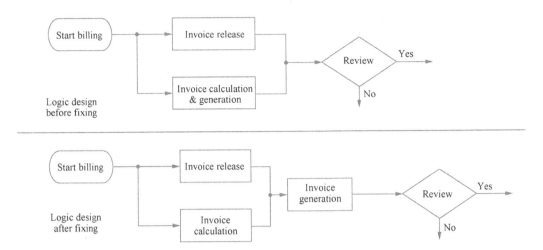

FIGURE 4.18 Flowchart represents logical differences.

After the business process design is finalized, we can also use the flowchart to show the flow in the web pages. We can simply understand that the focus of the business flowchart is the process of users completing their business value, and the process of web pages includes page navigation (jumps, etc.), and the main focus is to improve the user experience.

In the development process of our distributed team, the rational use of flowcharts can reduce the loss of knowledge in communication. In terms of "rational," does everyone in the team have some basic principles to refer to so that they can use good flowcharts when needed?

The start-up of the project requires a whole business flowchart in order to give all teams an overall view, let them know their respective requirement scope and the parts that other teams are responsible for.

In the process of development, when developers explain an implementation solution to others, especially nontechnical personnel, the flowchart is a good carrier. It simplifies the implementation of the code into a process, because nondevelopers only need to know what developers "want" to implement, not "how" to implement.

The testers first benefit from the above flowchart, because the flowchart has a very good effect on the display of business scenario and technology. During the testing process, identifying the business meaning in the business flowchart can inspire valuable test cases and also clarify the scope of the test. The flowchart produced by developers reveals the idea of implementation, and also has a certain enlightening effect on the hiding place of bugs. Will testers use flowchart to show their deep understanding of the system? To answer this question, let's first take a look at a question that usually occurs in a team: Who is the one know our program best, business analysts or testers? Business analysts do have the final interpretation of requirements, but testers are the ones who understand the behavior of our programs best. In addition to knowing how the program satisfies the user business value, testers must also not destroy the user business value at any time. Not all business scenarios have flowcharts for testers to use. When the scenarios that meet the user business value are relatively simple, and the abnormal situations are more and complicated, it is better to use the flowcharts in the test cases, so as to better express sad path, branch, and sequence.

4.2.4 Overall View of Project Requirements

We know that when a project starts, it starts with dividing the requirements and ending with the split of story cards.

When story cards are recorded in Trello or JIRA, we tend to get lost in a bunch of requirements list, cannot grasp the relationship between the story cards, and whether the boundaries of the requirements are intact. If we want to ensure the integrality of the functional modules composed of stories without missing requirements, we must organize all the story cards in a structure to show the logical relationship between them. These story cards have affiliation relationship, parallel relationship, and hierarchical relationship with each other, thus making any missing requirements easily identified.

This structure can be represented by a tree diagram (shown in Figure 4.4). Displaying the tree diagram requires us to write all the story cards first. At this time, except for the stories in the first iteration plan that have complete acceptance conditions, all other cards have not been specifically analyzed, and we cannot guarantee that each card is a definite need. Their current role is actually to occupy a place, and the place itself is to prevent the omission of requirements.

When I first participated in a project inception, Jolly Tan showed us the tree diagram of the project for the first time, which fully occupied a wall of our meeting room. After a week of requirements bombing, it was at this time that I finally had a clear understanding of the interrelationship between requirements modules and the requirements range for each function. This project was to continue to develop on the customer's legacy system. This tree allowed us to distinguish the existing functions of the legacy system, the tasks of the customer's local function team, and the tasks our offshore team which served as an independent function team.

After we started quickly at the time, we produced almost 100 story cards. Here is an example of our project that is split into 30 story cards. Let's take a look at the steps and precautions for manually drawing an overall view.

We can see the following information from the overall view (shown in Figure 4.4).

Primary and secondary relationship. The module function is the trunk of the tree, and the story card is the fruit on the branch. The type or priority the story card can be indicated by the logo on it, or directly by its color.

Iteration plan. The schedule of story cards in each function module.

Requirements scope. All functions that need to be implemented are below each functional module, and functions that are not in this scope do not need to be implemented.

Changes in requirements. The newly added functions and the removed functions are directly updated on the overall view. The removed card can be simply drawn with a big red cross, instead of being discarded.

The tree diagram is an output of the project's start-up phase. Does its life cycle end here? Does the agile team need to maintain it continuously? The manual maintained overall view can end up here, It accomplishes the purpose of a sense of ritual. Continuous maintenance requires high cost. Subsequent continuous maintenance needs to be carried out in the online requirements management system.

4.2.5 Expression of Requirements Stories

Speaking of graphical descriptions of requirements stories, at the level of user stories, some detailed content needs to be displayed to facilitate the transfer of information or to discuss based on the details of the information. In the offshore delivery projects I have experienced, no matter it is in the form of high-fidelity mockup or low-fidelity wireframe, it has the opportunity to be adopted by our team or customers. The expression of a requirement story usually goes through the following processes: sketch, wireframe, and then code implementation and testing.

For customers in a lower-level cooperation with us, they generally have their own user experience experts, and the discussion process of requirements generally does not require the participation of offshore teams. In this case, what the offshore team got is already very close to the mockup. At this time, our front-end development engineers only need to develop the implementation prototypes for these mockups through some development frameworks, such as HTML/CSS and other technologies. The mockup is almost exactly the same as the final software, and the information it conveys is highly accurate, which is of great help to the quality built-in.

Working with customers in a high-level cooperation is both lucky and challenging for offshore teams. The team needs to go through the entire life cycle of the requirements from generation to final delivery. Based on the principle of lean production, the understanding of design is shared between teams, that is, the principle of "just in time." At the beginning, the least authentic but least costly sketch form is used to collect as much feedback as possible. After the team has a basic understanding of the purpose and range of requirements, the user experience experts within our team can complete the wireframe.

Wireframes are mainly about content, layout, weight, interaction, and other things that involve user interaction. The principle of drawing a wire frame is that it should not contain too many details, we can only draw a schematic diagram of the page and highlight the key parts. Because of its low cost, we can continue to discuss and further collect customer feedback based on it, and repeatedly modify it until it becomes a result accepted by all parties. Its another advantage is to allow everyone to participate in the design process, whether it is technical or nontechnical personnel in the team, both of them can benefit from it.

When we start learning and using wireframes, experienced people will generally tell you to start with manual drawing. Simple tools such as pens, white paper, whiteboards, and sticky notes meet all our requirements. The average beginner starts here. In a company full of agile culture, when we sit down to solve a problem, we often say let's draw a wireframe. So, if you have the opportunity to visit the office of any mature delivery team, on every table and in every meeting room, there are essential items such as pens, hard cards, and post-it notes.

Using software tools to draw wireframes is more practical for the cooperation of offshore teams. First of all, the teams can easily share, and continuously update and improve the wireframes, which is an advantage that the paper media cannot match. Secondly, wireframe software tools usually support some typical page elements that designers can use directly. When it comes to software tools, there are really many excellent tools on the market, such as Sketch. But to my surprise, the tool used by many people around is Keynote which is very handy. After in-depth understanding and use, I found that Keynote also has many advantages.

(1) Keynote was born for presentation, and naturally has the advantage in this regard. It can properly support user navigation and clicking, we can use small pens to draw pictures with it directly, which is conducive to giving play to the talents of designers.

(2) It has good integration with other document tools; it is able to export multiple formats and easily embedded in a report.

(3) It eliminates business personnel's fear of technology, lowers the threshold of use, and increases the participation of personnel of various roles in requirements design.

Of course, Keynote also has many shortcomings. I just hope we can all understand that tools are only means, not the key to creating high-quality wireframes. We should make good use of them to explore everyone's ideas, to promote the team's communication on the demand side, which is the purpose of creating high-quality wireframes.

Figure 4.19 shows a real wireframe I have used. As can be seen from the figure, the regulations and implementation effects of the controls have been relatively clear.

TIPS FOR DRAWING WIREFRAMES

We must grasp the focus of expression when drawing a wireframe, since irrelevant elements will distract developers' attention. Stick to the essence of the schematic, and do not spend too much energy in pursuit of realism. Unclear points can be communicated directly on the wireframe until all parties understand and agree. So in essence, using wireframes is also a built-in measure to ensure quality.

FIGURE 4.19 Design effect of wireframe.

4.2.6 USE OF MIND MAPS

From the date of birth, the mind map has greatly reduced the loss of information in communication through the innovation of the information organization form. Its application is more and more extensive, it makes information processing easier and less likely to be missed, and it can be easily archived. The following are three typical application scenarios of mind mapping in distributed teams.

(1) Do business analysis to refine the original idea. When a requirement is not clear, it may be an idea of the boss, he probably wants something, and we need to sort out the specific details for him. In this case, we can first write the relevant points one by one on the paper, which is a divergent process. After almost all the points are listed out, we will then build an mind map document, which is an inductive process, that is, convergence. When we put together the problems of the same type, we can quickly optimize this topic and make up for the missing parts.

(2) Sort out the product functional structure during product design. Figure 4.20 is an example (part) of a project I had worked on, the task management function of a page is disassembled in this figure.

(3) When team brainstorming, write down the output with mind map format while discussing. At the end of the meeting, a sharing plan as shown in Figure 4.21 is produced.

The mind map also has many principles to ensure that it achieves the desired effect. One of the things I value most is to ensure that a branch only says one thing, because it is more conducive to its divergent effect.

4.2.7 DATA VISUALIZATION

"Let data talk" is a mantra often heard in the era of Big Data. To satisfy the boss of the customer team, we must pay attention to the statistics of the data that have appeared during the work, such

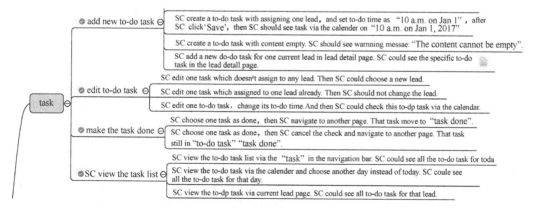

FIGURE 4.20 Using mind map for making meeting minutes.

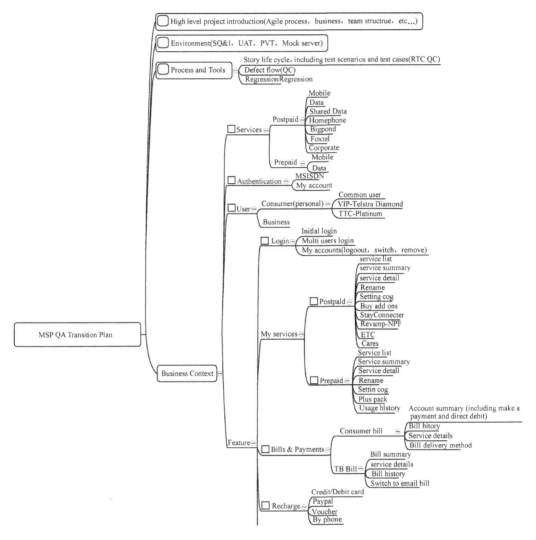

FIGURE 4.21 Mind map for requirements splitting.

as changes in response, and count out all unplanned tasks after the completion of the staged task. Its importance is self-evident, only the data are quantitative and real feedback on one thing. But the data themselves do not make much sense. Only by means of visualization can the value of data be better reflected.

For the offshore team, the first step in attracting customers is to make our daily work visible to them, and also make their daily work visible to us (it is more difficult, but we can strive for). Further, in the form of a chart, the trends and magnitudes of data such as the delivery speed of the two sides teams and the severity of bugs are displayed and compared. If necessary, we can collect the data of the teams separately. Draw a burndown chart and take picture to show it to the customer, so that it can also be used as the beginning of data visualization. However, to continuously attract customers, it is best to use tools to draw and send them a burndown chart template for them to use, try all means to give customers a sense of freshness. If the requirements of the offshore team come from the local team, then the offshore team is prone to lack of "overall view awareness." To prevent this problem, we can do one thing when we start the project: draw our requirements as a big tree (as shown in Figure 4.4), and depict each requirement card as a branch or fruit. The branches of the tree represent the relationship between requirements, and the fruits can be individual requirements. In the task management system, we can embody the relationship between cards (between functions) in another way.

Each visualization method must have its own unique features, bringing value to the team beyond space and time. How can everyone in the project team see the overall progress and status of the project? Combined with the actual situation of the team, think more about the data indicators in the team. For example, use Lead Time to measure the work of the team. How about giving up tracking story points? I have seen some teams give up estimating story cards and focus on their duration in Kanban to track their development progress. Of course, it requires extremely high trust in the team and team members.

4.3 USE VISUALIZATION TO MEASURE OUR WORK

The biggest advantage of visualization is that it is more intuitive for users. For remote customers or partner teams, large text descriptions are easily overlooked. Even if they are not ignored, the information reach efficiency will be below our expectation. If it is a visualization method, whether it is a table or a picture, we can quickly draw the user attention to the point of interest through forms such as comparison.

4.3.1 MEASUREMENT OF DEVELOPMENT AND TESTING WORK

If the working environment allows, it is recommended to visualize as many work results as possible, in addition to burndown chart, burnup chart, problems and defect trends, action plan produced by the retrospective meeting, and any other event calendars. Do remember we should not make any "one-time deal," we need to easily add new data after each iteration. I've seen too many teams interested in nice-looking visual charts, but when we really look at the contents, they are all outdated. Their excuses are varied: there is not enough space, we have to redraw the chart for continuous updating; the customer is no longer interested in status updating.

Don't make excuses for you laziness, but discover more visual highlights from your work. A simple comparison with before-after performance improvement, should it be counted as a visual method? The answer is yes. Many times the absolute value of some data is of little value to us, but the relative comparison has more meaning. For example, to improve the performance of a certain function module of a project, we say "the time to generate an invoice is 1 minute." For others, the information it expresses is a plain value, but if you are told that the previous value is 2 minutes, and then supplemented by a histogram, this information will immediately have a three-dimensional effect.

The purpose of using visualization is to provide help to the team during the work process and enhance communication with customers, not to report to the leader after the end of the project. What we need is timely and effective feedback. We can collect a large amount of data from the development and testing process, determine some indicators that explain our work effect or efficiency, and finally express these indicators in the most intuitive way to drive the final improvement needed.

4.3.2 SUGGESTIONS FOR MEASUREMENT OF TEAM WORK

When customers track the work progress of each team, why they use the burndown chart instead of the Gantt chart? The basic reason for not using the Gantt chart is that it does not have any value in the process of tracking tasks of agile, nor can it handle requirements changes. It only has the function of reviewing and reporting. For a team adopting agile development, if they cannot provide value to the team during the development process, it is a worthless task, which is for the sake of visualization.

Visualization is only used for the plain text description where it is difficult for the user to understand the scope and status, or it can deepen the understanding of some theories and practices. The purpose of visualization is to make the status of the team easier to see, so that we can take timely improvements. The purpose of our visualization is not to visualize for visualization. Visualization is not our purpose, the information conveyed through visualization and the responsibility we bear are the purposes for which we need it.

4.4 INTRODUCTION OF VISUALIZATION TOOLS FOR TEAM COLLABORATION

I have to say that electronic tools have many advantages.

(1) Synchronizing the status between teams, which prevents work errors due to human negligence.
(2) Properly managing the relationships and dependencies between story cards, as shown in Figure 4.22. Managing dependencies on the physical Kanban is basically based on the memory of team members and is prone to causing omissions.
(3) Saving the development records of the team in the system, which is helpful for the later statistics and review.

4.4.1 BRIEF INTRODUCTION TO MINGLE

It supports two types of card: one is called an epic, and the other is a so-called story card. The role of epic card is to represent a large functional block. We can use its hierarchical relationship with the story card to show the functional structure of the entire project delivery. If a type of story card indicates an iteration plan, we can use them to demonstrate the process of functional delivery.

Mingle provides a wealth of reporting functions; its reporting module contains a variety of burnup charts, bug status histograms, development status tracking histograms, and pie charts. Compared with the physical wall, Mingle can bring us the status history of all story cards, the history of content changes, and technically set some limiting conditions to achieve the purpose of process control.

4.4.2 BRIEF INTRODUCTION TO TRELLO

Trello is a good progress management tool. In addition to focusing on the current iteration, we can also view the entire delivery plan at any time. Trello is developed for multi-person collaboration, and also for providing integration with other team collaboration tools, which is very convenient.

FIGURE 4.22 Online Kanban tool for managing dependencies.

Trello has many Kanban plugins available. Although Trello does not provide the Kanban WIP restrictions, this does not prevent us from using it. We can use the Chrome browser plugin of Kanban WIP for Trello. We can set a WIP limit for each lane. When the number of story cards in a stage reaches or exceeds this limit, the color of the exceeded story cards will change to alert the user. So it does not really limit the number of WIPs. The limit could be exceeded according to special circumstances, but it clearly shows us.

4.5 SUMMARY

Many times, specific analysis is needed. How to weigh what to do and what not to do requires us to choose according to our own situation. One of the main purposes of visualization is to expose problems faster and more significantly. The roadmap can show the progress of all teams on a timeline, highlighting the time of each milestone.

Information flows between teams, and choosing the right carrier can effectively reduce the loss of information. Visualization is not only so simple to display textual things graphically, but also helps customers see as many situations as possible during the project development process, and vice versa.

We use visual symbols or charts to convey some information, but it is not that visual things are always more expressive than words. The combination of the two can achieve the effect of intuitive, accurate, and memorable information expression.

The visualization tools discussed in this chapter are some of the most basic tools. A deeper understanding of the basic tools is far better than a shallow understanding of advanced and complex tools. At the same time, most people do not pay equal attention to simple tasks. I think that the ultimate implementation of basic tools or methods is what our ordinary people should insist on. We may have encountered this scenario: There is a simple task which we should have done well, such as drawing a flowchart. If this is the case, it means that we have been passing by success, and it's time for us to wake up now.

5 Waste in Distributed Teams

5.1 WASTE CAUSED BY HUMAN FACTORS

Any work that deviates from the business value of the team is waste. As long as we individuals or teams do not complete a task or do things in the best way, all the people, events and processes that cause this result are the source of waste. For a team, its continuous improvement is to constantly find these root causes, and then find a suitable solution to eliminate this waste.

We can examine the waste in a team from several dimensions of individuals, entire team, process, and information. Of course, all of them are intra-team factors. We can also find ways to reduce waste from external factors, such as whether we can introduce some tools to make the teamwork more efficient.

Different cultural backgrounds and insufficient language ability will cause different teams to speak their own words, and each party cannot understand the other party's true intentions. For distributed teams, we cannot understand each other face to face. All we can do is prepare well before each communication, understand the context, and confirm after each communication.

Bad apple

I once led a team to test a customer's warehouse automatic picking system. The design of the test data involved some technical issues. Our team proposed a plan and reached an agreement with the customer, except for a young man named Liangliang in our team. Liangliang also proposed his own plan, which should be encouraged, but it seemed not that good as compared with the team plan which was already approved by the customer.

With his plan not adopted by other team members and the customer, Liangliang remained passive after we started work, and he often complained, throwing a question from time to time to show off the advantages of his own plan.

This had caused a bad influence on the team. The most direct performance was that whenever there was any difficulty he would jump out to dampen others' working passion, repeating that all these problems were avoidable if we listened to him. He never joined with others to figure out solutions. Later, Liangliang began to resist the tasks assigned to him, resulting in the failed completion of the entire task. Moreover, he took advantage of the company's flexible working system, either late for work or got off work early to avoid communication with others. Eventually, we had to ask him to quit.

You may have heard the story of "Bad Apple." A problematic individual team member is actually a typical "bad apple." If you put a bad apple in a basket of good apples, you will end up with a basket of bad apples. This is the "Bad Apple Theory." A person's attitude will affect a team, so if you want to make the team successful, you must first establish an aggressive spirit in team. Maybe Liangliang had a good intention at the beginning, hoping to contribute to the team, but a problematic employee can seriously wear down a project. How can we identify a problematic employee? This is not as difficult as imagined. You don't have to be friends with everyone in the team, of course, it helps, but a certain level of basic respect for individuals and careers is necessary for any team to function properly.

We need to observe carefully to identify the "bad taste" in a team, because it is difficult to obtain trust between remote teams, and the relationship is relatively fragile. We should try to avoid the damage of the bad apples as follows:

- Those who are content with superficial understanding, and always try to cover up their ignorance, instead of actively learning from their teammates. They may say "I found this solution on the Internet, I've made a try, it is workable" or "the logic of my code is too complicated to test."
- Those who keep complaining about the team's decision, and reiterate the old things after the team has moved on for a long time. They may say "I still think we should go back and revise the design discussed last month. The current plan does not work."
- Those who care least about the team's goals, especially at the key time points. For example, in a project I've worked on, we needed to show our test plan to the customer before an important deadline. The entire team was busy organizing test scenarios and test data, but one of the testers suddenly asked to take two days off, since he was about to participate in the union conference of an online game.
- Those who always criticize the shortcomings of other people's methods without giving their own solutions.
- Like scholars (tend to) scorn each other, there are people like setting barriers for their teammates subconsciousnessly.

As a member of a team, we all have to learn to identify "bad apples" and try to avoid being infected by them. If our team leader or project manager does not deal with the "bad apple" in the project team, then he is delinquent and we must remind him. A worse situation is that the leader of the project is a "bad apple," and then the team members are more or less contaminated with his bad habits. At this time, even if we continue to bring in new apples, we can't change the ending of a basket of rotten apples. In a leadership organization, it is more difficult to get rid of such a bad apple, and it requires higher-level leaders to find out the predicament of the team; but in a flat organization, it will be easier for team members to throw away any "bad apple."

We should also not be afraid to transfer (or even dismiss) the people who do not consider the benefit of the team. You can develop a person's skills, but it is difficult to develop his positive attitude. The longer these destructive people stay in a project, the greater their impact will be. They will gradually spread the "virus" to every corner of the project in the form of code, relationships, and communication. At that time, it is not easy to reverse the overall culture of the project team.

It is painful to transfer someone from the team. Many people have experienced such moments. We have to comfort ourselves that we are doing good for the project. Conversely, when we realize that we should have transferred someone away six months ago, we will feel even more painful.

We should start from eliminating waste and find the negative "energy" in the team to help him accumulate positive energy, that is, to help him grow. This is the system that a well-functioning team should have. Positive energy can maximize its value, negative energy will be suppressed, and negative energy that cannot be suppressed will be kicked out of the team. The negative energy in an offshore team will shake the customer's confidence, and make the positive efforts of the team in vain. As the saying goes, it takes ten days to build a wall, but less than a day to demolish it.

Bad ways of doing things form bad habits, and bad habits cause a lot of waste, such as insufficient communication and knowledge transfer. A newcomer is not very familiar with the business, he might have learned the algorithm of a requirement from another developer. After we program for a while and thought it was completed, but later we discovered that some of the previous business was misunderstood, and did not understand it until discussing it with the business analysts for a long time. After worked closely with all kind of people, I also found that some people's habitual approach to an uncertain thing is: uncertain; hesitate to ask someone; decided not to ask; make an assumption on his own; continue.

To develop a function, we need the cooperation of multiple people such as front-end, back-end, database, operation, and maintenance. If someone is not in place, it can result in an unsatisfactory development sequence. Sometimes the absence of one person will cause other people to wait.

The waste caused by human factors may be attributed to someone at the customer team. Since the people in the customer team are partly responsible for the whole project, if some of them are not active and lack of responsibility, it will cause many unexpected results. Especially in the case that their work shall be integrated with ours, and we do not fully understand what they are doing. Like Xiaoli in Chapter 3, he will slow down our work at any time.

5.2 WASTE IN INTER-TEAM COLLABORATION

As an offshore team, we should not only pay attention to the waste of collaboration between team members but also eliminate waste between teams, especially between distributed teams.

When our team conducts project reviews, we often use the starfish chart as a framework for our divergent thinking. Compared with the ordinary three thinking dimensions, the starfish chart has another two dimensions of "stop doing" and "doing less" which more about efficiency in team. Base on my experience, the results of these two dimensions usually have the following similarities:

- Stop doing: Start working before confirming the requirements; go home while the deployment pipeline is still red (failed state); communication with the customer by himself, others know nothing.
- Doing less: Open discussions and discussions without conclusions, passive communication, reconstruction approaching delivery, submission of untested code, too many meetings scheduled during core work hours.

In these problems mentioned in the two dimensions, waste is an important factor, which can be hidden in our actions and behaviors. If we want to pursue excellence in our work, we must pull them out from time to time. Retrospective meetings are a good way to help us think and pull them out. If there are people with agile coaching roles in the team, it is even better; he can help the team identify where the waste exists through observation.

The waste mentioned in the retrospective meeting is generally explicit waste, which is easy to identify. There is also a kind of waste that is implicit and difficult to quantify. It requires disruptive thinking or the introduction of people like agile coaches from outside to help the team identify and improve.

The following is an example for illustrating how waste is generated in teamwork.

A company provides free milk and coke, but when you see the already opened beverages in the refrigerator, you have no idea when they were opened. So you preferring open a new carton, and put this newly opened carton in the refrigerator. Other people in the same situation will do the same thing like you. Waste is generated in this way. There are several opened beverages in the refrigerator at the same time, sometimes the open milk cartons are kept there for days, and the coke is no longer coke. This situation will be even worse on Monday, more milk and cola will be dumped.

This true story is essentially an example of teamwork. Everyone who drinks milk and coke is working together to drink up a large bottle of milk and coke, which is equivalent to the work to be completed in our project.

In fact, it is not difficult to figure about the solution, either reduce the opportunities for cooperation, or let everyone learn to "cooperate."

- From the perspective of reducing cooperation, it is advised to use small packages to dissolve or reduce the "cooperative" relationship between people who drink milk or coke.
- From the perspective of promoting cooperation, there are places on the milk carton for anyone to mark the opening date. Everyone who opens the milk should do one thing: mark the opening date on it. This date information is provided to those who drink milk later. Opened milk generally needs to be consumed within 24 hours, then we can decide whether to drink or pour milk accordingly.

5.2.1 WHERE DOES THE WASTE COME FROM

The waste in the team is in fact astonishing, we either turn a blind eye to it or fail to notice it due to our habit. We shall learn to analyze the causes of waste from all angles, which will also be helpful in promoting team thinking.

Analysis from the nature of waste:

- Direct waste: We have to wait for the upstream team to complete their work, which may lead to our repetitive work and lower efficiency;
- Indirect waste: We've made useless functions (many people simply don't know if the things they made are useful); we've gone the wrong way (the solution turns out to be unworkable after a long-term development or fails to satisfy the customer); we've chosen the wrong tool (a small agile team chose a task management tool with a sophisticated process).

Analysis from the source of waste:

- Lack of trust: Other teams have already developed a similar function, but we insist on working out a new one on for our own;
- Lack of communication: Insufficient remote communication, deviation in interface understanding;
- A truth has multiple sources: Several persons from customer team can make decisions on requirements and solutions. If our team has developed a function with one of them, we are often challenged by the others, and have no choice but to modify it.

5.2.1.1 Waste Caused by Team Collaboration

- Waiting is the most common state in team collaboration. Many times it is caused by poor handling of tasks that have dependencies.
- Waiting is a common thing for distributed teams in different time zones and it is one of the biggest wastes. Waiting is more common when there is a problem that cannot be resolved immediately, and we have to stop the work at hand.
- Lack of effective communication, duplication of work, or the inability of the teams to integrate their respective work after it is done.

How to control the waiting problem between teams?

For example, in order to prevent indefinite and long-term waiting, in the e-mails sent to the remote team, we can say clearly when we need their reply. If there is no reply at a certain time, we will continue our work according to the first plan.

If we use Kanban, we need to use a blocker column in Kanban to manage the waiting tasks, and can remind us to supervise every day to release the dependency as soon as possible.

If there is a problem, try to describe the problem clearly at one time to reduce the need for the other party to reconfirm the situation.

Making simple things complicated, without using the accumulated knowledge of the team (that is, second-hand information), or spend too much to do something less valuable. At this point, do you feel a sense of accomplishment or waste in it?

5.2.1.2 Waste Caused by Different Time Zones

Due to the existence of different time zones, serious communication delays are often caused, so it is necessary to reduce the number of communication back and forth and strive to get things right the first time. For example, it is valuable for us to write sad path test cases in the acceptance conditions. When such a function is developed by a remote team, all scenarios can be considered from the beginning. This will definitely reduce the number of round trips between development and testing of this function.

In case of the collaboration between offshore teams, there are some non-strongly related factors in the waste caused by different time zones. It is necessary to arrange their work based on their different commuting time and lunch break, so as to reduce the waste in teamwork and increase collaboration efficiency.

5.2.1.3 Waste in Different Phases of Project

A business analyst will not analyze a requirement when he thinks about it. Instead, he will create a placeholder but not start the analysis until it is really needed. If a story card is analyzed before the delivery time is determined, it implies a certain amount of waste. Even if you are sure to do it at the beginning, but you may change your mind with time going on. In the end, this story card may not be arranged or the requirement of the story card itself has changed a lot.

5.2.1.4 Waste in Test Collaboration

When a problem occurs in the system, developers spend a lot of time, but find that this problem is caused by fake data. The test data are created by the team members in the system at will and used for quick verification, but they are not cleared after the verification, thus causing a specious error message to pop up later. In short, the "legitimacy" of test data is always very important.

Submitting a low-quality bug report also causes a lot of waste.

When there is a problem when we do an operation, can we just describe this step in the bug tracking system? This is not enough. To deal with such a problem, we must define the scope (conditions) in which it occurs, and this should increase the testing scope to related functions.

To define the severity of this bug, further testing is required. Is this problem a temporary one? Will restarting and reopening the window make the problem disappear? When this problem comes out, it only affects the user himself or it also affects others?

Therefore, the steps to reproduce when submitting a high-quality bug report must be accurate and unique, that is, they cannot be reproduced without doing so.

Sometimes we are unable to identify which team introduced the problems. When these problems come out, it is likely that they are not assigned to the right people. It is necessary to jointly maintain a list of known problems to query, because it is difficult for you to know whether other teams have solved similar problem in the past. If this is a known issue, it is a waste to conduct research from scratch.

Before getting a reply from the customer, we need to voluntarily stop a job instead of making decisions on behalf of the customer. When team members make a decision, it is not necessary for everyone to meet and discuss together to choose a plan. When encountering a problem, they should first analyze the problem and raise suggestions, instead of directly giving a solution to this problem. Most technical teams have such a situation. Without in-depth analysis, they hurriedly throw out a solution and make the decision.

Unreasonable things often come in pairs. For example, a young mother feeds her child in the morning, but the child does not listen to her, the child didn't have a good breakfast. As a result, the child cries hungry before noon, and the mother has to feed her child some snacks, which then disrupt the lunch. This whole process actually contains two things. If the child eats normally in the morning, lunch should also be unaffected, neither of these two things can exist. But what the mother does is to correct an error with another one. So waste sometimes occurs in pairs, and there are causes and effects. If waste is the "cause," there will inevitably be a corresponding "effect"; if waste is the "effect," there must be a "cause" for its occurrence.

Looking at teamwork from the dimension of time, in early phase of project, we may leave some pits and technical debts in order to achieve our short-term goals. When time passes, other team members will fill the pits and pay off the debts, it is an act lacking of teamwork awareness. What is the so-called "pit"? A person adopts a special solution according to his own preferences, but later newcomers are not easy to continue base on it. The solution lack of scalability and flexibility, and unable to adapt to business changes.

Any fragile solution may introduce unknown errors. If there are dependencies between methods or test code steps, unless we are familiar with the context, otherwise every time we change this part of the code, we will pay a greater price. From the perspective of developers, "smarter" solutions will result in more complex code and more difficult maintenance in the future.

5.2.2 Ways to Solve Waste

It's really hard not to waste because.
- Doing too much is a waste, such as over-design, over-development, and over-testing.
- Repetitive work is a waste, so we should reduce repeated construction. Although the reuse design between teams follows the design model, reducing waste is also one of its benefits.
- Doing something too early is also a waste. We should implement the just in time production and not to produce things that are not needed temporarily.

What should the team think about to eliminate waste in the process? They should consider objective goals and reduce the chance of waste; carry out some internal reform to reduce waste caused by human factors.

5.2.2.1 Just in Time Production

Produce the necessary things only when necessary. This is an important value criterion that the agile development follows.

The practical effect of doing so is to rethink the timing and frequency of activities and production. According to the traditional methods, many times before we start any design, we will conduct all the analysis in advance. Once design, development, or testing has begun, a large number of rework will result when new requirements or changes are discovered, or due to feedback. According to the principle of just in time production, we should focus on producing the necessary things only when necessary. Sometimes, at the beginning of the project, it is also correct to insist on just in time production. For example, a complex architectural decision will affect many dependent areas. Just-in-time production is not procrastination, it is necessary to distinguish its relationship with procrastination.

To drive production with requirements, only the requirements within the iteration plan will be produced.

5.2.2.2 Timely Collaboration

Work with the right people at the right time. The practical effect of doing this is to rethink how and when to cooperate. According to the traditional concept such as waterfall development, many times we work in a vertical way, and may discuss business with some key stakeholders, but until all requirements are ready, we will not discuss with anyone else. This often leads to decisions that disregard constraints and dependencies, leading to further changes and rework.

According to the principle of timely collaboration, we should identify and centralize the key stakeholders in the delivery field with the upstream and downstream key stakeholders. For example, inviting product managers to work with stakeholders in sales, marketing, billing, and customer support – of course there will be the representatives of the delivery team. This leads to better "joint thinking" and the opportunity to identify and mitigate waste earlier.

5.2.2.3 Effective Communication

There must be no ambiguity, when several teams collaborate with each other on a project. In order to reduce the limitations of the text itself to convey information, we often use examples, graphs, and other means to communicate when describing something containing abundant information and complex logic. Rich means of communication methods will minimize gray areas of communication.

Let customers reveal their thoughts clearly and completely at the beginning. We once sent a developer to the customer site to solve their problems in one day. However, the customer did not say that they still had two new problems at 4:00 pm that day. The management of this customer was bad, which we should take as bottom line to arrange and adjust our work.

5.2.2.4 Do It Right the First Time

Built-in quality and built-in safety from the beginning are the development concepts that many companies have been striving to implement in recent years. The actual impact of doing so is to rethink how can we ensure that our production meets our goals. When adopting the traditional methods, we usually follow the requirements document template and then transmit it for peer review before circulating it to a wider range of stakeholders. This often leads to filling chapters in order to complete the template, rather than focusing on what can represent business value.

In accordance with the "do it right the first time" principle, we must clearly define deliverables, acceptance criteria, and participants from the beginning. For example, how do we need to implement the solution? Is it a requirements document or a backlog that features priority, functional modules, and stories? When considering what we need to do to complete this, we should agree to the acceptance criteria, which makes us aware of the completion criteria. Finally, by inviting participation of key stakeholders as early as possible, we can verify and confirm our work as we progress.

5.2.2.5 Minimize the Steps of Process

There is no need for processes that are not valuable and helpful for teamwork.

The practical effect of this is to rethink the process we follow to support the delivery. When adopting the traditional method, we usually abide by the software delivery life cycle, which is defined by the project management committee. This means that we often make a fuss of our work. We do not challenge the status quo, but prepare documents for review meeting at every phase, but only find that the participants have not read these documents.

In accordance with the principle of "reducing steps as much as necessary," we strive to reduce or delete process steps that cannot add value. For example, advocating a risk-based quality policy, which makes the specification and testing of simpler areas more concise, and the specification and testing of higher-risk areas more detailed.

5.2.2.6 Manage Time and Reduce Waste

Apply the method of time management to manage the importance and urgency of the affairs and make our work more effective.

Use time boxes to limit our work, especially in case of any spike. It may be not so strict when making a story card, but we must report the progress in time. If we need to further extend the time or need to split a new story card, the team can make adjustments accordingly.

The stand-up sometimes causes waste, because this is not the place to solve problems, but the place to raise problems, just confirm the problems and the person in charge within the meeting. The content of a stand-up involves the matters yesterday (past) and today (present), we should avoid discussing future problems, since most of these problems are undetermined. In addition, some of the communication that should be on weekdays should not be left to the stand-up, which will cause a lot of waiting. Everyone in the team has a responsibility to supervise the rest team members, what the stand-up should talk and should not talk. A stand-up shall be as simple as a stand-up. Do not add the functions (such as discussing a requirement) of other meetings into a stand-up. Failure to control meeting time will inevitably lead to slack.

5.2.2.7 Record Waste So Everyone Can See It Intuitively

When working on a project in the past, we used a whiteboard to record our wasted time caused by the customer team. The purpose of this was mainly to play a defensive role, and the recorded time would be shown to higher-level managers, so that we would explain to them when they were reviewing our work with the customer team. The wasted time was mostly caused by the following reasons: the customer failed to comply with the continuous delivery rules, which prevented us from submitting the code; the interface was not done by the agreed time; the bug description was incomplete, thus causing a lot of time to reproduce it.

The recorded waste includes the cause of the waste and the wasted time, and the statistical period can be weekly or every iteration. Putting these contents in the weekly report, which will be a means for promoting both teams to solve the problems.

5.2.3 SUMMARY

The level of team self-management and self-driving should be well matched with the strength of managers tracking management. Once there is a gap between the two, waste will occur.

To save from communication, our team has done something that should be done by the customer team, is it a kind of waste? Who will maintain it afterward? It was convenient at first, but there will be more communication problems in the future.

Some offshore teams have more or less competitive relationships with the customer's local teams. All concerned teams shall try to reduce internal frictions, control their competition, and promote win-win cooperation.

5.3 WASTE IN THE PROCESS

The process is a method of doing things from the company level that everyone, each role, and each team must follow, in order to avoid the influence of subjective factors. The process is generally formulated from the perspective of management, so that all work can be controlled. But for every team, every role, every person, this must imply that there is something unsuitable for these people working on the front line. In accordance with the principle of continuous improvement, each team should always define areas for improvement so that the process can keep pace with the times.

We should start from the two dimensions of breadth and depth to reduce waste and turn cold words into actionable guidelines.

5.3.1 SHORTEN THE PROCESS

The development process of a distributed development project I once participated in had 19 steps, and each step required people in related roles to meet and then went to the next step. We believed there was a huge waste in several processes, since investing a lot of time could only produce limited value, and sometimes no value was yielded, only leaving a record in the system. As for the users perform recording, who also do not know the context, they were making a record for its own sake. In addition to this, many milestones needed all people together to work, which caused waste objectively.

Feedback is a core content in modern engineering practice. In order to improve efficiency, reducing the length of the feedback loop has always been the goal pursued by the team. If we examine these processes based on basic values, we can find that many workflows do not add much value.

In a team, especially in a distributed team, it is generally the testers and customer team members who provide feedback. They usually look at the problem with a scrutiny in their work. This is the resource we need to use. At the same time, we must encourage feedback from the entire team. This is the foundation of continuous improvement.

Many agile practices are essentially the guarantee of the feedback process.

- At the IPM, developers and testers provide feedback to business analysts, so as to improve the content of the requirements from the perspective of technology implementation and quality assurance.
- When developers start an desk check, testers and business analysts provide feedback to developers; and they shall try to find some problems before move it to test phase, so that developers can correct them in time and reduce rework.
- During a showcase, the customer team gives feedback to delivery team; and invite customer to experience the actual operations, so as to let them confirm whether their original thinking is implemented.
- Developers provide feedback to each other at the code review.

Sometimes we need to use white box, test coverage, smoke testing and other tools to obtain feedback.

Speaking of which, we have to mention the principle of fail fast. For example, the code design needs to traverse a set of data, and we will should return immediately when an error occurs, instead of throwing this error after the traversal is completed.

5.3.2 Simplify Complex Process

I was in a project which the customer team had a process like this: When reporting bugs, screenshots of them are required for each step and uploaded to the bug management system. When we asked why, the customer representative said that their leader might read the report, and screenshots would make him easier to understand. I did doubt such explanation, since leaders usually do not care about such details which cost a lot of time every day. Was his leader aware of this? Later, we told this customer this way: We will attach with screenshots when necessary. If they require all screenshots are taken, each person will spend at least one hour on average to do screenshots and uploading each day, which is a very high cost. Finally, we reached an agreement that each bug was accompanied with only one major screenshot. This event had finally passed, and I have never heard of the customer's leader ask about the details in this regard.

The complex process is synonymous with "more professional" in the eyes of many people, it is able to minimize the impact of human factors through strict control. In fact, simplicity is easier for technical teams to achieve success. Implementing simple solutions and simple processes can not only reduce the cost of management, but also liberate the creativity of the team.

5.3.3 An Important Way to Speed Up Progress

Time is the scarce and irreplaceable resource in the software development process, and its waste will directly affect the project progress. There are various wastes in the software development process, and rework is a common waste in this process. Avoiding rework not only helps speed up the development process, but also improves the quality of the software.

Some good practices in agile development, such as defining completed standards, pair programming, and test-driven development, can all help avoid rework.

- Define the completion criteria, such as quality requirements and outputs so as to avoid rework. Properly handle some "last mile" matters in the process to reduce such anticlimax waste.
- Pair programming and timely code review to prevent bugs from being discovered later and causing rework. Without code review, the worst part of the code represents the overall code quality level. After the code review, the code quality is theoretically determined by the most experienced person within the team. At the same time, it is very helpful for developers to learn from each other.
- Test-driven development and requirements-driven development will clarify requirements as early as possible to avoid rework caused by the introduction of bugs due to incorrect understanding of requirements.

5.3.4 OVER-DESIGN IS ALSO A COMMON WASTE

Over-design refers to making too many predictions for possible future changes in the design stage, and making too many limitations in the design of these predictions. As the saying goes, plans are not as fast as changes. It's a waste to prematurely deal with these changes that may not happen at all. Therefore, simple design is advocated in agile development. The so-called simple design is not zero design, but as simple as possible. In fact, there is no real design solution that can meet changes with constancy. If it exists, it must also be a simple solution. Because it is simple, it can be easily overturned and reinvented to adapt to changes.

It is very important for a team to formulate reasonable process rules. Usually, a manager spends too much time and energy on personnel management and task tracking, while team members waste time on trivial matters. Well-functioning processes can bring everyone together on the right path.

In addition to agility, lean theory also has some ideas to eliminate waste. The first is the waste of inventory. From the perspective of user value, the completed functions should be deployed and launched as soon as possible to help customers and get customer feedback. Therefore, if the functions that have been completed cannot go online for various reasons, it is a waste.

The speed at which the team responds to changes is very fast, and the lean team can adjust the requirements being developed at any time.

WAYS TO RESOLVE WASTE IN PROCESS

For the waste in the process, we need to establish the necessary feedback mechanism to identify these wastes in time. For some tasks that need to be done every day, we should strive to automate them to reduce repetitive manual work. Reducing the waiting time in the process can also improve our work efficiency. Some advanced technical practices, the establishment of a continuous integration environment, and the establishment of deployment pipelines also require serious consideration by the team.

5.4 WASTE IN INFORMATION PROCESSING

The organization of distributed teams poses greater challenges to the dissemination of information. The longer in transmission route, the increase in the storage location of information, and the increase in the proportion of written communication have more or less affected the efficiency of information reception.

5.4.1 Waste From Organizational Structure

If the project manager is out of office today, is it possible that lots of work cannot be carried on? When the local team is in another time zone, the members of the offshore team cannot get updated and complete information, then they are forced to wait.

If it is an organization with many hierarchical relationships, the leader usually has a great information advantage, and the frontline employees depend on the top-down information transmission in a certain sense, rather than direct communication with end users. In this state of opaque information, the information obtained by the ordinary members are incomplete, especially the understanding of other teams and the information provided by the customer. The consequence is that what we made is inconsistent with the result expected by users, and we have to rework to correct it.

Part of the information is missed while being transmitted layer by layer. People in different positions have a habit of "receiving information at their demand," so that they may interpret the information out of context; while managers tend to receive the information that they think is "correct," and so on.

One of the biggest disadvantages of this multilevel organization is that communication only occurs in an up-down channel, and the horizontal connection between different roles or functional departments are very weak. If we can't change the organizational structure, we can try to strictly enforce some rules in the team to comply with. Only in this way can we eliminate waste as much as possible while maintaining the organizational structure unchanged.

When someone is absent one day, normally the information transmission may be disconnected at his point. The e-mail state must be set as "out of office," so that those who send e-mail will know which person cannot receive the message. When we take the initiative to communicate with customers, try not to send e-mails to only one person, but copy as many related people as possible from the customer side and those from our own team, and make CC e-mail a habit. Besides, it is very useful to create the necessary mailing groups, which ensures that everyone receives the message.

When using the instant message tool for communication, try to discuss in the chat group as much as possible, and copy information when necessary.

If we can reduce the hierarchical structure level, promote flattening, and eliminate the opaque state of information, we can fundamentally reduce the length of some information flows. To change the control-oriented multilevel structure to a learning-oriented flat structure, and the work initiation point is changed from supervisor command mode to full staff initiative mode.

5.4.2 Waste in Knowledge Management

We often hold seminars on requirements or technologies, and I sincerely suggest to make two types of records: decisions made and action plans. You might say, do I still need to record if I have all attended meetings? Yes, you do. Who can guarantee that there is no substitution while the project is going on? Sometimes a written record is needed for the newcomers to take reference. It is applicable to both testing and development.

Team knowledge is not well maintained, especially some research results, which will cause some team members to learn it again later. The main purpose of management of team knowledge, that is, the accumulation of team knowledge, is to reduce the learning cost of subsequent team members. People's repeated researching is a waste, there is not only time cost, but also loss of knowledge. Since it is impossible to trace how much quantity is lost, it is easy to cause unpredictable losses when delivering.

Some people may say that this is an inevitable learning curve due to the loss of knowledge caused by personnel changes. It is the learning cost that newcomers must pay. But if the cost is too high, it is also a waste, so we still have to do some work to reduce the negative impact of this. After all, in the current software industry, team changes are very frequent. A complete roadmap of handover steps is indispensable. It must define the things to be done, the time arrangement, and the criteria for successful handover.

Sometimes the information transfer between people is not enough, a person spent a lot of energy to solve a problem, but found that it was researched before. It is possible to avoid this problem by managing team knowledge, sharing information in pair work, and actively communicating information. If you have any questions, you must speak them out. It sounds easy, but you have to overcome many obstacles when doing it.

We commend people-to-people communication over perfect documentation. Many people mistakenly think that they don't need documents. This is a relative concept. The correct understanding is that we cannot rely too much on documents. Documents must meet the need to preserve team knowledge. Too much and too little will cause waste.

What kind of knowledge management the team needs depends on whether it is convenient for people who lack knowledge, such as querying and searching, but also on the invest of team maintenance, whether the team can maintain the knowledge base and keep the latest content. If we can't do these two basic things, we don't have to waste energy on it.

We often encounter problems with test document management. I once worked with a large corporation which wanted to save all test case documents to JIRA. The purpose was to make it easier for managers to see reports and assist business personnel to do acceptance test with the completed functions. But the part of our automation is maintained in the code base, which means part of the test cases were copied into JIRA. There will be inconsistencies and conflicts in the replication. Over time, this type of problem requires more and more time to solve.

The waste in knowledge management is also affected by time. We should organize the received information in real time, and promptly reconfirm the information that may be missed or ambiguous. As the old saying goes, strike while the iron is hot. We'd better organize and improve the information as soon as possible, because after a period of time, it will be difficult for us to remember fragmented information.

5.4.3 Waste Caused by Too Much Information

Sometimes, something too much is really a waste.

Too much information or too many choices may hinder us from making decisions and causing procrastination. As the saying goes "less is more." For example, We often install a lot of fitness software on our mobile phones. Every time we find a good software, it will be installed. But none of them will be used. If only one fitness software is installed, it is highly likely to be really used. If there is one more choice, many people will hesitate, and each additional step of choice will prevent some people from continuing to move forward. This is the funnel theory for user retention.

Multitasking is not uncommon in work. But for the development team, the more business contexts that need to be mastered at the same time, the efficiency will be reduced when frequent switching. If it is an offshore team, the final result in the eyes of customers will be like this: the delivery time of each story card becomes longer and the delivery speed becomes slower. This is why Kanban has an important attribute of strictly restricting the quantity of WIPs, so as to reduce inventory.

When managing the team knowledge, if there is too much information, another catastrophic result is likely to occur: proliferation of versions. All distributed teams must use Wiki, Google Doc, Dropbox, and other online collaboration tools to manage knowledge, tools, and documents within the entire team to avoid duplication.

An offshore team usually maintains two story walls, a physical one and an online one. Many times developers will question why we need to move cards on two walls, track progress, and do the same thing twice?

Distributed teams have no choice but to have an online virtual wall, which has many benefits:

- Real-time updates between teams
- Support customers to see the progress of the team from time to time

- Generate reports automatically
- Retain historical records during the delivery process for future queries

So, can we give up the physical wall? Since all the information on it is also on the virtual wall? Before going further, let's look at the following scenarios:

- Open the webpage every time you move a card
- All of us have to be crowded in front of a screen to discuss problems
- Carrying a computer at the stand-up

Therefore, the physical wall is more convenient for the team, and you can see the whole picture when you look up. Its use is effective and vivid for the team.

5.4.4 Solve the Waste Caused by Information Processing

Promoting the sharing of existing information and making existing information work better is one of the important ways to solve the waste caused by information processing.

5.4.4.1 Passive Safety Mode Solution

Only organized information can become the knowledge of the team. Therefore, we need to define some rules for the teams to follow and turn information into knowledge. First, all requirements, including changes in requirements, must record on paper (in JIRA/Trello or Excel). Secondly, the logical part of technical implementation needs to be shown in a flowchart, which is beneficial to spread knowledge to nontechnical personnel. Finally, regarding the extraction and reserve of information, we must do it from the details. The conclusions of communication by any tool must be summarized and stored. The use of e-mails should make good use of keywords to facilitate future searches.

5.4.4.2 Active Safety Mode Solution

Develop the habit of active communication. When a message is conveyed to someone, he should not become the end of the message, but should be a new starting point and be conveyed in the way he should. Just like broadcasting, the purpose of it is to convey information to other personnel in the team, especially the relevant personnel. When the customer changes the requirements or poses other requests, inform everyone that joins in this work. When broadcasting is not needed, the information should be stored as knowledge, and the purpose is to share. In addition to the sharing of information itself, we sometimes need to go further, thereby initiating a task and putting it in the story backlog, waiting for someone to complete it.

Helping others is helping ourself. We should attend the meetings (including the stand-up) between distributed teams. In case of any missed information, it may cause us to do some unnecessary work or omit some work. Similarly, some of our information should also be updated to other teams in a timely manner, such as providing some bug investigation results to prevent them from doing some useless work. If the current work priority changes, it should be made known to other teams.

We generally pay more attention to our own needs and how to obtain information when needed. On the contrary, when we provide information that others need, we always passively provide limited content. After all, it is the party in need that dominates and takes the initiative. But it is equally important for distributed teams to ask others for their needs, and they need to be taken seriously and provide as much detailed information as possible.

5.5 INVISIBLE WASTE

Compare with visible waste, invisible waste will cause the repeatability of project failure. We want to repeat successful experiences, not failed ones.

5.5.1 GIVING SEA CUCUMBERS TO MOTHER-IN-LAW

Sea cucumber is a kind of high-end gift. In my hometown, anyone who can receive the gifts of sea cucumbers like to brag about. I bought a box of sea cucumbers at a price of several thousand yuan and gave it to my mother-in-law. She was so pleased, but begrudged to eat them like most people. Consequently, I happened to find them remaining lying in the refrigerator two years later, but the quality was not as good as before. I took them out and was about to speak, then my mother-in-law saw said to me in a hurry, "Don't worry, I'll not waste them!" "Mom, eat them quickly, they cannot be kept much longer," I said so, but what in my mind was that "they cost me several thousand yuan when buying, but now they were not worth few hundreds yuan."

It can be seen that the thing that costs you a big price remains intact, but it is not as valuable as before, and not many people can realize it. This invisible waste exists widely in our lives. The above example is that improper preservation causes the loss of its own value, while many deep-rooted thoughts and bad habits may cause us to disregard something, which is also a kind of loss.

The example of giving sea cucumbers is essentially the result of mind-setting.

Mind-setting, also known as inertial thinking, is that people always habitually thinking about problems in accordance with the previous thinking, just like the inertia when objects move.

Looking back at the field of software development, there are also some things that have not changed on the surface in our work, but many intrinsic values have decreased.

To find these wastes, we need to analyze a problem from both external and internal factors. The waste caused by external factors is mainly due to communication problems and insufficient knowledge, and the other is mainly due to our own reasons, like mind-setting can cause habitual errors.

With the iterative process and continuous integration of distributed development, the number of functions is increasing, and there are often cases where the stability becomes worse and the quality is reduced. This loss of quality is relatively hidden, difficult to quantify, and usually wasteful.

We may be kept busy every day, it seems that productivity is not wasted, but our time management is bad and do no work by priority, so the invisible waste is everywhere in our daily work. To avoid this issue, generally, our project team will briefly highlight the list of tasks with the highest priority for the day after the daily stand-up.

Therefore, the manager usually adopts the result-oriented management method to solve the problem and complete the task within a certain period of time, and will not invest too much attention on work process.

5.5.2 FAIL QUICKLY TO AVOID WASTE

Such examples often appear around us. For example, your supervisor asks you to log in a customer website and register your company as a supplier. You spend a whole day in preparing all materials, but after uploading these materials, you find that your company is an existing registered supplier. The problem here is that the premise we assume is not valid, and the instruction from supervisor is an action, not a goal, so we assume that this premise is valid. So before you take any action, be sure to distinguish the difference of the goal and the instruction.

Could the idea of fail quickly in agile practice solve this problem? First, we can write test scripts and run it, this test is bound to fail under normal circumstances, and then we can implement the function to make the test passed. Let's look back at the above example, following the similar principle, we first register directly and then get a failed result, and then prepare materials to try the registration again. But in fact you will find the existing registration at the first time.

Fail quickly principle does not mean that you can do something right away without thinking. There was once a project, one day the customer proposed an improvement plan and suggested the time of each operation, then we embarked on it immediately. We came to realize that we should not do so two days later. If we feel we should not do something, it may be because someone has done it before, or the customer's idea is not feasible, either technically unfeasible or conflicting with requirements.

5.5.3 Identifying Invisible Waste Requires Some Insight

Invisible waste is mostly difficult to record because it is difficult to attract everyone's attention. For example, if we are late for work, it is apparently a waste to the company, same as give short weight on market. On the other hand, we do come to work on time and guarantee 8 hours of work every day, but we do not concentrate on our work, we may browse a news website during working time; it is a kind of invisible waste since it is not as obvious as being late. There is another kind of more invisible waste, that is, inefficiency. When we work, we do not think problems deeply or work by trying our utmost. This waste is more difficult to quantify. Unlike visible waste, being half an hour late is a waste of half an hour of work.

In many teams, I often notice that some people will enter a more focused work state before and after work, as if the time before returning home is the most productive time of the day. Even though I also find that they often forget to do things that day. I am one of those "not quite positive," since I start thinking about closing the job at 5:30 every day: check whether everything planned today is completed and see what needs to be scheduled for tomorrow.

5.5.4 Invisible Waste: Unaware of Progress

At a retrospective meeting, someone asked such a question: "Why do we always keep up with the progress hurriedly in the last few days? Do we need an agile coach in the team?" In such a delivery cycle, the efficiency of the first half is not high, and the speed of the second half has kept up. It looks like we achieved the goal, but it sacrificed a series of tasks such as test coverage, delivery quality, and performance tuning, which could be opportunities for us do a better job.

What we lack here in essence is not an agile coach, but to find a way to make the progress visible to everyone at any time. I've found a phenomenon that every time our technical team encounters a problem, it is easy to think of it as a new job which could be solved by increasing manpower. As a decent technical team, we should think about whether this problem can be solved by a certain technical means. As far as the problems mentioned above are concerned, we can completely solve it with a burndown chart.

5.5.5 Technical Debt and Requirements Debt

The problem implicit in the technical debt is that its influence will slowly expand in the code base and is invisible. Developers are often forced to make a choice: pay down the technical debt or develop new features? With the continuous accumulation of technical debt, customers begin to complain about the slow delivery speed, and the pressure of project progress begin to drive developers to take a lot of shortcuts and "black technology" to increase the development speed. Sometimes this is counterproductive, further increasing the technical debt, and the delivery is still delayed, eventually forming a vicious circle of negative feedback. If we notice these conditions too late, the project will be in risk. The team must solve these problems as early as possible, gradually solve the technical debt, and even consider introducing technical forces from outside the team to specifically help the team deal with the technical debt.

Misunderstanding: Is refactoring an indirect waste? Why doesn't our team do things well at once? In the world of agile development, it is impossible for us to maximize some functional modules from the beginning. Iterative development will make the scalability of the code worse and worse, and embracing the nature of change will make our code overturned at any time. Of course, the fundamental reason is that customer's requirements are changing along with project progress. Sometimes the realization of the business is also due to the cost of implementation, so finally the online solution may not the optimal solution.

5.5.6 LACK OF PRIORITY

If there are no rules for priority, developers will randomly pick up jobs to do according to their own preferences. Prioritizing product functions and bugs is quite necessary. It should be particularly pointed out that learning to lower the function priority will be more conducive to the team's efforts in truly valuable places. Both the business analysts of the offshore team and the product manager of the customer team have a tendency to over-evaluate priorities. Some teams I had worked in even set all functional requirements to high priority, which makes the priority meaningless.

5.5.7 INVISIBLE WASTE IN DISTRIBUTED TEAMS

Using systematic thinking to think about the invisible waste of our team, and use mind maps to conduct divergent thinking. If the deployment pipeline fails, developers cannot submit new code, and testers cannot get the latest program to test. If this kind of thing happens frequently, the team should discuss a solution.

Iterative development can reduce invisible waste. Since iterative development plans only short-term goals to avoid doing things that may change in the future without analysis.

We implement agile development, and the core of delivering valuable functions is "user feedback." Without user feedback, we cannot adjust the requirements during the development process. It seems like all requirements are defined at the startup of the project and do not make any adjustment later. So we must convince customers to pay attention to auditing and let end users try out the functions that have been done. Without a benign feedback mechanism, it will inevitably cause some invisible waste.

What is the fundamental purpose of eliminating waste? This is a question that many people think is too simple to think about, and they can blurt out a lot of "correct" answers. At the end of this chapter, I raise this question, hoping that we think about several more dimensions, and then from the direction of each dimension, combined with the environment in which our team is located, start thinking deeply to find the answer. This is also a popular pyramidal way of thinking in management, which has a good effect on finding waste in the team.

- Dimension 1: the speed of delivery. Need to improve the work efficiency of the team.
- Dimension 2: satisfaction of team members. Need to reduce negative energy and avoid complicated work processes.
- Dimension 3: mutual trust between remote teams. Improve the professionalism of handling team collaboration issues and handle the information sharing between teams.
- Dimension 4: quality of delivery. Do a good job in collecting feedback, and build quality in and out.

Therefore, the team shall take some time to pay attention to the waste that cannot be quantified. By doing their utmost to find out these invisible problems, we must have an unexpected gain.

Agile practices are better methodology, even though we also need to identify waste. For example, have we extended the stand-up to a seminar, and has the stand-up calibrated everyone's situation in all aspects? Has our investment in test-driven development paid off?

In the case of testing. We usually spend more time in places that are not easy to test, rather than in places where users use more, which is wasteful. Important functions have not received corresponding attention, so the results must be lower than normal expectations.

5.5.8 CONSEQUENCES OF INVISIBLE WASTE

If we do not pay attention to invisible waste in the process of development or other pursuit of a goal, as we approach delivery, we will find:

- The project needs to be delayed
- Low quality or performance does not meet the requirements

- Low morale and frequent complaints
- No active collaboration between teams
- Increased customer complaints
- Many people ask to leave the team without knowing the real reason

5.6 DON'T TURN BDD INTO A WASTE IN THE TEAM

The emergence of behavior-driven development (BDD) incorporates many agile practices.

The first is the integration and upgrade of test-driven development (TDD) and desk check to ensure that the functions developed by developers will enable everyone to understand the requirements. Requirements-driven development (RDD) eliminates the desk check, that is, the manual on-site inspection steps after the development is completed; the test conditions are set by technical means, and they have been defined before development.

The second is to generate live documentation to ensure that anyone can find the latest instructions of the software at any time. This is an effective supplement to the requirements of the story card recording. The requirements on the story card are very time-sensitive. Extremely speaking, it can only represent the behavior of the software in the iteration period to which it belongs. The requirements reflected by BDD will always be effective, otherwise they will fail the test.

The quality of the designed BDD test cases has a great influence on its ultimate responsibility. They must be described in business language, and do not involve statements that have no business meaning, such as operations on webpage. The complex business part is described by examples. It is difficult to call BDD a decent BDD without SBE.

If the practice of BDD is adopted, but the advantages of BDD are not reflected, it will become a burden for the team. The cost of BDD is very high, it is a pity if it cannot be brought into full play. Many teams regard it as a fashionable selling point to implement, because its effect is difficult to quantify and evaluate, and there are customers who pay, why not do it? However, the value of BDD is to drive development in the form of requirements description. One is to ensure that the understanding of the requirements of all participants in the team is easy to calibrate. The second is to ensure that the developed functions are born to meet business requirements from the beginning.

Making BDD generate value is an important job to convince and guide customers under the conditions of distributed teams. From a lean perspective, our value is not how good we produce, but to avoid the generation of low-value things. The low-value things mentioned here include not only low-business-value things for users, but also a large cost invested in the development process. Yet there is no practice of value output. .

To ensure the value of BDD, the team should establish a feedback mechanism for BDD, so that it always runs around our expectations. We can do the following things:

We can use BDD to get feedback on requirements change as early as possible. We have a lot of practice in the development process to balance customers and offshore teams. But users (usually the selected user representatives) can only see the functions we deliver after going online. The feedback presented at this time is a bit late for the development team. Despite the agile development approach, we give the users the most valuable functions through small steps, iterative development, embracing change, and deliver them the most valuable functions in the end. Although we have embraced changes, we don't like to accept some waste during the process. Considering there will be user verification of our developed functions to accord with their daily business, can we deliver functions in advance to make it? The answer is ask user to take BDD audits, not just customer audits. Incorporate user representatives into the team, at least to ensure that the offshore team's business analysts, customer's product manager and designers can maintain close communication with user representatives.

Although the embracing changes mentioned above generate additional workload, customers are also willing to pay for them. However, if this part of the waste can be reduced, such as do it right from the beginning, is it to create additional value for customers? At the same time, this also explains why many projects need to be postponed, and many teams have to work overtime to reach the release time of customers. Because the actual workload we spend is equal to the workload of the function finally delivered to the user plus the workload of embracing change introduced.

This part of the workload in embracing change produces business value, which is the value generated by promptly correcting errors and promptly retreating from the cliff. But have we thought about eliminating these errors in the bud?

It is precisely because we hold the idea of "embracing change" as a value action. Instead, we will neglect to dig deeper into the underlying reasons behind the change, causing us to become dependent on the stage of user provide feedback. The initial stage is still based on the business requirements of the existing customers to communicate with their users in a centralized manner, or the final requirements summarized by the offshore team's understanding of the customers. After the development work begins, users' thinking will also change, constantly approaching the most real goal. BDD provides an opportunity to begin to intervene in the business verification phase when the requirements are refined.

5.7 SUMMARY

Waste is actually negative energy and negative assets in all aspects. It flows in our daily work. Some will cause direct losses to us, and some will cause indirect losses to us. For a team that advocates continuous improvement, the problems of waste cannot be taken lightly. These problems are like "throttling" in open source throttling. Open source without throttling cannot be called complete continuous improvement.

The cost of handling anomalies is definitely higher than the normal cost, and so is the social cost. Take a simple example, there are always some people parking on the sidewalk. The floor tiles on the sidewalk cannot bear the weight of vehicles and are often crushed, so new floor tiles are replaced frequently. Of course, the management department can erect isolation piles on the periphery of the sidewalk to prevent the entry of motor vehicles. These two schemes, which are adopted to guard against the behaviors of a small number of individuals, will consume a lot of social resources. If everyone abides by the law, such a huge investment will be saved. For the waste of large outsourcing teams, the same problem can cause greater waste, so it is more important to reduce exceptions and establish specifications.

The development team adopting the agile delivery method will always develop the released part, and the other parts have not entered the development link, so modifying the requirements will not waste any work. We can even say that agile development encourages us to modify the requirements when necessary, and we know that the requirements change is the most important reason for the failure of most nonagile outsourcing projects.

6 Self-Managed Offshore Teams

A traditional software development team puts more emphasis on planning and control. All individuals working on a project shall strictly abide by some norms, such as the use of milestone, and do a good input and output job at all stages. Any unfulfilled output will preclude the next-stage work, because throughout the software life cycle, the impact of defects at the early stage is much larger than that at the later stage. In pipelined development, the waterfall model defines developers as workers on the pipeline. Since developers at all stages only access things within their own scope of work, their understanding of customer requirements is of different extent. Therefore, developers are more resistant to changed customer requirements than designers. On the positive side, the development is carried on according to certain criteria, even if there is staff turnover, some new ones will fill the gap in a short time. That's why managers prefer the waterfall model, while developers hate it for its constraint of their creativity.

The self-managed offshore team needs to be people-oriented. Compared to the document-oriented waterfall development, agile development highlights human creativity. In development of details, individuals can play a subjective role and use their skilled techniques and development model, rather than machine-based development, which is easy to stimulate the interest and creativity of team members. All project participants need to continuously achieve iterative and continuous personal growth from communication and meetings with customers.

Self-management does not mean that there is no demand for the team. Just as rights and obligations always appear in pairs, so the message to the team should be like this: "you are a completely self-managed organization, but you must implement TDD and regular reviews, etc."

Many teams do not lack regulations and norms, but a self-control and self-management ability in a loose environment. Self-managed teams have high requirements for team members in terms of soft skills. This chapter lists some very effective methods. Anyone who wants to build a self-organized offshore team cannot bypass these points of thinking in order to succeed.

6.1 THE INFLUENCE OF TRADITIONAL CULTURE ON THE TEAM

Due to the influence of traditional culture, Chinese teams or teams from different countries are accustomed to command and control management. Team leaders make the decision and other members of the team execute it. There will be many hindrances in implementing agile development in such a team. In an agile team, there are certain requirements for the self-management ability of team members, and it is also a necessity. When completing a task, if we have to make choices and decisions, we must put the opinions of the particular executors first, not the leaders.

Chinese people are used to maintaining a harmonious relationship with their partners to avoid conflicts. This has affected the way offshore agile teams work in offshore delivery, including iterative planning, iterative reviews, and daily agile work. People are used to reserving their opinions because we cannot adapt to an environment where we might make mistakes, even if it doesn't matter we make mistakes in such an environment. Agile development requires everyone to speak out where is the problem, which is contrary to our traditional culture, because Chinese pay special attention to showing respect to others, not making others embarrassed, and they are ashamed to express any unpleasant advice in front of others.

Ken Schwaber is the founder of Scrum.org and one of the creators of Scrum. In his blog, he mentioned the cultural obstacles encountered in the implementation of agile thinking in China. He has observed that some people who are used to focusing on predictability will encounter difficulties in an agile environment. For those who are used to predictability, they hope they can make detailed plans for future goals. After that, their job is to use human and material resources to make their foreseeable future a reality. People with agile thinking know that for such complex and creative work as software development, such things as predictability are impossible, so the results are usually very bad: poor software quality, delays in planning, wasted funds, and low morale.

Many companies outsource projects to China, they also want to reduce costs by adopting agile development. But in fact this development model actually requires high-quality team members who are more costly than you think. Therefore, as long as everyone still holds the simple idea that agile development can reduce costs, it will be difficult to implement this development model in China.

In an offshore team, expression is also a big problem. Being too modest, we will not speak out loudly and confidently even if we are certain about something. Being too humble, we dare not take on a task even if we are confident of doing well. We just put our back into working, and rarely take the initiative to express ourselves and show the ability of our team. Under the influence of a low-profile and restrained culture, the offshore team may give up their own ideas and follow the other party's plan, although their ideas are much better. In contrast, a local team, despite a flawed plan, will fight for it by arguing with the other party. So in reality, if you want to find a solution when dealing with these two teams, the best way is to maximize the advantages of their plans by combining the positions of both parties.

We also have a bad tendency: compared with soft skills, we care more about hard skills. As a member of a distributed team, each of us should exercise our expressive ability, because the project manager will not take over all the communication on behalf of the team. Overseas customer teams understand that our work is largely based on our expression, both in oral and written forms, rather than directly seeing the results of our work, which is also one of the limitations of the delivery based on remote cooperation.

If we don't express ourself carefully, it will bring us a lot of losses:

- A good job is unable to be fully visible
- Unable to fully obtain the trust of the customer, resulting in the task assignment inconsistent with the actual situation when the tasks are distributed between the teams, that is, the customer has reservations for us
- Complete a job with questions due to insufficient communication
- When we ask the customer to cooperate with us for certain joint tasks, he may misunderstand our requirements and causes greatly reduced effect. What's worse, he may complain that the work of offshore teams needs to be improved.

Learning to undertake is a required course for everyone in the team. When facing difficulties, we may say "I don't know much about this part" or "We were not responsible for this part." We should not be afraid of failure or taking responsibility, but thrive on pressure, "Let me try it," "Let me try again." Even if we fail in the end, we should say "I've tried my best, trust me," instead of looking for some objective reasons.

The worst traditional team I have ever seen is like this: team members have no incentive to ask questions and discuss issues. When they find it is not likely to complete the task by the schedule, they still remain silent or make no suggestions to the supervisor for improvement.

Therefore, as a member of the offshore team, when working with other distributed teams (especially teams from Western countries), we should try to avoid the following situations:

- Accept a proposal that is not fully satisfactory out of courtesy.
- Retain your views during team discussions.
- Making fun of other's flawed opinions. Everyone's environment may be different, and we need to think about whether there is something we do not understand. The correct method is to further confirm with the other party whether there is something to be ignored, or special consideration is required.
- When you notice a potential problem, you may feel it has little to do with yourself, so you say no word about it. In fact, as long as it is related to the team or any team member, you cannot get away with it since you are also one of them.
- Do not join in the discussions with the English speakers for fear of poor expression. We should try to express ourself even if we are not skilled in speaking English. Others understanding that English is not our mother tongue, so they usually take the initiative to confirm with us and help us express our intention. With these experiences, we can improve our English, and it will not take long for us to find ourselves more and more relaxed in attending such meetings.

Of course, if we understand that some of our own habits will have some negative effects, we will try to overcome them in a targeted manner. Many teams are struggling to overcome these agile resistances, and I have heard many encouraging news. When we give every ordinary team member certain powers to make decisions within their controllable scope of responsibilities, their activity and enthusiasm will be ignited. We also understand that while exercising power, we also have equal responsibilities. Therefore, when making a decision, we have to be more careful and do more research than before to be confident in making choices for ourselves and the team. In this process, everyone's sense of responsibility will be slowly established. Finally, in addition to the project manager, everyone will learn to be responsible for the entire team.

When we have more sense of responsibility, more courage, and more confidence to make reasonable decisions, we can also reduce a lot of waste, because we do not need to wait for the local team to make a choice. Of course, if we often make decisions rashly, or make decisions that exceed our capabilities since we do not have any context, this trust may be lost at any time.

The formation of both habits and culture is a process. At the beginning, we will encounter many difficulties, starting from small things will establish confidence and bring reputation to us.

From my observations over the years, there are many trifle things to pay attention to, we can take the below ones as example:

- Get rid of the habit of not being punctilious and pay more attention to details. For example, do not make unnecessary laughter at meetings.
- The traditional thought of scholars scorning each other is not desirable. Don't look down on your teammates. As long as you work together in the same team, you have the same goal to work hard for.
- You must learn to be punctual, avoid being late for meetings, and make preparations in advance.
- Don't do things too casually.
- Don't be too sensitive, this is also a lack of confidence.

Some people want someone to tell themselves what to do, and some people always want to direct others to do things. Don't worry, in a team composed of such people, the entire organization will be well-regulated.

With different cultural background, people have different ways of solving problems. Although the blending of culture and habits is not done overnight, it is very helpful to understand the differences between them for daily cooperation. But we do not advocate deliberately catering to each other.

6.2 THE DRIVING FORCE OF THE TEAM

As early as 1954, Drucker proposed an epoch-making concept: management by objectives. Its core idea is to give up command-driven management and embrace goal-driven management. Fundamentally speaking, management by objectives changes the manager's job from controlling his subordinates to setting more objective standards and goals with his subordinates, and letting the real executors accomplish it on their own initiative. These commonly recognized measurement standards prompt the executors to manage and control themselves with objectives, that is, self-evaluation, rather than evaluation and control by outsiders. This idea of Drucker is considered to be the basis of self-organization and self-management advocated by modern team management.

Today, more than half a century later, this idea is still not outdated, but also has a broader applicability. With the development of agile and lean thinking, management by objectives has played a role as a banner and benchmark for team members in the project to exert their subjective initiative. Because the team's objectives are the same, it's easier for everyone to stay motivated. Although we all know that there is an objective to be defined in the project, and also the team members have agreed on the objective, but how can we achieve the objective?

Objectives and Key Results (OKR), which is very popular in software companies, is a new type of management by objectives. It decomposes objectives into teams and individuals within the organization, and defines some key events to measure the achievement of objectives. This structure of objectives ensures that everyone's objectives are consistent and clear through the organizational relationship of the objectives, and what the team's overall objectives are and where they play their role.

OKR is indeed simple and effective, but in addition to the method itself, the person who executes the method is a more important factor. For a team, in order to have the ability of self-driven team, the formation of a team cannot be underestimated. People with weak self-discipline and those who do not set goals for themselves will encounter great challenges in the self-management team. Management theory still believes that management cannot change a person, and even self-managed organizations cannot do this.

The organizational structure and organizational culture of the team determine whether the self-management team can continue to operate. It sounds abstract, but any successful organization must have its inner power to support it. Once this power weakens or dies, its organization will inevitably fail. So this section will show how to build an offshore team and indicate the source of spiritual motivation to team members.

In response to the above problems, combined with the organizational structure of the distributed team, and according to the team's objectives and personal responsibilities, we shall explore the source of the team's driving force from the aspects of team culture and horizontal organizational structure. Everyone shall first understand these requirements before they have them demonstrated in daily work, and it is possible to build an internal driving force for the offshore team.

For offshore teams, customers cannot sit and work with them every day, so building a team with self-organization and self-management is more important for the healthy operation of the project, which can effectively reduce the management costs of the customer and the contractor. The ultimate goal is to improve work efficiency.

6.2.1 WHERE DOES THE DRIVING FORCE COME FROM

In a broad sense, the driving force of a team may come from all team members, the cultural atmosphere created by these people, their way of doing things, and the role of team leader.

A team may find the sources of driving force anywhere at any time. We have to be keen to discover them. Self-managed teams need to start from little things and develop step by step, so that quantitative changes can be transformed into qualitative changes, just like blades of grass can be twisted into a strong rope.

The practice of distributed teams in the use of information is focused on facilitating the dissemination of information. They should avoid letting managers act as a microphone for them, which makes sense for them to develop a transparent communication habit. After the team is flattened, the sharing of information by team members is a network structure, and everyone has an equal opportunity to get all the information. The traditional organization is a linear structure, and anyone can become a bottleneck in information dissemination.

6.2.1.1 Objective-Driven

When working with projects, all milestones defined are actually phased objectives. This is usually the objective we set together with the customer, and it is also the result of the refinement of the entire project objective. But not all tasks can be taken as milestones. A task with no requirement for time means that it is not a real task to be completed, but only a landmark event. Regarding the test coverage target of a software development project, test execution is a subtask, and adding test code is also a subtask, but completing the test coverage target is not a subtask that really needs to be completed. When making plans and tracking plans, a subtask of completing the test coverage target is often added, but the duration is often set to zero. The purpose is to check this time point, which is a sign of the end of the entire test task.

The purpose of the milestone setting is to calibrate a procedural task with a conclusive mark, so that the task has a clear start and end point. This series of starting and ending points becomes a milestone that guides the progress of the entire project. In the progress tracking process of project management, as long as the milestone events can be completed on time, the progress of the entire project is also guaranteed.

The delivery team must have long-term and short-term objectives. Short-term objectives are better controlled and managed. But how can we achieve the long-term objectives? The long-term objectives seem like a high-score user story, or a large functional module that has not been refined. A large objective will make the executor unable to start, and get awestruck. Therefore, the first step is to divide the unrealistic tasks into reasonable small tasks. As long as we can complete small tasks every day, we will get closer to that large objective.

Each project should have its own objective, and each team member should also have his own objective. If they can't set their own objectives, the project manager, as a team leader, should say what to expect from everyone, and make it as an objective, pressure, or incentive. At the same time, this objective should be constantly reviewed to become a constant pressure.

We need to set a realistic and normally challenging objective. If we set our objectives according to our good wishes, we will inevitably experience the setback again and again.

6.2.1.2 Team Culture

Building a team culture is a big topic, which is hard to be thoroughly elaborated here. Don't worry, we will only talk about the "tip of the iceberg" of team culture, that is, how to mobilize an atmosphere of active sharing, active problem-solving, and active responsibility bearing in the team.

In fact, I always want to say "formation" of team culture, the word "building" is easy to make people feel the existence of external forces. It is the personnel within a team that are interested in form their team culture.

Everyone has heard of "creating a team culture," and we need to turn this into a viable approach. One of my important work in writing this book is trying to find some practices that can help the team.

In a self-managed team, no one will come to you to "help" you. You need to take the initiative to ask for help. Do not wait for others to do something for you; otherwise, you will be kicked out of the team quickly.

(1) Authorization. We require all people to take the initiative, even to reach the level of obligations, which requires empowering team members. Doing a good job in authorization is like switching on the light mentioned in the Toyota production method. The one who switches on the light knows what kind of decision he can make under what circumstances.

Command and control will not work for smart people, so we need new methods. Learn to authorize is one of them. Executors will find a way to do it themselves, all we can do is to verify the results.

A self-managed organization needs a highly trusted authorization system, which can promote everyone to automatically take responsibility and pursue collaboration. We emphasize that team members should create value independently. In such a team, benefits shall be shared rather than enjoyed by certain individual. Trust and authorization are the greatest pressure on the team, and sharing is the best control.

(2) The authority culture of the team. Don't be afraid of authority after getting the authorization. In the art field, someone without extraordinary talent cannot exceed his master. But in the technical field, it is common for apprentices to surpass masters, so bold authorization is required.

The authority of the team comes from distributed and multilevel authority. The authority of traditional enterprises is a top-down authority, equivalent to the authority of administrative orders. The authority of the current self-managed team is a kind of bottom-up authority, process authority, and expert authority. In any aspect, becoming an expert is the authority in this regard. There must be authority within the enterprise, but it is no longer the same pattern: the single and top-down administrative order is outdated, now every team member has the opportunity to become authority. This is also a feature of a fully functional team. Everyone has their own role positioning and strengths.

(3) What is culture? Culture is that team members have strong self-discipline ability and can complete their work spontaneously. For teams with self-reform and learning ability, continuous self-reform and innovation is the eternal theme. The team can accept fresh ideas and things, and can also help a newcomer enhance his professionalism.

6.2.1.3 A Sense of Security

The sense of security for a team is that when anyone on the team wants to share their thoughts, they should not feel troubled or worried.

"Everyone is important" in a self-managed team, and everyone should be respected. With this idea, everyone in the team will be happy to share their knowledge and be brave enough to undertake some challenging tasks. The self-managed team believes that regardless of the results, the teammates have done their best under the conditions at that time. Because they trust each other, when team members make mistakes, they give each other understanding and encouragement, rather than pass the buck and blame each other.

Of course, the sense of security does not mean that the team is used as a safe haven. It is inevitable that the teams will collide with each other when they are learning from each other. They may present challenge, but not attack others.

6.2.1.4 Internal Driving Force

As a self-organizing team, the normal operation of the entire team needs a force. This force is not imposed from outside, nor is it a command from the leader, since such a force is relatively rigid and passive. To maintain vitality and enthusiasm, the team needs internal driving force. But where does the internal driving force come from? Let's start with a few issues that the software delivery team will encounter:

- Generation of requirements
- Changes of requirements
- Discovery of bugs
- The deadline requested by the customer

When a new requirement is generated, study the reasons behind this requirement, what kind of solutions can quickly meet this user requirement? How about its priority as compared with the current requirements? How to revise the release plan? When a requirement changes, how much impact does the change have on the team's workload? Has it caused a waste of completed work? Does the development plan need to be adjusted?

When a bug is found, the priority of bug processing is higher than that of normally developed function cards, and developers need to deal with this bug first. If possible, he has to hold on his work in progress. Bug tracking, processing, verification, and closure are all handled priority by the team.

When a customer requires a function to be included in a package to be released next month, discuss with the customer which previously planned function can be replaced. In addition, the test plan also need to be adjusted accordingly, besides functional test part, especially need to evaluate whether nonfunctional tests in the test plan will be affected.

The above are some typical events in the software delivery process. These events are just signals, and seems to trigger a series of tasks to be completed. In another dimension, people with different roles in the software delivery team also need to drive themselves. The following is a detailed analysis of the driving force from the four dimensions of requirements, development, testing and DevOps.

6.2.1.4.1 Requirements-Driven

In each iteration, there is a product backlog to be completed. The backlog reflects the amount of work the team promises to the customer. This number is entirely determined by the development team. The workload can only be determined by the development team itself, and the product manager or anyone else cannot impose more workload on the development team. The amount of work depends on the team's estimation of story cards and the development speed of the team counted in past iterations.

6.2.1.4.2 Development-Driven

The test code in TDD also belongs to development work. A failed test drives developers to complete all functions, so that the test code can pass, and the developers' work could be completed. This also means that the implemented functions are able to satisfy the requirements.

The pace and speed of development drives the team's delivery speed. When developers get a new task, they will work with other personnel to examine the details of the requirements, eliminate all ambiguities, and then quickly break down the task to estimate the rough workload. When the work is completed, the relevant personnel must be brought together to review whether the completed function meets the business requirements. At this point, the developed functions begin to drive testers to begin acceptance testing.

6.2.1.4.3 Test-Driven

The essence of test is to feed back the software quality to the development team. The functional bugs, performance, and security issues raised from a testing perspective will be added into the product backlog as individual tasks.

After the test is completed, testers will decide which functions can be shown to the customer, which functions can be released, and which bugs must be fixed. It is the testers that are duty-bound to make these decisions which are needed by the team, not the managers.

6.2.1.4.4 DevOps-Driven

Another problem brought by iterative development is that when the team is developing new functions, it is also responsible for maintaining the production environment that is already online. Outages, data loss, and business interruptions are all issues that the team needs to resolve immediately. Some are problems with environment configuration, and of course there are also problems caused by code implementation. If it is the latter, it needs to be fed back to the development team as soon as possible. When necessary, these problems need to be fixed on the branch and deployed to the production environment as quickly as possible.

DevOps will often expose some design problems, which affect the stability of operation, and other nonfunctional problems, because these problems cannot be simulated in the test environment.

Some customers will request to include the function of event tracking in the function, so that they can collect user data, analyze the users' behavior, and count the effects of some key functions. The feedback results of these data will greatly affect our subsequent requirement arrangements and development plans.

6.2.2 Establish a Flat Organization

The characteristic of a flat organization is that it replaces mature and complete management with a high degree of autonomy. Everyone is authorized to make important decisions by default, it sounds like "a general in the field may refuse his lord's command." Here it means that each solider can make his own choice according to the situation in the battle. To ensure the occurrence of these situations, the organization needs that each team member can receive the exact same information, and each member can use the same methodology to face challenges and solve problems. When faced with choices, it is more important to define the options available than to make choices.

To flatten the management of a team, it is necessary to ensure the free flow of information, which is an unshakable premise. Everyone must make their own judgment based on the information they have. The consequences of any individual's monopoly on information must be influencing the judgment of others. In addition, flattening also embodies the word "fast," that is, to quickly respond to changes: make fast adjustment in case of changed requirements; fast fixing of bugs; fast failure to verify our assumptions.

If we use a team collaboration tool, such as Slack, even one-to-one online communication between team members must be conducted in public. This will bring a lot of benefits, and others can join in quickly to supplement this communication. We also need to manage groups of various communication tools. When a project starts, we create a new group, and when the project ends, we close the group. This method of communication is much simpler than e-mail, and the information covered is more comprehensive.

In a flat organization, team members need to share information and understand what other people are doing. Eliminating information asymmetry becomes crucial. What each one does must be as intuitional as possible for most people, and common values are conducive to others to make correct judgments.

Knowledge accumulation is also important for flat teams, but it is important to avoid fighting for oneself. For example, the team must have the same understanding and judgment on the same type of problem, if we can further summarize some applicable cases for the current situation, it will be the wealth of the teams. Knowledge summarization is more valuable for offshore teams where staff changes are usually frequent. The project manager in the team is responsible for calibrating the understanding of all offshore team members, and trying to unify the knowledge as much as possible at the beginning. The beginning refers to when the problem first appeared. In the process of dealing with this knowledge, it is necessary to actively and constantly communicate with other teams or individuals, there must be some unexpected gains if we are lucky.

Teamwork should follow some skills, such as planning tasks at different stages, long-term adherence to some good practices to form habits. The team must have a set of dispute resolution mechanisms suitable for their common ground while reserving differences. Ideally, team members must be able to naturally reach some consensus, otherwise "managers" will always appear quietly to help us coordinate our work, reach consensus, or appear angrily to blame those who have not completed the work.

Isn't a full-functional team a flat team? There are some misunderstandings. The flat team does contain many functions and is composed of people with many functions. What a full-functional team pursues is that everyone in the team can assume the functions of other roles in the team at any time, so this is not necessarily related to flattening.

The flat company structure brings a more agile company and a more open environment. At the same time, it also gives everyone in this ecological environment more responsibility and trust, that is, everyone is capable of self-control, self-management, pursuit of self-excellent, and excellent software. When people have a lot of autonomy, they have a strong instinct to avoid disappointing others. Flat organizations should amplify this instinct.

Nonflat organizations have to bear relatively high management costs, although at high costs, the effectiveness of the organization is not good. In traditional organizations, the project manager represents all people, all roles, and communicates with the customer, he seems like the interface between the team and the outside, but he sometimes becomes a stumbling block. The tasks of the members of the organization also come from the managers, and the leaders will assign the tasks to everyone below from top to bottom. In a flat organization, everyone and external customers can achieve peer-to-peer communication, and the task acquisition requires everyone to identify and pull the task actively.

6.2.3 PEOPLE ARE THE CORE OF AN ORGANIZATION

THE STORY OF LIANGLIANG

First of all, Liangliang is a very smart person. When he found that the team's approach was not good, he would challenge it, but he was unable to give a better solution.

Over time, he gave everyone the impression that he talked about it every day, but he never turned his ideas into reality. His attendance record was also very bad, his excuse was that he did not have much work to do. Because of his bad performance, I couldn't believe that he could do something good for our team. Later, I no longer assigned any task for him. Without executive power, such an empty talker is impossible to do a good job in a team. Maybe he is more suitable to act as Party A? But who knows?

Therefore, the self-managed team does not place all of its energy on the operation of the project itself. The talents in the team are the basis of its self-management. With qualified and reliable personnel, the output of the team could be guaranteed. Among them, initiative and execution are decisive factors.

6.2.3.1 Initiative

Self-driven teams have high demands on individual initiative. What if someone in the team is not motivated to actively ask for a task? We need to conduct self-management training within the team, the purpose is to foster everyone's awareness in this regard. However, it may be unlikely to achieve the goal by just talking to everyone. Some people can do it as we've told them, but what about others that are insubordinate? Is there a better way?

Team members should develop the habit of active thinking, take the initiative to do things, and reduce their passiveness. Everyone in the self-organized team needs to coordinate with other colleagues to determine the daily tasks, rather than waiting for the assigned work. Promote more communication within and between teams, especially face-to-face communication. For example, try to find some work to do during communication at the daily stand-up. If someone needs you to debug an interface, you have to reserve some time to do this day. If testers need to fix a bug right now, the relevant developers have to temporarily put down their work and help deal with the bug.

Don't just think, do it boldly. Taking the first step is sometimes difficult, but once this is done, many things will become natural.

6.2.3.2 Execution

Execution refers to the situation that one accepts a task, or get a task in whatever means, and full completes this task 100% without the supervision of anyone else. He can actively inform others the progress of the completion, ask for help when encountering problems, and cooperate with other relevant personnel to work out the solution.

Execution is sometimes a sign of responsibility, instead of being asked by leaders from time to time and still unprepared when integrating or cooperating with others. If these situations often occur, it is necessary to deal with these disruptors or "disintegrators" of the team's driving force, because they have become the negative assets and negative energy of the team.

6.2.3.3 "Initiative+Execution" is the Basis of Pull Work Mode

As a member of an offshore team, if you want to do your job well, you need to be able to find the job you need to do, you cannot wait for the customer or the project manager's arrangement. Even if it is impracticable, you should accept the work assigned by others. But if you still need others to inspect your work from time to time, you are unqualified, since the driving force for the work should be yourself.

When the team encounters some problems, including some plans, actions or only some suggestions mentioned in meetings, the actions to be taken should be decided by person in charge of execution.

For the responses in other aspects, such as rotation in personnel, we have the responding concepts of pair programming and whole team responsibility. We will not put all eggs in one basket. With transparently defined responsibilities and sufficient communication, everyone can access to the maximum contextual knowledge to the maximum extent. These agile ideas, organizational power and even the application of some technical means (continuous integration, continuous delivery) are also guarantees for the efficiency of distributed teams.

If the team members do not take their work as a career worth fighting for, then flattening will give them the reins. Moreover, if the team members do not have enough abilities to stand alone, flattening will leave a gap for team collaboration. This is a reality. The above two types of people are widely present in our team. If not, the team does not need personnel management. The project manager of a flat team needs to identify the people who have no enough ability or will, and then take the following measures:

- Focus on training these people, give them advice and opportunities to grow faster
- Give other people some feedback, promote their self-adjustment, and feedback their conditions to the human resources office, so as to put some pressure upon them

When mobilizing the enthusiasm of everyone in the team, never lose the objective of the team. Although the team may take some actions to achieve the objective, we always remind ourselves what the objective is. Many times we may mistaken the actions as the objective itself, such as to keep the team busy and let the teamwork overtime. If these actions are taken as the objective, the team will go to a low morale and fall into a dead end, unable to turn around.

6.2.4 Does a Flat Team Need Leadership

Leadership refers to the ability that leads everyone to achieve a goal, and do things more efficiently and effectively with fewer detours. It is not easy to possess leadership, it is a kind role model like taking the lead in the first line. Leadership is not a qualification to become a leader in the traditional sense, in which only needs to issue orders by the side, all the specific work is undertaken by others.

Leadership is mostly seen when a coach of the team guides the team members on daily work. Both an independent agile coach or a project manager can have leadership.

An important starting point for leadership is to promote the team to make effective decisions. How to get all team members to agree is also an important skill. Some team leaders will make decisions on behalf of the team, which is an incorrect approach to quick success. Just like the star players in a team, the real leader is to cascade the whole team and exert the overall strength, rather than choose to be a lone hero and go it alone. It seems like football or basketball, it's an ultimate team sport, just like all outsourcing projects.

How does a flat organization make decisions? From leaders and customers make decisions to all team members sit together to discuss problems. Each side has its own unique advantages: The front-line team knows more technical details, and the leaders have the resources needed to solve the problem; while customers are aware of the requirements of end users. A comprehensive solution should be made by giving full play of the advantages of all parties, but discussions must be organized, otherwise an agreement cannot be reached.

Everyone may have different opinions. The purpose of discussions is to find an optimal choice in the current situation within a given time frame and under the allocation of existing resources (or available resources). Everyone must remember that it is not a perfect choice. In a flat organization, most decisions are made through this kind of team discussion (not excluding the authoritative decision of experts), and finally made in a way that is accepted by most people.

Leadership is not something inborn or acquired overnight. In this flat organization, the decision-making comes from the group wisdom of the team. In the case where everyone has his own idea, he shall find ways to persuade others to support him. In this process, whoever gets the most support for their ideas often gains more leadership. Therefore, this is implicitly produced in the process of constantly proving himself.

Many practices or activities appear to exert collective power, such as brainstorming. Brainstorming is a way for a flat team to gather the strength of the whole team to explore deep-level problems. Brainstorming needs to be logical, with a theme as the main thread, rather than disorderly imagination. The retrospective meeting in agile practice is actually an efficient brainstorming process. In this process, we must pay attention to the following points: each section must have a time limit and cannot be diverted unchecked; there must be a facilitator that guides everyone to discuss specific problems, give specific examples, and record everyone's problems; there must be output; the fierce collision of opinions is conducive to bringing deep thinking and digging out the root of the problem.

Is there a conflict between leadership and teamwork?

Many technology firms often advertise that the people they are looking for need strong leadership and a good team spirit, especially the good team work spirit as I've described above. So many people have such questions: Does having strong leadership mean being domineering and aggressive? Is there a conflict with teamwork?

I specifically interviewed many people in charge of consulting and outsourcing on this issue. Leadership and teamwork are not contradictory at all. In a service outsourcing company, our work style is project-based, and we need to work with other team members, so teamwork skills are required. Everyone needs certain leadership skills. The leadership skills mentioned here are not the same as strong command, but that we must understand how to manage various resources, manage our partners, manage our superiors, and manage our customers. The phrase "working together independently" circulated in offshore teams refers to the need to have both leadership and teamwork skills.

Of course, self-organization is not without organization and without responsibility, and self-organization also needs to bear responsibility. In a self-managed team, greater ability is accompanied by greater responsibility. The team leader will also act as a catalyst. Although sometimes he does not directly complete the task, he can lead the team to a better result through his own method.

6.2.5 Transform Traditional Organizations to Self-Managed Organizations

Disruption is a common vocabulary in the current Internet industry. In particular, the Internet industry has used technology to disrupt many traditional industries. The self-managed model is also subversive to the traditional enterprise management model, but it is to subvert the traditional business organizational structure. Can we say that as long as enterprises are used as platforms to divide small business units and use the Internet self-managed model to develop traditional enterprises, we can improve our competitiveness and live a better life?

This is a new requirement imposed on enterprise organizations by changes in the external environment. At the same time, inside the organization, the management of knowledge employees also requires the change of traditional vertical control management or authoritative leadership, that is, transform into a new management method with the purpose of stimulating the value creation vitality and self-management ability of knowledge employees and stimulating the vitality of the organization. It sounds easy, right? But it is very difficult for a mature enterprise, because it requires the organization to carry out structural innovation.

Take Haier for example. Haier is a traditional manufacturing enterprise. Haier people are borrowing the development of the Internet to explore an innovative path. They have broken the boundaries between departments and formed a profit center (essentially transformed into a business-centric), which is actually a full-functional independent team. They have indeed made great progress. However, this process will certainly not be smooth sailing. This is a process of finding a synergistic value from the disordered structure to the ordered structure through continuous self-adjustment and interaction with the external environment, information, and energy.

Sometimes the advancement of technology itself, like the popularity of microservices architecture, has also brought about changes in the organizational structure within the project. The changes brought about by this technology are so radical. In the previous model of division of labor for functional teams, each team must adopt a technology stack, while the team based on division of microservices can adopt different technology stacks, as long as the communication interface is specified. This architecture minimizes the cost of communication and reduces the coupling between teams. The microservice architecture seems to be tailored for distributed teams. A service can correspond to a distributed team, and each microservice can be delivered by an independent team.

Self-organization is a distributed and multicenter control method. In a self-organizing state, "deauthorization" and "decentralization" will naturally occur. According to business requirements, everyone can become the center or even CEO. It should be emphasized that everyone can become the center does not mean that everyone is the center, but that each of them has an equal opportunity to do so. In other words, "decentralization" does not mean that the center is completely unnecessary, it just changes the original centralized center and turns into multiple control centers.

6.2.5.1 Recommendations for Traditional Middle Managers

Flat organization transformation is not simply removing the middle layer, but putting all team members into one layer. The first thing for middle managers to do is to change the concept of traditional management theory, from the management based on issuing command and assigning task (which is also one of the characteristics of multilevel management organizations) to the management where team members actively ask for tasks. Middle managers must also change their minds, become a coach in the team to help and coordinate team members, and refind their own position, otherwise their position in the team will become awkward.

We can start by creating the rules and regulations of an organization and let the rules and regulations replace the previous managers. It should be noted that the rules and regulations should not be too rigid, but rather framework-based, giving the executors space for thinking and autonomy. A self-organized team needs process and normative rules and regulations, just like a country with a strong legal awareness still needs laws. The existence of rules and regulations is not to punish anyone, but to avoid the appearance of a team governed by a man and a team that depends on being management.

6.2.5.2 Three Stages of Self-Management Transformation of the Delivery Team

The first step of team transformation is very similar to many learning scenarios is to "reserve": learn the excellent practices of the predecessors step by step, and lay the foundation for team transformation through continuous practice. The second step is to "break": combine some of the team's own circumstances to make some trade-offs. Through the application of technical practices, we will deepen our understanding of technically solving problems. The third step is to "improve": carry out more innovative activities on the basis of easy assessment of the effects of the completed work.

(1) Start with iterative development, use Kanban to visualize teamwork tasks, and do basic agile practices. At this stage, we need to make good use of iterative development to discover delivery risks in a timely manner; use Kanban and other agile practices to make information more transparent and establish a new communication culture.

(2) Focus on technical practice, improve test coverage, and achieve continuous integration. At this stage, a process framework is established through technical means and automated means. The purpose is to allow the team to focus on business value in future delivery activities, rather than solving various problems in the middle, thus ensuring long-term objectives.

(3) Establish a feedback mechanism that can independently evaluate the energy efficiency of various activities to achieve continuous improvement. The team has changed from applying various practices to being able to combine the project itself and innovate its own solution. And from a series of successful experiences of its own, the team can extract the general method and spread it outside the organization.

6.2.5.3 Does the Team Misunderstand MBO

MBO means "management by objectives," but any people distort it into "management of objectives" and "setting objectives for teams and members, and implementing assessments based on the results." This has caused many companies to fall into serious misunderstandings when practicing MBO. Companies spend a lot of time on "setting and breaking down objectives" when drawing up their annual business plans at the beginning of each year. Since the achievement of these objectives is associated with employee assessment and income, companies have to constantly "bargain" with their employees regarding the setting of objectives, and finally reach an agreement in the "letter of responsibility." When this series of cumbersome work is completed, does it mean that these companies are one step closer to achieve their objectives? Unfortunately, the answer is "no."

The achievement of objectives depends on two factors: whether the objectives setting is correct, and whether employees have adopted correct and reasonable manner of working. Just as the premise for successful pass of the college entrance examination includes investigating which university is most suitable for yourself, and investing plenty of time to accurately grasp various knowledge points and problem-solving ideas. MBO not only includes the "premise," but for offshore teams, the "actions" taken for achieving the objectives are more in line with their vital interests.

After setting an objective, quantify the big objective into small ones for different teams. Each teamworks for its small objective. After all of them complete their work, will they get the big objective expected at that time? According to Dr. Deming, when implementing MBO, we must unfold and divide the company's objective into the objectives of each component or department. We usually assume that if each department achieves its target quota, the entire company's objective will naturally be achieved. In general, however, this assumption is not established because departments are always dependent on each other. In other words, the efforts of different departments cannot be simply added up to become the overall performance of a company. On the contrary, the respective process of achieving of objectives among departments may bring a lot of contradictions and conflicts.

The relationship between distributed teams should be cooperation, not competition. Any misunderstanding of MBO will cause competition (internal friction) among the teams, which ultimately hinders the achievement of the big objective. The big objective of the entire team must be placed above the small ones of their own team. During the cooperation between distributed teams, the objective of each team is to guarantee the achievement of the big objective. If one team encounters a problem, other teams shall try to find a solution from themselves. The old MBO concept is suitable for traditional manufacturing enterprises, but it has also been replaced by Toyota's lean production theory.

6.2.5.4 Three Levels of Self-Management

At the first level, when you encounter problems, you know whom to ask. Although this way of obtaining information is not good, since it may occupy other people's time and disrupt their work.

At the second level, you can find the information you want by searching, after that you have to spend time having the obtained information summarized and organized. At this level, although the extensibility of the information is good, it requires you to spend a certain amount of time, and have a strong initiative.

At the third level, your working environment is designed based on your intuition, it will guide you to the next step of work, presenting the information you need. This requires everyone in the team to share the same values, and the way they conduct themselves in relation to others.

At present, the environment we face is a chaotic era of qualitative change, an era of subversive innovation, and an era of uncertainties. To adapt to changes in the environment, companies must have a self-adjusting ability, self-adapting ability, and self-repairing ability, or "continuous improvement" which is a buzzword in the Internet industry, that is, organizations constantly get feedback in a process from disorder to order, thereby repairing, perfecting, and reconstructing a new order.

6.2.6 FLATTENING IS NOT A PANACEA

Employee growth is the foundation of flat development and the policy that needs to be adhered to for a long time. When a new employee has just entered the team, he will not become a qualified member of the self-organizing team right away. If everyone is a piece of paper and someone is a piece of white paper, we can tell him directly how to write this paper and what the format is. He shall add the content by himself, learn, and accumulate knowledge and experience by himself. Some people seem like the paper written with content, but the format is not what we want, and it needs to be adjusted to match the paper of others. Finally, some people with too much content on their paper may share it with others.

There is also a contradiction between flattening and rapid growth. How to give employees advice and feedback to promote their growth is also one of them. In the case of ordinary companies, it is their leaders who pay attention to employee growth and give them suggestions. But in a flat organization, the project manager is mainly responsible for the project functions, and it is unrealistic to expect him to take care of this matter. This requires employees to be reminded from time to time, giving each other suggestions and feedback. In general, when we leave a project, we will invite others to provide feedback to ourselves, so that it is easy to clearly see our performance in the project in the eyes of others.

If you want to hire engineers with great potential but lack practical experience, the team cannot maintain an absolutely flat structure. They need more experienced people to lead them, teach them skills, and train them to become excellent engineers. In many companies, a newcomer will be arranged to work with a "buddy" who is from the same team. These people are responsible for helping newcomers understand how to do things correctly and also helping them integrate into the team more quickly. The purpose is to give newcomers a good start. Perhaps six months after joining the company, the newcomer will have a more complete understanding of the company and his work, and he will have a definite objective. We will let this newcomer choose an experienced person in the company as his sponsor. Those who act as a sponsor may come from another team or play a different role, as long as the newcomer feels that this person can help him do career planning and benefit his personal growth. The sponsor will meet with the newcomer regularly to understand his growth over time and his confusions, so as to help him make a continuous plan.

6.2.6.1 Buddy/Sponsor: To Solve Cultural Inheritance in a Flat Team

The buddy's responsibility is to help newcomers integrate into the team and into the company as soon as possible. Their work focuses on values, and does not include specific business or technical assistance, but conveys the company's way of doing things. For example, how to set an objective, how to meet the requirements of the company, and how to collect feedback. Therefore, the buddy is a person appointed by the management of the company from top to bottom to help a newcomer, while conveying the company's expectations to him. This kind of relationship mainly exists within half a year after the newcomer joins the company. The main solution is to let the newcomer quickly prove himself in the right direction, find the defects in his work in time and help him to improve, and evaluate whether he is able to become a regular employee in this process.

The role of sponsor is to use his work experience and the inheritance of the company's culture to help a regular employee to make a career plan, so that the his career plan is as consistent as possible with the company's strategic policy. Building a relationship with a sponsor is a long-term activity, and every formal employee in the company will have a sponsor. Because of the service outsourcing model, each project team within the company is highly independent, so it is easy to cause different teams to have different working styles and cultures. In order to ensure the company's unified culture and service standards, some cross-team channels are needed to promote horizontal communication. A sponsor from a different team undertakes some of the horizontal communication duties. Anyone can choose a sponsor from any team as long as they feel that the sponsor can serve as their professional role model. The sponsor will communicate regularly with the sponsored object to find his problems in work through communication and help him solve the problems.

6.2.6.2 How to Find Someone Who is "Responsible" for a Thing in a Flat Organization

In a traditional organization, when we encounter a problem, we can find the leader of our department or the relevant department to solve it. In a flat organization without any "department," whom should we look for? Under normal circumstances, we can ask those who are most closely related to our problem to help, even if we are looking for anyone around us. If he can't solve it, he will definitely find people around him to consult again. In this process, a radioactive information search method is presented, with high efficiency and large radiation. When this problem is solved, there is also a good by-product, that is, a lot of people know how to solve this problem. Therefore, when the same problem is raised again later, the efficiency of its solution will become higher and higher.

A flat organization culture itself will reduce communication costs and also minimize the occurrence of problems: have a strong desire to serve others. When you find a potential problem, in order to prevent it from becoming a time bomb and damaging your teammates, you will actively isolate the danger. You can record it and put it in an obvious place for everyone to take a notice of it. You can also add a note to the problem, all information can be inevitably found when encountering this problem.

In addition to organizational and communication skills, technology can also be used to reduce the occurrence of "trouble" through more friendly implementations, such as designing self-explanations for all issues. This principle is relatively easy to understand technically. For example, when an error message appears, the message itself contains an explanation of which team to contact to solve such a problem; or, like the navigation process design in software, we can reduce external thinking and focus on the problem itself.

Conditions for establishing a self-managed organization: Team members know the objective of the entire team, their position and responsibilities in the team, and can drive themselves to perform their responsibilities. Self-management embodies initiative, as described in Agile Statement to pull the work, without the need for others or leadership to drive you.

Improve the execution of offshore teams. Complete the planned workload on time and ensure its quality and quantity. For each requirement story card, in addition to the acceptance condition itself, it cannot be counted as "truly completed" unless the bug in this part is fixed.

Focus your attention and hope on the internal driving force and self-driving ability, not on the external force.

6.3 SHAPING THE PROFESSIONALISM OF THE TEAM

The internal strength and external performance are equally important for an offshore team.

Simple outsourcing projects have been evolved into professional service companies; their professionalism not only comes from the use of most popular technologies and practices, but also the ability to apply them well in routine work and from project inception to the end.

Professionalism, a high-end word, is defined differently in different industries. How do you define professionalism in the field of offshore delivery? Professionalism is reflected in the ability to find and solve problems. Does it also lie in the upper limit of the value reflected by the offshore team? What decisions can we make? What decisions cannot be made? Of course, as a team that needs to communicate closely with customers and communicate frequently, letting customers feel our detailed high standard is also crucial to customer satisfaction. When customers need to report to their leaders, they can easily think about cooperation details with examples, and also a process where we complete milestone events, implement solutions, address various difficulties, and gradually fulfill our large objective.

6.3.1 TEAM CAPACITY BUILDING

Let's start with the management of the team's knowledge warehouse. The knowledge warehouse can be the method to solve the problem, but more is the result and conclusion of problems. As an asset of the team, the knowledge warehouse is of great significance for maintaining the service level of the team, and can determine the "capability bottom line" of the team to a certain extent.

Accumulate second-hand information to effectively avoid the situation where you need to touch the stones and cross the river every time you perform a task. For example, every time we upgrade our financial system, all the preparations to be done are the same, so they should be solidified. As another example, every time we build a branch office, the financial system must be updated accordingly. When faced with the same problem, newcomers need to do the same thing and solve similar problems. The process of the collaborative work of each distributed team in a project, which finally also become the knowledge and consensus of the distributed team.

The difference between capacity building and knowledge warehouse building is that one is "to teach people how to fish" and the other is "give fish to people." So we have to talk about the issue of teaching people to fish.

The ultimate goal of team capacity building is to continuously improve the team's ability to solve future problems. Anytime we encounter a problem, we will have the way to solve the problem. Specifically, you can try to use four-quadrant, radar chart, and pyramid thinking methods to analyze the problem. The four-quadrant method can help us think in multiple dimensions. Radar chart incorporates four quadrants, which is essentially four quadrants, but its focus is on highlighting the results of performance in all dimensions. Pyramid thinking can help us to conduct structured inductive analysis on the characteristics of sequence, top and bottom, primary and secondary.

The troika of thinking mode is divergent thinking (mind mapping), parallel thinking (six thinking hats), and pyramid thinking. Divergent thinking is fairly common, the carding of the product functional structure is usually drawn out with a mind map. Parallel thinking is very effective in the requirements assessment, allowing people in different positions to think from different angles. Pyramid thinking is used in scenarios such as product planning, project reporting, and phase summarization; it has a strong universality and is especially suitable for product managers and testers.

In general, we should not interpret things from a single dimension. For example, when we want to a car, its space, safety, power, appearance, and fuel consumption are all factors to be considered, and then find a model that best matches our needs. Offshore teams have a more limited perspective than local team, so they should better maintain an open mind and accept multidimensional thinking when encountering problems.

6.3.2 FORM GOOD HABITS

Only by forming a habit can our professionalism become sustainable and reproducible.

Many things require training. It is as simple as prioritizing things. Things that depend on third parties must be done first, because they are easily overlooked and delayed.

It is necessary to cultivate pull-mode work habits in offshore teams. To achieve this goal, the premise is to maintain a proper backlog. The backlog must have a priority attribute. With these prerequisites, the pull-type working method has a foundation for starting. Based on these conditions, customers can have confidence in the remote offshore team. Some teams are relatively independent, and they have their own backlog. But distributed teams, such as integration groups, need to work with others and then pull some of the functions to be done from the shared project backlog.

Proactively solve problems. Many people do not really understand it. There is a project that keeps people working until midnight every time it goes online. Overtime work uses fatigue tactics to solve problems. We should focus on solving the root problem. The overtime compensation method can only be temporary, but it is our pursuit to solve the root problem. For example, the code freeze time is advanced one day, and there is sufficient time to test and go online. A stable online launch is much less risky than a rushed online launch, and the price paid is only a few fewer functions, which is still worthwhile.

Arrange your plan by splitting story cards. If the plan is not split into small tasks, it is easy to fall into the swamp of procrastination.

In his *The 7 Habits of Highly Effective People*, Stephen Covey argues that the habits of proactive, begin with the end in mind, priority, win-win thinking, empathy, and constantly updating can help people improve efficiency, and become a highly effective person. For offshore teams, they shall apply agile development and transform their daily behaviors, and eventually make them a habit.

Develop good habits. What are the good habits? Conscientiousness, responsibility, time concept, self-summarization and self-improvement, conscious accumulation of knowledge and experience (take notes), and organizing materials to make them become your own knowledge (disorganized into organized).

Good habits are often complementary to good culture. The offshore team creates a culture for sharing among the teams. In addition to the direct benefits brought by the spread of knowledge, it will also indirectly enhance mutual understanding and more exchanges.

6.3.3 THE POSITIVE IMPACT OF PROCESS STANDARDIZATION WITHIN THE COMPANY ON THE TEAM

If we are in a large-scale outsourcing company, it makes sense to establish standardized processes within the company. It can establish basic guarantees for numerous projects within the company, improve delivery efficiency, and reduce delivery risks. As any project team in the company, it must also think about how to interact with the company-level standardized processes and how to take into account the customer's work processes.

The standardization here means: As an offshore team, have we met the company's requirements and reflected the company's service standards? Specifically, does our agile practice reflect value, rather than float on the surface, is it adhering to effective communication and simple design?

Maybe not every team needs a strict standard, but there must always be something that is relatively stable, "guarding" for later people, so we have quickly established the project (inception) to form a standard, and the project weekly risk reports and project closures have also become standardized.

After we have accomplished our work, we need to further evaluate the results. If the things we have done are not effectively evaluated, we cannot say whether we have achieved a success, and there will be no targeted help for future improvements.

After the basic "PDCA" is done, we will then start "PDS (standardization) A," which should be continuously improved. Just like the understanding of agile and programming must be deepened, and eventually the successful process can be standardized, and it can be promoted to the company level. This can also be regarded as a feedback of the growth of the team to the company culture.

Specialized risk control can also be standardized, such as the risk control of project, because the time when the project goes online is a very important time point. The team's deployment plan must have a bottom-line version, that is, the worst plan to prevent the situation that has to be rolled back after the rush to go online. How to do a good rollback, the development team and the DevOps team must divide the work reasonably and collaborate efficiently in order to minimize the impact of the rollback.

The outsourcing companies I have worked in have very limited knowledge sharing between projects, and it is difficult for them to promote good experiences, let alone the company-level standardization of process. If you have similar experience, you must find ways to change this situation. I feel that for most software outsourcing teams, there should be more leadership than management, and the team leaders should take the initiative to tell everyone what to do. Some people think that strictly following the standards is a waste of time and too easy to compromise. This is typical phenomenon that someone shoots off his mouth but compromises in practice.

6.3.4 BECOME AN IMPORTANT CONTRIBUTOR IN THE PROJECT

The comprehensive ability of team members must reach a certain level.

When the team staffing is not mature enough, the team leader or builder should intervene in everyone's work more frequently, for the sake of training talents. After the team matures, there may be a diversified and multicenter situation, and then the team leader shall delegate power to team members to let them solve problems in a self-organized manner. The project manager acts as a supervisor in this process: provides guidance and assistance to individual members at the beginning, and then let them work on their own after they are strong enough. The life cycle of a software outsourcing project is mostly like this: In the early days of team formation, everyone is not familiar with each other, and someone may be inexperienced. At this time, the project manager and senior employees need to pay attention to other team members, and help them become familiar with some practices and quickly grow up. As they grow, the project manager may assign some tasks to them and let them complete them on their own, and he will shift his focus to periodic reviews. Then the project is carried on step by step with team members more familiar with each other. At this time, the project is likely to end. Each outsourcing project goes through such reincarnation, the only difference is the length of the reincarnation cycle.

Admittedly, teamwork skills are not invincible. These skills alone are not enough to fully satisfy customers, but make them feel that the team is manipulating for self-interest. Given this, it is necessary for the team to remain professional. The important contributors in the team represent the upper limit of the team and also confidence that the team can solve major problems.

It's odd that those who practice agile development rarely talk about it directly, because these things are taken for granted to themselves. But it may sound like something new for customers. A team shall be able to explicitly explain all matters that it takes for granted, which is of great significance for other teams, especially the customer team.

6.3.5 HOW TO DEAL WITH DOCUMENTS

Document bear an important responsibility in communication, especially in case of collaboration with offshore teams, documents are a carrier of communication used more frequently than telephone and video conference.

We all met the following circumstances: When someone hands over his job to a newcomer, he may forward him a bunch of documents for him to learn. Most of the knowledge is already recorded in the documents, but they are frequently asked about within the team. Here I want to stress is that we shall pay attention to both the form and the content of documents.

Regarding the form of documents, in many projects I have worked on, the documents were managed by the requirements of code. Each update must be checked into the version control system, so that the people in different teams have access to the latest documents, which has greater significance for teams who cannot confirm the problems face-to-face in real time, and ensures that everyone gets the latest version of documents.

Using wiki online editing tools to manage team knowledge is also a popular method. wiki is not inherently structured, and this freedom is a great advantage. The team can define a suitable structure according to their needs. We only need to exercise moderate management and make full use of its link and search functions to build an information base shared by the team. Don't worry, its learning cost is very low, and it is often learned once and benefited for life.

Let's talk about the content again. Many people say that the code is the document, I agree with them. Code is the most accurate document that records the current behavior of the software. However, as a document, the code is inefficient because it is only open to developers.

So is it easy to prepare user documentation? Every time we are preparing to write a document, we will face a dilemma: If it is written in great detail mainly for satisfying the new users for the first time, users who have a certain understanding do not like to read; if it is written like a simple list mainly used as a reminder for relatively experienced people, it cannot meet the needs of new users for context. Make full use of index, abstract and details in document, will make everyone's life easier.

We all agree that the management of document content in any project must be maintained in accordance with the standards of an active document. The branch of a document must be maintained permanently, and do not copy documents at will, which causing the proliferation of documents of different versions. For the content of the document, the large text will make it difficult for people to read, and it is easy to have different understandings. A really good document should be the one that allows users to understand the content in the least amount of time and get impressed. Such a document should be the best combination of pictures (including diagrams), flow chart, and a small amount of text description.

The waste in documents is also worthy of our attention, because writing detailed documents is really time-consuming. The energy you've consumed in an article is enough to let you explain to a newcomer dozens of times face to face. The challenge that newcomers encounter most of the time is not that they don't know what they don't understand, but they don't know what they need to understand. In fact, as long as you know where you need to figure out, then you can find a way or find the appropriate person to learn. So all we need is to know these points which help us concentrate on the main points, and we can define a range for each point to explain the goal.

Now that the design is in the limelight, the design is beginning to have an impact on the documentation. The prevalence of minimalism and the extreme emphasis on user experience have also reduced user demand for documents from another aspect. Many times users do not need documentation to tell how to use this software. Through good design, we can use this software based on our common sense and use the software's internal navigation.

6.3.6 Doing Simple Things Well is Professional

Many offshore project personnel do not check their e-mails in advance when they attend the stand-up meeting every morning. As a result, at the beginning of the stand-up, the information of the local team and the offshore team is not calibrated. Since the stand-up is usually on the morning for the offshore team, the result is that our information is always lagging behind at the stand-up. If this is the case every day, the customer experience will be very bad. Is this problem difficult to solve? Of course not, we can use our mobile phone to quickly check the e-mails in advance. Could it be that the company put the communication subsidy into the salary, and it seems that company has weakened its support for mobile office and also the employees' awareness?

6.3.6.1 Details Make a Difference

We usually know how to do things right. But when there are multiple solutions, the key is to balance all the options.

There is a principle called "first time, first place," which means doing things right the first time, and solving the problem where it first occurs. Improve your ability to do things in one step, don't think that you will continue to do this in the future. However, is this contrary to agile thinking?

Do we have to go through detours to know what to do? Is there some way for us to find the correct route without going through unnecessary processes?

Many times it is too casual and insufficiently prepared. For example, to attend the weekly team meeting with the local team, we must be fully prepared and planned before the meeting, and even the contents of the preparation should be evaluated internally.

Many times I feel sorry for our team members, because we are only one step away from becoming "professional," but easily lost such an opportunity. For example, many times we do small things consciously, but we never pay enough attention to them, but deal with them casually. When updating the task status, we should make things clear at one time, solve a problem and check similar problems proactively, instead of waiting for the customer to point out new problems.

The shared system must be updated in time, and the remote team cannot see our physical wall, so the online task management system must be updated in time.

We advocate professionalism, it first of all refers to hard skills. When it comes down to soft skills, they shall also reflect professionalism. For example, when we are about to send an e-mail to confirm a matter. If the time difference is relatively large, we can get a reply the next day. When we first send this e-mail, we must describe the matter as clearly as possible; otherwise, when we rely the next day, it is the customer that asks us to further confirm our question.

We shall think ahead of the customer. When customers want something, we must prepare it in advance, do not wait until they ask about it. In the project delivery process, we often need to go online frequently, and open to customers for testing. When we send a message to customers to tell them which version of the package can be tested, a list of known issues with that version should be attached. This can effectively avoid harm to user satisfaction and free users from wasting time on known issues.

Each project can stimulate many good practices. For example, on a project, unless everyone's laptop needs to be used, all personal laptops are placed on another table, and the development machines used for pair programming are all placed on one table, which can effectively avoid distracting our attention and increasing the efficiency of working hours. For the same reason, using WeChat as a team communication tool is also easy to cause distractions. Later, the team used Slack as a team communication tool which is much better for attention.

We know that efficiency is doing things in the right way, and the effect is doing things right. For an offshore team, it is often not up to them to decide whether to do the right thing. Relatively speaking, we need to spend more energy on doing things the right way.

Do the right thing, do something right. This is a truth that many people know, but they always fail to follow this principle, and just ignore it habitually. What hinders this last-mile practice?

Based on the above understanding, let's think about how to deal with important and urgent matters. Limit the time spent on urgent matters, and identify things that are not really urgent, because spending too much time on them will have great side effects and fail to deal with important matters in a timely manner. Doing the right thing is more important than doing it right.

Tips for answering open questions from customers or other teams. When there is no fixed answer to a question, you have to give your own opinion. Open questions cannot be accurately answered, such as the coefficients of the best case and the worst case in burndown chart. Before using it, we cannot prove that a number is the best for our team. We often refer to an empirical opinion or other's recommendation. We can use it first, according to the principle of continuous improvement, get a coefficient suitable for our team in a short period.

Decisions made in a state of passion should be slowed down. This is what I associate with the phrase "passion crime." The decisions a person makes under the influence of the environment and personal emotional state are often more radical. To avoid making a final decision at this time, you need to calm down first. You may feel good at the time, and thinks that the plan is enough, but notice its adverse effects later. Or, you can't think of it when you do it, and you regret it a little afterward. Of course, this regret just disappears in your mind quickly.

In retrospect, for anything, generally we will prepare for the beginning, but we will never prepare for the end, just let it end naturally or passively. One of the responsibilities of the project manager is to "tear down" the offshore project properly. "Tear down" is not just for software, it is suitable for applying loan, purchasing a car or house. "Tear down" properly will benefit the later work.

6.3.6.2 Find the Reasons behind the Problem

For offshore teams that need to face customers, don't give out problem solutions to customers before finding the root cause of the problem. When a problem occurs, the first thing we should do is to find out the real cause of the problem, and then find a solution to the cause of the problem, instead of giving solutions randomly based on our experience. Customer asked us for a solution, not a suggestion.

The company I used to serve can be regarded as a professional software service company. A basic job of everyone is to fill in the timecard. But every week someone always forgets to submit his timecard, which really should not be what a professional company should have. In order to ensure that everyone submits on time, we will send e-mail reminders to all those who have not submitted, plus SMS reminders, but even doing this, we still did not solve the problem. This matter even triggered many big discussions in the company's internal mail system. Every time everyone is actively proposing solutions, some say fines, and some say developing a tool to automatically submit timecards. Not to mention the effect of these schemes (fines hurt morale, automatic submission brings legal risks to the company), no one is thinking about why these people did not submit the timecard on time. Some people have considered one more step than others, and counted how many people did not submit the timecard each week on average, and how the impact was. Most of the people who forgot to submit each week were mostly recidivists, while others were casual offenders. If you average me with a billionaire, I am also a billionaire. Even if the data are accurate, the data calculation is still in the wrong direction.

The user experience in filling timecard is not good, and the financial system using these log data is not easy to use. First, the user needs to manually associate the two systems in configuration. Because of the complexity, everyone will receive an English version of the guidance e-mail to do this when they taken on the job. Not surprisingly, this program did not achieve the desired effect, because every once in a while a lot of complaints were received.

If you encounter the above problems, you can actually create a technical support ticket and ask for help. If this is a problem dealt with by technical support, we will focus on this issue, not too divergent. As for the complaint for reimbursement system not easy to use, this is another problem, which can be reported on the company forum. At the same time, we think about the reason behind this problem, why is this system designed so? The financial staff needs to import the reimbursed data into our financial system, so that we can charge customers in time and calculate the cost of the project. If we don't connect the two systems, we have to enter the data manually. Given the size of the company, this is an impossible task.

It's not just newcomers in the workplace who make the mistake of starting to work without understanding the root cause of the problem. Someone likes to say it should be done in a certain way, which is a typical way to make a decision based on guessing, and confuse the real situation with your imagined situation.

6.3.7 THE TEAM SHOULD BE ORIENTED TOWARD BUSINESS VALUE

Strengthening the way of thinking with business value as the core can improve the effectiveness of all aspects, whether developing or testing in the project.

When the team guarantees product quality, the first thing to ensure is that the main process of the business function is working properly. When we consider the normal path, we usually only analyze it from the perspective of technical realization. In the context of full-scale business value drive, we have to analyze from the business perspective which is the normal use case path.

The offshore team should also focus on business value, because we are a functional team. The offshore team will be independently responsible for part of the function development, and the responsibility to pay attention to this part of the business value of the function should be borne by itself. What are the criteria for the success of the offshore delivery team, stacking the functions? Of course, it is to deliver projects that meet the users' business value.

6.4 MAKE INFORMATION TRANSPARENT

The selection of management is probably the most powerful change in an organization, since the tone of the entire organization is set by those people. In fact, transparent behaviors do not happen naturally among those in power, and management is rarely produced because of their ability to create a culture of straightforwardness. But now everything has changed, willingness to listen to his opponents has become the trait of a true leader, which is also one of the criteria for many organizations to find future leaders.

Unfortunately, companies with a multilevel management structure respond slowly to problems. A company with this structure can be said to adopt the "push" model in Kanban theory – a model cannot give play to the subjective initiative of individuals. The multilevel management structure will result in the monopoly of information and impede its free flow. In order to increase information transparency, we must break information barriers by reducing the levels of management.

In a project team that implements the traditional management model, a great advantage of being a manager is to possess information. His subordinates, those who lack information, have to comply with his arrangement. In contrast, in an agile team that worships flatness, a manager is not like his counterpart in a traditional team, but a component of the team where all information is commonly owned. However, information sharing is easier said than done, since we subconsciously think that ownership of information is a privilege to govern others.

Many visualization methods can help make information transparent; they are good practices, but far from enough for one hundred percent information transparency. We need to change our subjective consciousness to realize information sharing in an organization.

"Don't be evil" – code of conduct in Google. What is "evil"? In my opinion, controlling information in a team is evil since it creates barriers to others.

6.4.1 BLOCKED INFORMATION FLOW IN TRADITIONAL TEAMS

Business organizations shall increase information transparency, which has been advocated for years, but not many substantive results are achieved. I've heard more than one company managers say that their corporate culture seems to "keep everyone on a self-enclosed mushroom farm." An authoritative research agency once interviewed a group of business executives, more than half of them admit their corporate culture is not transparent, and less than half of them depict their communication as opaque as if there are clouds covering the sun.

Organizational transparency has both rational and ethical significance for it enables companies to operate more efficiently and effectively. In all organizations, management attempts to hoard and control information since they believe it is the source of power. Management sometimes believes that access to information is a special power and benefit, and a privilege that distinguishes themselves from ordinary employees. Such leaders think themselves to be smarter than other team members, so they only need to know how to use sensitive and complex information, but only if they are interested in doing so. Some of them even prefer information opacity so as to keep their awkward mistakes a secret.

A team shall be decentralized and free from dominated by a single leader. "Decentralization" here means to replace one center with multiple centers or different centers at different times or occasions, which depends entirely on the operation of the team.

Let information flow freely, what does it mean? One of my former employers is a role model in this regard: each employee has equal access to the company's quarterly financial statement, status updates of multinational teams, and human resource requirements in branches in foreign countries. Although not everyone is interested in all the information, it at least sends a signal that a company can do well in information transparency.

The counterexample to information transparency is information asymmetry, which is commonplace in stock market. It is always hard for ordinary stockholders to learn some useful information of a listed company in time. Whenever the information is disclosed, it is far too late. There may be two reasons for such situation: One is the huge amount of information, which makes it impossible to sort out the valuable information the first time. The other one is that the institution that controls the information keeps us in the dark intentionally.

6.4.1.1 What to Do If the Amount of Information is Too Large Overload?

With limited energy, no one is able to grasp all the information, just like no individual team member can take on all the work of his team.

- Learn to select information. We must obtain the information that helps us perform our responsibilities.
- Properly manage the obtained information by indexing, which helps us promptly locate the information when needed.

6.4.1.2 What Shall We Do If the Information is Occupied?

We can make information nowhere to hide by utilizing working process and visualization. The morning stand-up meeting enables each of us to inform others of what we have done and planned; and the code review before getting off work enables us to learn about the design and code completed by others. We can use Kanban to make the project status and progress clear to everyone at a glance. The one-way flow of task cards on Kanban reminds the responsible person of each link to pay attention to the content of task cards, and the tasks without enough information will be highlighted.

Horizontal communication is encouraged between teams to avoid all information from being conveyed by a single manager. If the information could flow directly between executors, there will be fewer links for information exchange and less possibilities that information is stuck at a certain point.

The businesses of offshore teams are regularly updated. Therefore, their business analysts shall, at regular intervals, inform other team members of the businesses finalized over a given period. The advantage of doing so is to ensure that no one will deviate from the established businesses when communicating with customers, which will build up customer confidence in offshore teams.

6.4.1.3 Are Senior Managers More Likely to Make Mistakes?

Technical teams are notably different from traditional teams, for example, even the most experienced managers have some blind spots in their knowledge. The traditional teams usually do their jobs with reference to precedents, just like the workers on an assembly line that only care about correct execution. In contrast, the technical teams are engaged in innovative activities with many decisions made by executors; since the information may be controlled by a manager or a business analyst who only makes decisions at the business level, they must explain a certain business to developers clearly enough so that the latter can work out an optimal solution for function implementation.

Managers of traditional teams are eager to eliminate uncertainties, while those of technical teams prefer conveying the information completely and correctly, so that the executors can respond to an uncertainty in the right way, which is especially important for software delivery – a process where uncertainties are everywhere.

6.4.2 Challenges against Information Transparency

6.4.2.1 Upward Communication

Now that a self-managed team is a flat organization, why there is still upward communication? Let me first explain the angle of thinking here. We advocate flattening for it avoids the drawbacks in a hierarchical relationship, just like we don't report work to the project manager at a stand-up, but update information to everyone else in parallel. However, not everyone is obliged to process information, there are special personnel responsible for coordinating the work of teams, external communication, processing and filtering information, so as to save the time of others on information selection and guarantee the entire team to be concentrated on priority tasks.

It is true that the relationship between organizational justice and job performance is complicated, but it is worth being examined from multiple perspectives. Telling the truth to an authority is not easy, there shall be a brave speaker and a modest listener. In all organizations, such as families, ball games, companies, and government agencies, we like to hold back the unpleasant truth, just like we only want our parents to hear good news about us. Of course, it does not mean we don't trust them. On any occasion, a speaker takes on considerable risks to reveal the truth. If we can communicate with higher-ups frankly, and if a team can challenge their own assumptions publicly, it will lay a basis for information transparency in a team. Managers shall play an exemplary role: share information with others more actively, listen to different voices, dare to admit their mistakes, and articulate their expectations for others.

When team members are asked to write down what they want from their leaders, "trust" is always at the top of the list. That's why the first item on the agenda of a project restrospective meeting is always the safety check. If leaders are frank and sensible, then they are sure to act as they speak and unlikely to change their minds from time to time. Team members will receive such signals that our game rules will not change and important decisions are not made arbitrarily. These guarantees will exempt team members from future worries, and motivate them to make extra effort and actively collaborate with their managers in achieving team goals.

In order to create information transparency, we have to practice unpleasant conversations sometimes. Candid communication is beneficial most of the time, but when we talk about some difficult topics without reservation, it may cause serious unintentional harm. For example, managers feel embarrassed to notify the employees doing unsatisfactory jobs that they have failed the performance appraisal. Likewise, we seldom provide negative feedback to leaders, since we are worried about the forthcoming negative assessment.

Is there any way that helps us deal with unpleasant communication? Here are some tips for us to bear in mind. The most important thing is to avoid harming others, strengthen mutual understanding, and put ourselves in others' shoes, otherwise it may stimulate the defensive reaction of others and result in irrational communication. From this starting point, we will have more smooth communication.

6.4.2.2 Downward Communication

Let's first look at an interesting test. Researchers from NASA once asked in-service pilots, copilots and aviators to operate a flight simulator, respectively, for the purpose of testing their response to an accident in the critical 30–45 seconds. Although typical pilots can take an action immediately, they are more probable to make a wrong decision than other more open-minded pilots, since the latter usually ask other crew members before taking any action: "We've met a problem, what do you think we should do?"

This kind of information opacity or noncommunication will cost us a huge price. Research institutes have reviewed many aviation accidents and came to the conclusion that "the various errors that led to an aircraft crash are in fact the erroneous teamwork and communication." A pilot may know something important, but he rarely tells other pilots. Therefore, pilots need to change their minds. They should know that communication is not a means to issue an order, but the most articulate and transparent means to share information with others. Team leaders shall take the initiative in downward communication, which will maximize the collective strength of the entire team rather than individuals.

Common values and assumptions are of great significance for sustaining a group. The issue of transparency not only exists in the relationship between a leader and his subordinates (the leader does not listen to others' opinions or the subordinates dare not tell the truth), but also exists in the contradiction between individual opinions and group thinking (individuals are at a loss when besieged by group thinking). Although many organizations have specifically discussed how to deal with group thinking, it is a pity that it remains widespread in the conference rooms of companies of all sizes.

Everyone must understand that admitting mistakes is a normal action in communication. Wise managers dare to confess their fault, which not only makes critics speechless, but also encourages other team members to admit their own failure. In this way, even unpleasant information can flow (especially upward and downward flow) unimpededly inside the team.

In the case of downward communication, the sources of information shall be diversified. Managers shall try hard to keep from being self-reclusive, since a person with a limited outlook will never make himself a senior manager. For all well-trained engineers, consultants, and managers, when they want to explore into a problem or a culture, the best way is to find all kinds of information sources to balance biases. Similarly, the team member responsible for coordination needs to communicate all matters (including annoying criticism) with everyone else in a polling mode, so as not to be biased by the opinions of certain individuals.

6.4.3 HIGH TRANSPARENCY IS AN IRREVERSIBLE TREND

While managers are learning to improve information transparency, they have found it increasingly difficult to withhold information due to the popularization of the Internet, especially the online communication channels such as Weibo, WeChat, and forums on news platforms. For example, one day in 2007, a popular blogger posted that a chemical plant was about to be built in Xiamen, a beautiful coastal city in southeastern China's Fujian province, which provoked opposition from local residents, thus forcing the local government to reassess the environmental impact of this project and finally built this plant in a remote town far away from populated areas. If the same incident happened ten years ago, the plant would be built before local people became aware of it. Now the speed of information dissemination on the mobile Internet is too fast to be imagined, and similar events keep emerging in endlessly, so to speak, preventing information transparency through human intervention is a mission impossible.

The above example illustrates that extensive information sharing is critical to the effectiveness and social responsibility of an organization. This is why successful managers encourage and even reward openness and objection, since the straightforward advice, though sounds unpleasant, may guide them to make right decisions. Realizing genuine transparency requires our constant attention and precaution against any act of concealment. So it is necessary to build a safe organizational structure that protects the people telling the truth from being retaliated or punished. Regarding a project team – I believe that everyone has a good intention and wish their team become better and better, there shall be sufficient information sharing, which is basis for building trust among team members, and trust is the premise for stimulating their work enthusiasm.

6.4.4 INFORMATION TRANSPARENCY FOR OFFSHORE TEAMS

A product backlog shall be visible, transparent, and unambiguous to all members, and show the next-stage work scope of the Agile team. This backlog contains a large amount of information, including the information caters to our need. Since such information has been refined for several times to eliminate redundancy, we shall lose no time in finding it out for fear of any information loss.

In a delivery team, developers decide how to do a job, while product manager decides what is going to do. It is a duty for personnel playing different roles to provide useful information to others. To make sure of transparency in a distributed team, one sub-team shall try to learn about the work content, progress, and even plan of other sub-teams. It is a two-way information communication for a team, so this team must have a strong initiative and holistic thinking. It means that the personnel playing the same role in different teams often update their work progress and product functions.

The use of Kanban can make project information transparent and visible, and facilitate team members to track each other's work progress and improve their collaboration. A team must have an objective, go live dates, and milestones. A burndown chart can be drawn to show a trend line towards the release date, which seems like a road map that leads us to fulfill the objective.

Information transparency is a necessary condition for running a flat team and for everyone to make their own judgment. Otherwise, we have to invite the team leader for making a final decision.

6.5 JUMP OUT OF THE COMFORT ZONE

"Life is like a box of chocolate, you never know what you are going to get." We should be brave enough to face up to all uncertainties in our life, why not a project team sometimes goes against the wind to try something new!

6.5.1 FIND THE COMFORT ZONE

In the comfort zone, we will be exposed to a familiar environment, doing assigned work every day, and feel contented. If we are members of an offshore team, in the comfort zone means that we only need to complete the tasks assigned by the customer on time, and regularly report our work to him, but never take a step outside the zone.

Such a state is quite harmful in the long run. For individuals, keep staying in the comfort zone will impede them from gaining experiences along with increasing years of working, which will delay their personal growth and even destroy their career. For teams, keep staying in the comfort zone will make them unable to create greater value, which is not conducive to further cooperation with customers. In the short term, customers may prefer working with such teams for saving cost, controlling risks, and reporting work to their boss without further explanation. But software development itself is an innovative activity, which is substantially different from Apple's outsourcing product manufacturing to Foxconn. If the offshore teams are indulged in the comfort zone and make no active input, their working achievements will disappoint customers, while customers expect offshore teams to take remedial action on their own. If things go on like this, customer satisfaction is sure to decline.

Our offshore teams can confirm that we are trapped in the comfort zone if we are in any of the following states:

- The customer feels satisfied with our current work and requires no further improvement, so we will not take the initiative to do so.
- We are doing everything by strictly following the customer's instructions. Even if we have found something questionable, we will not confirm it with the customer, nor give him any feedback.
- When some new technologies, tools or practices have emerged, we prefer turning a blind eye to them, rather than investigate them and then recommend them to the customer.

When staying in the comfort zone, every one of us, especially the project leader, has the responsibility to break the "peace." We should first come to realize the negative impact of the comfort zone, that is, to know why we should jump out of the comfort zone and how do so.

6.5.2 Why Should We Jump Out of the Comfort Zone

We desire for perfection, like children want to get a perfect score on their tests. It is a habit formed in our childhood. But unfortunately, the more desperate we are eager for perfection, the easier for us to procrastinate. Many of us like to make a bunch of plans, but hardly carry them out one by one. According to the principle of least action, we must take the first step toward the established goal in spite of all difficulties, take the second step after making adjustment according to the feedback, and then repeat the process of "implementation – feedback – adjustment," so as to fulfill the goal in several iterations. In each iteration, we can find our progress. In short, we shall be the one that is capable of self-improvement, not the one always strives for perfection.

For everyone in the team, jumping out of the comfort zone is an important way to achieve self-motivation. If we are only doing everything within our ability, we will never make progress.

The team leader shall admit that beneath superficial rationality there are many irrational forces that may undermine the operation of his team. For the sake of self-protection, our team members will activate social defense which may transfer, alleviate or eliminate our anxiety, but it may preclude us from jumping out of the comfort zone. Sometimes we have to bear some risks for jumping out of the comfort zone: either individuals or the team may resist changes or hide some problems in order to avoid or expose certain things they are not good at.

6.5.3 Team-Motivated to Jump Out of the Comfort Zone

Jumping out of the comfort zone includes making constant improvement to do a better job:

- Help every team member to fully understand the business through frequent internal discussions.
- We shall keep doing lots of jobs by applying the iterative development model.
- Conscientiously organize the daily code review meeting, and make sure to implement the outcomes of the meeting, including the modifications that need to make to the code.

All teams shall track the project progress, discover problems at any time, and take the initiative to improve the quality of deliverables, rather than satisfied with the current situation. Each team shall put all tasks into a task management system, even including the tasks such as technical surveys and preparation of test data which cannot yield any tangible business result. This task management system is used throughout the delivery process to visualize everyone's tasks, so as to motivate them to complete their tasks without delay, rather than end up with nothing.

Competitiveness and executive ability are the foremost self-requirements of all teams. Competitiveness means that all team members are competitive, and their personal ability is unquestionable. When a team undertakes a particular project, both competitiveness and executive ability are indispensable. Now that it takes a lot of courage and impetus to jump out of the comfort zone, it is difficult for a team with poor executive ability to do so.

In each team there must be a safe environment, which means that some errors of their members are tolerated. When some of them attempt to jump out of the comfort zone but fail to make it, the team shall not blame them or investigate their responsibilities, but help them to sum up experiences from the failure, either tell them to stop loss in time, or provide them with some suggestions for the next attempt.

6.5.4 Self-Motivated to Jump Out of the Comfort Zone

Jumping out of the comfort zone is a process of overcoming oneself which is not an easy task. This means that we have to change our fixed pattern of thinking and dare to do things beyond our reach. Therefore, making mistakes is inevitable in this process. No one can make sure of success when doing something challenging. We should not be afraid of failing, since making progress in practice is our ultimate goal.

No matter how busy we are, we should spend some time every day thinking about how to improve our work. For example, we may spend an hour in each work day to review our recent gains and losses in work, find the places where we did not do well, and think of ways to perform better in the future. The best way for personal growth is self-motivation and self-management, which can yield twice the result as compared with the influence of external impetus.

When working in a project team, we may ask to change the status quo. For example, Someone wants to work on a more challenging project, someone asks for operational support and assistance, or someone suggests introducing a new tool to help the team and customers solve certain pain points. All of these demands for trying something new are endeavors to jump out of the comfort zone.

In traditional companies, generally every employee has a line manager, you can directly go to him. But such a line manager does not exist in a flat organization, what should you do? The answer is to find the right person for advice, there must be someone who occupies a certain position or plays a certain role that can help you. If you want to be shifted to another project, consult with the delivery supervisor; if you need help for some personal matters, talk with the HR officer; if you have questions about career planning, discuss with the team instructor or the senior employee that you worship. Don't expect that there is an available organization in your company that automatically jumps out to solve your puzzles whenever you are at a loss.

Self-motivation means to leave one's comfort zone to meet challenges, like working on something new and even difficult. For example, most IT engineers in software industry are introverted. This kind of people like staying alone to "recharge themselves." And they feel quite at ease when staying quietly if they have no work at hand. If an engineer intends to enhance his prestige in a technical community, he has to join in community activities frequently and even share his work experiences with his peer. At first, he may feel nervous and often make mistakes. As he keeps urging himself to persevere, he will definitely perform better and better, and finally get used to this state and rise to the occasion. Therefore, motivation is not only applicable to the operation of things, but also to the persons who want to try something meaningful, even if they feel uncomfortable at the beginning.

6.5.5 KPI-Motivated to Jump Out of the Comfort Zone

Each company has its own graded criteria for performance assessment, so every team member shall refer to these criteria to identify which grade we are in at present. Based on an accurate positioning, we will have a direction of efforts, then we can define some achievable objectives, and put into action to satisfy the higher-level criteria. It is a process where we jump out of the comfort zone to challenge ourselves.

Everyone in the team may set monthly, quarterly and annual objectives for themselves. If possible, we'd better invite a more experienced person around us to help us decompose each objective into several tasks, and guide us to measure the achievement of an objective in each stage.

The objectives we set shall be achievable. Let's draw an analogy, an apple that we can pick through some efforts tastes sweeter than those at our hand, but we may lose interest in those out of our reach. In this sense, we should be brave to encounter challenges, and free to give up a fruitless endeavor.

6.5.6 Summary

When we are capable of doing a job with skill and ease, it means that our personal ability has reached a certain stage or we have entered into the comfort zone. If we want to keep moving forward, we have to jump out of this comfort zone, improve our abilities in all aspects, and head for the next comfort zone. Excellent team members usually have this way of thinking to jump out of the comfort zone.

We often see that armless people are extremely nimble on their feet, I'm sorry that that example is a bit offending. I only want to express that our potential is far beyond our own imagination, but we will never know it unless we have a try. Keep staying in the comfort zone may stifle our creativity. On many occasions, when we are forced to do something, we will be amazed at our talent and ability.

6.6 WHAT DOES A PROJECT MANAGER DO?

Let's first look at a case.

There was a project manager whose team was entrusted to develop a web app. His team was made up of about ten developers, three testers, and one business analyst. He assigned tasks like this: divide the requirements to everyone after they are teased out by the business analyst, and ask them to estimate when they could finish their tasks; then input the overall delivery plan into an Excel spreadsheet; and finally determine the delivery time of each requirement by combining the customer expectations with the time spent on integration and testing of some requirements.

Each developer knew very well what they should do by each time node. As long as their estimated delivery time was close to the customer expectations, the project manager would not raise any objection.

Everything should have gone well, but unexpected problems kept coming up. Late delivery happened most of the time. Whenever the project manager asked the team members about their progress, he would be told "I'm almost finished, the back-end part is done, I only need to add a search function to the front-end part." But in fact hours or even days had passed before the delivery. Of course, there were on-time deliverables, but the developers would not have them tested until the last minute, even though they were simple enough to be completed much earlier. It was probably because they wanted to buy some time to relax themselves after days of working overtime.

Apart from this, there were other things that made the project manager worried. Newcomers often encountered problems, but they would rather make aimless attempts than ask for help. A developer was too persistent in bringing about a perfect architectural design, so he spent much time refactoring code and then resulted in a tight schedule. Some developers who were transferred from a different project were asked by their former colleagues to help solve problems, which distracted them from their current jobs. The project manager had discovered more than once that a developer was fixing bugs for his previous project.

The project manager asked about the work progress of each developer from time to time, and even more frequently when the planned delivery time was approaching. Such an overseeing action made developers feel stressed to work against the clock. He was used to allowing them to work on their own schedule as long as they promised to finish their tasks on time, but it began to dawn on him that things were becoming uncontrollable. He had been conscientiously tracking the completion progress of each requirement, but it was of no use in revealing the underlying problems.

The above case is an epitome of the work status of most project managers of software delivery teams. Every day they are weighed down by a variety of problems, but they are so powerless that they have to passively wait these problems to emerge and then solve them at any time.

In an era where traditional management philosophies are prevalent, because of asymmetric information, knowledge, and tools, individuals are unable to realize their goals all on their own, but employed by an organization that fulfills its benefit goal through top-down control.

But in the age of the Internet where everyone accesses to information, knowledge, and tools on an equal footing, the role of individuals is further amplified. When an organization wants to achieve its goal, it relies more and more heavily on individuals to create value and share value. It is no longer an employer of individuals, but their partner.

In this process of transformation, the role of manager has changed from exercising management and control (through directive or autocratic management) to providing services to individuals, in order to help them keep a good mood while working, and stimulate their potential to create value and share value. Individuals sometimes cannot notice the existence of their manager, so they are no longer at his beck and call. Now the project manager of a software team is mainly responsible for accumulating experiences and domain knowledge by relying on his company's resources, so as to help his team avoid making mistakes, and fulfill their common objective at the minimum cost and in the most efficient ways.

By implementing the agile management model, a project team will be fully empowered to work for its established objective, which is a thorough transformation from the management model centering on the project manager. Directive management is replaced by cooperation, mutual respect and humanistic care, thus forming a self-organizing team in which everyone is open-minded and responsible. With the help of Kanban, either physical or electronic whiteboard, this agile culture is visualized in daily management process.

There is one thing that you must avoid. Do not say that middle management layer and project manager are no longer needed, and they'd better resign or become an agile coach. Don't be so childish! Self-organizing teams are not built overnight, and delayering is not as simple as excising the middle management layer, but transforming it into the execution layer.

For example, Google CEO Larry Page made a bold decision after the number of his employees had reached 400: fire all project managers to keep the company agile and free from being bureaucratic. But things went contrary to his wishes. A few months later, he had to rehire project managers and reposition their role by learning lessons from this setback, and found that all project teams become more vibrant and productive.

All excellent offshore teams need a project manager, even though they are highly skilled in self-organization. In these teams, the project manager is no longer a pure manager that reports work to the boss every day, but an indispensable member of the team, he takes charge of both internal and external coordination, and takes up some specific jobs at critical moments.

Is it necessary for other team members to know what the project manager does? The answer is "yes." As I've said, project manager is part of a team, all of the rest people have the opportunity to deal with him. After learning the positioning of the project manager, every team member will better cooperate with him and each other, bear in mind their responsibilities, and make concerted effort to build a stronger team.

6.6.1 What Does a Traditional Project Manager Look Like?

A traditional project manager usually has the following characteristics:

- Assign tasks like issuing an instruction, and seldom interact with team members when they are carrying out their tasks.
- Being responsible to his boss. Every day he makes a work report to his boss, but he only reports what sounds pleasant most of the time. Anyway, the boss will not oversee the internal affairs of the team in person.
- Transfer information in the team, but sometimes block the free flow of information.
- Busy with all kinds of communication every day, and unable to be concentrated on the principal business.
- The knowledge reserve of the team is easily out of control. All of the data and documents are stored in E-mails and computers of team members, and the file versions are in a disordered state.
- Spend too much in communication, that is, track the project progress by holding regular meetings to hear work reports made by relevant personnel, instead of using visualization tools to display their work achievements.
- Pay no attention to reflection on the work and accumulation of knowledge after a project is started.

In general, the process of project management is divided into five stages: startup, planning, implementation, control, and closeout. At each stage there are some points that deserve to draw the attention of the project manager. The content of management covers project scope, schedule, cost, quality, human resources, communication, risks and stakeholders. Every factor must be rigorously planned. Any unplanned change to the project must be approved before it is implemented.

Traditional management model is rigid, leader-oriented, and process-oriented, rather than people-oriented, which suppresses the thinking ability of team members.

In addition, traditional management model controls project risks at the early stage: all risks are qualitatively and quantitatively analyzed during the planning process, and the response scheme is written into a document; some task plans even include risk treatment. But risks are uncertain, front-line staff often fail to adopt appropriate measures to deal with an unexpected situation.

6.6.2 Project Manager of Self-Organizing Team

A traditional project manager takes up a lot of specific work, including analysis of requirements and determination of technical solutions. But in a self-organizing team staffed with product manager or business analyst and technical director, is there still much work left to project manager?

An offshore development team possesses all the characteristics of an ordinary team, yet it must pay special attention to communication with customers, which happens to be the area of expertise of project manager. Good customer relationship management plays a vital role in improving customer satisfaction, controlling project risks, and maintaining long-term cooperation with customers.

What the project manager of a self-organizing team should do? How does he differ from his counterpart accustomed to directive or autocratic management? The first difference is that he retreats from micromanaging every aspect of his team. In a flat organization, everyone must take his initiative to acquire tasks, update progress, communicate with those outside of the team (customers) and share information with them.

The project manager of a self-organizing team is more like a scavenger. Whenever his team encounters an obstacle, he will stand out to help team members remove obstacles and interferences, so that they can keep working on the project and meet the deadline.

He must be good at finding problems. For example, our help documents and user manuals are scattered and unorganized. To find out what we need from such a mess is tiresome. The project manager should notice this problem in time, and then figure out a better way for managing documents.

He must be far-sighted. Whenever taking over an important job, he must prepare a detailed plan based on his experiences, in a bid to mitigate risks and guarantee work efficiency.

He must know how to organize the teamwork. After his team is built, he shall first define the mission of the entire team and ensure that everyone understands the top concern of the customer.

A qualified project manager of a flat team shall meet the following requirements:

- A good coach
- Ready to authorize others to take up specific jobs, instead of dealing with everything in person
- Explicitly tell all team members that the company cares about the benefits of everyone and rewards those with achievements
- Productivity and achievements-oriented
- A good communicator
- Guide team members to do career planning
- Have a clear vision and leadership strategy
- Skilled in providing help or advice to team members
- Able to guide others

Unlike a traditional project team where project manager thinks for the entire team, a self-organizing team allows everyone to make plans and decide work methods, while the management refrains from excessive intervention in specific work of team members. If project manager always makes decisions on behalf of team members, they will gradually give up active thinking and depend on their superior for direction.

In the case of agile project management, the delivered software is allowed to contain risks before the project is formally closed, and tasks are scheduled according to the priority of risks. When responding to changes in requirements, agile team evaluates development work on basis of workload rather than man-hours, which differs from traditional team. In other words, agile team prefers relative estimates to absolute estimates when evaluating development work, which can leave enough room for risk control. Moreover, with participation of front-line staff, and through experience sharing and brainstorming, a small-sized team is turned into an independent organization for solving problems in a better way.

6.6.3 Importance of Project Manager to His Team

As coordinator in his team, project manager must always remain sensitive: keep an eye on the work of team members, so that he can detect those slacking off at the first time, and then pull them back to their normal work state. Project manager also needs to organize some internal activities to smooth the information flow. It may slow down the project development pace in the near future, but reduce unnecessary waste in the long run. When holding a meeting, if team members' divergent thinking is out of control, he shall bring everyone back to the major topics. He shall sense the "bad smell" in the team and take measures to reshape the team culture. How to build an intangible team culture? The first thing to do is to ask everyone to stick to the practices that they have agreed, and promise not to lower the requirements.

It is no exaggeration to say that creating a team culture is the ultimate goal of project manager. The culture here represents ideologies such as values and product concepts, but they must be based on the consensus on such factors as quality, priority, working hours and time management.

Project manager also has the responsibility to integrate everyone into his team and grow together. Based on the size of his team, project manager shall have a one-on-one dialogue with each team member once a month or every two months, in order to know well their work state, guide them to set achievable and staged goals, and help them keep improving themselves to fulfill these goals, which constitutes a strong support to realize the objective of the entire team.

Flat teams also need a person to coordinate their work. Although we encourage those who release requirements to take up the coordination job directly, this responsibility usually falls on the shoulder of project manager. What needs to be avoided is that team members may develop the habit of relying on project manager to deal with everything.

In addition to project progress and KPI, project manager must keep a close watch on the persons in his team. He will be shocked and perplexed when a member in his team who has been working the most positively and conscientiously suddenly jumps ship, but it has become a trend in today's workplace. Data have shown that more than 40% of company employees said they want to get a new job since they feel gloomy about their future, and over 30% of them said the primary reason was that they cannot get along well with their direct supervisors.

Most project managers can do an excellent job in monitoring task achievement and pushing forward project progress, but few of them can maintain a good personal relationship with their team members. Therefore, project manager should not only care about the KPI of team members, but their individual development expectations. He can encourage them to talk about their career planning, even if it may be a long-term one, which is a kind of incentive for them to devote themselves into work. When showing concern for every team member, project manager shall back his words with actions, instead of paying lip service. For example, project manager can create some opportunities for team members to receive trainings or serve as tutors in training camps. Not all training courses are full-time, team members can attend those open in their spare time. Project manager can also introduce some useful courses, data and resources for everyone to study on their own. In the real work environment, when getting caught in some difficulties beyond his reach, project manager can ask for help from his team members and make it through with them, which will motivate all team members to unite as one, and get along better with each other in the future.

Project manager shall be accustomed to predict problems from the perspective of the entire team, which is essentially a kind of prospective thinking and available to fall into the category of risk control. It is necessary for project manager to think problems by "beginning with the end in mind," which can be illustrated by the example of a logistics management system mentioned in preceding part of the text. While putting functions online one after another, the project team had remained careful in ensuring the compatibility of subsequent functions with existing data, and carried out data cleaning at the end. Once a function for automatic calculation of goods arrival date was about to be put online, before that the dates were subject to manual updating, so the project manager immediately asked the responsible person whether the manually updated data could be further processed after this automation function was open for use.

In the case of offshore delivery, the top priority is to deliver products that meet the customer expectations, but project manager should not forget his team members. To satisfy team members will satisfy customers indirectly. If you are with a full-featured team but lacks of cohesion, what you are doing is not to create exciting products, but complete iterative tasks, you are sure to leave this team when receiving an intriguing job offer. Project manager needs to make everyone believe that his team is a promising platform where they can realize self-fulfillment. Only in this way can he retain talents and enhance the overall strength of his team.

As the saying goes, do not do to others what you don't want to be done to. But what is more important is that do not force others to do what you've done. Quite a number of managers seem like a control feak; what they themselves have done, they want others to do the same, and take it for granted. They always say righteously that "I've worked overtime, how could my people still get off work on time?"

Taking and giving seems to be two contradictory things, but it's not. Asking others to do what you've done is also an act of taking. People falling in love often complain that "I love him/her so much, but he/she doesn't love me enough." You can love someone as much as you like, but you shouldn't count on them to love you back in the same way.

Project manager is responsible for the composition and adjustment of team members. He shall build offshore teams according to the characteristics of a project, pay attention to the rapid integration of new teams and periodic rotation of personnel, and even take the initiative to change some team members. He has to make offshore teams and the local team at the customer site as cohesive as possible, complete the transition from "me" to "us," and lay the foundation for continuous delivery in the future.

Project manager has enough reasons to replace some team members with those more combat-worthy, at least new faces means changes, which may impress customers with their sincerity. Moreover, each project manager has to think about what team members can get from this team, which is the decisive force that maintains the stability of the team on the whole. Successful management of a project team will not be roses all the way. A designed road map can also get the team to go astray. Self-organizing teams are not "free-range," project manager sometimes has to put some pressure upon the team and make everyone no longer unrestrained.

Everything project manager has done is ultimately designed to equip team members with the following work habits and philosophies:

- Dare to make attempts without fearing making mistakes or criticized by others
- Complete tasks on time and up to standards
- Clearly aware of their roles, plans and goals
- Your job is meaningful and helpful to the team
- Make progress every day

6.6.4 IMPORTANCE OF PROJECT MANAGER TO CUSTOMERS

The contact of project manager of offshore teams with customers can significantly reduce the communication cost of the latter. It is difficult to handle the internal coordination of offshore teams in a remote way, so project manager of these teams can give customers a lot of help.

Project manager usually has synchronous multithread operation, so coordination is one of his important skills. He has to coordinate the teams of both sides to keep the same pace, maintain clean interfaces during integration, and urge them to reach consensus on all issues.

An important task of project manager is to control requirements. The original scope of requirements is determined before the project is started, and the workload is also estimated at that time. Software development is different from traditional projects, it cannot be completed strictly according to the customer requirements as provided for in the contract, because unexpected things and requirements changes happen from time to time during the delivery process. In this case, project manager must deal with the newly-added requirements separately and invite the customer to write down his new requirements, which is a self-protection means of the project team. Otherwise, all project team members will be exhausted and demoralized.

In terms of managing customers, project manager must carefully listen to their views of the project from the beginning. If they do not think there is any difficulty in the project, they are likely to raise their expectations later, thus increasing pressure upon the team. Project manager must tell customers of the difficult points of the project clearly and unambiguously, so as to make them more empathetic. Managing customers differs from managing his team: project manager must try to lower customer expectations, but raise expectations for his team members.

There is a viewpoint that offshore software development belongs to service industry, which is endorsed by industry insiders, while project manager is foreman in this industry. He must get along well with the key stakeholders at the customer side and try to learn everything about them, in order to pave the way for future negotiations. The key stakeholders have a big say in project solutions, so project manager sometimes has to give in to them to bridge the differences between the customer team and the local project team.

A major weakness of offshore teams is that they lack opportunities to show themselves, and their members are not good at self-promotion. So project manager is obliged to have their achievements fully displayed at each showcase. Since most R&D personnel are not very talkative, project manager shall take the initiative to communicate with them and work out ways to show what they have done in a more straightforward manner. Moreover, project manager shall record the project testing plan and send it to all relevant persons, so as to remind every team member of their duty and enhance customer confidence in the project quality assurance scheme.

Project manager shall be a good copywriter so that he will be capable of fully displaying the project results to customers, and in the meantime indirectly help customers to report to their boss. In terms of copywriting content, it is better for project manager to have the project results quantified in diagrams and tables.

Project manager of offshore teams shall be used to working under pressure. It is an official rhetoric. To put it a little crassly, he must be thick-skinned enough. Unlike developers whose pressure comes from technical realization and business requirements, project manager is forced to deal with all types of people involved in a project. No wonder it is said a project manager capable of withstanding pressure and reproach will acquire more resources, and even make their mistake sound less serious and then reduce it to nothing at all.

Customer management is not that difficult. Although not everything that project manager has done is sure to please customers, he can find ways to make them willing to accept an unwanted result.

After undertaking a fixed-bid project, requirements inflation will become a headache of project manager. Requirements inflation mainly indicates newly-added requirements and inflated existing requirements (there will be increased workload during project implementation, because the workload estimation at the beginning is only made with the simple implementation method). In addition to recording these requirements, project manager must distinguish if there is any job that is ought to be done by customers themselves. For example, customers will invite all distributors to join a UAT before the system goes online, and it is in fact the job of their project manager specialized in UAT.

There may be unlucky circumstances where customers never take the initiative to communicate or remain silent even if they have noticed something go wrong. Project manager shall manage to put all problems on the table, so that the two sides can see clearly which one is to take the responsibility. Take Project L for example, an engineer in the customer team did not update the data field along with our development progress, causing users to complain a bad experience with an application we've developed, because a completed executive function was unable to display any data.

Only by solving the major concerns of customers can project manager ask for their concessions in other aspects. He may help customers to talk difficult users into something, or upgrade the professional knowledge of their team members. For example, when doing the user persona for Project L at the early stage, we collected rich information about a key user named Andrew, including his age, thinking pattern, and behavioral style (is he interested in details, experience, or data?). On this basis, we designed a more flexible user interface which made him quite excited. Later, when our team was stuck in the technological difficulties of a requirement, we communicated with him, and he decided to lower some performance requirements, which was to our surprise.

In the process of working with each customer, project manager shall carefully observe if there is any likelihood for new requirements, which seems like "digging holes." But it has two benefits: On the one hand, if a new requirement is inserted into the current delivery cycle, we can make higher point estimates for workload, for the purpose of helping the customer to apply for additional budget, and also balancing our inflated existing requirements. On the other hand, if too much fund is invested into the current delivery cycle, there will be less profit, then some new requirements will increase our chips for a second-phase project. The customer himself may have thought about it, what we are doing is to urge him to make up his mind.

6.6.5 Successful Project Manager Shall Be the Coach of His Team

Offering assistance to team members in knowledge management is within the duty of project manager. And more importantly, he shall maintain the work style and means of communication of his team, then each team member, especially newcomers, will find it easier to learn the domain knowledge of the team and adapt to its work and communication style.

How to manage the team's knowledge library? This question relates to the content of our work.

Knowledge management has three dimensions, namely, individuals, offshore teams, and the entire team. We once cooperated with a four-people customer team (including three consultants), which should have been a pretty cushy job. However, we repeated the solution to the same problem again and again, because when one of them got a reply from us, he didn't share it with his team members, forcing the other people to turn to us for help. Later, I reflected this matter to their responsible person and advised him to strengthen their internal knowledge sharing, which saved time and improved work efficiency of both sides.

If one person in the team has learned how to solve a problem, then his teammates are assumed to have done so; otherwise, the phenomenon of "reinventing the wheel" will be repeated. This is to build a knowledge library for the team so that newcomers will take over their job as soon as possible in case of any staff turnover. And the knowledge library can be submitted to customers together with the deliverables. In addition, a skill library also needs to be built to collect all people's skills that are required by the project. Both knowledge and skill collection and storage plays an important role in personnel management. To accomplish a project, we must pool the wisdom and strength of the entire team, rather than individuals.

Project manager is porter of knowledge, and the last-mile one. He centralizes the knowledge of individuals into that of offshore teams, and then builds a knowledge library of the entire team.

How to manage the work style and communication means of the team? This question concerns how we work.

A self-organizing team must adopt a pull-type work style. When addressing a problem, the true source of this problem shall be identified by implementing the first-reception liability system. Only in this way can the team maintain normal functioning without supervision. With respect to the details of managing the project process, project manager shall examine the problems themselves, rather than direct against certain individuals. As long as everyone improves the process, they can keep doing a better job in iterative development.

All matters at the team level shall be visualized. Traditional project manager stores all information in their head, and assigns tasks to team members who have to wait passively for their work arrangement. In contrast, project manager in self-organizing team shows the team-related information to all team members to motivate them to work proactively. Before task assignment is finished, all the information about business background, priority, and dependency is already prepared.

Project manager is "goalkeeper" of a project. Upon receipt of the customer requests, he shall first learn about their intention, determine task priority and tactics, and then assign tasks. Being a qualified goalkeeper, he shall make sure that everyone in his team is working for the same objective, observe the performance of all players on the field and substitute some of them if necessary, reduce the occurrence of chaos and address risks, or act as forecourt player himself if the problem is still there in the end.

6.6.6 SUCCESSFUL PROJECT MANAGER SHALL LOOK AT LEADERSHIP IN THE RIGHT WAY

The term "leadership" is often misused in China, since it is not exclusive to specific individuals. Everyone needs to have leadership when showing themselves or rendering services to his team, because a project team needs different leaders at different stages. At the stage of business analysis, the leader is business analyst or product manager. At the stage of development which is a technology-driven process, it is R&D engineer that determines the implementation plan and solves the technical problems. At the stage of product release and testing, it is test engineer that takes a leading role.

For example, NBA teams are associated with the term "leadership." Although they have star players that attract fans, it is usually role players that make a team invincible. In post-game interviews, they'd like to tell audiences who is their leader on the field and who is their leader in the locker room. Everyone has a chance to play a central role at different moments or play a pivotal role in different scenarios and occasions.

Unlike "leader" which is a fixed title of a person, leadership may belong to different people at different stages. On a certain day or during a certain period of time, if a task is completed under the leadership of someone, thus fully showing his authority, then it can be said that he is the team leader at that time, while project manager is no more than a common role in the team. And in fact, project manager doesn't play any prominent role in an agile team.

Of course, self-organizing teams are not perfect. Someone powerful and paranoid may take advantage of a loose management environment to hold the power of discourse. In the end, a self-organizing team will be at the mercy of a strong person. If this person has no leadership at all, it may lay hidden dangers for conflicts. So project manager must take notice of the signs that some team members are deviating from the right direction and correct them in time.

6.6.7 SUCCESSFUL PROJECT MANAGER SHALL PROPERLY RESOLVE CONFLICTS

Handling different types of conflicts is an opportunity for project manager to demonstrate his coordination skill.

(1) **Direct conflict.** To achieve one's own objective by sacrificing that of others, or refuse to give up one's own interests for protecting those of others. This kind of conflict occurs between project team and customer team, and between local team and offshore teams, or even inside the same team. For example, before a project is started, the customer agrees on a simple development approach, and says user experience is not important, since this system is for internal use only. But when the product is about to be delivered, he keeps asking for better user experience, which has caused inflated requirements. At that time, the project team is hardly able to deal with any increased requirements, so the project manager has to reject the customer request by showing him the negotiation records of the two parties.

(2) **Avoidance conflict.** Someone may ask whether "avoidance conflict" means the conflict no longer exists. In fact, the conflict is still there. Both sides know that the conflict is only covered up for fear of escalating into any head-on confrontation.

(3) **Accommodation conflict.** In order to establish and maintain cooperation, one party would rather support the plans of the other party, even if they don't like them. They can sacrifice their own interests for sustaining the cooperation. Is it a genuine cooperative spirit? No, of course not. Their consent is usually not based on mutual trust, but a kind of superficial harmony. So this situation is still classified as kind of conflict. Maintaining false harmony is undesirable, one party may pass the buck if any problem takes place, then the innocent party has to sigh out: there are too many tricks, we shouldn't have been so naïve!

(4) **Compromising conflict.** When both parties to a conflict give up something and share benefits together, it means that they are ready make compromises: face up to the conflict together and accept a solution not 100% satisfactory. The prominent characteristic of making compromises is that both parties will give up something. Then they can achieve their basic objectives, and their team members can maintain a good relationship. But it doesn't mean the conflict is settled permanently. Why is that? It is because their objectives are not fully realized, and it is not certain whether the compromise will lead to a win-win or lose-lose outcome. Moreover, project manager has to keep a close watch on the long-tail effect of the compromise for a period of time.

(5) **Replacing conflict with cooperation.** Project manager shall take account of the interests of his party and the concerns of the other party, in order to achieve a win-win result. Both parties shall carefully think about their concerns and more options, especially those nonpreferred options that can also achieve the ultimate goal, such as exchanging space for time. For example, a customer wanted us to develop a system for him to replace the existing cloud service which was about to expire half a year later. In order to meet the deadline, we deleted some unimportant functions after evaluating the development plan with the customer, and postponed the development of some low-priority functions. It was by this way that we successfully put the system online by the specified date.

6.6.8 WHAT TO DO

"Self-organizing" does not mean that the team is free from any management; instead, it means that it does not need the traditional type of higher-ups. Offshore teams must help customers reduce the costs in management and communication, which requires project manager to play a good coordinating role within offshore teams for avoiding the hidden costs that are hard to quantify.

6.6.8.1 Contribute to Company Management

Project manager needs to monitor the project, including its progress, scope, and costs, as well as quality. Balancing the relationship among the first three points is the most important job of project manager. Besides, he has to deal with some trivial matters such as determining transportation and hotel costs, travel subsidy and group building expense, and even recording all team member's working hours every day.

6.6.8.1.1 Good at Discovering and Solving Problems and Also Making Decisions

Project manager shall be acutely aware of the problems mainly about personnel, progress and risk identification in a project.

Project manager shall see through the appearance to perceive the essence. For example, if an employee gets off work at 18:30 every afternoon, does this suggest that he is not working hard? Of course not. Project manager must ascertain the truth that this man starts working at 12:30 which is still lunch break, while his colleagues do not start working until 13:30, so he is working much longer or he seems to be off duty at 19:30. Moreover, it can be assumed that he is working more efficiently, because those who have a strong sense of time hate being slacking off.

Project manager shall be a man of good judgment. He knows for sure when to do and what to do, and which task has a lower priority (it is easier to remove the low-priority tasks than those high-priority ones).

Project manager shall calibrate the information of all parties. For example, if some hotfixes are needed after a system goes online, he shall consult the established criteria to confirm which hotfixes are available and which are not.

6.6.8.1.2 Plays an Organizational Role in the Team

Project manager shall organize team members to offer and collect feedback frankly and forthrightly, and put everything on the table. Two programmers can never write out the same codes for the same function. The delivery of software products is essentially a process of design, that is to say, coding is designing, which calls for flexible organization, and such flexible organizational work requires the participation of project manager.

Essentially speaking, the job of project manager is to communicate with different people on different occasions again and again. When dealing with all sorts of people, project manager shall pay attention to discovering problems and seizing the focal point. Do not count on team members to actively report what they have known. Project manager shall take the initiative to ask them for valuable information.

Project manager shall report information to higher-ups who make deployment at a higher or overall level. What they need is a work report, rather than intervention with the specific work. Every week project manager has to summarize all kinds of information, such as the number of points completed in this iteration and the remaining points, the overall progress, the team members that have asked for leave, obstacles and the reasons for each obstacle, and the deadline for resolving each risk point.

In the process of pursuing long-term goals, project manager shall keep an eye on the changes in this process and constantly assess the impact of these changes on the benefits of the team in the long run. As the saying goes, those who do not plan for the future will find trouble at their doorstep.

Some problems are better resolved at the management level for the following reasons: on the one hand, project manager can ward off some pressure from customers, so that team members can keep working with undivided attention; on the other hand, project manager can observe the unprofessional performance of his team members immediately and urge them to make self-improvement, which will maintain the customer confidence in his team.

6.6.8.2 Focus on Products

As result of the rapid development of the Internet industry, customers have become more stringent for product design and user experience. Although offshore teams are farther away from end users, project manager still need to collect user feedback on their products, instead of turning a deaf ear to user comments after completing the product development.

6.6.8.3 Lead the Team to Get on the Right Track

Being an administrator or an agile team's project manager, his most important job is to establish a mature process for his team. This process is the right track for self-organizing teams, then everyone will give their subjective initiative into full play, do their work by following the rules of the closed-loop feedback control, and adopt all sorts of means for continuous improvement. Project manager can employ some useful tools to improve management efficiency, such as PDCA Cycle, 5W2H Principle Analysis, SWOT Analysis, SMART Principle, Two Eight Rule and 5S Management System.

6.6.9 How to Do

After learning about what project manager should do, now let's talk about how he does his work.

In general, the communication and feedback between technicians and managers are not enough. In order to solve this problem, a project manager once established a monthly feedback mechanism when working on a project. He asked every team member to raise three questions on Slack or WeChat: How can I help you do a good job? How can you do a better job? How can the team make everything easier for its members?

The first question urges us to do one's own job well, which will benefit the teamwork. The second question reminds all team members to improve their job performance. The third question denotes that everyone is entitled to the assistance from their team. It seems that each question raises only one specific requirement, so they are easy to be satisfied in a month. But as time goes by, a big problem will be solved several months later.

Project manager shall make sure that the conclusions of monthly topics for discussion are recorded in the online documentation, so that the existing topics may become reference for the new ones and prove that everyone has done his own part. The review of topics demonstrates how to operate a remote team, because it allows project manager to get feedback on all the matters that make his team members more enjoyable. For example, if you have to visit the customer site frequently and stay there for a long time, your personal credit card may be maxed out. It could be no more embarrassing when you swipe your card to pay for a dinner and only find insufficient balance. So it is better for offshore teams to ask the company for a business credit card, and let the company pay off their credit card debts uniformly, which will solve their worries for business trips. Don't look down upon such trivial matters, they are part of humanized management of a company and able to bring everyone a comfortable work experience.

In order to a good job in visualization, project manager may start with the simplest visualization tool of Kanban which enables every team member to see the work progress of others, so that they will have a sense of urgency.

Being manager of a project development team, one of his top concerns is completion of tasks. So he mainly cares about whether the assigned tasks can be finished on time, whether the project progress has deviated from the original plan, is everyone getting down to his work and are there any difficulties. Likewise, in a software development team, the assignment, tracking and management of tasks is the main duty of the team manager.

Project manager shall coordinate task arrangement to guarantee that team members are doing right things within the prescribed time. For example, when the date of showcase is approaching, he shall ask developers to concentrate their efforts on finishing certain story cards for showcase, so that business analysts can display perfect functions to fight for the maximal satisfactions of customers.

The technical research for a task card shall be arranged reasonably. The scheduling of a technical research should not be too early, since any change in the later period may make it invalid and cause unnecessary waste. A recommended approach is that do not schedule the technical research for the task card in the next iteration until the end of the current iteration.

Offshore teams usually have a high turnover rate of personnel. If there is a personnel change after a project is started, the most difficult thing is to make newcomers fully and clearly aware of what is to be done. For this purpose, the knowledge owner (senior employee) shall develop a detailed plan for transmitting knowledge to the knowledge recipient (new employee). The handovers shall be carried out according to this plan at the beginning. After the newcomer becomes acquainted with the business or technology of this team, he is encouraged to ask questions until he can understand all the important matters, it is at this time that the handovers are finally completed.

In a distributed team, its project manager must set a rhythm of cross-team collaboration, although each sub-team can determine its internal working process. A benign rhythm of collaboration is fairly important: extending the product launch cycle may make team members fed up with their work, but shortening the product launch cycle may increase uncertainties to the project delivery. As such, in the case of remote delivery, quite a number of project teams prefer a product launch cycle of every two weeks.

Project manager shall be fully aware of the process of agile project management, and able to explain to others what is agile management. Before the project is started, he shall reach consensus with technical supervisor on iteration plans, functional modules and main acceptance conditions without going into too much detail.

The life cycle of a project is divided into several stages, so project manager may have different responsibilities at different stages.

6.6.9.1 Initial Stage

At the beginning, project manager is unfamiliar with his team members, so he has to get to know everything about the project, whether they are important or trivial. It is after a while that he can gradually transfer some specific jobs to his team members and concentrate on the matters that entail relatively high risks. This is also a process of risk control and risk elimination.

It is difficult for project manager to transit from 100% participation in management to minimal participation and it is also unlikely for him to withdraw from project management all at once. A feasible approach is that he transfers tasks to others step by step to withdraw from management by in-depth participation. It means that he must learn to delegate something to subordinates and manage the project through some indicators or milestones.

How should project manager solve specific problems in a project? For example, if the problem of Single Sign-On (SSO) is unsolved after several iterations, he must reflect upon himself: How about the current state of this function? Is it in need of substantial improvement? Are there any sub-tasks? Which ones are accomplished and which ones are yet started? For those unstarted ones, how long could they be finished? If there are no definite answers to these questions, project manager must call in all developers to have a discussion and pool their wisdom to find a solution. If this remains impracticable, he has to contact external forces for assistance.

In the first half of the project, it is necessary for project manager to strictly monitor the work progress and eliminate various risks in both people and requirements. Otherwise, these risks may turn into real problems in the second half of the project.

6.6.9.2 Later Stage

When approaching the sprint stage of a project, a reasonable timetable shall be developed and visualized to show to all relevant personnel, so that customers will see the hard work of offshore team members, and every team member will know what they are going to do in this critical stage.

Project manager shall develop a Master Test Plan (MTP) before putting a feature online. To put it simply, he needs to get fully prepared: based on a determined timeline, arrange all tasks by using backward induction, define the time points and designate responsible persons. At each time point, project manager must check the completion status of tasks and confirm whether the plan is strictly carried out. Take Project P for example, team members first made a To Do List based on the timeline, and then figured out the dependencies and sequential order of all tasks, set the deadline for completing each task, designated the person responsible for each task, and defined the completion status of tasks, thus forming an executable instruction file.

Project manager is responsible for his project, no matter it is under traditional or agile management. But the ways of taking his responsibility are different. In traditional project, the output of the team is usually attributed to the leadership of project manager. In an agile project, the output of project manager seems to be insignificant, which is particularly evident when Kanban is used to demonstrate other people's concrete deliverables.

- **Development output:** completed and workable features
- **Requirement output:** split story cards and specified acceptance conditions
- **Test output:** bugs and versions of software available to be put online
- **Design output:** interactive design that meets business requirements

6.6.9.3 Manage Requirements

For the business analyst with the offshore team, his main duty is to fully introduce the customer's businesses and expectations to developers. This is not as simple as carrying information from one place to another. If there is no such person interpreting business analysis, it may become an additional burden undertaken by project manager. There shall be reasonable division of labor and collaboration between business analyst and project manager: the former examines the business value of the requirements themselves, while the latter cares about the project implementation plan, workload, priority, iterative planning, and product testability.

Project manager may invite business analyst to join him in making the work plan for each iteration, and see to the size of story cards split by business analyst, since a right size of story cards is important for iterative planning.

The scope of requirements must be properly controlled. New requirements may come out in the development process, some are definite, but some are equivocal, how can we deal with these vague requirements? For fear of dissatisfying our customer, we must come to an agreement with him by the means of visualization, such as the Priority Pyramid. More importantly, do not try to muddle through. If we turn a blind eye to something ambiguous at the moment, it may breed more problems in the future, just like the saying goes "you can run but you can never hide."

Each project manager shall learn about the baselines of a project, such as the context and details. Take Project L for example, although the business analyst joined the team in the middle of the project delivery, his knowledge of the requirements soon exceeded that of the project manager three weeks later. As such, the project manager had to reassess the project baselines: for the parts to be completed by someone independently, he only needs to know the overall requirements and work progress; for the parts requiring multiparty collaboration, he has to serve as the last line of defense.

Any difficulty in developing a user story will force us to spend an unexpected longer period on its development. Generally, such difficulty, which costs a long time and consumes the existing resources of the team, is a typically separate problem like SSO, uploading or downloading of report files. In that case, it is better for project manager to invite a domain expert from outside the team to help them address this problem as soon as possible, which will help the team save its own human resources.

In connection with my past delivery experiences, I don't think it is wise for project manager to take over the job of testing, because his concern on project progress may impel him to make compromises in product quality, which will lead to a discounted delivery in the end.

Fewer requirements will make a project more sophisticated, while more requirements may cover up the genuine project highlight. Since fewer functions can bring users a better use experience, it is necessary to reduce the quantity of requirements and work harder on the high-value ones. A survey shows that 60% of the functions in a product are rarely used after going online. Project manager shall find them out and try to have them reduced, which will become added value of the project.

A project can be successfully completed even if it has no project manager, which is proved in many delivery cases. The cost of project management is very low, some daily affairs and necessary coordination can be handled by ordinary team members. Nevertheless, it is true that a project led by project manager differs from the one without leader.

After working in software outsourcing industry for years, I've found that few projects can carry on as smoothly as planned. In contrast to manufacturing companies that can implement a fixed production plan, the development of software, as an intellectual activity, is hard to strictly follow the established plan since unforeseen incidents occur from time to time during the entire delivery process; therefore, project manager must be good at making dynamic adjustment, which may be progress, scope of requirements, priority, or all sorts of resources.

6.6.10 PAY MORE ATTENTION TO PROJECT RISKS

Each project is unique because of the existence of uncertainties. The verified and quantified uncertainties are known as risks. Project manager should take the initiative to predict what may go wrong, which is his unshirkable duty. After identifying risks, project manager will play an important role in risk management by guiding his team to avoid or mitigate risks.

One of the important jobs of project manager is to represent the project status in a simple and explicit manner. An ideal tool for visualizing project progress is burndown chart on which project manager should faithfully mark the start date, completed work, and estimated remaining working hours, which is a form of supervision to guarantee the project progress. The workdays of each iteration should be visualized to become a reminder to both project manager and his team members, since they are an integral whole working for the same goal.

Finding a balance among the dimensions of scope, schedule, cost, and quality is a professional means for a project manager to reduce risks. The personnel risk in a project also needs to be controlled. Project manager should take into account of various personnel matters, such as who is going to have a baby, who will take annual leave, etc.

Delivery team is relatively vulnerable or passive. For example, customer may complain about a certain problem, because he has found a real case doing better on the same problem, which makes delivery team unable to refute. From the perspective of delivery team, it may find mistakes of customer while working with him, but it usually remains silent and makes correction on its own instead of pointing them out. This kind of workstyle shall be rectified; otherwise, customer will never know about the pains of delivery team, and even amplify its minor faults.

6.6.11 SUMMARY

In the past, project manager had been busy with managing his project team, but nowadays project team is capable of self-management to a certain extent, so he has shifted focus to management of customers. Inside his team, project manager creates conditions for team members playing different roles to solve specific problems on their own. For example, he shares information with team members, updates the progress of project-related matters, and makes it known to everyone in a timely manner, for fear that team members may make hypotheses if they have no access to information.

There is no doubt that project manager still has bright prospects. But he needs to improve himself according to the above requirements, such as deciding project plans resolutely, and caring about his team members in addition to the project itself. Or else his value will be no higher than a foreman that passes on a message between proprietor and constructor.

Everyone is encouraged to think about problems and come up with solutions, but in the end they have to listen to the one that has the final say.

6.7 DEVELOP A WHOLE-TEAM AWARENESS

First of all, we need to understand that whole-team consciousness is rooted in full-functional team, which is also a consensus in the field of offshore delivery, especially for teams that adopt agile development. In terms of communication, full-functional team greatly reduces the communication between offshore teams, since its communication mainly exists inside each separate team. In terms of teamwork, if offshore teams do not make concerted efforts, it will be difficult for them to achieve the goal of delivering high-quality products on time.

In this section, we will learn the ways to exert the power of the entire team, give full play to team members that perform different functions, and achieve our common objectives through closer teamwork.

6.7.1 THE WHOLE TEAM SHALL CORRECTLY UNDERSTAND REQUIREMENTS

The first thing is to clearly understand the three concepts in product requirements.

- Business requirements: the requirements proposed or specified by "customer" according to offshore teams.
- User requirements: the requirements of the consumer group that actually uses the products that we've developed. There is always a certain purpose behind user requirements, in other words, all requirements are born to solve problems. To this end, there shall be a set of strategy for dealing with functional requirements.
- Functional requirements: the functions of the products we've developed must be able to satisfy both business and user requirements.

If we are developing a terminal sales system for an automobile brand, then the automaker, such as Mercedes-Benz, is at the side of business requirements, all of its agents and dealers are at the side of user requirements, and the development team is at the side of functional requirements. An important task for the business analysts with the offshore team is to transform both business and user requirements into functional requirements for developers to work with.

In practice, we often mistaken business requirements as user requirements, and customers sometimes take their requirements as those of users. For example, the business representatives of an automaker take it for granted that dealers will use a system in a way as they've imagined, instead of doing any user survey, and in the end the user feedback that they've got is mostly complaint. Therefore, it is so important to distinguish genuine user requirements from customer supposition, and customers shall take the initiative to confirm what users desire for; otherwise, they may have to deal with annoying requirement changes in the later stage.

Take another example about automobile sales system. The business requirements, which are presented by a luxury brand car company, are as follows: contact with the manufacturer to collect the inventory data of all dealers; and contact with logistics companies to make sure when the cars can be delivered to dealers. The aim of these requirements is to acquire accurate sales data as many as possible, reduce communication with dealers, and raise the efficiency of the entire process.

For each dealer or 4S showroom, their requirements involve management of the information of the customers who have entered their stores, management of orders, management of the approval process for bill signing, and analysis of customer conversion rate. The aim of these requirements is to standardize the signing process, guarantee transparency of in-store information (fast query of inventory models and their configuration), and facilitate data analysis and KPI assessment.

Here let's talk about a concrete example:

- Business requirements: the cars already sold may not be resold by other salesmen.
- User requirements: all the sold cars may not be found in the inventory pool.

■ Functional requirements: upon receiving the deposit and confirming the order, the vehicle number corresponding to the order shall be hidden in the inventory pool.

I once met a customer who asked to "add a function for manually modifying the vehicle information in the order." If we did so, it would take about five workdays to complete a version iteration and put it online. But we decided to find out why the customer intended to do so. It turned out that "the latest information about the cars on spot sale is incapable of automatic synchronization," which was attributed to the logic of design, since we thought all the cars were delivered to the dealer's warehouse, the vehicle information would be fixed and free from further change, but we had overestimated the quality of the customer's data. Later, we spent one workday on canceling the state verification during synchronization to circumvent this problem.

This example tells that if we fail to figure out what customers really want and do as what they say, we cannot provide them with much value. Instead, at hearing customer requirements, if we could put ourselves in their shoes, we will get twice the result with half the effort.

After understanding the connotations of user requirements (the problems they want to solve) and business requirements (the solutions to solve users' problems) and distinguishing them from each other, everyone in the delivery team should play their respective roles in developing product functions satisfying both customers and users.

6.7.1.1 Business Analysts

As mentioned above, it is necessary to fully distinguish user requirements from business (customer) requirements, only in this way the work to be done by offshore teams can satisfy the two sides, and avoid requirement changes and resource waste in the future.

Business analysts will first break down large functional modules into small user stories. As entering the stage of product development, business analysts will explain the business requirements to developers and testers, so as to make sure that no one has any doubt about these requirements.

In general, the quality control of requirements is to turn vague requirements into clear ones, which can avoid repeated communication and excessive interference into the process of strategic planning. Consequently, it will be more likely to raise work efficiency and reduce resource waste, as well as develop high-quality and forward-looking strategies, and divert to chain-like and hierarchical development instead of being limited to the transmission of business requirements between points.

6.7.1.2 Development Engineers

Development engineers or developers shall fully comprehend the functional requirements provided by business analysts, do a good job in task decomposition, set a technical architecture after knowing what they are going to do, and think about business expansibility after satisfying the existing functional requirements. Upon completion of functional development, developers shall immediately call in business analysts and testers to join in acceptance check to ensure that these functions accord with the business requirements.

The technologies to be selected are associated with the way of teamwork. From a technical standpoint, microservices and split services are conducive to distributed agile development.

6.7.1.3 Test Engineers

Through process guarantee and quality assurance, the business requirements can be finally achieved. The entire processes, from business analysis to function development, from development to testing, and then to user testing, is under strict quality control. Test engineers or testers shall try to find out bugs for the sake of users, because when they are about to test a user story, it is theoretically taken as satisfying the business requirements. At this moment, testers shall confirm if these bugs may bother different users in different scenarios.

The kickoff of new story cards and the acceptance check of the development environment aim at clearing up misunderstandings about the business requirements, since such occasion where all project-related personnel are present could not be better for calibrating everyone's perceptions.

In the final analysis, everyone in a project team should fully comprehend customers' business and do not be restricted by their own job duties. Wherever we are in the process of project implementation, an misunderstanding of requirements may ruin the ultimate goal of our team. Despite fancy functions and stable performance, any product that deviates from business or user requirements is a defective one.

6.7.2 THE WHOLE TEAM IS RESPONSIBLE FOR QUALITY

The small-step iterative development mode is able to spread the risks of large-scale development going live, so the risks of the entire project are dispersed into each iteration. Then it will be enough to focus on the core function of each small iteration at each stage; automated testing and regression testing will guarantee the overall quality of each online delivery.

Agile development is a method and process specially invented for agile teams according to their characteristics. Such development mode is targeted and already verified by countless projects or teams. The agile development practices of offshore teams are under the supervision of project manager to ensure smooth project implementation, because poor implementation will cause both project progress and quality to go wrong. Whenever there is a conflict between progress and quality, on no account can we give up quality.

As far as I can tell, in many projects, especially those employing agile development mode, the biggest challenge is the quality assurance of frequent deliveries. The usual response is to strengthen testing which is indeed necessary. But it is worth noting that better quality is ascribed to the design of technical architecture and high-quality codes instead of being obtained through testing, and they are the key essentials of iterative delivery. Agile development is based on a series of built-in quality practices, which are the biggest value of this development mode in addition to its feature of spreading risks.

Each team member has his own duty, it is natural for them to think about problems from their own standpoint. For example, a customer once asked my team to add a new field ("country and place of delivery") in the system. It was so easy that we only needed to merge the two existing fields and display them together. But in the eyes of technicians, users could get all information by selecting two fields, why did the customer still want a new one. In fact, it was out of consideration for actual business operation where two fields needed to be merged. For example, when exporting data to generate a report, if "country" and "place of delivery" are separate fields, the manual data sorting will make the report more aesthetic.

We shall pay attention to product testability throughout the process of materializing the requirements. In addition to testers, developers also need to care about the acceptance check of their work. Whenever they sit together to have a meeting, such as kickoff of a new story card, they should discuss which performance tests are required and where third-party integration tests are to be introduced. The acceptance check of the development environment is also an opportunity for us to know more about the test cases written by developers.

When developing a process-oriented system like an auto sales terminal, we shall pay great attention to the handling of abnormal paths, which in essence indicate any operations that exceed the shortest workflow. Another focal point is data, especially the integrated data, we need to guarantee the accuracy of the data at entry point and exit point by following the principle of "easy entry, strict exit." Moreover, we shall first define the "rules of the game" with the integration team: we give them the data as they've required, if they find something inconsistent with their requirements, they can try to fix it on their own; if they fail, we may modify our interface to avoid inflicting the overall interests.

The purpose of testing is not just for finding bugs. For example, the unit testing written by developers is not to detect bugs, but ensure the security of iterative development and then drive out the correct implementation code; and integration testing is to ensure that different developers and different development teams could submit code frequently and realize continuous integration.

Proper use of tags in test documents will help testers quickly understand the designed test scenarios, eliminate misunderstandings, and improve communication efficiency:

- To mark types of testing (smoke testing or regression testing)
- To mark function modules (selectively run tests for certain functions)
- To mark purpose of testing (eliminate misunderstandings of code logic)

To what extent the bugs will impact users' business? Testers shall have a clear idea of this. They must bear in mind that business value is the key to providing better services to customers, rather than thinking only of functions of a system.

6.7.3 Development Practice

The code design of offshore teams shall be capable of self-protection at the points with an outer interface, and in line with the principle of "easy entry, strict exit." Moreover, on the premise of guaranteed testability and verifiability, the code design shall be convenient for isolating bugs in later period and locating bugs more quickly.

6.7.3.1 The Boundary between Built-In Quality and Built-Out Quality: Code Warehousing

Code review must be easily operable based on the code warehousing process. If possible, the review process shall be accompanied with automated inspections such as code scanning, encoding specification and security scanning, as well as continuous integration for automated testing, so as to ensure of adequate quality inspection of code before its warehousing. After that, it enters the stage of special QA testing, and it will focus more on the "outside" business scenario testing.

6.7.3.2 Philosophy of Code Co-Ownership

The codebase of a team is not suitable for individual contracting. First, there will be risks from personnel change. For example, if someone quits his job, then the tasks assigned to him will come to a standstill for some time. Second, the monopoly of certain code by individuals will impede the communication and collective learning between team members, and make them spend more time on resolving problems.

Well, which kinds of practices are conducive to establishing the code-sharing philosophy?

Pair programming can not only promote the efficient communication between developers and produce a multiplying effect, but also facilitate knowledge sharing and code co-ownership. If different people could join in pair programming in a regular manner, it is sure to expand the scope of code co-ownership.

Code review is a process where one developer gets to know the code written by others so that he can quickly get started when he is asked to modify other developers' code. In addition, developers shall try to find bugs in the code and help their colleagues to improve the program design.

If each story card is split into fine granularity, more people will get access to the same fragment of code. In contrast, large granularity of story card will to some extent keep developers from communication when writing code.

6.7.3.3 Continuous Integration

As a mature practice, continuous integration, on basis of automated code building and automated testing, mainly employs a unified code repository and frequent integration to achieve the purpose of obtaining a stable and available software at any time. From the perspective of customers, continuous integration is able to reduce delivery risks.

What challenges does continuous integration pose for offshore teams? What are the peculiarities of offshore teams?

- A unified code repository determines that local access is available to one team, while other teams can only have remote access. Therefore, poor network conditions may interrupt the work of some team members and even tread on the entire project schedule.
- Through frequent submission, distributed teams can find conflicts and errors in their understanding in time, which will motivate them to strengthen communication at the code level.
- Distributed concurrent construction reduces the waiting time by creating concurrent servers.

The most important thing in continuous integration is communication. We need to ensure that everyone can easily see the system status and the latest modifications, while customers can query the project progress through the continuous integration server. Although continuous integration is a difficult process that calls for technical improvement, resource investment, teamwork, and culture cultivation, all of these efforts we've made will pay off after this process comes to an end.

Presently, the Internet industry has kept developing in full swing, offshore teams are often asked to be capable of frequent deployment. If continuous integration is applied, it will eliminate the biggest obstacle to frequent deployment.

6.7.4 Awareness of System Security

In most people's view, it is testers that should assume responsibility for product safety, since they run various tests which are ought to include safety test. But if there was a dedicated security team, then people would start arguing that the security team should guarantee product safety – top priority of the team. However, these viewpoints are harmful misunderstandings. If we take safety as a responsibility borne by individual team members or a separate team, a passive atmosphere is likely to be formed: someone may think product safety has nothing to do with him and choose to act as an onlooker. This atmosphere will generate lots of negative effects such as the safety problems are hard to be detected and resolved promptly, most team members have no chance to exercise their safety skills, and measures for safety improvement are hardly carried out within the team.

Unlike the traditional practice of relying heavily on certain individuals or security team to safeguard product safety, industry insiders advocate the concept of "built-in security," that is, split security responsibilities among team members and let each of them do his own part in solving security issues. In this way, everyone will shoulder the responsibility for maintaining product safety and make positive efforts in this regard.

Business analysts shall, while analyzing business requirements, get a whole picture of product safety. If they are incapable of doing so, they can work with technicians to complete this task. In terms of developers, they shall consciously avoid security risks in the process of encoding, and assist testers to run security test on products. As a result, before the products are handed over to the security team for security review, some safety loopholes are already discovered and repaired, or circumvented during the business analysis. By this time, product safety is to some extent guaranteed, and more time is won for the security team so that they can

Through this way of sharing responsibilities, all team members will be more united in dealing with security issues, and they are ready to take the initiative to improve their security capability. More importantly, this approach will strengthen collaboration between team members and between development and security teams, thereby gradually forming a virtuous circle in teamwork.

6.7.5 SUMMARY

Although we praise highly the whole-team consciousness, it does not mean that every activity has to be approved by all team members. On several occasions, technical director and agile coach directly put their plans on the table and ask team members to carry them out; after a period of time, they will invite all team members to make comments and suggestions based on their personal experiences. This practice has been proved more efficient.

If a team does not have a core leadership and let everyone act on their own, then efficiency will be out of the question. For example, one problem may have multiple solutions which are only different in their pathways, but in the end all of our efforts are to no avail, it is because no solution is generally agreed and smoothly implemented. It is true for large teams and even for the small ones consisting of less than ten people.

Although the flat self-organizing team pursues knowledge sharing and technology co-ownership, this does not mean that every team member has to be an omniscient, but that he can access to the information that he wants at any time.

We advocate co-ownership of both team and project, everyone should do good to his team and project, instead of showing himself in front of leaders. A team should remain democratic and inclusive, allowing team members to oppose the decisions made by leaders. A team should assume responsibility as a whole, otherwise it will be unworthy to be a collective.

6.8 FEEDBACK IS A PROPELLER FOR DISTRIBUTED TEAMS TO ACHIEVE CONTINUOUS IMPROVEMENT

It seems that we human beings are only interested in going straight ahead instead of looking back. If we could draw lessons from history, then many tragedies, especially wars, are likely to be avoided.

6.8.1 WHY SHOULD WE VALUE FEEDBACK

The core of agile development is to achieve continuous self-adjustment and self-improvement through feedback in a highly collaborative environment, with emphasis placed on collaboration and feedback. Collaboration, which is the basis of feedback, exists between project team and customers and between team members.

Feedback refers to an instant summary of lessons for guiding future work; it may exist in any link of development, such as code quality control, automated testing, deployment, project scheduling, requirements changes and customer acceptance. Even if we've gone afar, as long as an error is detected, we shall look back to examine what we've done. Feedback shall be made as soon as possible: the sooner we get feedback, the faster we can confirm that we've gone the wrong way. If everything goes well, we are sure to have more confidence; otherwise, we should make adjustment promptly to minimize resource waste. If there is something wrong with our starting point, we will go too far on the wrong track as time goes by, and spend too much on getting back on track. Since it is so, how can we build a feedback mechanism to discover abnormalities in the first place?

When it comes to feedback, we have to talk about the Deming Cycle or Plan-Do-Check-Act (PDCA) Cycle. As far as I know, the vast majority of project teams can only complete the first two steps, which means that they are doing the work in front of them single-mindedly without reflecting on what they've done, let alone making adjustment and improvement.

As long as we observe carefully, we will find that feedback exists in all aspects of our work and life. Its essence is to reduce the possibility of making mistakes by learning from past experience, so that everything we do in the future will become more and more smooth. Our Chinese ancestors have left us so many wise sayings in this regard, such as "drawing lessons from history and gearing to the needs of the future," "lessons learned from the past can guide one in the future," and "never forget why you started, and you can accomplish your mission."

Now let's take a look at what offshore teams should do to ensure of feedback.

6.8.2 Key Points in Making Feedback

As one of the quintessences of agile development, feedback is a means of self-management and continuous improvement for project teams. With feedback at its core, self-managing teams can discover problems on their own, and continuously improve themselves through internal motivation.

6.8.2.1 Feedback on Personnel Performance

Giving feedback to individuals requires some skills. First, inform him of what went wrong or not good enough. Second, recommend him how to make correction or improvement in a timely manner. Finally, develop a habit of giving feedback to others actively and continuously; it is better to point out the problems at the spot, rather than having them exposed in the final assessment. The purpose of feedback is to improve the work efficiency of individuals or teams, not for their performance assessment.

There shall be a suitable pathway for making feedback on the work saturation of team members. The team staffing can be adjusted in time based on feedback (every team shall confirm if it has timely and effective feedback). Weekly or daily work report is the easiest and the most direct feedback pathway.

We often ignore an important activity – speech rehearsal. Software engineers are mostly introverted and not good at expressing themselves, especially on public occasions. Improvisation in showcase is unrealistic, they'd better learn how to give lectures by making his teammates as audiences, collect their feedback and then make necessary adjustment. Practices have proved that the feedback on speech rehearsal can help improve the effect of formal speech. Getting fully prepared is the only way to become a confident speaker. The contents of speech rehearsal, which may be technical sharing, progress reporting or presentation of achievements, shall be able to bring out the best in the team.

One of the most formal feedback is the project retrospective meeting during the iteration process. A staged review can expose problems in the team in a timely manner, then all team members can make concerted efforts in finding solutions, and take actions to have these problems effectively addressed.

In terms of the project review on a team basis, its focus is problem-solving and continuous improvement, rather than finding out who is to blame. After discovering any problem, the work priority of the retrospective meeting is to ensure that this feedback problem could be effectively handled by distributed teams.

It is beyond doubt that project review can expose many problems, but some problems should not be discovered until the review. Are offshore teams aware of this matter? In addition to the retrospective meeting, are there alternative ways for offshore teams to find problems?

For offshore teams, they should pay special attention to the following two types of feedback:

(1) Feedback from customers to offshore teams. After some staged results are achieved, customers like to send a thank-you e-mail to offshore teams. It is a mere formality, but it shows their recognition of offshore teams and willingness of maintaining this cooperative relationship.
When dealing with some typical customer feedback which is usually negative, we have to keep patient. We shall first make explanations to the customer, and then take corresponding actions if the feedback problem is confirmed.
My project teams have received the following complaints from customers:
- Spending too many resources on code design, thus slowing down rate of development.
- Some team members are not capable enough, making a simple task unfinished on time.

- Overall progress is behind schedule and showing no signs of improvement.
- Product quality is deteriorating.
- Not taking initiative in communication.
- A high turnover of staff.

(2) Feedback from offshore teams to customers. It is a mission impossible for most offshore teams, mainly because they don't think it will benefit themselves. But it should be clarified that this feedback is not a complaint, but to make customers feel that our offshore teams take them as our members, and we hope to provide them with assistance as much as possible and create value for them.

Giving feedback to customers can also ease the pressure on offshore teams, because the responsible person of the customer team can learn about the true performance of his team from a wholly new perspective – feedback from a third party. We can point out the shortcomings of the customer team, which is an indirect way to show the level of trust between our two sides. Real trust is not built on everyday greetings.

6.8.3 FEEDBACK ON PROJECT

The feedback on code review made by development team, in addition to showing each developer the bugs in their code, is a kind of output feedback to test team. For example, through a brief discussion, developers can find the function part that may be affected by the new code submission, which is a reference for testers to determine the direction of test execution in the future.

Effective automated testing can correctly feedback the quality level of the software. Continuous integration is another way to provide feedback to the development team about integration, and it is both fast and frequent.

The continuous product tests run by testers, together with the bug report to be submitted later, are also feedback on product quality. This feedback, which is manifested in bug descriptions in the report, is in essence to inform developers of the quality of the code they've written. An accurate description can guarantee the quality of the feedback itself.

For the sake of project management, we can use some tools to get feedback on project progress. Burndown chart is in essence feedback on development progress, making all team members clearly see the project status and current trends. Although we can also use Gantt chart which is more suitable for waterfall development model, changing requirements will invalidate the entire Gantt chart.

Many times, the bug analysis made by the team ends up with nothing definite, it is because close-loop feedback remains absent, making feedback and consensus unable to yield any effect on future development. In view of this, we must ask ourselves a question when making bug feedback: the reason why we investigate bugs is to find out how things went wrong, and how can we draw lessons from this bug feedback to prevent these bugs from repeating themselves in the future.

User feedback is the most direct way to obtain product feedback. Although offshore teams are far away from users, they can get feedback through a variety of technical and nontechnical means. When online functions are not complete, user feedback can hardly be accurate, which is not expected by offshore teams. How to get more valuable feedback at this moment? Generally, effective user test does not start until all functions are put online, but it will be too late to make feedback. Therefore, it's better to switch on new functions and switch off unfinished functions at the same time, only in this way can keep users to concentrate on completed functions.

The product operation based on phased launch will inevitably produce some valuable feedback. There is sure to be some feedback on user operation from the production environment, so project manager shall urge his team members to improve product design and reduce the occurrence of such problems, thereby easing the burden of DevOps.

Customers with available conditions are advised to use the special call center services, which will make users provide feedback on bugs more easily, and facilitate development team to get the summary and analysis of these bugs and then adjust the future delivery plan accordingly. The call center, with mature solutions, may help development team mitigate part of the interference from users and filter out useful information.

Feedback is quite important, and the way of remote collaboration determines the output of offshore teams is the greatest value. After getting feedback, offshore teams must work out solutions to all problems and take actions to have these problems resolved. It is a process that tests the wisdom and working philosophy of offshore teams.

7 Customer-Oriented Offshore Teams

For the offshore teams that are engaged in enterprise software delivery, providing good customer service is their eternal topic. Staged delivery of products is no doubt a rigid requirement, but in the process of achieving this goal, maintaining benign interaction with customers is also important, which helps offshore teams learn the thoughts of customers, improve their cooperative relationship, and accumulate valuable hands-on experiences for team members.

Each team is about to encounter the following problems. They shall learn a multidimensional way of thinking, face up to the difficulties of diverse types of projects, and find appropriate solutions. There are always ways to overcome difficulties as long as you do not give up.

- **Across-team synchronization:** How to make all teams move in the same direction instead of restraining each other.
- **Cooperation with customers:** How to set realistic expectations for customers and satisfy them without over-commitment.
- **Types of projects:** Are there any different strategies for dealing with different types of projects, either charging a fixed amount or charging by per man-day? How do these strategies affect the daily work of each team member?
- **Release plan:** How to develop a release plan and prioritize story cards across multiple iterations and multiple teams.
- **Frequent release:** How to guarantee product launch within the given time and ensure product quality?
- **Product DevOps:** Software delivery is never a one-time solution. How to smoothly deliver software to the DevOps of the customer team.

7.1 ESTABLISH MUTUAL TRUST WITH CUSTOMERS

First of all, we must be aware that a solid customer relationship is never won by good luck, but unremitting efforts and sincerity. Sometimes we may bring some bad news to customers, and sometimes we may fail to perform well when showing our staged work result to the head of the customer team (e.g., the system that we've developed either goes wrong or reacts slowly). It is wishful thinking if we can still have a good customer relationship at this moment. More than that, even if the product itself is reliable and we have been doing a good job, is it certain that remote customers can accurately understand what we want to convey? In short, both soft and hard skills are required for building and maintaining a good customer relationship at work. If we fail to get along well with our customers, smooth project implementation cannot last long, our communication will become increasingly difficult and our mutual trust is likely to be ruined, making the project doomed to failure in the end.

To build a bridge of trust between offshore teams and customers, the delivery of high-quality staged work results is undoubtedly important. Moreover, it is equally important to exceed customer expectations and improve customer experience in the delivery process.

It is difficult to deliver software in distributed projects, since the difficulties in communication can easily lead to misunderstandings, errors, waste of time and resources, and even confusion. Once there is mistrust, the project will soon come to an end.

7.1.1 OBJECTIVES

During the operation progress of the project, customer management is a continuous task, which is the duty of every team member who deals with customers. A reliable customer relationship has a positive effect on project implementation, and several realistic goals can keep the team from getting lost:

- Cooperate closely with customers by speaking frankly with them and by collaborating with them in solving problems.
- Let a trustworthy customer relationship become a valuable asset of the team.
- Make customers fully aware of the project status so as to avoid unexpected events.
- Win back customers who do not trust us in a timely manner.

7.1.1.1 Establish Close Cooperation with Customers by Being Frank with Them

Maintaining customer relationship is a long-term task. It is far from enough to impress customers at the beginning, what is more important is to win their trust through each cooperation and communication with them. Our offshore teams must stay professional, because the key reason that we can draw different customers, despite of their unique requirements, is that they have confidence in our delivery capacity. We need to convey such information to our customers that we have both competence and confidence to fulfill each delivery.

Speaking from the perspective of customers, what they desire is professional service which includes not only the final deliverable, but also the experience in cooperating with offshore teams. To obtain trust from customers, we shall show them our professional performance, and collect information about their stakeholders (e.g., whether they have a great influence and whether they support the work of offshore teams).

At the inception stage of a project, we shall introduce our work style to customers for cultural matching. We shall remain active while working, whenever someone (either with the project or customer team) poses a problem, we shall keep tracking it, instead of acting like a hands-off boss. By adopting the PDCA approach, customers can see our ability to solve problems and fulfill tasks, not just the ability to discover problems.

In the process of collaborating with customers, the most recommended way is to reduce inefficient modes of communication, and directly employ the fastest modes of communication. We should not be bogged down in the minutiae, and remember when should we jump out of details. In communication with customers, the information we are trying to convey should not contain too many details so that customers are free from worrying about the details brought by us.

Don't be afraid that we are not perfect when working with customers. We should not start building a customer relationship until everything is ready, but take the first step to win customers and then improve ourselves through cooperation with them, which accords with the philosophy of lean customer cooperation. The traditional concept is that we should "put our best foot forward" in front of customers, while lean customer cooperation requires us to show our "true colors" and sincerity to customers, and make a concerted effort with them to become perfect. A close cooperative relationship built in this process is especially valuable to customers.

When we do a good job as we always do, customers will make nothing of it, but once we make a mistake, they may take it "unforgivable." Therefore, we should show our cards one by one, which is a kind of professional skill and a strategy for presenting ourselves. By following the principle from simple to complex, we can accumulate our work results, which is conducive to building the trust of customers. It will help us avoid a crisis of confidence when encountering greater challenges in the future. In short, we should pay attention to solving problems and showing our staged results, which will raise morale of both customers and our team members. Achieving landmark achievements one after another is as sweet as enjoying the fruits of our labor.

Professional players and fitness coaches have enviable physical quality which is obtained through years' exercise. Soft skills like emotional intelligence and mentality can also be improved through exercise, but their results are hard to be quantified, in other words, they are invisible. By the same token, if customers cannot see any tangible benefit from the things not quantified, how can they agree to pay for them, or how much they should pay. It is a difficult issue, but if we have already earned the trust from customers, we can win their consent without making extra efforts to prove our capacity.

7.1.1.2 Customer Trust is a Kind of Asset

As nonprofessionals, customers may present requirements irrelevant to software performance, stability, or security, so we should take the initiative to think of these requirements on behalf of customers, rather than waiting for them to surprise us. In addition to these requirements that are mostly nonfunctional, we should also recommend to improve software design for ensuring better user experience, and evaluate which requirements are technically achievable and which ones are not, and then estimate the workload of those achievable ones.

Our performance in the early stage of the project must be good enough to convince customers that we are fully capable of offshore delivery. Two of my projects are typical examples in this regard: The first one was that we persuaded a customer (a Beijing-based auto company) to outsource its software development to our offshore team in Wuhan. The second one was that our project team, which was working for a large logistics company, left the customer's site in the middle of the project to return to our headquarters where they started remote delivery. In these two cases, the heads with the customer's team were at first suspicious of such remote delivery, but in the end they found our performance impeccable.

As long as we firmly trust each other, even if there is any dilemma in the future, customers will tend to adopt our recommended solutions.

7.1.1.3 Avoid Accidents

Of course, outsourcing industry is still a service industry. In line with this thinking, we cannot make customers feel that offshore teams are as unpredictable as the "Black Box Testing." Efficient communication is a useful tool to avoid this circumstance. Everyone in the team should know their own status and the status of the whole team at any time, and keep abreast of status updates in real time. We should frequently update our status to customers, which is a way to show our respect to them.

Good offshore teams must be able to maintain transparency. Take Project B for example, we rapidly provided Party A with deliverables through every two weeks of iteration, and promoted its decision-making on development of businesses and IT products. Compared with a German supplier's nontransparent black-box practice through three-week iteration and delayed delivery in the end, our better performance won Party A's recognition and it preferred us to the German supplier to fully take over the background development.

Good collaboration within offshore teams can also increase customer confidence in them.

When undertaking fixed-bid projects, we must carefully record the new requirements. Whenever we find out a requirement beyond the work scope, we shall e-mail the customer and let him confirm this matter. Everyone in the team cannot only bury themselves in their 8-hour duties per day, but also keep a close watch on the changes of requirements. If there is any newly-added requirement that is beyond the original scope, it will bring risks to the final delivery.

7.1.1.4 Win Back Customers Who Have Lost Trust in Us without Delay

If someone with the customer team lost trust in us, we have to try our best to win him back. But it is a long-term restoration task in need of some techniques. Distributed teams shall first ensure visibility of the project, if we fail to demonstrate the development results of the project continuously, the customer is prone to interpret everything done by remote teams from the most negative perspective, and our project may be halted because of this.

There are some tips as follows for us to increase customer trust in us:

We can invite the customers who lack of trust in us to join in our team events. In general, distrust originates from the feeling of losing control. Therefore, we can invite them to participate in our showcase of staged results and solicit their comments, and even invite them to attend our daily stand-up. Even if these customers still feel dissatisfied, we shall keep asking for their feedback, only in this way can we accurately locate the points for improvement.

When asking for useful feedback, if we ask some general questions like "What do you think of this project?," then we can seldom receive an insightful reply. Our questions must be more specific, such as "What is your biggest concern?" "What do you think is the highlight of this design?" "If we can change one thing in this iteration, what do you hope to be?"

We can celebrate the landmark achievements of our team with great fanfare, and even show our small gains. Customers are likely to be drawn to negative issues, even if they are not intentional to do so, and affected by prejudices. Therefore, whenever we have gained some accomplishments, it is important to make them known to everyone concerned.

When encountering any problem or obstacle, we should promptly inform customers of this matter. If the work of offshore teams is interrupted by some people, it is especially important to make it known by the customers who are suspicious of us. Of course, we do hope these customers could directly help us overcome obstacles. Seeking help positively from the other party is able to build up mutual trust.

Both progress and obstacles shall be clearly visualized with the helpful visualization tools such as burnup chart and burndown chart. We should highlight the obstacles through whatever means so as to have them resolved as soon as possible.

We advocate "push" not "pull." Our project manager can check the control panel to find the information he needs, but don't expect the customers who have lost trust in us will do the same thing. We have to send work report to them in the form of "push message," which is a means of communication that they are accustomed to.

We shall make sure that the customers who do not trust us can easily contact with remote teams. Not everyone of them holds a leading position, if they could easily get answers from a chat channel or from a phone call with remote teams, they will feel much more comfortable.

We should endeavor to establish a multichannel customer relationship. For the customers who have prejudice against offshore teams, they are unlikely to publicize the achievements of offshore teams within their customer team. A multichannel customer relationship can spread the news about offshore teams as widely as possible, so that the information exchange between teams will not be selectively filtered.

Successful delivery can obscure many negative problems of offshore teams. Therefore, if there are risks in time limit or budget of delivery, we must do our utmost to have these risks eliminated.

7.1.2 BUILD A TRUSTED CUSTOMER RELATIONSHIP

The fundamental objective of software development project is to make it easier for customers to carry on their work, and it is important to ease the worries of customers about project implementation. To this end, we have to take the following three steps when encountering difficulties:

(1) Ask customers open-ended questions directly.
(2) Give customers several options and let them make a choice.
(3) Help customers make a choice and tell them our tendency and basis.

This is the only way for the growth of every offshore team. In this process, we will provide customers with more and more value.

Managing customers is also the key to maintaining their trust. The first step in customer management is to manage their time. Some customers are always in a hurry, while others may be a slow-coach. We cannot dance to their tune, especially we cannot wait for their instructions every time. We need to be clear about what we are going to do and how to do it, and the things we can do without their cooperation.

We should help customers and our team members adapt to changes. A project plan may change all the time, which depends on the environmental volatility of each team and the characteristics of the project. But it still necessary to have a plan, since it is able to drive conversations around priorities, interdependencies, and team productivity. Requirements may exceed team productivity all the time, that's why our team and customers shall work together and make decisions after difficult trade-offs. To carry out planned activities, our team has to adopt an empirical method, just like the operating mechanism of weather forecasting.

For fear of uncertainties, we'd better not make many commitments at the beginning. With the gradual elimination of uncertainties, we can deliver more functions to customers than we've promised, rather than make over-commitment in advance which may lead to late delivery in the end. In this way, customers will feel more satisfied even though there is no difference in the final deliverables.

We cannot always trust customers. For example, at the beginning of the project, customers may say that what they care the most is progress instead of quality, and warn us repeatedly to complete all the functions on time and don't be afraid of bugs, since they can have them fixed after product launch. However, if we do as they say, we will end up miserable, because in the event of uncontrollable product quality, customers will blame us for pursuing speed regardless of quality. It is in line with most people's psychology: when their top-priority requirement is satisfied, they will shift attention to low-priority requirements. Another situation is that the work of the customer team depends on the work of ours, then they will be more likely to vent their anger on us, so we must develop an alternative plan for the bottom line.

We need to build and maintain close communication and cooperation with customers, but how close they should be? Every team member is encouraged to communicate with others, of course, it is on the basis that everyone knows how to communicate, when should they act as an entire team, and when should they think about problems from the customer perspective.

7.1.3 Tips for Establishing and Maintaining Customer Relationships

We'd better know the personnel composition of the customer team and everyone's limits of authority, so that we can discuss work with the right person and steer the project in the right direction. Moreover, we shall identify stakeholders of the customer team, and the person that has absolute discourse power in a certain aspect. Our business analysts and project manager shall pay special attention in this regard. And we should learn about the different concerns of stakeholders, then we can determine which kind of output can cater to them.

We can draw up a communication plan. To deal with different stakeholders, we can build a variety of communication channels in different teams. After the project is started, we can have a fixed form of communication based on the output of some teams. The contents of communication are, respectively, about story list, project status reporting, risk identification, and bug assessment.

We can organize some informal communication activities. We shall seize all opportunities, such as paying them a visit, having dinner with them, or having fun with them in the bars, to make friends with customers, which will quickly bring us close and build mutual trust. For example, Beijing Xiaomi Technology Co., Ltd. – pioneer in developing a mobile phone operating system based on the Internet model and known for its unique "fan culture," shouted to "make friends with our users" at its inception, which blurred the boundary between "merchants" and "consumers," and enabled vendors and buyers to interact in a credible environment free from commercial interests.

7.1.4 Summary

Generally, a failed project is not attributed to technical failure, but to loss of customer trust. In order to maintain customer trust, we shall actively communicate with them at the customer site to make a good impression on them; moreover, we shall make sure of continuous and on-time delivery to make them confident in our capability.

For our offshore teams, we shall deliver workable programs as early as possible, and then deliver new functions in a regular manner to maintain customer trust. In this process, we can take a shortcut, but we can never take crooked ways.

7.2 WHAT SHALL WE DO WHEN AT ODDS WITH CUSTOMERS?

When different teams, including offshore teams and local teams, insist on their own plans, how can they help customers make decisions?

7.2.1.1 How to "Oppose" Customer Opinions

It is normal to oppose a plan or an arrangement, but we must give constructive suggestions instead of making an objection for objection's sake. And these suggestions shall be based on careful preparation. Even if a suggestion is a simple and clear, we should be able to explain why we recommend it, otherwise customers may think that our decision is made arbitrarily.

7.2.1.2 How to Get Prepared to Convince Customers

Whenever we have to resolve difficult problems, we must convince ourselves that we are capable of doing so before we convince our customers. Don't be satisfied with a smattering of knowledge. If we don't have full assurance to address a problem, we must seize this opportunity to learn some new skills. Without adequate knowledge and skills, we should not try to convince customers, or else our attempt will be counterproductive and damage the reputation of offshore teams.

7.2.1.3 How to Resolve Differences

The further away we are from end users, the more likely we are to misunderstand and move in the wrong direction. When we disagree with customers, it is possible that neither of us is right, the only way out is to invite the referee (end users) to make final judgment.

Sometimes our disagreement is no more than a misunderstanding. The communication process is like information falling through a funnel: the information is input in a form but output in another form. No wonder a lot of information is lost in this process.

I happen to think of an entertainment program where a team of five or six people standing in a queue to hand on message one by one, and everyone was only allowed to communicate with the persons before and behind him. The host showed a message to the first person who would describe it to the one behind him, those after him would do the same until the message was conveyed to the last person. If the answer of the last person was exactly the original message, they would win the game. Hardly no team could win victory, but this show still made audiences laugh all the way through since everyone's description was totally unrelated to the original message. Now that the loss and change of information in the process of transmission is unavoidable, we have to constantly verify whether the obtained information has changed, so as to form a closed loop of information.

What can we do to make us and customers come together with one mind?

7.2.2 SETTLE DIFFERENCES

7.2.2.1 Business Requirements

The contents of requirements must be thoroughly analyzed, and their external impact should also be taken into account, which is to remove the breeding grounds for differences. A qualified business analysis shall meet the following conditions:

- Ensure that the realization logic of these requirements is feasible;
- Requirements must go through end-to-end refinement to confirm whether there are any points not examined or interpreted;
- Estimate the implementation cost;
- Confirm whether these requirements conflict with the logic of existing products, and;
- Deeply understand the value of these requirements.

In addition, we also need to think about the requirements from the perspective of an entire project, such as the scope and priority of requirements which are likely to cause differences. Here is our solution: the scope of requirements should be tracked from the beginning with the online document editor, everyone has access to real-time information, the dependencies of all requirements are clarified, and the acceptance criteria should accord with the specific requirements of users. We should evaluate the priority of requirements together with customers. Although we can satisfy the hard requirements of customers, we need to remind them of the impact of doing so, that is, certain functions have to be pushed back.

When doing software outsourcing services, there is a high probability to contact with the business personnel in the customer team, they are better at dealing with different people than all members in offshore teams. In negotiations, these business personnel are easily to gain a great advantage, and beat us in a "reasonable" manner even in situations where we have an even chance of winning. We have to learn some skills to deal with these customers with "a silver tongue," otherwise our team will be taken advantage of. For example, in case of any difficulties, we shall take the initiative to make all information transparent so as to "shut the mouths" of customers. All discussions with customers must be recorded by e-mail and sent to them in time to block the channels through which they can play freely.

7.2.2.2 Technical Realization

In fact, most customers only have two requirements for their project: development speed and software quality (including requirements quality), which are focus of our work.

Customers usually do not know much about the specific implementation of software development, so they may think the process of technical realization too easy or too complicated. If there is a lack of information transparency, customers may be surprised to see how simple it is or astonished to find how hard it is. We are not sure this outcome is good or not, but we do believe that not everyone wants to have an experience like riding on a roller coaster.

In the process of technical implementation of software, the cost of handling abnormalities is definitely higher than that of handling normalities. Everyone knows that many institutions and resources are put in place for a minority of people who do not follow the rules, those who observe disciplines and laws and work hard seldom consume public administrative resources. For example, huge social capital has been invested into management of shared bicycles: special parking lots are segmented for fear of random parking; there has been endless operating cost for buying new bicycles or repairing vandalized ones (the maintenance cost incurred by bicycles is quite small in case of normal use). We should make customers get psychologically prepared to abnormalities, so as to prevent them from getting too angry at offshore teams, especially their speed of delivery. Therefore, the tests on abnormal scenes are the most energy-consuming.

How can offshore teams make sure of their work progress and 100% completion of the planned workload? It is definitely challenging.

7.2.2.3 Results Verification

The common A/B Testing is able to facilitate companies to adopt a variable decision-making model for making decisions in most cases. In the traditional sense, A/B Testing can only be run with at least two product versions: version A is the original version, while version B is the version we think may be better than version A. We can run the A/B Testing in a variable decision-making process, if version A is proved to be better than version B, we can simply close version B and then return to version A. The A/B Testing can even help us recognize when we need to apply the "irreversible decision-making" model.

The A/B Testing can not only accelerate decision-making, but also help empower team members to make decisions. It is not simply a test, but a user study that allows data to help us make decisions and convince all teams. Using some technical means to assist decision-making instead of relying on leaders to make decisions is a manifestation of the work style of self-managing teams and characteristics of their decision-making process.

Regarding the results verification, I need to tell a story: In every iteration, we will present our work results to customers who will show these results to users, and then users will immediately try the completed functions in a UAT environment and get ready to make feedback. Our expectation is that users will test these functions to see whether they can meet their job requirements, then give us feedback and inform us whenever they meet any problems. However, users may mistakenly think that our UAT environment is the same one for their previous UAT test, so they carry on trying these functions in a production environment. As a result, users (attaching great importance to the integrity of test data and functions) give us feedback on deficient data and missing functions, without knowing that the data are to be completed and the noncore functions are to be developed in the later stage, it is because we usually complete the core parts of all functions in the first place, and then have them optimized one by one, rather than delivering an integral functional module every time.

The delivery team hopes to get valuable feedback as soon as possible. If user test only brings additional workload and their feedback is of little reference value, then we can call off user test. Instead, users can be invited to our showcase meeting, just look around without hands-on operations, and wait for official launch of the system designed by experts and then manage to adapt to it.

7.2.2.4 Teamwork

We shall first confirm the top concern of customers: results or process. The focus of IT project management is results and process. Mental work cannot be quantified and managed as easily as manual labor which is paid by piece/hour; and it is not simply to finish an assignment, but to analyze and solve problems. The ability of an individual is by no means perfect, it is a team made up of talented individuals that is invincible. Therefore, we are in favor of human-based management: creating a comfortable environment where everyone is in love with his work rather than taking it as a means of livelihood, and self-motivated to work harder and insist on improving themselves.

Offshore teams usually care more about results and ignore process. Owing to its nature, distributed teamwork is characterized of paying attention to process, which is able to avoid big differences. The teamwork of the customer team is no much better, that is, there are different voices inside the customer team. Therefore, whenever a disagreement arises, we should try to collect the opinions that are on our side and properly respond to dissenting opinions.

Disagreements can result in bad mood. We must pay attention to emotional management and concentrate on solving problems. There are various reasons for making us frustrated. For example, customers repeatedly ask the same question, go back on their word, changes their requirements at will, or a certain team member is held responsible for an error made by the whole team.

When we have any unhealthy emotions, we must learn to overcome ourselves and keep calm, otherwise we may regret it later. At the same time, it is also dangerous to make decisions when our mood is unstable. It is probably a radical decision. When we experience great mood swings, we can take the following actions:

- Strengthen communication and identify real responsible persons to avoid "unjust cases."
- Put aside the things that make us struggling and think about them until we have calmed down.
- Transfer the job at hand to another person.
- Do not get emotional when we find the fault is made by customers, since our bad mood may get ourselves become scapegoat and suffer losses in the end.

7.2.3 CUSTOMER OPINIONS DETERMINE DELIVERY QUALITY

No matter how many indicators we have set, how many forms we have checked, how much code we have reviewed, and how many tests we have written, the only important thing to customers is properly working software. Relative to code quality, performance, design, and usability, customer feedback is the only factor that determines quality. We need to adapt to review our output from the customer perspective.

This involves the intrinsic value and commercial value of the same thing. The reason why the focus of customers is different from ours is that they are more interested in business value than intrinsic value.

I want to explain this problem in terms of the historical status of porcelain and glass. These two things appeared at different historical stages, which determined their status in people's hearts. Porcelain can be used as tableware and cup, etc., glass can do the same, and it boasts a much lower cost and an additional property of transparency as compared to porcelain. But we always think that porcelain is more high-end, and glass is only a symbol of cheapness. This is the reason why glass has the same intrinsic value with porcelain, but lags far behind in commercial value.

Offshore teams interact with local teams every day and have to work like one team. But different teams are affiliated with local companies or branches, and each has its own boss. Therefore, when dealing with some thorny problems, they must be aware of the dividing line between adherence to principles and dogmatism.

We must cooperate well with the people of other teams while working, just like we are in the same team, but do remember that we still represent our own company, and it is our inescapable responsibility to safeguard our company's interests. For example, increased requirements for fixed-bid projects require our more input. We should not only focus on a matter itself, but also on the environment where the matter exists. All matters can be adjusted with changes on the environment, and different environment determine to what extent these matters can be adjusted.

In the process of collaborating with customers, it is common to make compromise, but we shall have a road map to get back on track, instead of making concessions again and again. Everyone must understand that compromise is an expedient tactic. For example, we may reduce test coverage in exchange for development speed, which will incur a "technical debt," so we must backfill this gap as soon as possible.

Is pair programming necessary from beginning to end? The criteria for our judgment is to see whether it has additional value. We should judge whether a pair of people can share knowledge, and whether they can get any valuable sharing. Simple code stacking may make other people sleepy or too bored to check their WeChat updates.

Regarding how to embrace change and respond to changes in customer requirements, it is necessary to distinguish the middle line between changed and unchanged. When we embrace change, we must distinguish between unnecessary changes and at the same time help customers avoid paying for unnecessary things. Keep asking yourself if you have created value for your customers, then it will be easier for making decisions.

7.3 DELIVERY PROJECTS CHARGED BY MAN-DAY

For this kind of project, the customer pays according to how many hours our team members spend. Most overseas outsourcing projects in China adopt this approach.

Customers of these projects will bear more risks and pressures. But the benefits to them are also prominent. First, customers will have stronger control over requirements, including scope and priority, which can be adjusted flexibly at any time. Second, this type of cooperation is suitable for projects with high requirements on user experience, and customers can control the satisfaction of user experience. For a fixed-bid project, the total quantity of requirements must be fixed. Any change in the scope of requirements requires customers to adjust the budget, and the rework of the project also needs to be paid separately. If a project with a high requirement for user experience is a fixed-bid one, then we and our customers will inevitably have a dispute over user experience which is a requirement with a vague boundary, and the real situation could be even worse.

In terms of recent years' projects, few of them have a fixed scope of delivery requirements when they are started. In order to satisfy users in the end, project teams have to collect user feedback during the development process while adjusting the direction of the product. In this way, they can not only make the product functions as complete as possible, but also optimize user experience as much as possible. Most user feedback cannot be submitted until users have seen product effect or tried the product in person; therefore, a fixed-bid contract is not suitable for software development projects.

For projects where customers pay by per man-day, offshore teams also need to pay attention to the progress. As with fixed-bid projects, the story card estimated results also represent the team's commitment to customers. And customers are also concerned about the pace of development, it seems that faster development may mitigate the risk of going over budget.

Sometimes the developers of offshore teams have some autonomy in deciding the level of a function in a technology stack. Especially for front-end developers, by adopting different technology stacks, the effects produced are different, and it is not necessarily possible to achieve the effects that customers want. Of course, it may exceed customer expectation. As a member of the professional software service industry, we should be brave to face challenges and show our customers what the best delivery team looks like.

Since the development team only develops the part of the requirements that are released, while the other part is not developed at all, so there will be no waste arising from changing requirements. It can be said that agile development model even encourages us to modify requirements for the sake of promoting development. In the past, the modification of requirements was the main reason for the incompletion of software outsourcing projects.

This service model makes it easier for offshore teams to live in the comfort zone. No matter it is for the growth of individuals or for the entire team management, efforts must be made to make everyone jump out of the comfort zone.

7.4 FIXED-BID DELIVERY PROJECTS

The contract of a fixed-bid project must contain two points of relatively fixed requirements and a delivery date. Many customers, especially domestic ones, tend to sign such contract because it can pass on part of the risks to the supplier. Therefore, if offshore teams are working on a fixed-bid project, they will bear greater pressure.

Developing this kind of project is not complicated. But unlike the ordinary man-day projects, we still need to pay attention to the following five factors:

- How do we measure the size and price of a project?
- How do we manage requirements changes?
- How do we manage customer expectations?

- How do we manage risks?
- Commercial factors

7.4.1 Estimation of Workload and Price

When we take over a fixed-bid project, we need a relatively accurate estimation of its overall workload. Although we know that more manpower and more time spent in estimation will generate a more reliable estimated result, we have to complete the process of estimation as soon as possible, because the result is still an estimated one no matter how much we have invested.

In response to the above thinking and in order to meet the requirements of domestic customers, ThoughtWorks, as an initiator and leader of agile development model, after working on quick-start projects for years, created and practiced a method for agile development teams to properly deal with fixed-bid projects. This set of methodology for quickly kicking off projects is known as "quick start," which requires project teams to define requirements with customers through in-depth collaboration in the shortest time (usually two to three weeks). In this process, it is also necessary to confirm the scope of each requirement and include necessary buffer for fear of different risks. However, this method is not suitable for the projects that fail to fix all requirements at the time of kickoff.

In the case of a fixed-bid project, the estimation of its workload is no different from other ordinary projects. The content of such estimation covers story card list, business analysis, arrangement of iteration plans, testing strategy, and workload, which are irrelevant to the type of project.

The particularity of a fixed-bid project is that the uncertainty in this process is more important, because our delivery team bears more risks. For a project with an original estimate of 1,000 man-days, should we quote 1,200? In this way, it can help us cover up some additional investment. Any additional resource input that exceeds the planned budget will reduce the profit of the project. If the profit is lower than a certain level, the project will be taken as a failed one. The worst case is that the project seriously exceeds the budget, but we still have to keep working by investing additional manpower and working hours.

All the requirements we plan to deliver come from the output at the inception of the project. Of course, we do not need to do a simulation operation of the entire project requirements, and then produce a distributed result set. There is nothing magical about the process of completing this fixed-bid project. We expect that the final result may be an interval, so it is best to estimate three results (minimum, most likely, and maximum). This is of vital importance because the possible results will directly affect the business negotiations of the project. To put it simply, we can get a less scientific result but with reference value by simply looking at the sum of all minimum, most likely, and maximum values. Table 7.1 shows the three results I have obtained in a project:

According to estimates, if everything is normal, we need to invest 283 man-days. The most optimistic estimate is that it will take 203 man-days to complete the project (such as which parts are expected to be reused), and the most pessimistic estimate is that it will require 477 man-days to complete (if all possibilities have become real).

This is how we can digest unexpected situations in a scientific manner. Obviously, compared with time- and resource-oriented projects, in fixed-bid projects, the handling of unexpected situations is more important. At the stage of estimation, a common response is to add some buffering, such as

TABLE 7.1

An Actual Result of T-Shirt Estimation

Estimated Minimum Man-Day	Most Likely Man-Day	Expected Maximum Man-Day
203	283	477

an increase of 20% on the estimated result. If a fixed amount is involved, a fixed price premium is usually added at the end to make up for the inherent risks we assume as a supplier.

For estimating a fixed-bid project, the following factors are in need of special attention:

- **Unexpected situations caused by uncertain requirements.** Even if the requirements are determined, we do not have enough time to have them refined to contain all the details of acceptance conditions. By estimating the most likely value, we will have an accurate understanding of the parts with clear requirements. Even so, we should remain cautious to leave room for the unknown situations. Even there is the worst case, that is, customers ask to increase requirements, we should be able to remove the story cards (which are within the scope and not less than the new workload) out of the requirements scope without increasing the budget.

- **Nonfunctional requirements are easily missed in fixed-bid projects.** Whether it is from the required cost input or from the perspective of contract, our team needs to consider as much as possible when starting the project, especially the nonfunctional requirements. When it comes to the resources invested, according to the contract, it is crucial for us to define the completion indicators of the project. As we said before, one of the risks of doing a fixed-bid project is that the project is not completed by the deadline. At that time, unless there is a clear definition of the end of the project, it is easy to get involved in disputes with the customer, that is, whether the system is currently "acceptable." When negotiating the previous plan, we should discuss and record all nonfunctional requirements. These can include many indicators such as response performance, MTBF, failover, throughput, disaster recovery plan, and supporting documentation. Large-scale workload may be hidden in this area, and its scope should be clearly determined before signing a fixed-bid agreement.

- **Acceptance criteria.** The key factor for success is to clearly define the project as a whole, that is, what constitutes the minimum successful delivery which can be accepted and paid for by the customer. Moreover, the acceptance criteria should also specify the project phase. Without clear indicators to measure success, it will cause different expressions by all parties, which is also one of the reasons why the relationship between offshore teams and customer team eventually falls apart. Although politically ambiguous statements will help both sides seek common ground while reserving differences and the basis for cooperation, clear indicators for a project are the basis for cooperation.

- **List of requirements stories.** When the contract is signed, it means that we have reached a consensus with the customer, and the story list represents the scope of the project requirements. This list of requirements must be used as a strict baseline to monitor changes in requirements, including increases and decreases. If the scope of requirements increases significantly, this list can be seen as evidence that is beneficial to us.

- **Start this project.** Start-up speed is crucial in all projects, especially fixed-bid projects. The initial environment setup takes a lot of time for the team. We have to make sure that these tasks have been included in the estimated quotation to the customer. Otherwise it will definitely affect the expected deliverables in the first few iterations. We can directly find someone outside of the team that specializes in deploying development environment and continuous integration environment, which will cost one week, while our team members can concentrate on technical research and requirements development to ensure the productivity of the team. One of my teams had suffered a loss in this regard. The team members were inexperienced in setting up the environment, they had to spend time in learning special techniques for doing so, which greatly affected the project progress, forcing us to take remedial actions through several iterations.

- **Estimated checkreview.** All estimates require an independent third-party check, and the entire release plan also needs to be checked to reduce errors. We usually invite experienced technical directors in other projects to review our team's estimated results. In addition to an additional perspective, we may also get some ready-made technical experience, such as the similar SSO function which has done by other teams.

- **Both architectural and technical aspects need to be fully considered.** We need to assess our technical risks, which are part of the risks we have to bear. When necessary, we can create some technical cards and put them in the list of story cards.
- **Manage dependency.** We should strictly manage the dependency of requirements on the customer side. If the customer team is responsible for delivering a part of relevant things or integrated upstream and downstream things, these issues must be specified in the contract with defined responsibilities and obligations of all concerned parties, as well as important time points. We should pay attention to the progress of these issues from beginning to end. Don't let the other party's obligations affect our work, and notify the customer in writing as soon as the impact occurs.

7.4.2 Management of Fixed-Bid Projects

A basic issue surrounding fixed-bid projects is the cost for completing the project, which includes all human resources investment and travel expenses. We need a tool to manage these costs quickly and easily. By inputting the data that have occurred and the data that are expected to occur in the future, we can learn the cost and time of the entire project as much as possible. This has a good real-time management significance for whether the project has exceeded budget or other risks. This tool can support the continuous data updating, and each time the data are updated, the result is closer to the real cost of the project.

While implementing a project, when it is found that the delivery is prone to be delayed, we need to increase manpower to enhance project progress or persuade the customer to increase budget. The bargain-hunting and cost-diluting practices in the stock market should be adopted to increase a small amount of workload and trigger customers to increase budget as much as possible, so as to strike a balance between project delivery and customer satisfaction. In the past, in order to help customers increase their budget, we once added an integrated function module. The purpose was to help other departments of the customer's company to easily access to logistics data, so we obtained a budget of 500,000 yuan from other departments, it was in this way that we completed this project with a tight budget.

7.4.2.1 We Should Know about Team Members

If you have become a member of such a project, I'd like to say "congratulations," you have chosen a challenging path, you will not be satisfied with doing your job perfunctorily, you cannot help caring about the scope, cost, and schedule of the project. Because of these characteristics, everyone in the team must have a unified understanding. Although we can continue to promote agile and collaborative team culture, we must strictly manage some changes. It is particularly important to note that our focus must be on the minimum functions to meet customer requirements. We should make a basic estimate of the story cards of original requirements. It is of vital importance for business analysts and developers to ensure that the changed requirements do not exceed the originally estimated workload. Of course we will encounter some occasional incidents, so we should always remain careful, especially in the early stages of the project. Team members need to know clearly whether the changes have increased or decreased workload. In addition, it should be emphasized that any work that exceeds the original requirements shall be recorded and signed by the customer. Of course, it is not to say that we are dogmatic and never willing to compromise to the scope of customer requirements. If the workload is not large, it can also be digested within our offshore teams for the sake of maintaining customer relationships. For example, in a $3 million project, it is unwise to resolutely refuse an additional three-day workload. If the customer intends to increase the budget for the added requirement (highly recommended), we may think about to agree with him or use some tactics to win more budget.

Beyond the scope of the original requirements, we should also think about the functions that bring more value to customers, and bear this in mind all the way. Especially for small-scale projects, if we could find new value points, we will not only help customers achieve business growth, but also bring us more cooperation opportunities. This process is dubbed as "digging holes for customers." Don't forget that many customers are willing to pay for changed requirements or separately pay for all newly-added requirements, which is the essence of fixed-bid project contracts. Customers often accept risks arising from fixed-bid contracts, because they think their scope of requirements are satisfied. But in reality, they will never have a correct scope of requirements.

7.4.2.2 What Business Analysis Needs Attention?

For an ordinary agile team, business analysis follows the principle of punctuality. Normally, we only analyze short-term development tasks (one or two iterations) for developers. Although this work style is quite good, our experience shows that in fixed-bid projects we need to change this line of thinking, try to minimize unpleasant temporary situations, and ensure a relatively accurate cost for project completion. One way to achieve this goal is to start these analyses in advance so that we may have at least five iterations ahead of time, and ensure that the analysis of less clear definitions and high-risk functions is completed in advance. Of course, we may have to increase communications with customers, because they may fail to promptly respond to such large-scale requirements story cards.

7.4.2.3 Make Good Use of Original Story Cards

These story cards are most probably produced at the start of the project. The list of requirements given to our delivery team actually represents the scope of the requirements and should also include our estimates. All of this information must be contained in the contracts signed with customers. After all, customers have defined the scope of the project, which is a fixed-bid project should have in traditional sense. As business analysts, we should also conduct an expansive analysis of these original requirements story cards to estimate the workload of each requirement and the overall workload in a worst-case scenario. In this way, we will have a more comprehensive understanding of the scope of project requirements.

After project inception, we produced the requirement list, and every requirement followed with prerequisite and agreed effect achieved. Any requirement that deviates from these requirements during the development process must be counted as an increase in requirements, which should be carefully recorded and e-mailed to customers for confirming their details in each iteration.

These original requirements cards are valid for everyone, including developers. Each of our story cards corresponds to some assumptions. If you ignore them, you are likely to do something outside the scope of the requirements. These things can be beyond the vertical scope (it may be a real function better than the expected one) or beyond the horizontal scope. But your extra effort is an additional cost for the team. So, it will be too late when project manager asks about it that you realize you have taken the wrong path.

7.4.2.4 Monitor Progress

The process used by all ordinary time resource-oriented projects to track progress is still applicable to fixed-bid projects. The key to a successful fixed-bid project is some additional rigorous means and process of progress management. Through early analysis and emphasis on changes, there is no reason that we cannot successfully and flexibly deliver fixed-bid projects. As discussed earlier, we need to have a clear understanding of the possible conditions and risks included in the original plan. In fact, each of our story cards has a most likely estimated workload, plus a buffer to cover the uncertainties in the original estimate. The most critical task is to effectively manage potential contingencies.

When the project progresses to any particular iteration, we will find, for example, that the estimate for a particular set of stories is 10% greater than the original estimate. Then we need to consider: Is the expansion of requirements systemic? Whether all the original requirements story cards are underestimated or there are expanded requirements for some story cards?

Make sure that all new requirements are added to the original list of requirements, but they must be clearly marked. These cards are not part of the team's original scope of delivery, but we still have to estimate it and complete it. At the same time, we and customers need to know which requirement is a newly-added one.

7.4.2.5 An Agile Way to Handle Changing Requirements

The traditional fixed-bid project contains a lot of ahead-of-time analysis, so we all understand the accompanying strict scope control. All tasks that are not in the original requirements list will be treated as a requirement change. In the world of agile development, it is important to adopt a more flexible approach, because we cannot simply take all changes in requirements as formal requirement change and exclude them from our plan, which is contrary to the fundamental principle of agile development. Although we recommend that we keep following the agile principle, we have to think about the resulting cost increase. We have two options, but both of them need to be negotiated with customers at the beginning of the project. One option is to increase budget to complete the new requirements, the other is to replace the original requirements by the new ones with the same workload.

In the early stage of the project, if some rules are not defined and some consensus is not reached, disputes will certainly occur in the later stage, because customers focus on business, while we care about cost. If requirements cannot be adjusted at all in the middle of the project, this does not meet the principles of agile and lean. In the process of developing Project L which was a logistics management system, we designed a data matrix template for all logistics routes. There are thousands of routes worldwide. At the beginning, it was agreed that the routes worldwide were to be designed by only one template (proposed by the person in charge of the European region). However, two weeks before the official MTP, the user responsible person in the Asia-Pacific region expressed opposition to this template because the KPI focus of his region was somewhat different from the European region. According to the contract, we could refuse to do this kind of work beyond the specified scope. If we did so, we would have a successful project, but we would ruin a product and a customer relationship. In the end, we helped the customer apply for additional budget for another requirement and included our two-week workload (to redesign the routes) into this new requirement.

Since the requirements will always change, it is better to make the product smoother instead of promising not to change requirements. It is necessary to work hard to understand the characteristics of development, and adopt the idea of high cohesion and low coupling when designing products. High cohesion means that a functional module preferably only completes an independent subfunction and performs it well. Low coupling means that the modules are as independent as possible, with few connections and simple interfaces.

Based on the above ideas, we have seen the perfect interpretation of microservices which are a way to split functions from an implementation perspective.

- Independent team. In a single application, most people in the development team need to know all the parts of the application even if they only develop a small function. They must cooperate closely with other teams in deployment planning, version control, data migration, etc. In the microservice architecture, each microservice is built around a small business capability and managed by an independent team. The team only needs to know the interfaces provided by other services and stick to the interfaces provided by it. Each microservice should be deployed independently.
- Only do one thing and do it well. Microservice architecture is also similar to the principles of Unix philosophy: do one thing, do it well. This is a principle that has proved to be fairly valuable, and it is also one of the reasons why Unix systems have not become obsolete decades later. Microservices should be designed to do one thing, but can handle all possible situations.
- Fault isolation. Imagine if an error occurs in the report generation module in our application, but we need to close the entire trading application, which is a very serious consequence. If the

application is based on a micro server, the report generation module will fail and only occupy that specific function. Users who have not generated reports will not even notice any abnormalities in the system, and the core business part of the application can still work. This is the result of loose coupling between micro servers and can now be achieved with this architecture.

7.4.2.6 Decisions on Changing Requirements

Regardless of the exact implementation of the changes, the premise is that a definite organization or individual must be able to determine this change. There are many ways to do this, but no matter which method we use, it must have the following characteristics:

- Participants must have the right to agree to the changes. This includes the decision to replace old functions with new ones, and the recognition of changes in budget caused by changed scope and spending.
- The level of change agreed by the Change Control Committee must be known and agreed by all parties.
- For possible changes that cannot be agreed, there must be an agreed way to report to superior leaders.

7.4.2.7 End a Fixed-Bid Project

Offshore team must understand what is the end of a project. There is no doubt that this is part of the commercial cooperation and is a key success factor of a project. The most significant cost overrun on a fixed-bid project is that the project continues to exceed the expected end date. As such, in order to maintain the size and development speed of the team, it is usually necessary to increase manpower in the development process.

On the other hand, if a project cannot get a beautiful ending, a common problem is that the final definition of the acceptance conditions in the original contract is not clear enough, or in some cases certain definitions in the original contract are not correct, or there are matters without agreement. Find the points that the team has ignored as soon as possible, clarify the goal, and make up for everyone's work as early as possible.

We must ensure that both parties understand what the end of a project is, which is usually some form accepted by customers. There are some things to consider when defining this end criterion:

- What is the accepted time point for project delivery? Should it be the time when it is deployed to the production environment after development is done or sometime after it is deployed to the production environment?
- In the end, how many bugs are acceptable in the system? Don't be too optimistic or too pessimistic, otherwise we may end up like this: we have to continue to maintain a large number of human resources, and continue to fix endless bugs after the end of the contract, and this should be the work of customers' DevOps.
- Which nonfunctional requirements have we agreed with our customers? Business analysts must discuss these indicators with developers, otherwise it may become a difficult problem later. For example, there was a performance problem in exporting data to an Excel spreadsheet in Project L. Finally, we consulted with the customer and agreed on using the CSV format.
- Make a knowledge transfer plan with the customer.

7.4.3 BUSINESS CONCERNS

Managing customer expectations has always been a top priority in project management, especially for fixed-bid projects. Although our team has always strived to achieve what customers want, and let both parties clearly understand their responsibilities from the beginning. Our team needs to understand that requirement changes need to be managed in a more controlled manner, and we should work harder than ever to produce the smallest acceptable functions that meet customer expectations. Customers need to understand that new requirements are outside the original agreement, we need to have control over changes and may ask for additional budget. We can generate a new budget for changed requirements which will be easily managed, but the key is to ask customers to increase the budget. Both parties need a more complex and detailed process for change control, which must be fully understood at the beginning of the project and under careful management. Ideally, these precautions must be determined at the contract stage, at the latest in the first or second week after the project is started.

In addition, in the process of transforming the delivery plan into a business proposal, we should consider the following matters:

- What do we know about our customers' business realms?
- How familiar are we with the technology to be used in the project?
- What is the appropriate size of the team?
- Do we have to worry about the scale of the project?
- Do we have to agree with the burdensome and complicated nonfunctional requirements?
- Have we conducted an ahead-of-time risk assessment of our customers?
- Are the key success factors clearly defined?

If we use agile development, it will be difficult to talk about the cost of project with customers, because if a project has a fixed total price, it means that the workload of the project is fixed, then the outsourcing team would not be happy to see modified functions according to the agile development philosophy.

7.4.4 RISKS OF FIXED-BID PROJECTS

It needs to be reiterated that projects with uncertain requirements are not fit for a fixed-bid contract.

However, what if we unfortunately take over a fixed-bid project with uncertain requirements? At the beginning of some projects, due to various reasons such research errors or uncontrollable changes in requirements, the workload greatly usually far exceeds the initial estimate.

What shall we do? To transfer to another project? This is not what a decent offshore team member should do. Don't worry, there is a risk response strategy for this type of project. Members working on fixed-bid projects need to keep the following points in mind:

- The key definitions for project success that we have agreed with the customer must be consistent with the goal, and the project manager shall disseminate this information in his team.
- Every team member must be aware that it is of prime importance to complete all the functions agreed upon, so we must pay attention to project progress and make sure the committed workload be completed within the prescribed time limit.
- The fixed-bid project must have continuous risk management, and the risk assessment should be started as early as possible, even if it is the early stage of the project that has not started. We can invite customers to join in our preliminary work when necessary, since our two parties shall bear risks together.
- If offshore teams undertake a fixed-bid project, and the risks therefrom are greater than the projects charged by per man-day. But the risks are usually not exposed in the early stage of the project, so we should not let down our guard.
- Whether the change in requirements exceeds the scope of the requirements specified in the contract, it requires more careful management and strict comparison. Properly managing these boundaries is the cornerstone of a successful offshore fixed-bid delivery project.
- The fixed-bid project places great emphasis on minimizing the acceptable functions to be completed so as to fulfill the contract on time. But we still hope that customers will be satisfied

with the delivery in the end. All functions that are not really necessary should not be included in our plan. Moreover, all of the new requirements that customers want must be subject to change control, because this may generate additional costs.

■ For a fixed-bid project, maintaining the scope of project requirements is already a remarkable achievement for an ordinary offshore team.

7.4.5 SUGGESTIONS, TIPS, AND POSSIBLE PITFALLS

Fixed-bid projects often involve "soft" delivery (such as evaluation, analysis, etc.). On the surface, this is like a sweet deal, and the risk is much smaller than delivering software. However, if we do not clearly define the scope of the analysis, the content of the document, and follow up after the evaluation is completed, we are prone to be stumbled. An accurate understanding of what will be delivered is critical to creating estimates and managing effective completion of project. Ideally, you will need to conduct frequent audits with customers from the first day to the completion of the final delivery to confirm that they meet their expectations.

We need to seriously consider the following points:

■ At which stage the software is to be handed over to the customer (code freeze, user acceptance testing, or customer team can fully accept the software)?
■ What is our responsibility for solving software bugs?
■ To which environment does the software need to be deployed?
■ What are the other requirements related to the software, such as installation and configuration management?
■ Avoid adding resources in the later period of project, which will increase the cost of contextual communication, except for relatively independent modules.

At the beginning of the project, we must make sure that customers of fixed-bid projects are able to increase the budget. If they confirm that the budget will not increase, we should increase a certain percentage of premium when we start quotation.

To make matters worse, a large quantity of requirement changes occur at the later stage, because it is at this time when customers start seeing and using the software, and coming up with new ideas. It is frequent to see requirement change in the last minute, that's why overdue projects and excess budget have become commonplace.

If the customer has a legacy system, and we still need the functions of this legacy system, we can make the assumption that the legacy system is working properly, provided that once these functions are abnormal, the customer will have his developers to resolve these problems. If the customer does not any developer to maintain this system, we must make the assumption that this part of functions does not work properly.

7.5 CONNECT WITH CUSTOMER'S WORK

The connection between offshore teams and customers mainly occurs in the two stages of project initiation and closure. If the development process needs to be closely coordinated with customers, frequent communication with customers is required throughout the entire project cycle.

At the stage of initiation, we mainly take over the requirements from the customer's business personnel, determine the design plan and technical development plan with the customer, and then a delivery plan is generated.

At the stage of closure, the deliverables are transferred to the customer's DevOps department. But there are times when we have to think about the final deliverables at the initial stage of the project.

7.5.1 PROJECT INCEPTION

In the early stage of development, offshore teams should work closely with the customer team, mainly for formulating some guiding rules to facilitate the future cooperation of all parties. Moreover, offshore teams should establish a good relationship with customers and win their trust. In short, it is a process of laying the foundation, setting the direction, and clarifying responsibilities.

7.5.1.1 Determine the Scope of Requirements with Customers

This task is the top priority during the project start-up phase. So the business analysts have to maintain close communication with the customer's business staff.

In the early stage, the product function should be decomposed, and each function point should be decomposed layer by layer to ensure that nothing is left in the future. The method of decomposing tasks cannot only be used for business analysis, but for other purposes. When we feel that a job is too difficult to start, we can also use this method to clarify our thinking.

The smallest work unit obtained through decomposition has a separate business meaning, which is known as "user story." Only at this granularity can we estimate the workload and arrange the delivery plan.

7.5.1.2 User Experience Requirements

This is what we've said that the assumptions on which we estimate the workload for implementing a function. These assumptions must be listed clearly in writing and handed over to the customer as part of the requirements.

The user experience is the same, the level of customer attention will seriously affect the workload of technology implementation.

7.5.1.3 Prioritize All Functions with Customers

Our team usually visualizes priorities (see "Priority Pyramid"), and then hangs Kanban on the wall near the team, reminding us which things are more important.

Winning is at the starting line is of course important, but it is the one who first crosses the finish line is the real winner, since it is the criterion for judging results.

THE PROCESS FOR RECUSING A PROJECT

No achievement can be made without effort.

The failure of cooperation must not have been caused in one day. Many problems have already occurred in the early stage, and must be resolved without delay. In the initial stage of cooperation, due to the unfamiliar working habits of each team, it is easy to work separately.

We once had a customer from an overseas telecommunications company, and their development team had an independent design team that was specifically responsible for producing design prototypes for various project teams. But it was not closely working with the people in our distributed team, let alone had any direct communication with the developers responsible for implementation. Isolation between teams prevented business analysts from accurately defining the requirements, plus the design team often delayed in submitting design drawings or even had them frequently changed. Developers often saw requirements and prototype diagrams do not match at all, thus forcing them to increase communication with responsible persons, which in turn affected the working status of every team.

Facing the above situation, we had to report the matter to the higher management of the customer, and ask them to designate a designer to communicate with us and ensure that this person can communicate closely with our product manager.

The customer team must have someone who can make a final decision. This is the key to our successful communication with customers. Sometimes even the customer team can't figure out who's going to make the final decision. This is not a joke. When a problem arises, everyone discusses it for a long time, but no one makes the final decision. At that time, we thought of the realization of an interface for business requirements, and feedback this opinion to the customer's product manager who said that he had to discuss with the design department. After we met the head of the design department, he was also ambiguous and said this matter needed to be discussed with the product manager. The most direct impact on our offshore team was that this requirement could not be fulfilled, or it would be redone after completion. The rework rate of the story card in the first iteration was as high as 90%. Only the navigation buttons on one page were free from being changed, and almost all other business requirements were asked to be rewritten. This was only the processing flow of single-line requirements within our business scope. When cross-business line requirements were involved, there are more uncertain requirements, such as approval process and customer lead query, which became even more ambiguous.

After we entered the real delivery iteration, the seminars to provide product solutions were also carried out simultaneously. The product was constantly adjusted. After the business analyst analyzed a requirement, confirmed it with the product manager and transferred it to developers, customer regretted the next day and he had to reconfirm and modify the requirement with developers, wasting a lot of manpower and time. The product structure had also changed a lot, and the business logic involved had been fine-tuned. A few days later, our team was annoyed, so we suggested sorting out the main business processes first, and tried to persuade our product manager to start with the simplest product category, walk through the important business logic end to end, and define the scope of the first release, not wait the customer first analyzes a part to a perfect state before proceeding to the next story.

In addition, we were also trying various methods to help customers improve the development process. Some had achieved obvious results, for example, improving the efficiency of meetings, and shortening to no more than 15 minutes; changing the habit of customers in doing anythings ambiguously, and clearly visualizing requirements and progress; correcting some of the errors in agile practice, the estimation must be consistent and conducive to arranging a reasonable delivery plan; simplifying the testing process and reducing waste.

Identifying problems of project in time and proposing some solutions in a targeted manner is the only way to prevent the project from sliding into the abyss step by step.

In the past, customers were keen on the promotion of various tools. But I have witnessed too many failures in this regard: a manager promoted a tool in his company, but this tool had a specific way of operation. As a result, it failed to solve problems, and even hindered other efforts to solve problems. Tools should help us prevent known errors and remember repetitive tasks, rather than not replacing thinking itself. We expect to see the effect of customers' assessment tool to determine whether we will keep using it. But customers have found that many tools are too costly to use, and there are alternatives that can also yield benefits, showing that customers have become more and more rational.

7.5.2 PROJECT IN PROGRESS

7.5.2.1 Management of Requirements Backlog

Requirements will always be the focus of entanglement between offshore teams and customers. Although the product is constantly updated and iterated, the requirements seem never diminish but keep increasing. At this time, we need to use the tool of requirements backlog to manage these endless requirements, and all distributed teams must share the same requirements backlog.

The requirements backlog have a continuous impact on the iteration plan. When requirements are included into the plan or removed out of the plan, we shall to discuss this matter with customers and reach agreement with them. Some people may question the significance of the iteration plan, but professionals understand that if the plan fails to keep up with the changes, they will work even harder on planning, since making no plan entails greater risks. The prerequisite for planning is to first clarify the project scope, which jobs are necessary and which ones are not. If we get confused at our duties from the beginning, this project can hardly succeed.

Although the requirements backlog is used for collecting and managing various customer requirements, it is not simply a record of requirements. In this requirements pool, every requirement is attached with a reasonable label. Our requirements need to have the following information to help us make better decisions and plans.

(1) **Source of requirements.** During the implementation of a project, offshore teams will not actively explore new requirements, which is the duty of the product manager with the customer team. We will passively get some requirements from customers, and then actively probe into these requirements to gain an in-depth understanding of business value.

The DevOps department will summarize the problems frequently consulted or complained by users. We can study these problems with our customers, sort out some tasks that can reduce the burden on DevOps, and add them into the requirements backlog.

Some design problems such as interaction discovered by the testers of offshore teams can also be submitted to change requirements. Usually, such problems require customer confirmation and have a relatively low priority.

(2) **Business value behind requirements.** We should properly record the business value of each requirement. If we can switch to the user-oriented way of thinking, it will be of vital importance for choosing an implementation approach to fulfill business requirements. Customers often meddle in the affairs of offshore teams by giving them a direct implementation plan instead of the requirements containing business value. However, this implementation plan is usually neither the most efficient one nor the lowest-cost one. We have to explore the real business value behind requirements to determine the most available implementation plan.

(3) **Priority.** Many IT divisions often provide multiple project services to other divisions in the same company and external customers at the same time. For more than once I had seen staff working on a low-priority project while ignoring a project that deserved more attention. This is why there should be a project manager. He can let team members know which tasks should be prioritized and when the priorities should change. An industry insider once said, "clearly communicating project priorities can help delivery team avoid detours and no longer have to worry about what to do."

7.5.2.2 Customer Knows Project Status in Real Time

Ensure transparency and guarantee that customers can intuitively see project progress and difficulties whenever they want to do so. Kanban and other visualization tools are the primary tools, but maintaining the software availability in the acceptance test is the best way to maintain customer confidence in the product. Even if the progress seems smooth, customers will not feel totally satisfied since they have no hands-on experience of the product.

Report to customers regularly through various regular meetings and weekly or monthly e-mail. But we cannot throw all information to customers without processing. How to process information is also a problem we have to think about. In the report to our customers, we may include lots of figures and charts which can fully show our professionalism. But different people may get different information when reading these data and charts, so we have to fully interpret these data for customers, ensure that they can easily understand the meaning behind the numbers without too much thinking.

We should make full use of all sorts of informal and irregular communication opportunities. We can have a chat with the head of the customer team anytime and anywhere. It is not an exaggeration to say that sometimes the effect achieved in this way is better than scheduling a formal meeting.

The effective means of information communication, from high to low, is face-to-face, video software, telephone, instant messaging tool, and e-mail.

7.5.3 LATER STAGE OF PROJECT

In the final stage of project development, development and DevOps teams need to work closely together to make the project transition smoothly from development to deployment. The development mainly focuses on functions, while DevOps mainly aim at solving any problems encountered by end users. Since agile development adopts the way of simultaneous development and launch, many times the work of development and DevOps is combined.

Project ending is the final step to complete a delivery project. A beautiful ending can avoid a lot of entangled problems, especially the problem of payment collection.

We usually have a formal acceptance document for project delivery, which is shown in Figure 7.1.

Type	Deliverables	Delivered or not	Qualified or not
Requirements sorting	Project quick start report	Yes	Yes
Experience design	Sketch source files (mobile and PC)	Yes	Yes
	Design style guide (mobile and PC)	Yes	Yes
Customized development	WeChat browser mobile version Web site source code	Yes	Yes
	WeChat browser mobile version UAT deployment	Yes	To be test
	Package the P2P Web interface as the source code of RESTful Web API	Yes	Yes
	4 sample pages for the PC version of the Web site	No	
Mobile development framework products, implementation and training	HTML5 auxiliary development tools (including source code and documentation)	No	
	Native auxiliary development tools (including source code and documentation)	No	
	SimpleDemo, HTML5 debugging aids (source code)	No	
	CoralDemo, Native part of HTML5 small app store	No	
	Coral-demo-mock, the mock server of the HTML5 small app store	No	
	App-scanner, HTML5 small application example	No	
	Barcode-scanner-plugin, Native plugin example	No	
	Sign-demo, sample signature script	No	
	CI server setup and script documentation	No	
	Coral comprehensive documentation on use, maintenance, management, etc.	No	
	NPM, Bower, Git private server construction and documentation	No	
	Mobile development framework training materials	No	

After verification, Party A confirms the deliverables that Party B has delivered.

Signature of the person in charge of Party A: Date:

FIGURE 7.1 Project deliverable acceptance document.

Offshore teams shall keep doing a good job till the end. After handing the product to customers, they shall teach them to continue operation and maintenance. Since the functions of making logs in the system are important to reduce the burden of operation and maintenance, these functions must be taken into account at the beginning and during the implementation of the project, in order to convince customers to pay for these functions.

How to deal with project delay is also part of the project progress management at the later stage. Increasing manpower and reviewing the requirements are our options. For the inflated part of the requirement change, we must clarify with customers, explain the reason for the delay, and strive to reschedule.

7.5.4 OTHERS

In addition, the collaboration with the customers' work will inevitably cause some challenges by customers. Based on past experience, these challenges are mainly manifested in low quality, backward schedule, incomplete requirements, and technical difficulty. All these aspects should arouse our attention. Of course, being criticized by customers cannot simply be understood that our team is not doing well. We must always believe in our team. But, can we do better?

7.6 HELP CUSTOMERS TRANSFORM INTO AGILE TEAMS

Some projects include content for agile transformation of customers in addition to delivery activities. We must help customers make efforts in capacity building, thinking transformation, process improvement, organizational structure change, etc.

There are usually two types of such customers: one is the enterprises accustomed to traditional development are about to adopt agile development, and the other is the enterprises that have completed or just started agile transformation. Both of them need our guidance and correction.

7.6.1 CAPACITY BUILDING

We can cultivate the fast-learning ability of customers, because the process of doing a project is a learning process. In short, the process of offshore delivery is also a process of continuous improvement.

Learn from continuous feedback and find problems, such as thinking about what prevents the team from continuous improvement. Is it because customers hate changes or our teams have made any mistake? For a place that needs improvement, and learn to think systematically. Having a good idea is only the first step, we also need a plan and carry out actions. Execution plays a decisive role.

The transitional period is a great opportunity to challenge and remove some legacy tools from customers' organizations. In addition, a large number of opportunities also help us find some seed players in our customers. The cultivation of seed players plays an important role in the final successful transformation success of customers, making the communication between offshore teams and customers simplified, increasing the willingness to transform within the customer team so as to generate a better chemical reaction, making the final transfer of the project much smoother.

To quantify the agile transformation of the team, we can know how far we are from the successful transformation. Customer performance management should also be adjusted accordingly to make it suitable for these ideas and to demonstrate the transformation of customer team and distributed team.

7.6.2 HIGHLIGHT THE ADVANTAGES OF AGILE DEVELOPMENT AND SOLIDIFY THE BELIEFS OF ALL PARTICIPANTS

Whether it is the head of the customer team or the teams directly involved, we should start with the following aspects to convince customers that the road we lead is correct.

7.6.2.1 Embrace Change

When it comes to agile development, we all know that it can adapt to changes in requirements, but it does not mean that our requirements can be changed at will. Once started, no one welcomes any change in requirements. And, in most cases, this change refers to the time when the requirement is in story backlog and not taken by developers

Of course, we can stop developing user stories that need to be changed and re-examine the latest requirements when necessary, even if we have already started development. According to the latest estimated points, adjust the story card of this iteration, even if the completed part needs to be changed, we can roll back the previous changes, add a new story card, and arrange this latest requirement change into backlog.

In short, agile development is to always deliver the most valuable function in every iteration. Whenever it is found that the originally planned function has lost value, it must be replaced. The later this work is done, the more waste will be generated.

Can we still change requirements when using the traditional waterfall development model? Waterfall development needs to be carried out in stages, and after entering the development stage, the requirements will not change. Since all the functions to be delivered are listed in detail in the stage of business analysis, when we are about to start the work of development, the analysis of all requirements is completed, and no one will think about the requirements in the future. Only when the customer finds that there is a major omission in the requirements (the problem in user feedback after product launch) will the requirements get changed. But in this way, all the development process needs to go through again, which will cause a huge extra cost in time and resources. This is not the worst case, and the ending of more cases is that the change of requirements has to incorporated into the next development plan. And the next plan may be a year later or come to nothing.

Therefore, in the face of changing requirements, agile development boasts more advantages than waterfall development. The essence of agile development is to develop the smallest available product, the end user will use it immediately, and then give feedback to the development team. We will then adjust the task of the next iteration based on customer feedback, because our iteration itself is based on constant changes, ready to be adjusted at any time.

7.6.2.2 Reduce Delivery Risk

One reason why agile development has become more welcome is that from the beginning to the final delivery, all people are working hard, and their workload is relatively balanced. The full participation of testers and test-driven development can ensure product quality. Waterfall development, which is staged handover working mode, features a state of "some people are terribly busy and others are sitting around" at each stage; the hidden waste of labor costs is also serious in the whole process. Figure 7.2 compares the workload of team members with different roles in different stages during the entire delivery cycle. Figure 7.3 shows the distribution of total workload of the waterfall and agile development teams during the entire delivery cycle.

In brief, agile development is an iterative and incremental development mode that takes the evolution of user requirements as the core. In terms of agile development, the construction of a software project is divided into multiple subprojects, and the results of each subproject are tested and have the characteristics of integrability and performability. In other words, a large project is divided into multiple small projects that are connected but can also be run independently and completed separately. During this process, the software is always in a usable state.

Apparently, there is a qualitative difference between agile development and waterfall development. The former adopts an iterative development model, it does not predetermine the requirements of users in advance, but first makes some prototypes to allow key users to experience, and then continue to modify and adjust based on user feedback. Throughout the R&D process, the initial design and final design of the product are often different.

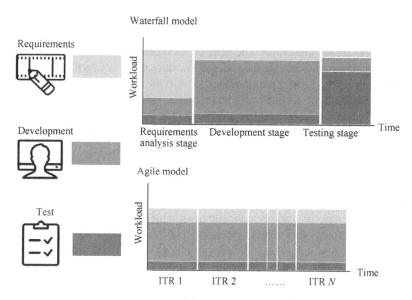

FIGURE 7.2 Workload distribution by team and stage.

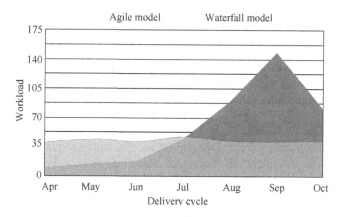

FIGURE 7.3 Distribution of total workload based on different development models.

According to lean theory, team members should forget their roles and do what the team needs them do most. This is challenging for managers and ordinary team members to do the most important work rather than allowing them to work most efficiently. Many times this is for short-term goals, but it affects long-term productivity. Therefore, it also reflects how to balance individual efficiency and organizational efficiency.

7.6.2.3 Legacy System

If you ask a developer if he wants to work on a project with a legacy system or a completely new project, he will prefer the latter one. No one likes to develop on legacy systems. Putting aside personal preferences, when we get a legacy system, how can we help customers develop something new based on an old foundation?

The legacy systems are all in debt, and the first is technical debt. The technical debt of a legacy system includes lowered code requirements, requiring architectural adjustment and optimization, test failures and corresponding reparation, more modules without test protection, and no performance requirements for quick launch, all of which aim at get the functions put on online quickly. In addition to technical debt, the legacy system also has requirements debt, that is, those accumulated requirements changes without response. The agile development model uses continuous feedback to make up for these requirements debt. In the end, the overdue and unsatisfactory requirements design in the system is replaced by the user requirements to meet the latest business.

In addition to responding to technologies and requirements, it is also our direction of efforts to use the automated function testing to isolate and protect the legacy system and shorten the feedback cycle of test to the development team, so as to establish continuous integration and deployment pipelines for legacy systems in the end.

7.6.2.4 Process Improvement

Any one of us, when entering a project, may start working at any stage of the project. But no matter at what stage, when we discuss agile development, we must start when the requirements have just arisen. Why should we clarify this matter? Because when we talk about agile generally, it indicates agile development model, which seem to be mainly related to development. In fact, agile needs to run through the entire software delivery process and requires the participation and cooperation of all activities.

We should determine the scope of minimum requirements for each functional module, sort them out according to priority of each functional module. We cannot listen to the customer to complete one functional module at a time, nor should me modify each module for every iteration. Although there is perfect automated testing as a guarantee, it is still risky. It is best to complete an independent functional module in two to three iterations. This requires the iteration manager to consider various factors and find a balance.

Figure 7.4 shows a roadmap for the function delivery from 1 to 100 of one of my projects. We start from the most core and most value-generating function, rather than complete one function and then go to the next. Note that the word "enhancement" indicates the noncore part of the function.

The requirements panorama is exhibited on a requirements tree, see what it looks like in Figure 4.4.

Process improvement must adopt a step-by-step strategy. We should first assess the customers' current situation and their objectives, list all improvement actions and planned output accordingly, and then execute each improvement action in stages. There may be periodic retrospective and review for adjusting the plan at any time. It can be seen that process improvement is actually an agile delivery process.

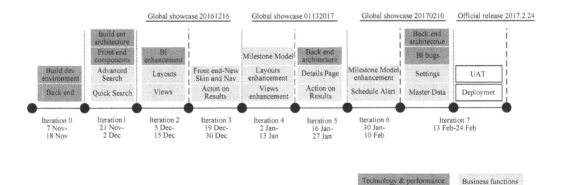

FIGURE 7.4 Delivery plan.

7.6.3 ESTABLISH CROSS-FUNCTIONAL TEAMS

In traditional enterprises, departments are generally divided according to functional attributes, and various departments will collaborate to complete projects. However, the cost of cross-department collaboration is obviously too high. When products need to collaborate frequently across departments, such a model is obviously inadequate. At this time, the company will inevitably expose the problem of low development efficiency due to such issues. At this time, the establishment of a virtual cross-functional team led by the business department or the core department is a matter of course. Cross-functional teams can effectively solve the problem of frequent collaborative communication during product development. In such a team, the personnel in charge of development, testing, and business analysis can directly communicate with each other face to face. More frequent communication and less information distortion will avoid departments from arguing back and forth.

Doing a project requires the coordination and operation of various functional departments (teams). The coordination cost and communication cost of non-full-function teams are very high. Only the barriers between functions are broken, and a small full-function team is established to put communication within the team, the capability of coordinated operations can be truly improved.

7.6.4 SUMMARY

After all, the main responsibility of offshore teams is delivery, not specialized agile transformation consulting. Many times we undertake a project of a customer with a relatively traditional work style, and he also wants to adopt the agile way of working. But we can only let him see and learn by exerting limited influence and by making some achievements. Some customers have already begun to implement agile model themselves, then we can help them to identify the authenticity of agile practice.

At different stages we can instill in customers different things like focusing on business value, reducing waste, simplifying processes, continuous improvement, team building, information sharing, etc.

My experiences have shown that all the well-functioning projects are similar, it is the problematic ones that are different. Delivering any offshore project is a learning process, and doing a good project is always a systematic process.

It is said that distance creates beauty, and we must make good use of the advantages of offshore teams, strengthen the spread of good news, and at the same time control the disadvantages of offshore delivery, and manage and eliminate the adverse effects.

8 The Future of Distributed Teams

The rapid growth of global IT service outsourcing business has driven the rapid development of the global IT service outsourcing industry. Although domestic outsourcing service companies have sprung up like mushrooms, problems such as shortage of talents, team management, distributed collaboration, and others have always plagued the development of the industry. Solving these problems is a key element that every team and every outsourcing service company has to solve, and it must keep pace with the times.

8.1 PEOPLE IN OFFSHORE TEAMS

People are the first element in an organization. Which attribute does a person want to show, to what extent does he want to show, what motivation is behind it? When we make a product, we can easily generate the consciousness of ownership and do everything we can. But how do we cultivate this sense of ownership when doing outsourcing projects? One benefit in an outsourcing team is that you can choose to join the projects and technology stacks that you are interested in. Of course, this involves two-way choices between projects and engineers. If offshore teams can narrow the distance between customer and create value to end users through hard work, the sense of satisfaction and achievement will inspire them to do better.

Agile development has higher requirements for team members, especially developers. They shall have good communication skills, a humble attitude, and an enterprising spirit, which happen to be the reason that makes many teams discouraged when facing the challenge.

In offshore teams, individuals must learn to adapt to constantly improved personal skills and process.

8.1.1 Manage Personnel Change

Offshore teams should pay attention to the sustainability of team members, but the frequent personnel change is the characteristics of offshore team. There are many reasons for personnel change, some are the need to optimize the composition of the team at different stages of the project, some are planned team replacement, and others are the overall team migration. Whether it is active or passive, it is fundamental to manage team knowledge in the process of change.

8.1.1.1 Knowledge Transfer

Look at newcomers through the eyes of veterans. For example, if you often take the subway, you will be familiar with the rhythm, that is, when to get on quickly and when to wait for the next one. If you don't take the subway very often, it will be difficult to distinguish the length of platform ringtone and the interval between platform ringtone and subway ringtone, and the time interval from the ringtone to the closure of compartment. Now let's look back to the team, as an old team member, we are already familiar with the team and take for granted many things. Therefore, we should be enough patient enough with new members to help them get started as soon as possible.

We should do a good job in project knowledge inheritance. The project's overall knowledge is important. We can use the project introduction, technical architecture diagram, and project roadmap to help new members rapidly get to know about a project.

Manage environment as code is another good practice. After new developers run a few commands, a development environment can be quickly established locally. It is very important to get all up-to-date contents, which can ensure the comprehensiveness and correctness of knowledge. In theory, newcomers can start working immediately.

8.1.1.2 Team Migration

The migration culture of internal projects of software outsourcing companies also reflects the variability of outsourcing projects, both passive and active changes will occur. Now domestic software companies are also showing a multicenter trend, which help companies hire more talented people from many places.

A trend is that outsourcing teams are shifting from first-tier cities to second-tier cities, since the labor cost in first-tier cities continues to rise, while the labor reserves in second-tier cities are getting better and better, creating conditions for such migration. We need to create conditions for this kind of migration, otherwise, it may result in loss of knowledge, declining technical capability of new teams, and mounting risks in projects.

A team that actively seeks change will have higher productivity and creativity, while a changeless team will become inert and deprive the team of motivation. This is the biggest impetus for enterprises to support team migration except for cost considerations.

8.1.1.3 How to Maintain Team Culture Amid Personnel Change?

Offshore teams often face this situation: one person has made achievements in the team, such as building a complete testing framework, but he is then replaced by a newcomer. Will this testing framework lack maintenance and the value of the result drop sharply? Personnel change in teams should be considered in terms of maintaining the sustainability of team plan.

How to help newcomers quickly integrated into a team? We'd better draw a roadmap to make them get familiar with the job left by their predecessors. Project manager shall do his own part to help newcomers integrate into this team.

Personnel change, especially recruitment of newcomers, can be a catalyst to expose problems in a team more thoroughly, while these problems may be difficult to attract attention without personnel change.

Distributed teams should maintain a uniform level of professionalism, which means that there is an available code of conduct for newcomers to follow and to stick to the philosophy of "we are one team."

Recruiting new people may make existing team members feel anxious. When their work is to be handed over to newcomers, we should make sure that they know it is a part of the project development. If possible, before these things happen, develop a handover schedule, and distribute it to those concerned, set expectations for each task, and ensure transparency when making any changes.

Regardless of how to maintain the loyalty of a project, the loss of best talents in a project from time to time is inevitable. We should not prevent it or delay its occurrence, but to actively find ways to deal with this inevitable situation. Usually, the technical difficulties at the early stage of the project have been investigated, the necessary specifications have been established, and the process of cooperation between teams has been formed, what we should do at the later stage is compliance since the risks are already greatly reduced. After reaching this state, even if some key team members choose to leave, the project remains safe, and the established standard team culture will have a strong digestive ability to accept new members.

8.1.1.4 Create New Culture Amid Changes

All successful projects start with finding the right persons, and the project team members only take responsibility when everyone starts to trust each other. On the contrary, if we have no trust in some members, then the only solution is to keep monitoring at them to do things.

Everyone is unique, and everyone has their own advantages and disadvantages. Although we tend to seek like-minded people, teams with talents with different styles and different advantages are much better. The advantage in a certain field may become a disadvantage under certain circumstances, and a team that combines the advantages of all sorts of talents will be more powerful. Although different strengths can lead to conflict, members in a healthy team can appreciate the differences of each other, not hate each other.

When selecting team members, there is also a common situation where too much emphasis is placed on ability. Of all the successful teams we have encountered, no one has all the necessary abilities at the beginning. In fact, we found that the team itself is a powerful mentor to cultivate its members with necessary skills. Therefore, when selecting team members, the development potential and proven ability of candidates should be given equal attention.

Putting people at the first place, motivating everyone, giving them the environment and support they need, and believing their ability to complete the work, which are necessary conditions for creating a unique team culture.

Implementing the three-in-one team culture of learning, practice, and sharing is the best team cultural atmosphere I have ever experienced. It is a decisive impetus for the growth of team members and the establishment of a learning organization. Mastering theoretical knowledge through learning, testing the effect of learning in projects, summing up, and then sharing with the outside world, this is a virtuous circle.

8.1.2 Pay Attention to Personal Performance

Be sure to use KPI as a guide for personal career. Many people will ignore this problem, and the pursuit of their goal is limited to the work of the project. Others are not doing projects that are of interest to them, but they have not brought this out. They devote considerable energy to things that are of interest to them beyond the project. These two types of team members work hard and seriously, but they do not match the company's KPI, the result is that their performance results are much lower than their expectations, which is also a loss to their company.

8.1.2.1 Find the Best Hitting Point

"The best hitting point" is a term in sports, which means that the conditions in all aspects are particularly well matched, and athletes can achieve the best results. In our work, we need to find these three points that "I like," "I'm good at" and "valuable." When we find that we are doing something that combines the three points, we can achieve a good result in very little time and bring more value to ourselves and the company. In this way, we may become those who work especially efficiently in the eyes of others. How to find our own best hitting point? Simply put, find projects in areas of interest and choose popular or skilled technology stacks. But what does "valuable" mean? It is a means being able to produce results and enhance your influence.

8.1.2.2 Invest in People with Offshore Teams

We can invite experts, either from the outside of the team or from the same company, into our team to help everyone locate problems, and thus improve the ability of engineers. For example, maintaining high-quality code can obviously improve productivity. Or we can apply for a certain amount of training funds to facilitate self-improvement of each team member.

In addition, regular retrospective meetings and team-building activities are also one of the ways to improve team efficiency and ability. Since technologies have kept improving, our team shall remain in a state of being improved. To this end, we shall motivate every team member to learn new skills, and it is necessary to make everyone feel valued and respected.

8.2 REMAINING PROBLEMS IN FRONT OF DISTRIBUTED TEAMS

Speaking of problems, in order to facilitate understanding, we can divide the problems into three categories: simple problems, complex problems, and uncertain problems.

1. Simple problems
   The turnover of personnel creates risks for project delivery. If there is frequent personnel change in distributed teams, a lot of contextual information will get lost in this process. Only lucky enough can we have vertains in project teams to pass on their wisdom to newcomers.

   Inactive communication in distributed teams is shown in two aspects: On the one hand, they will not take the initiative to create opportunities for communication. On the other hand, they wait for others to ask questions or wait for problems to be exposed on their own.

   The above two types of problems are quite common for distributed teams, and both of them are simple problems. If your team does not have an available solution to the above problems, you should come up with standard and fixed solutions as soon as possible. In the case of personnel replacement, a standard and planned handover process is required. To improve the communication between teams, you should set up time for regular communication and fixed communication matters.

2. Complex problems
   Distributed teams have to deal with some complex problems as follows:
   Time management requires that each team is doing the right thing at the right time.
   Customer management and control over expansion of requirements are priorities of offshore teams. These two problems are especially troublesome in fixed-bid projects.
   Unsuccessful quality control. Quality problems seem like a systematic engineering. It is never a simple task to locate the problem scenario and find a way to improve quality.
   Relative to simple problems which can be solved by certain means, when facing complex problems, we often have many solutions, but we cannot simply measure the effect of each solution. We need to do some extra work to show the effect of these solutions. The best result is to use technical means, because the problems solved by nontechnical means will always leave room for bargaining.

3. Uncertain problems
   Both simple and complex problems are foreseeable problems, and mature teams should have ready-made solutions to deal with them. What is really tricky and can bring risks to the team are unforeseen problems without any available solutions.
   There are no standard solutions to uncertain problems. For example, do offshore teams have long-term goals? What value does it bring to customers? Everyone on the team also needs to think about what the project can bring to themselves.

8.2.1 MANY PEOPLE SAY THAT AGILE PROJECTS CANNOT BE OUTSOURCED

Distance and time difference are likely to make the agile development model lose the labels of close collaboration, self-management, quick kickoff, rapid delivery, and time limit.

Different geographical distribution of teams has increased the complexity in implementing the agile development model, making it difficult for teams to communicate in daily their work, backlog status, problems, and obstacles. However, in the past few years, lots of confident software outsourcing service providers have transformed their teams into agile teams based on iterative software development and delivery, and also made targeted adjustments. Therefore, some leading IT vendors have also slowly adopted new agile outsourcing services.

I have heard of some companies which have adopted an agile development model have achieved success in offshore delivery. The general public view is that the teams doing agile projects must sit together, but an experienced project manager of offshore teams told me that if your team members cannot work in the same room, agile development will be the best way for software development. Especially for distributed teams, they value communication frequency and efficiency.

Skills will never be burden. Let's learn follows techniques for doing outsourcing projects with agile development model:

(1) **Make adequate preparations.** The stand-up meeting with customers or other teams is currently only available through instant communication tools or video conferencing systems. Imagine that it takes ten minutes or more each time to find a meeting room, and then it takes ten minutes or more to dial in, all participants will get impatient. Establishing a stable video-conferencing venue and system will create conditions for distributed teams to practice agile development. This system can also keep the camera on all the time during working hours, and it can be used as an uninterrupted video system. Of course, the precondition is the time zone conditions should allow us to do so.

(2) **Start with small steps.** Realestate.com is a leading real estate information service company in Australia. The shortage of talents in Australia has caused the company to seek overseas resources to ensure it innovative competitiveness. They have not outsource the development work before, so they first hired the android develop team with 5 people and established work mode for distributing teams, then in the after one year, the delivery team extended to three teams and total twenty-five people.

Even in the United States where there are plenty of talents, some small and medium-sized startups have decided to adopt offshore agile development because they have to compete for local software talents with companies such as Apple, Facebook, and Google. These small and medium-sized companies value the technical capabilities of offshore teams more than cost factors.

In my opinion, each separate development team should have 3–7 developers, so as to ensure that everyone's work is more effective and easy to evaluate. We should also be prepared to tolerate the team's poor performance in the first few iterations, because many problems will appear at the beginning. An iterative cycle should be no longer than two weeks, and it has proved that this is the smartest way to balance development rhythm and requirement granularity.

- **Consider a mixed delivery model.** When researching software outsourcing, S&P said that the popularization of agile development has brought some development work back to the homeland. Therefore, the customer chose to pay more for the offshore partners to provide more on-site personnel. In this way, at the customer site there will be the customer team and the vendor team, which will constitute a half-and-half team of local and offshore personnel. This seemingly mixed delivery model maximizes the negative impact of distance on agile practice.
- **Active management.** In theory, agile model should be a systematic and flat approach to software development. But if you are an outsourcing team, especially offshore outsourcing team, you need to actively manage agile model, unify the level of agile practices of different teams, and let everyone collaborate on the same level. Offshore teams need a project manager. As a project manager of a self-managing team, his job content is greatly different from his counterparts with traditional teams.
- **Training offshore teams.** It is very difficult for an outsider to understand a business independently. Because of this, especially at the beginning of a project, the customer will allocate a special budget for inviting people from offshore teams to join in business training. A deep understanding of business will have a significant impact on future cooperation. In addition to business training, technical communication is equally important.
- **Choose the best offshore partner.** Many traditional IT service providers have established mature waterfall development models (such as CMMI) in customers' companies, but they

have not established and improved their agile delivery capability. For example, less than 20% of outsourcing projects in Inforsys and Tata, famous consulting firms in India, use agile model. Multinational companies such as Hewlett-Packard and IBM have similar proportions of overseas delivery projects in all agile projects. But some consulting companies and outsourcing service providers (such as ThoughtWorks) are building their own delivery centers based on agile model. It is difficult to hire an offshore IT service provider to finish delivery with agile model unless it has successful experiences in this regard.

- **Consider time difference.** It helps to schedule daily meetings in some overlapping time zones. When communication is not thorough and lack of contextual information, the team needs to wait for local customers or experts to come online to answer questions, and some work will be stalled.

8.2.2 Management and Improvement of Domain Knowledge

If we lack of domain knowledge, there will be greater risks that the functions we deliver will not meet user requirements. Many people overlook the effect of understanding customer business in doing a good project. These activities include research on user behavior in the field of this project, define typical user portraits and conduct user behavioral analysis, and then feedback on business analysis and testing to guide their work.

Build a knowledge-sharing system to bring out the power of collective wisdom. Because of a knowledge-sharing system, all knowledge such as the domain knowledge of the team can be opened to everyone, so that the knowledge level of the team can be maintained at a very high level. It is better to let users find what they want on their own. We can set up mail groups and concentrate important and intellectual mails in public places. Members who join later can easily find them on their own.

Continue to grow and establish a knowledge framework to achieve the goals of reducing delivery risks and costs. For key areas such as continuous integration, automated test methods/framework, and agile requirements management, standards should be established first. These are the core of team knowledge. We can effectively reuse the previously accumulated knowledge framework and form an effective teamwork, rather than relying on a limited number of top experts. I believe that it can also bring value to our customers while forming large-scale development and reducing inner team cost.

INTEGRATION OF DEVELOPMENT TEAM

The development plan designed for a customer is like this, 5–8 development teams will be arranged to work in parallel. Each of them is responsible for their own module development, and they need to frequently perform system integration and joint debugging. They hope to follow the operation idea of product integration. Each module forms its own functional team and implements the product manager responsibility system. Each product team is equipped with product manager, business analysts, test engineers, designers, and developers. Every member needs to be responsible for the overall success of the product. Each product team shall be highly cohesive and low-coupling at the organizational level. When considering the overall integration of the system, the independence of each team shall be ensured to avoid unnecessary horizontal communication.

Pay attention to observe customers' safety regulations, many customers will ask everyone on offshore teams to sign a confidentiality agreement. We can't disclose customer requirements in external forums and other places, nor can we post the code for discussion. The tools we use are also specified. In many cases, data cannot be stored on servers on the external network.

8.2.3 EFFECTIVENESS OF OFFSHORE TEAMS

When the size of the team develops to a certain extent, how to improve the effectiveness of the team will become increasingly important. We can consider from experience learning and from standardized work practice to ensure that mature results could be applied, and there will be no repeated invention of wheels.

Learn to expose problems, successful projects are the same, but failed projects are in different forms. The failure of one team guarantees that other teams will not follow the same path.

Use technical means to solve problems, for example, use virtualization tools, so that developers can get an environment anytime and anywhere, and then start working quickly.

Even in small teams, communication and getting along with team members is often difficult. However, in the world we live in, the communication of details within the team is an increasingly indispensable factor towards success. And those tools that can reduce the complexity of communication and assist in the development of more robust software are undoubtedly a huge boost for distributed teams. This is why technologies such as Docker deserve our in-depth understanding.

8.2.4 LEARNING FROM HISTORY AND FACING THE FUTURE

Looking back at the processing enterprises which were characterized as "processing with materials, assembly with supplied parts, processing with supplied samples, and compensation trade" in the 1980s and 1990s, then we can foresee the future of outsourcing industry. Processing companies that had been settled in the status quo have already declined and vanished. Outsourcers will continually look for lower-cost contractors, some labor-intensive enterprises (such as Nike) have set their sights on Southeast Asia. Outsourcing must embark on the road to innovation, attempt process innovation, or find the soil to breed products. Of course, some OEMs now have their own brands.

Outsourcing companies are similar to the OEMs of that age. If you want to win the future, you also need to form your own core competitiveness. You must either nurture your own products or cultivate your unique ability.

8.3 THE FUTURE OF OFFSHORE TEAMS

There is no big talk.

This is a beautiful era of innovation, and many companies need innovation and digital transformation. The customer's responsiveness to software systems is also becoming higher and higher. At the same time, in order to meet the continuous development of the business, we also need to adapt to more complex challenges.

Outsourcing has been a buzzword in the IT field for many years. When companies have ambitious business goals to complete and their own employees are not enough to accomplish this goal, they will choose to outsource. According to relevant surveys, the use of overseas developers in the process of enterprise outsourcing software development in 2017 increased exponentially.

At the beginning of 2017, Deloitte released a survey on outsourcing. The data covered all aspects, such as which companies will choose to outsource; which projects will be outsourced; and the growth of outsourcing in various industry sectors. The areas covered by the survey are consumer products, industrial products, financial industry, healthcare, IT, and media. Interviewees include heads of companies in different divisions, such as IT, human resources and finance.

Among them, the outsourcing ratio of IT division was the highest, reaching 72%, and outsourcing software development has become the most popular business model for enterprises. The report also pointed out that outsourcing increased by an average of 20% from 2014 to 2016 in all divisions surveyed. Most people gave a definite answer to whether they would choose to outsource in the future.

According to interviewees, at the beginning, they were unfamiliar with the remote development team, and were suspicious of the relationship and working mode between the two parties. However, as outsourcing services gradually mature, more successful cases emerge, they are confident in convincing their boss to engage remote development teams to complete project, and they are quite optimistic in the success of the project.

With the development of the Internet and communication tools, it becomes easy for individuals to work at home for a day.

8.3.1 Reasons to Hire a Remote Development Team

An important option for this Deloitte survey is "Why did you hire a remote development team." The answers to this question are shown in Figure 8.1.

59% of the respondents said that they want to cut cost, while hiring a remote development team means that the company does not need to hire a large number of software engineers for software development for a long time. In addition, hiring a remote development team can enjoy more professional services at a lower price, and in addition to paying salaries for their own employees, their insurance payment is also a large expense.

57% of the respondents said that outsourcing is to enable existing internal employees to focus on their core business. For example, a project of CRM software development may require a small internal IT team to concentrate on development for several months, and the developed system may be imperfect with various flaws, which will affect the company's business.

31% of the respondents said that using remote development teams can solve capacity issues. Other reasons include that they need experts to improve their companies' service quality as quickly as possible, and relative rapid "reparation" of the critical nature of business needs.

Another 28% of the respondents said that in order to obtain intellectual capital, each region has its own unique way of thinking and expertise, so remote development of this method can gain more knowledge.

Judging from Deloitte's survey report, companies are pleased to hire a professional remote team for project development, and said they will increase the proportion of outsourcing in the future. We can basically think that outsourcing will be a universal and permanent practice.

The future of service outsourcing industry is bright. The digital development of different industries aims to simplify process and improve efficiency. But these companies usually don't form their own teams, and opportunities for offshore outsourcing teams come. Lots of people are required to

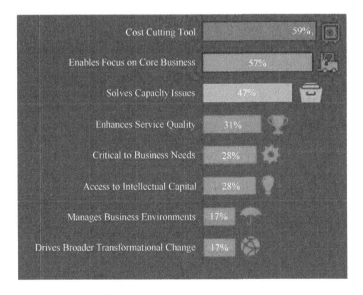

FIGURE 8.1 Deloitte's findings on offshore outsourcing.

develop a project, but only a few people are needed to enter the operation and maintenance after development. Using outsourcing is the most cost-effective solution. Of course, we cannot wait for these prospects to come while doing nothing. Outsourcing companies need to be fully prepared. To receive innovative contracts, we must continuously improve our domain knowledge and delivery capability by devoting ourselves into an industry and a domain, and even nurturing our own products and tools. To provide domain solutions, it is necessary to accumulate talents, knowledge, and cases.

8.3.2 International Competition

The following is my experience of changing spectacle lenses.

Before long when I changed myopic glasses, I learned that lenses are divided into different light transmittances. Good lenses have higher light transmittance. So I decided to change to better "lenses" this time. However, after I tried these high-end lenses, my eyes were uncomfortable, and I felt the light was too strong and too dazzling. Finally, I realized that my eyes had adapted to the low-light transmission of ordinary lenses. But everything before my eyes are actually more brighter than I had seen. And I had been no aware of that till then.

Many times we cannot see the essence of things, so we simply accept facts. Subverting traditional thinking requires us to make changes, especially changes in thinking. Even if our start is not as high as that of our competitors, as long as we can see what others cannot see, and have the courage to try some practices that do not seem to be routine, we will have a higher probability of success and innovative development. As for the extent of development, no one can predict, only to wait and see.

When it comes to the word "outsourcing," it may sound low-end. But in fact, the nature of service industry is procurement, that is, companies hand over part of their operating processes to others. Therefore, purchasing some services from outside is neither low-end nor high-end, but domestic outsourcing companies mostly offer low-end jobs, even the branch of large multinational companies. We can position the Shenzhen branch as supplier of core software and high-end services, while the Shanghai branch is engaged in low-end maintenance and plan implementation.

In recent years, the overseas M&A and business expansion of domestic sci-tech companies have increased, and they will also encounter problems of coordinated development. In the future, this form of work for distributed teams will only increase in number, instead of decreasing. What we have to do is to move from the so-called low-end to high-end outsourcing services in this process.

In June 2017, Shanghai branch of Infosys, a well-known Indian IT service provider, was officially established and put into operation in the Shanghai Minhang Park. Vishal Sikka, CEO of Infosys Shanghai, said that the information technology service industry is undergoing profound changes and iterations, and the rapid development of AI has brought both opportunities and challenges. Infosys is facing a transformation from a labor-intensive information technology outsourcing service company to an AI service company.

Amid the international competition in the software outsourcing industry, in order to obtain more competitive advantages, we also need to start with reducing communication costs and improving efficiency through standardization.

8.3.3 Assist Digital Innovation in Traditional Industries

Forerunners in some traditional industries, the streamlining and more effective analysis achieved through digitalization have eliminated some manual processes, and improved work efficiency and user experience. More and more traditional enterprises will need digital services, but few companies with strong and visionary plans will form their own teams.

Citibank gave a high-profile comment at the feedback meeting of Pivotal, "we are no longer a bank, but a Silicon Valley company. It is a technical organization. This technical organization just happens to do banking as well. Now our mindset is more towards our customers than bankers."

When this book was about to be finished, I saw a piece of news from the Circle of Friends on WeChat: "Bank of China and Tencent co-founded a joint laboratory for technology and finance." Similar laboratories have also been established by major technology firms and financial institutions. It can be seen that the trend of using technological innovation to promote the development of traditional industries has been formed. Other industries will also reach this intersection. Software outsourcing companies have excellent technology and talent accumulation, and should actively participate in this trend to show their skills, coupled with a more suitable method for remote collaboration, and they are sure to have the comparable competitiveness of Internet companies.

According to media statistics, in the 2016 annual report of China Merchants Bank (CMB), some high-frequency vocabulary appeared, highlighting the bank's new strategic direction: "Fintech" (11 times), "IT" (11 times), "digitization" (7 times). Li Jianhong, Chairman of CMB, said at the annual results conference that the bank has invested more than 5 billion yuan in IT in the past, leading the level of investment among all Chinese banks. A new round of scientific and technological revolution is poised to take off. The emerging technologies represented by the Internet, big data, cloud computing are accelerating integration with traditional finance, which not only brings new impetus to the reform, development, and transformation of the banking industry, but also has caused certain pressures on the advantageous areas of banking industry, and made information technology the key for financial institutions to resist risks and enhance competitiveness. In the future, the evolution path of CMB's financial technology strategy includes three steps: networking, datamation, and intellectualization. The bank will set up special technology funds, increase investment in financial technology and in infrastructure such as mobile technology, cloud computing, big data, and AI, and pay close attention to the latest progress and innovative applications of new technologies such as blockchain.

The opportunity for combining technology and finance has been opened, and there will be more gates in the traditional field in the future. Outsourcing companies should actively demonstrate their advantages and assist different industries to use digitization to innovate or transform. Of course, in the process of digital transformation, the IT team should not only follow the business department, but to drive business innovation through technological innovation and explore the driving force of technology.

8.3.4 AGILE MODEL OF OFFSHORE TEAMS

Offshore outsourcing projects have the characteristics of short duration and wide business coverage. The accumulation of domain knowledge sometimes does not work quickly, we need some basic norms and principles. To provide mature and stable delivery services, participate in the wave of digital innovation, and ensure that each project has a mature and standardized process that can be followed from start to delivery, we need a mature agile delivery model. Only when a standardized and generalizable practical model is formed can reproducible success be produced.

Agile development pays attention to the participation of customers. We have different delivery solutions to different degrees of participation, and the delivery strategy should be adjusted accordingly.

The first level of distributed teams is simple offshore delivery. Customers do not participate in specific work, but only accept results. Offshore teams need to strictly follow the technical manual to complete their work, and do not make creative input.

Based on this situation, we can adopt the following strategy:

- Iterative development, delivering available software in stages.
- Introduce the necessary agile practices, but the technology selection should be conservative and the future operation and maintenance costs should be considered. Choosing the appropriate phased delivery cycle is favorable for collecting end-user feedback during the development process. Business analysis runs through the entire delivery process, and requires customers to have business experts work with offshore teams to determine solutions.

- This kind of delivery must define the staged deliverables in the beginning. When doing showcase to customers, this is almost the only opportunity for customers to understand us, and it is also the most important moment. The showcase includes, but are not limited to, design scenarios, previews in advance, topical cohesion and guidance, preset questions. The first one is particularly important and also reflects our understanding of the business.
- With the goal of creating a baseline product for development, we will gain a lot of competitive advantage when serving similar customers in the future.

Today's customers increasingly need to get user feedback during the development process and adjust the requirements design at any time, which requires that offshore teams can also keep up with this delivery process. Ensure that offshore teams have sufficient technical accumulation in continuous delivery, frequently and automatically package a workable version which is also a high-quality version that has been tested.

The second level is based on continuous integration of distributed teams for delivery. We need to introduce more agile practices, such as test-driven development, code review, application of continuous integration tools, and the implementation of the test pyramid theory.

At the same time, what we have to do is not only to provide delivery services, but also to help customers bring them an overall change in software development and concepts. Let the IT and operations staff of the customer enter the team and take the role of development and operation. In this way, the operational efficiency after the project is transferred can be greatly improved.

In terms of release plan and working methods, many companies used to use relatively large software, and a relatively large team was responsible for distributed development. Now large software or a large team is outdated, it is small teams that are responsible for many different and small services. Meanwhile, each team has its own release cycle, and the correlation between them is not very strong, that is, each part is a microservice, and each team represents a microservice.

8.3.5 PRACTICE OF INNOVATION WITH CUSTOMERS

We often hear these sayings that companies do not know how to innovate, they have no achievements in product development, and they are unresponsive to business changes. This brings up a question, which part is going wrong? What are the key factors to consider when innovating in a large organization?

Generally, the factors that restrict innovation are indefinite business goals, unnecessary competition for priorities, localized performance measurement criteria, and definitions of success. The traditional management approach to control the behavior and output of personnel in the organization; in a highly competitive and rapidly developing commercial environment, it will inevitably produce the ability to stifle innovation and delay the organization's response.

So, what elements are needed to release the energy of innovation in enterprises?

- **Super execution power.** Top-down promotion in the organization is essential. For any innovative initiative to be successful, participants need to be encouraged to invest wholeheartedly, even if they require support through the requirements of an executive order. At the same time, the innovation of the new measures also determines that all executives need to be given the mission to explore and provide as many new ideas as possible.
- **Flexibility of innovation strategy.** Encourage customers/users to participate in and jointly create innovative activities, and participate regularly throughout the development process. Regularly feedback what you are designing for your customer. Close the feedback loop with them, keep learning, and keep moving forward.
- **Changes in organizational structure.** If you want to make full use of innovative networks, companies must also make organizational changes, which means ensuring efficient collaboration and information sharing throughout the organization. Mechanisms in this area include

collaborative thinking seminars, organization-wide portfolios, and cross-functional work-day activities, so as to meet and build relationships with others in the organization. Leaders must seek opportunities to increase the exchange of ideas between business units as much as possible.

8.3.6 SUMMARY

There is no single answer for companies to meet the challenges of innovation, but I always remind leaders to consider the following points:

- Ensure that innovation has a strong executor throughout the organization. If leaders are not willing to support, success can only be progressive at best.
- Understand the organization's own strengths and weaknesses, flexibly choose an innovation strategy, and then make adjustment when you have made it clear what is feasible and what is not.
- Don't stifle innovation and traditional business indicators, such as ROI. Adopt short iterations to quickly verify the impact of innovation on the business.
- Making it easy for people to share what they do and what they learn face to face, thus opening up networks of collaborative organizations, and encouraging people to build their own ideas rather than destroy others' thoughts.
- Establish an entrepreneurial culture within the company, find and authorize people to do this work, and make them as successful as possible to further promote business change.
- Make long-term investment commitments because revolution requires time, support, capital, and protection, so only then can momentum be established over time.

The successful organization is constantly delivering functions to users to test the design to understand what is effective and what is unsuccessful. Not every innovation attempt will be successful, but those who pass the test will have a huge impact on the future destiny of the company.

8.4 OFFSHORE TEAMS MUST PREPARE FOR TECHNOLOGICAL CHANGE

In the software field, from DevOps to Docker, it seems that a new technical term will appear once in a while. To put it simply, the technology trend can be summarized into four fragments:

- **Integration of development and operation**, which means that operations and software development are now combined.
- **Continuous delivery**, in simple terms, means that every commitment made by a software engineer can be deployed immediately.
- **Microservices**, which is now not based on large software units, but on small software units, and each microservice is to do its own release, the dependence between each other is relatively low.
- **Container**.

Because of these trends, the past and present development models have shown some differences:

- In the past, we assumed that there must be a reliable infrastructure, but now we assume that cloud infrastructure is fragile.
- In the past, if the development was fast enough, the code would be released every three months, but now the release is early release, frequent release, and continuous release.
- In the past, developers often said that these source codes were completely ok in my environment, but why didn't they work in other environments? Now DevOps and software developers

are in the same environment and in the same team, and they are very clear about each other's responsibilities.

- In the past, relatively large software was used, and the correlation between them was relatively high; now it is relatively small software is used, and the correlation between them is relatively low. One of the biggest secrets is that developer and DevOps person work together, so they can arrange release so quickly.
- In the past, release was a great event with high risks, and everyone had to be prepared. This meant that despite a large number of testers, there were still many bugs not discovered in time. Now through the deployment of micro-applications, many independent units are formed, and they can have rich functions through a simple application server.

In many organizations, the driving force for change is often from the upper levels. In a centralized organization, all power belongs to superior managers. Another meaning for all powers belonging to superior managers is that all responsibilities are also borne by superior managers. In this way, there will be an individual who "takes high risks and responsibilities" within the organization, rather than a team that jointly bears risks.

IT technology gives enterprises a great competitive driving force, such as BEKE, Diamler, Although many traditional companies have begun to establish their own R&D teams, they will also use external talents and hire external consultants to carry out digital innovation. Either ask a high-end consulting team to help your own team to perform disruptive design, or ask an external delivery team for low-cost delivery, or learn the engineering practice of an external mature team to help their companies' long-term development.

Among the many reasons for choosing a microservice architecture, the most important one is that teams can work at different speeds between systems without affecting other team members. We also expect that the team can independently decide how to implement the service in the best way and realize the business requirements faster. If we want to organize a team in the above way, then our system architecture will start to evolve into a microservice model. At the same time, in order to gain this kind of autonomy, each microservice should have its own database, and the database should not be shared between services.

8.5 LOW-COST OFFSHORE DELIVERY IS A NO RETURN ROUTE

The cost of labor in countries that provide offshore outsourcing services is constantly rising, and the path of making profits solely on price factors will be increasingly narrower. At the same time, the price is also the source of the outsourcing problem, since the harm of low-cost competition is very great. The "AOKAI" cable incident in Xi'an is a good example. In order to get the contract, the company bid at a low price; after getting the contract, in order to obtain profits, the cost was reduced by cheating on workmanship and materials during the delivery process.

On the surface, the low-cost bidding strategy was to save money for customers, but it was essentially harming them. At in the later stage, in order to make up for the quality defects caused by cost reduction, the total cost would far exceed the initial quotation, and the decision makers in the customer's company that supported outsourcing were screwed. Let customers understand that the unit price is high but the real total price is not high, it is a required course for every presales person.

As a member of the offshore delivery team, our focus should be to consider how to improve the delivery capability of individual members and the entire team, and how to ensure that the delivery quality does not shrink. This is the ultimate goal to truly help customers reduce costs and obtain value. Don't forget that the process of software delivery is also a process of establishing process and standardization.

When software outsourcing first took off, the wages of Chinese programmers were relatively low. For example, a good Java development engineer was paid a price higher than the market price (such as 5,000 yuan per month), and then the product was sold to a US customer at a price of $15 per hour

($2,500 per month). With such a profit, outsourcing was feasible, and there was almost no need to worry about cost. Even if we might eventually lose some customers, we still had enough money to pay the team wages.

The situation is different now.

Today a good Java developer may earn more than 20,000 yuan per month. In addition, there are all sorts of benefits for developers, such as insurances, free fitness membership, free lunch, paid vacation, and paid sick leave. At the same time, the price of Java projects has not grown as fast as labor costs. Now even if you earn $40 per hour (which is unlikely), your monthly income will be $6800, but your spending will be close to $4,000, meaning that your profits are greatly reduced. Of course, don't forget that there are also office expenses, taxes, computer equipment, administrative staff, team building, and other expenses. Due to the small profit margin, once a key customer is lost, the outsourcing company will face great risks.

From a cost perspective, the outlook for IT service outsourcing is not optimistic. But everything must be viewed from two aspects. At present, in the IT market, cloud computing, big data and AI are in full swing. Capital and personnel are swarming to these hot industries and products. If anyone can do cost control and targeted service solutions that are close to customer requirements, and ultimately build their own advantageous brand in IT service outsourcing, even if they make a baseline product with cost advantage in a subdivided field, it is also a good thing.

8.6 SUMMARY

Remote delivery services will exist for a long time. This industry attracts many young people with ambitious ideals. This is one of the few industries in China that is relatively integrated with the international standard.

In recent years, Apple's President Cook frequently visited China. Apple has built four R&D centers in China. It is not just an interest in the Chinese market. In an interview with the media, Cook said that Apple's original intention to establish an R&D center in China was to use some of China's advanced technologies (such as TD-LTE[1]) to go global. Cook also mentioned that "China has many talented graduates. We also hope that they can join the China R&D Center in the future." This also represents the direction and future of distributed teams.

In the past, delivery was entirely based on customer command. After entering the Internet era, customers are not necessarily experts. We need ways to help customers tap the requirements of end users and help customers create valuable products.

NOTE

1 Today, China has become a leader in TD technology.

Postscript

I have come to understand a truth after finishing this book: like actors never watch their plays, authors do not read what they have written.

This book took me almost fifteen months. The process of outlining, text writing, proofreading, and revising seemed like an endless ordeal. I was even fed up with such paperwork when it was nearing completion. That's why I can feel for a game software QA who hates playing the game he has tested.

If you don't think the above matter is a big deal, you must be a tough-minded person that can win the victory over yourself. In an agile team, you can do a project retrospective on your own. A retrospective meeting is no more than a venue for you to exchange ideas with your teammates and other teams.

The topic of offshore delivery deserves our full attention, because in the context of flourishing technical services, the skills in this regard are about to exert to unexpected effects. However, these effects are often overlooked since they are hard to be quantified. This is the main reason that I decided to write this book. I've gained so much from the field of offshore delivery in the past decade, I think it is time for me to give back to society, even if I'm ashamed to show off my incompetence in writing.

Offshore delivery is part of globalization. It was initially a simple means of worldwide procurement and supply. With the changes of the times and the development of innovation, today's global collaboration needs to break through the limitations of time and space. And we all believe that the trend of genuine distributed cooperation is just beginning.

This book is a highly practical guide although it has neither disruptive innovations nor groundbreaking viewpoints, what it contains is a detailed summary of what I've learned from dozens of software development projects, such as how does the daily offshore delivery work look like, how can project manager and team members playing different roles do a good job, how to make sure of on-time delivery, how to choose appropriate development models, how to avoid or mitigate risks, and how to satisfy capricious customers and even create more value to them.

Being one of the pioneers in China's offshore software delivery, I don't want current practitioners to repeat our past mistakes or waste time struggling with the form of offshore delivery, you can just step on our shoulders to do more valuable things, which is worth of my ten years of perseverance in this field. Well, pull yourself together and get started to pursue user value and business innovation in the realm of offshore delivery!

References

[1] Millett S, Blankenship J, Bussa M. *Pro Agile .NET Development with SCRUM*. CA US, Apress, 2011.

[2] Kniberg H. *Scrum and XP from the Trenches*. Beijing: Tsinghua University Press, 2011.

[3] Elbeheri A. Burn up vs. Burn down Chart. https://www.linkedin.com/pulse/burn-up-vs-down-chart-alaa-el-beheri-cisa-rmp-pmp-bcp-itil [March 15, 2016]

[4] Brodzinski P. Why Burn-up Chart is Better Than Burn-down Chart. http://brodzinski.com/2012/10/burn-up-better-burn-down.html [October 11, 2012]

[5] Maineri S. Why You Should Use Burn-up Chart in Agile Instead of Burn-down Chart? https://www.linkedin.com/pulse/why-you-should-use-burn-up-chart-agile-instead-sebasti%C3%A1n? [July 5, 2016]

[6] Mo L. The FANCY Approach for User Story Analysis. https://www.linkedin.com/pulse/fancy-approach-user-story-analysis-mo-li [October 15, 2016]

Index

abandon, 40
abbreviation, 11
abide, 65, 167, 179
abnormal, 152, 223, 237, 248
abreast, 133, 233
abroad, 61
absence, 35, 136, 163
abyss, 250
accessible, 17
accident, 71–72, 202
accommodation, 215
accompany, 3
accomplishment, 165
accumulate, 194
accustomed, 90, 179, 209, 211, 234, 253
acquaint, 7
acquisition, 11, 69, 187
adequate, 27, 224, 236, 263
adhere, 117
adverse, 25, 28, 30, 39, 89, 117, 199, 257
advocate, 45, 117, 121, 181, 198, 202, 225–226, 234
aesthetic, 223
affiliation, 153
affirm, 47
algorithm, 162
ambiguous, 26, 58, 172, 219, 242, 250
ambiguously, 250
ambitions, 9
ambitious, 4, 18, 265, 272
arbitrarily, 202, 236
assessment, 1–2, 18, 34, 58, 96, 191, 194, 202, 206, 221, 227, 235, 247, 250
assumption, 105, 118–119, 163, 191, 248
asynchronous, 25, 27–29, 94
auditing, 77, 176
authentic, 154
authorization, 183–184
axis, 46, 131, 140–141, 143

BA, 7
backlog, 36, 48, 80, 86, 99–103, 122, 131, 135, 139, 167, 173, 185, 195, 203, 250–251, 254, 262
balancing, 22, 126, 213
baseline, 62, 242, 269, 272
benchmark, 109, 143, 182
beneath, 205
beneficial, 53, 58–59, 86, 173, 202, 242
bidding, 43, 271
boundary, 59, 86, 117–119, 236, 240
brainstorming, 138, 155, 189, 210
branch, 77, 135, 152–153, 155–156, 185, 194, 197, 267
burndown, 130–131, 140–149, 156–157, 175, 198, 204, 220, 234
burnup, 130–131, 140–141, 146–149, 157–158, 234

calibrate, 36, 97, 99, 177, 183, 216
candidates, 54, 88, 261

capture, 48
cargo, 71–72
caring, 220, 243
Carnegie, 1
carrier, 152, 159, 196
carton, 27–28, 163–164
cascade, 188
chain, 5, 31, 222
characteristic, 66, 123, 140, 151, 186, 215
characterized, 25, 69, 98, 100, 238, 265
charge, 4, 9, 16, 48, 54, 67, 84, 167, 188–189, 199, 208, 245, 257
checklist, 119
circle, 15, 22, 49, 175, 225, 261
circulated, 189
circumstance, 16, 29, 83, 233
clarification, 56, 120
classification, 16, 69–70
classified, 215
classify, 47
CMMI, 1–3, 5, 263
coefficients, 146, 198
cognition, 106
coherent, 21
cohesion, 110, 211, 245, 269
cohesive, 211, 264
collaborate, 4, 25, 56, 66–67, 75, 86, 93, 108, 124, 132, 136, 167, 196, 202, 257, 263
collapse, 22
commercial, 43, 236, 239, 246, 269
commitments, 64, 100–101, 235, 270
comparison, 30, 129, 157, 247
compatibility, 78, 119, 211
compensation, 195, 265
component, 191, 200
composed, 3, 153, 181, 186
comprehend, 18, 222–223
comprehensiveness, 148, 260
conceal, 17–18
concept, 1, 10, 41, 57, 77, 83, 85, 88, 102, 105, 115, 118, 166, 172, 182, 190–191, 195, 225, 232
conception, 21
concessions, 32, 213, 239
concise, 167
conclude, 41
conclusion, 27, 51, 57, 83, 194, 202
conclusive, 130, 183
concrete, 219, 221
concretization, 28
concurrency, 15
conduct, 30, 37, 52, 73, 90, 165–166, 176, 187, 192, 194, 200, 244, 248, 260, 264
conflict, 32–33, 83, 116, 151, 189, 215, 223, 237, 261
confusion, 232
conscious, 195
consecutive, 147
consent, 15–16, 25, 39, 215, 233
consequence, 9, 58, 113, 171, 245
constitute, 4, 6, 95, 263

construction, 10, 92–93, 166, 225, 254
constructive, 125
consulting, 10–11, 92, 189, 257, 264, 271
contradict, 29
contribute, 161
convention, 121–122
conversion, 221
convince, 15–16, 32, 92–94, 149, 176–177, 233, 236, 238, 253
coordinator, 32, 210
cope, 105
corporation, 172
counterpart, 7, 200, 209
courtesy, 181
credible, 236
criterion, 1, 3, 43, 166, 246, 249
criticize, 162
CSS, 153
CSV, 15, 246
cucumber, 174
cumulative, 142
curve, 46, 70, 131, 140–141, 151, 171

damage, 22, 51, 76, 162, 236
DC-10, 71–72
deadline, 68, 109, 162, 184, 209, 215–216, 219, 242
dealer, 221–222
debt, 44, 175, 239, 255–256
debug, 187
decades, 245
deceived, 20
decent, 175, 177, 247
decentralization, 190
decline, 108, 133, 144, 204
decrease, 103, 122, 133, 147
deduce, 29, 89
defects, 14, 16–17, 21, 30–31, 51, 57, 65, 68, 73, 77, 80–82, 179, 193, 271
deficient, 238
Deloitte, 265–266
Deming, 49, 68, 191, 226
demo, 49
demolish, 24, 162
demonstration, 104, 115
deploy, 78, 123
deprive, 260
desktop, 49, 77–78, 86, 98
desperate, 205
destination, 100
destiny, 270
destroy, 152, 204, 270
destructive, 89, 162
detected, 109, 225–226
Dev, 7
deviate, 73, 107, 113, 144, 151, 201
device, 119
DevOps, 10, 14, 75, 109, 185–186, 196, 228, 231, 246, 248, 251–252, 270–271
devote, 56, 210, 261
diagnosing, 149
diagram, 14, 132, 134–135, 144, 153–154, 260
dialog, 93

Diamler, 271
differ, 29, 35, 209
digest, 102, 241
digitized, 11
digress, 38
dilemma, 197, 233
diluting, 243
dimension, 176
Dingding, 66
discarded, 143, 153
discipline, 77, 89, 182, 184
disclaimer, 45
disclose, 264
discrimination, 33
dispatches, 59
dispute, 186, 240
disrupted, 19
dissatisfied, 22, 34, 234
disseminate, 146, 247
dissenting, 238
dissolve, 164
distinguishes, 200
distort, 191
distortion, 78, 257
distract, 33, 66, 154
diverge, 46
diverged, 84
divert, 11, 22, 222
Docker, 123, 265, 270
DOD, 2
downtime, 92
DTS, 17
dubbed, 244
dynamic, 6, 65, 220

ecological, 186
economic, 6
edge, 10
edit, 65, 83
element, 31, 94, 259
embark, 105, 116, 265
embrace, 182, 239
empathic, 28, 33–34
encoding, 224–225
entrance, 21, 118, 191
enumerate, 47
enviable, 233
epic, 158
equivalence, 120
equivalent, 48, 104, 149, 163, 184
erroneous, 202
escalated, 105
essential, 16, 56, 66, 121, 154, 269
eternal, 25, 116, 184, 231
ethica, 200
EU, 5
evolution, 22, 85, 254, 268
evolve, 151, 271
executor, 130, 183, 270
exempt, 202
exert, 60, 85, 110, 182, 188–189, 221, 273
expense, 216, 266

expertise, 13–14, 209, 266
explicit, 36, 163, 220

facilitator, 38–39, 45–46, 48, 95, 189
facts, 13, 32–34, 267
fade, 52
failover, 242
fake, 165
fancy, 223
fatal, 71
fatigue, 195
feasible, 88, 112, 174, 218, 237, 270, 272
feature, 10, 50, 78, 184, 218, 223
fidelity, 16, 120, 131–132, 153
filters, 68
Fintech, 268
fixedbid, 239–241
flexibility, 4, 166
formulate, 170
forthcoming, 202

Gantt, 157, 228
garbled, 15
geographic, 29
GitHub, 69
granular, 118
graphic, 129

Haier, 190
halfway, 14, 60, 69
halted, 234
hammer, 71
handy, 95, 154
Hangouts, 66
harm, 198, 202, 271
harmonious, 33, 179
harmony, 83, 215
haunt, 136
headlines, xx
Heroku, 69
hesitate, 60, 163, 172
Hewlett, 264
hinders, 191, 198
hints, 66, 135
huddle, 39, 50–51, 85, 96, 108
hypotheses, 220

IdeaBoardz, 67, 96
ideally, 19
ideologies, 210
idle, 137
IE, 119
ignited, 181
illusions, 37
illustration, 112
IM, 56
imagination, 107, 189, 207
immediate, 27, 41
IMP, 100
impatient, 263
impede, 5, 200, 204, 224
imperfect, 266

impetus, 205–206, 260–261, 268
implications, 46
implicit, 126, 163, 175
imply, 91, 168
impose, 185
impression, 59, 62, 187, 236
improper, 17, 37, 174
impulsive, 24
inability, 164
inaccurate, 26, 30, 39
inadequate, 257
inappropriateness, 109
inbox, 69
incapable, 35, 89, 222, 225
inception, 58
incident, 71–72, 203, 271
inclined, 145
incompetence, 273
inconsistency, 107
inconvenience, 44
incorporated, 254
incur, 239
index, 133, 138, 197
indexing, 201
indicator, 19, 24, 96, 125–126, 133
individuals, 114, 207
induction, 37, 218
indulge, 22
informal, 38, 45, 51, 57, 235, 252
Infosys, 267
infrastructure, 63, 268, 270
inherent, 65, 242
inquiry, 27
inspect, 188
inspire, 9, 152, 259
instability, 93
instinct, 187
instructor, 206
integral, 150, 220, 238
intelligence, 233
interference, 222, 229
intermediate, 142
interrupt, 71, 225
interval, 76, 145–146, 241, 259
intervene, 26, 99, 178, 196
intrinsic, 174, 239
intuition, 192
invalid, 54, 217
INVEST, 44, 102
IoT, 5
IPM, 9, 16–17, 29, 39, 41–42, 44–45, 58, 83, 96, 98,
    101–103, 108, 141–142, 169
irrational, 202, 205
irregular, 108, 252
irrelevant, 23, 33, 70, 104, 154, 233, 241
irresponsible, 94
isolating, 97, 224
iterated, 250
iteration, 39, 96, 102, 144, 153

jam, 32
joint, 56, 62, 109, 167, 180, 264, 268
journey, 84, 103, 132

kickoff, 223, 241, 262

label, 70, 251
lagging, 197
laid, 92
landing, 71, 127
landmark, 11, 183, 233–234
lane, 159
lasting, 53
layout, 6, 125, 132, 154
leadership, 90, 162, 188–190, 193, 196, 209, 214, 219, 226
leads, 92, 104, 166–167, 188, 204
lean, 29, 68, 70, 85, 154, 170, 177, 182, 191, 232, 245, 255
legibility, 65
legitimate, 107
liability, 214
liberate, 169
lifting, 23
linear, 183
logistics, 58–59, 64, 76, 113, 211, 221, 233, 243, 245
logo, 153
logs, 25, 97, 124, 253
longitudinal, 151
longterm, 193
lowpriority, 147
loyalty, 260

magical, 241
magnitudes, 156
mainline, 77
majority, 226
Manifesto, 65, 88
manipulating, 196
manually, 94, 123, 153, 199, 211, 222
manufacturer, 4, 71, 221
meaningless, 40, 46–47, 89, 141, 176
measurable, 16
mechanisms, 11, 186
memo, 72
mentor, 261
merchants, 236
merge, 223
messy, 123
microservice, 22, 190, 245, 269–271
migration, 78, 245, 259–260
milestone, 53, 67, 101, 125, 159, 179, 183, 194
mindset, 13, 267
minor, 220
minority, 50, 237
mislead, 140, 145
Mo, 118, 275
mockup, 153
momentum, 270
MoSCoW, 142
motivation, 49, 64, 146, 182, 206, 227, 259–260
MTP, 218, 245

NA, 105
naïve, 215
narration, 37

narrow, 37, 259
NASA, 202
native, 34, 111
natural, 121, 187, 223
nearly, 82
negative, 8–9, 28, 33, 46–47, 71, 89–90, 107, 113, 123, 162, 171, 175–176, 178, 181, 188, 202, 204, 225, 227, 234, 263
neglect, 32, 178
negotiable, 44, 112
node, 50, 85, 113, 149–150, 207
nonfunctional, 14, 17, 19, 82, 116, 119, 185–186, 233, 242, 246–247
NumberComparator, 121
NumberComparatorTest, 121
numerous, 6, 195
nurture, 265

object, 2, 143, 151, 193
obligations, 179, 183, 243
observed, 62, 180
observer, 96
obsessed, 25
obstacle, 209, 216, 225, 234
obvious, 72, 143, 175, 193, 250
occasion, 8, 17, 99, 202, 206, 223
occasional, 100, 104, 243
occupied, 4–5, 153
occurrence, 37, 83, 95, 166, 186, 193, 214, 228, 260
odd, 196
offer, 211, 216, 267
offline, 40, 51, 96, 107
offs, 190, 235
offset, 107
OKR, 182
omission, 61, 127, 135, 153, 254
ongoing, 95
optimal, 9, 175, 189, 201
option, 17, 46, 148, 245, 266
origin, 87, 95, 123, 147
outline, 14
outwards, 71
overlap, 28–29, 53, 66
overrun, 246
oversee, 47, 208
overview, 30, 66
ownership, 77, 100, 102, 200, 224, 226, 259

package, 20, 76–77, 115, 123, 185, 198, 269
pain, 15, 25, 61, 78–79, 117, 206
pale, 107
panel, 113, 234
panorama, 256
partially, 16
participant, 39, 100, 150
pathway, 227
pattern, 109, 184, 205, 213
PDCA, 49, 68, 111, 195, 217, 226, 232
peer, 167, 187, 206
pending, 103
perceived, 130
permit, 50, 66, 102
persist, 93

persona, 57, 78, 118, 213
phenomena, 13
phenomenon, 175, 196, 213
phrase, 189, 198
pile, 76
pipeline, 77, 82, 87, 133, 163, 176, 179
pitfalls, 248
placeholder, 165
platform, 7–8, 40, 81, 211, 259
plug, 34, 84, 148
plugin, 159
PO, 7
pondering, 20
portfolios, 270
portrait, 13
postGL, 107
postpone, 109
precedents, 201
preceding, 211
precisely, 144, 178
predecessor, 2
predict, 77, 113, 130, 145, 211, 220, 267
preliminary, 34, 73, 103, 247
prematurely, 170
premise, 64, 75, 88, 138, 174, 186, 191, 195, 203, 224, 246
prevail, 26
preview, 38
prime, 247
prioritizing, 21, 79, 195
proactive, 10, 195
probe, 22, 251
procedure, 100
profound, 107, 267
proportion, 5–6, 170, 266
Pros, 30
prospect, 6
prototype, 16, 120, 132, 249
provision, 30
provoked, 203
punctual, 181
puzzle, 46
pyramid, 112–113, 115, 194, 269

QA, 7, 137, 224, 273
quadrant, 194
qualification, 5, 188
quantitative, 32, 145, 156, 182
quarrel, 94
query, 20, 76, 113, 165, 221, 225, 250
Quip, 65
quiz, 34
quota, 191
quotation, 43, 242, 248, 271
quote, 45, 241

race, 8
racers, 127
racing, 34
radar, 194
radical, 190, 198, 239
random, 109, 237
ratio, 8, 265

receipt, 14, 214
reception, 111, 170, 214
recipient, 25, 29, 35, 105–106, 218
reconfirm, 164, 172, 250
reconstitution, 14
recovery, 242
rectangle, 149
recurrence, 30, 72
redraw, 157
refactor, 123
reimbursed, 199
reimbursement, 62, 199
releasing, 133
reload, 113
reluctant, 79, 89
remarkable, 69, 248
rendering, 214
renew, 20
replicate, 108
reprioritize, 32
reschedule, 253
rescue, 73
resign, 208
resist, 161, 205, 268
retrospective, 39, 45–46, 96, 163
reveal, 105, 131, 141, 167, 202
rigorous, 22, 112, 114, 244
roadmap, 23, 78, 114, 159, 171, 256, 260
ROI, 270
rollback, 78, 196
rotate, 55
route, 63, 113, 147, 170, 198
routines, 29

sacrifice, 45, 215
sample, 43, 78, 80
SBE, 120, 177
scalability, 166, 175
scatter, 87
scratch, 165
seamless, 53, 97
sector, 6–7
seemingly, 89, 263
segments, 102
selfmanagement, 142–143, 182
selfmotivation, 205
selforganization, 208
seminar, 29, 61, 176
serial, 8
shortcomings, 17, 154, 162, 228
shortcut, 236
significant, 68, 111, 246, 263
sketch, 153–154
slogan, 45
SMART, 217
specification, 119, 121–122, 149, 167, 224
spectacle, 267
speculation, 121
spike, 167
sponsor, 192–193
stack, 18, 75–76, 90, 103, 133, 145, 190, 240
stakeholder, 14, 16, 19, 27, 140, 147
standpoint, xvii, 28, 33–35, 89, 222–223

standups, 41
startup, 79, 176, 208
stead, 26
straightforward, 121, 203, 212
sub, 3–4, 7–8, 53, 85–86, 112, 120, 204, 218
supervior, 3
supervise, 61, 111, 139, 164, 168
supervision, 187, 214, 220, 223
supervisor, 26, 43, 70, 171, 174, 180, 196, 206, 218
supplementary, 84
suppresses, 209
supreme, 16, 35, 45–46
surprisingly, 199
surrounded, 62
surrounding, 243
survey, 35, 73, 219, 221, 265–266
suspicious, 26, 233–234, 265
symbol, 239
synchronize, 69, 97

tackle, 92
tactic, 239
tags, 224
takeoff, 127
talent, 10–11, 184, 207, 268
TDD, 16, 117, 126, 177, 179, 185
tear, 94, 199
technical, 75, 237
territory, 31
theoretical, 141, 261
thrive, 180
throttling, 178
ticket, 199
tier, 6, 260
tiles, 178
timecard, 199
timeline, 20, 109, 159, 218–219
trajectory, 141
transaction, 11, 92
transparent, 40, 67, 88, 183, 191, 200, 203–204, 237
typically, 219
typos, 125

UAT, 23, 57, 73, 213, 238
UI, 120
unambiguous, 19, 203
unavailable, 35, 41
unavoidable, 236
undermine, 18, 205
unfold, 191
unforeseen, 220, 262
unforgivable, 21, 232
unfortunately, 9, 205, 247

unfulfilled, 179
Unicom, 20
unpredictable, 23, 73, 117, 171, 233
unsolved, 218
unstable, 125, 239
urge, 68, 84, 90, 212–213, 216, 228
utilize, 112
utmost, 175–176, 234
UX, 120

vacancies, 151
vacation, 136, 272
vague, 219, 222, 240
vain, 21, 162
valid, 8, 174, 244
vanished, 265
variable, 57, 238
varies, 8
variety, 8, 67, 73, 78, 124, 158, 207, 228, 235
vendor, 73, 106, 263
verifiability, 224
viable, 183
vibrant, 208
videophone, 34
viewpoint, 39, 212
vigorously, 5
virtualization, 10, 123, 265
virtuous, 15, 225, 261
virus, 162
vocabulary, 189, 268
void, 121
volatility, 235
volume, 71, 140
voluntarily, 165

walls, 138, 172
ward, 216
wasting, 25, 97, 101–102, 198, 250
waterfall, 117, 126, 151, 166, 179, 228, 254, 263
weakens, 182
whom, 14–15, 192–193
Wiki, 41, 65, 136, 172
WIP, 130, 135, 139, 159
Wireframe, 132
workflow, 68, 137, 139, 223
worships, 200
worthless, 157
worthwhile, 86, 195

Zendesk, 69
zero, 120, 125, 131, 142, 146, 148, 170, 183
zone, 7, 45, 89, 171, 204–207, 240, 263
Zoom, 66

Printed in the United States
by Baker & Taylor Publisher Services